Transgressive Typologies

Harvard-Yenching Institute Monographs 103

Transgressive Typologies

Constructions of Gender and Power in Early Tang China

Rebecca Doran

Published by the Harvard University Asia Center
Distributed by Harvard University Press
Cambridge (Massachusetts) and London 2016

Printed in the United States of America

The Harvard University Asia Center publishes a monograph series and, in coordination with the Fairbank Center for Chinese Studies, the Korea Institute, the Reischauer Institute of Japanese Studies, and other faculties and institutes, administers research projects designed to further scholarly understanding of China, Japan, Vietnam, Korea, and other Asian countries. The Center also sponsors projects addressing multidisciplinary and regional issues in Asia.

The Harvard-Yenching Institute, founded in 1928, is an independent foundation dedicated to the advancement of higher education in the humanities and social sciences in Asia. Headquartered on the campus of Harvard University, the Institute provides fellowships for advanced research, training, and graduate studies at Harvard by competitively selected faculty and graduate students from Asia. The Institute also supports a range of academic activities at its fifty partner universities and research institutes across Asia. At Harvard, the Institute promotes East Asian studies through annual contributions to the Harvard-Yenching Library and publication of the *Harvard Journal of Asiatic Studies* and the Harvard-Yenching Institute Monograph Series.

Library of Congress Cataloging-in-Publication Data
Names: Doran, Rebecca, 1982- author.
Title: Transgressive typologies : constructions of gender and power in early Tang China / Rebecca Doran.
Other titles: Harvard-Yenching Institute monograph series ; 103.
Description: Cambridge, MA : Published by the Harvard University Asia Center, 2016. | Series: Harvard-Yenching Institute monographs ; 103 | Includes bibliographical references and index.
Identifiers: LCCN 2016001278 | ISBN 9780674970588 (hardcover : alk. paper)
Subjects: LCSH: Women--China--History--To 1500. | Women--Political activity--China--History--To 1500. | Politics and literature--China--History--To 1500. | Women--China--Identity--History. | China--Politics and government--581-907. | China--History--Tang dynasty, 618-907.

Index by Anne Holmes and Rob Rudnick, EDIndex

♾ Printed on acid-free paper

Last figure below indicates year of this printing

20 19 18 17 16

Contents

Acknowledgments

This book would not have been possible without the support and help of many people, and I would like to express my deep gratitude for their generosity and assistance.

First and foremost, I would like to thank my devoted and dedicated professors at Harvard for their inspired guidance, support, and wisdom. Stephen Owen's erudition, generosity, and intellectual curiosity have been an inspiration over the years. I would also like to thank him for first awakening my interest in Chinese literature and for continuing to inspire my studies. Xiaofei Tian has been an erudite, inspiring, and dedicated mentor and model, and her careful reading of my work, perceptive comments and suggestions, and generous offering of new perspectives have improved this manuscript, as well as my approach to scholarship overall, in uncountable ways. Wilt Idema has also been a supportive and inspiring mentor, and his close reading of my chapters, his astute suggestions for revisions, and his encouragement have greatly motivated me in the process of preparing the manuscript. I owe much to Waiyee Li for her intellectual and personal support during my years at Harvard and beyond. This book could not have existed without the examples that my teachers have set to follow. I am also grateful to the Fairbank Center for providing me with a summer grant to conduct research in Xi'an.

I deeply appreciate the careful and insightful comments and suggestions offered by the two anonymous readers of this manuscript. Their recommendations improved the manuscript immensely and challenged me to rethink and develop my ideas at the same time that their meticulous readings saved me from errors.

Many teachers and friends at Harvard, Reed College, and the

University of Miami have enriched my academic experiences and generously contributed to my intellectual progress and personal development in myriad ways. I would like to thank Alexei Ditter, Ariel Fox, Jing Jiang, Lu Yang, Suzie Park, Hongyun Sun, David Wang, Zhang Chen, Yingzhi Zhao, and many others. I would like to thank my parents, my partner Ileana, and my sister for their enthusiastic support, kindness, and constant encouragement.

—R. D.

Abbreviations

The below abbreviations are used in the footnotes.
For full publication information, consult the bibliography.

BSS	Meng Qi 孟棨, *Benshi shi* 本事詩
CFYG	Wang Qinruo 王欽若, *Cefu yuangui* 冊府元龜
CYQZ	Zhang Zhuo 張鷟, *Chaoye qianzai* 朝野僉載
DTXY	Liu Su 劉肅, *Da Tang xinyu* 大唐新語
FSWJJ	Feng Yan 封演, *Fengshi wenjian ji* 封氏聞見記
HHS	Fan Ye 范曄 et al., *Hou Han shu* 後漢書
HS	Ban Gu 班固, *Han shu* 漢書
JS	Fang Xuanling 房玄齡 et al., *Jin shu* 晉書
JTS	Liu Xu 劉昫 et al., *Jiu Tang shu* 舊唐書
KTCXJ	Zheng Qi 鄭綮, *Kaitian chuanxin ji* 開天傳信記
KTYS	Wang Renyu 王仁裕, *Kaiyuan Tianbao yishi* 開元天寶遺事
LNZ	Liu Xiang 劉向, *Lienü zhuan jinzhu jinyi* 列女傳今註今譯
QTS	Peng Dingxiu 彭定求, *Quan Tang shi* 全唐詩
QTW	Dong Hao 董浩, *Quan Tang wen* 全唐文
SJ	Sima Qian司馬遷, *Shiji* 史記
SS	Wei Zheng 魏征 et al., *Sui shu* 隋書
STJH	Liu Su 劉餗, *Sui Tang jia hua* 隋唐嘉話
TPGJ	Li Fang 李昉 et al., comps, *Taiping guangji* 太半廣記
TPYL	Li Fang, comp., *Taiping yulan* 太平御覽
TSJS	Ji Yougong 計有功, *Tangshi jishi* 唐詩紀事
TYL	Wang Dang 王讜, *Tang yu lin* 唐語林
WS	Wei Shou 魏收, *Wei shu* 魏書
WYYH	Li Fang et al., comps., *Wenyuan yinghua* 文苑英華
XSS	Kong Pingzhong 孔平仲, *Xu shishuo* 續世說
XTS	Ouyang Xiu 歐陽修 et al., *Xin Tang shu* 新唐書
ZZTJ	Sima Guang 司馬光, *Zizhi tongjian* 資治通鑑

Introduction

The second half of the seventh century in China was marked by the rise to power of Wu Zhao 武曌 (also known as Wu Zetian 武則天 or Empress Wu 武后; 624–705), who would, in 690, become the only woman before or since to take on the ritual position and prerogatives attendant upon the title of emperor.[1] Already during Wu's lifetime, the uniqueness of her rule was widely recognized and understood in terms of her gender. In the years after her death, as the legend of China's only woman emperor grew, writers and thinkers continually reaffirmed, evaluated, and sought to explain the exceptionality of her power. Beginning in the twentieth century, shifting gender politics have led to positive reevaluations of Wu Zhao, but, with some exceptions, her uniqueness was throughout the Tang through Qing period cast in pejorative terms as "aberrance," deviance from the correct state of affairs.

Wu Zhao is the most prominent of various female figures who dominated the political and cultural arena during the late seventh and early eighth centuries. The condemnatory evaluations surrounding Wu Zhao have likewise followed the "next generations" of women leaders, who came to power during and directly following her rule. They include her daughter, the Taiping Princess 太平公主 (d. 713); her daughter-in-law, Zhongzong's 中宗 (Li Xian 李顯; r. 684, 705–10) Empress Wei 韋后 (d. 710); Zhongzong and Empress Wei's youngest daughter, the Anle Princess

1. I follow Bokenkamp, Rothschild, and others in referring to Wu Zhao by the name she chose herself. See Bokenkamp, "A Medieval Feminist Critique," 390, note 1; Rothschild, *Rhetoric, Ritual, and Support Constituencies*, 1, note 1; and Rothschild, "Wu Zhao's Remarkable Aviary," 84–85, note 1.

安樂公主 (684?–710); and Shangguan Wan'er 上官婉兒 (664–710), the granddaughter of the famous poet Shangguan Yi 上官儀 (d. 665) and a member of the innermost political and cultural circles during Wu Zhao's reign.

In the years between the death of Wu Zhao and the ascension of her grandson Xuanzong 玄宗 (Li Longji 李隆基; r. 712–56), these women consolidated their economic and political clout and formed factions as they vied to fill the power vacuum left by the absence of Wu Zhao. The faction headed by Empress Wei and the Anle Princess sought to have Anle named heiress apparent and was opposed by the Taiping Princess, who joined forces with her nephew, the future Xuanzong. In 710, following the sudden death of Zhongzong, Empress Wei and Anle attempted to take power but were executed in a counter-coup launched by Taiping and Li Longji. In the ensuing years, a rivalry developed between Taiping, who held the loyalty of a sizable and important faction at court, and her nephew, who took the throne in 712. Xuanzong, claiming that his aunt planned to stage a coup against him, destroyed Taiping's faction in 713 and ordered her to commit suicide as a preemptive strike. Over time, Wei, Anle, and Taiping would, like Wu Zhao, become memorable figures etched onto the literary-historical landscape and described according to particular typologies of feminine power and excess.

The calligrapher, painter, and poet Yang Weizhen 楊維楨 (1296–1370), writing over six hundred years after the Anle Princess was killed by opposing forces in the counter-coup of 710, was captivated by the iconic image of her death. He wrote of how, unaware of the approaching violence, she stood before the mirror completing her toilette.

> Copper drums at second watch, stars like snow,
> beneath the spring clouds of her low-hanging curtain her dreams begin to unfold,
> As the thousand cavalry of the imperial guard give out their battle cry,
> she paints her eyebrows, paints her eyebrows before the break of dawn.
> Forming dragons coil, flying simurghs dance,
> the person in the mirror is the heiress apparent.

She paints her eyebrows, not heeding the warning of the long-haired nun.[2]
paints her eyebrows, paints her eyebrows – what is it for?
The edict for the unlawful appointment of officials is not yet finished,
as blood suffuses the Third Master's blade.[3]

銅鼓二鼓星如雪, 帳底春雲夢初熟,
羽林千騎開殺聲, 畫眉畫眉天未明,
結龍蟠飛鸞舞, 鏡中人皇太女.
畫眉不鑒長髮尼, 畫眉畫眉將何為?
墨書未罷斜封旨, 血浸三郎三尺水.[4]

This image captures a key motif in retrospective denunciations of Anle and her powerful female contemporaries, that is, materialism or personal adornment and obliviousness to historical precedent. It also suggests a certain degree of romanticization of the princess as a figure in history and historical myth. Readers familiar with the Hebrew Bible will be reminded of the death of Jezebel, the Phoenician queen of Ahab. When Jehu raised a coup against the house of Ahab, Jezebel, awaiting her death, "painted her eyes, attired her head," and verbally dressed Jehu down; her response to certain death appears as a moment of admirable dignity in the life of a figure who is otherwise reviled in the biblical narrative as a foreigner and overly dominant woman.[5] Unlike Jezebel, the Anle Princess seems to be unaware of her impending doom, but the similarity in the imagery used to portray powerful female leaders is nonetheless intriguing.

In his *Xin Tang shu jiumiu* 新唐書糾繆 (Errors in the New Tang History), Wu Zhen 吳縝 (fl. 11th/12th c.) points to this episode, recorded

2. The "long-haired nun" is Wu Zhao, who, as a member of the harem of a deceased emperor, was a nun for a brief period following the death of Taizong 太宗 (Li Shimin 李世民; r. 626–49).

3. *Sanlang* 三郎, or "Third Master," was the child name of Emperor Xuanzong, chosen because he was third-born among his siblings. *Sanchi shui* 三尺水, literally "three-foot-deep water," is a poetic kenning for a sword.

4. Yang Weizhen, "Anle gongzhu huamei ge" 安樂公主畫眉歌 (The Anle Princess Paints Her Eyebrows), "Tieyai yongshi zhu," in *Tieyai gu yuefu zhu*, 5.13a. Unless otherwise indicated, all translations are my own.

5. 2 Kings 9:30, NRSV.

in the Anle Princess's eleventh-century *Xin Tang shu* 新唐書 (New Tang History) biography, as one of the historical "errors" that he is attempting to rectify in his work.[6] Wu Zhen's cross-examination of other relevant passages in the *Xin Tang shu* reveals that the coup was unleashed at night; he thus concludes that the Anle Princess would not logically have been putting on her makeup (a morning activity) at the time she was killed, and the famous eyebrow-painting scene is thus a clear instance of an unfounded (*wang* 妄) statement.[7] At this remove it is not possible to determine whether this episode is grounded in historical fact; we might also note that the princess may have needed to begin getting ready "at night" for the dawn court. Yet Wu Zhen's analysis does point to the romanticized nature of the passage, the way in which it makes the Anle Princess's death into a scene of historical high drama beyond the purview of fact versus fiction.

Yang Weizhen's treatment of the Anle Princess's last moments also points to the ongoing fascination with her and contemporary female power-holders in sources dealing with the period spanning the complex and tumultuous courts of Wu Zhao and her sons Zhongzong and Ruizong 睿宗 (Li Dan 李旦; r. 710–12). The fascination is in no small part connected to the identification of the period as a unique political-cultural space dominated by powerful female figures. As the basic trajectory of Wu Zhao's rise to power is well known, I will provide only a brief outline here.[8] She initially joined the palace harem in around 640, when she was in her early teens, as a low-ranking concubine of Emperor Taizong

6. *Xin Tang shu* was commissioned by Emperor Renzong 仁宗 (趙禎; r. 1022–63) of the Northern Song 北宋 (960–1127) and was compiled by a committee of historians headed by Ouyang Xiu 歐陽修 (1007–72) and Song Qi 宋祁 (998–1061). The history was completed and submitted to the throne in 1060.

7. Wu Zhen, *Xin Tang shu jiumiu*, 13.168.

8. For accounts of Wu Zhao in the official histories, see *JTS* 6.115–33 and *XTS* 76.3474–85. Detailed discussions of Wu's rise to power and policies as ruler are provided by, among many others, Guisso, *Wu Tse-t'ien and the Politics of Legitimation*, chaps. 3–9; Guisso, "The Reigns of the Empress Wu, Chung-tsung, and Jui-tsung (684–712)," 290–332; Twitchett and Wechsler, "Kao-tsung (reign 649–83) and the Empress Wu," 242–89; Zhao Wenrun and Wang Shuanghuai, *Wu Zetian pingzhuan*; Lei Jiaji, *Wu Zetian zhuan*; Li Juan, *Wu Zetian*; and Wang Hongjun, *Wu Zetian pingzhuan*. For a broader discussion of Wu Zhao's biography in relation to Tang gender discourses, see Jowen Tung, *Fables for the Patriarchs*, 57–72.

太宗 (Li Shimin 李世民; r. 626–49). According to traditional sources, after Taizong died she observed the custom of concubines following the death of their emperor and briefly became a Buddhist nun. Taizong's son and successor, Gaozong 高宗 (Li Zhi 李治; r. 649–83), supposedly visited the convent where she was cloistered and became enamored of her. Gaozong's interest matched the schemes of his Empress Wang 王后 (d. 655), who arranged for Wu to be recalled to the palace in order to take the emperor's attention away from another concubine, Xiao Shufei 蕭淑妃 (d. 655). Empress Wang's plan had disastrous consequences for Xiao as well as for Empress Wang herself. Wu proved highly adept at palace intrigue; she eventually supplanted both her rivals, who, according to the standard historical narrative, were hideously murdered at her command. Wu succeeded in having herself declared empress in 655, and as Gaozong suffered from waning health leading to periods of incapacity, she gradually assumed greater control of the government.

After Gaozong's death in 683, the couple's son Li Xian briefly assumed the throne as Emperor Zhongzong, but he was soon exiled following a clash with high-ranking ministers. In the ensuing seven years, Wu Zhao crushed two poorly executed rebellions against her. The first one was started in 684 by Li Jingye 李敬業 (or Xu Jingye 徐敬業; d. 684), the exiled Duke of Ying 英公, from his base in Yangzhou 揚州, and the second was spearheaded in 688 by a group of senior princes of the Li-Tang royal house in the context of the power struggles between the Li and Wu clans and Wu Zhao's perceived promotion of the Wu clan over the Li. The rebellion was launched shortly before the princes were due to answer a summons to court, which they feared was a trap that would lead to their imprisonment or execution. During this time, Wu launched a campaign of legitimization involving political, ritual, and cosmic symbolism; the circulation of works, including Buddhist sutras, that glorified and predicted her rule; and a purge of her enemies. Traditional sources describe the purge as a reign of terror against all members of the Li house, carried out by the empress's gang of "cruel officials" (*kuli* 酷吏). The multi-level legitimization campaign led to the establishment, in 690, of her own dynasty, the Zhou 周 (690–705). During the 690s, ancestral temples to the Wu house supplanted those of the Li-Tang house, and Wu Zhao became the only woman to rule in her own right as emperor.

The rule of a female emperor created an unprecedented situation, and in the mid- to late 690s, the issue of succession was hotly debated. Wu Zhao's nephews Wu Chengsi 武承嗣 (d. 698) and Wu Sansi 武三思 (d. 707) each sought the designation of heir apparent and the continuation of a Wu ruling house, but they were opposed by powerful ministerial factions at court. By the turn of the eighth century, Wu Zhao had recalled Zhongzong to the capital; it seems that she had already resigned herself to the impossibility of continuing the Zhou regime after her own death. In 705, a coup of high-ranking ministers forced her abdication, and the throne returned to the Li clan. She died later that same year. Nevertheless, after Wu Zhao was gone the domination of the court by members of the imperial in-law (*waiqi* 外戚) clans, especially female figures from the Wei and Wu families, continued to characterize the ensuing regimes of Zhongzong and Ruizong. Intermarriage between the Wei, Wu, and Li clans led to a complex and incestuous brand of court politics. The Anle Princess's first husband was Wu Chongxun 武崇訓 (d. 707), Wu Sansi's son. After Wu Chongxun's death, she remarried his and her cousin Wu Yanxiu 武延秀 (d. 710), Wu Chengsi's son. The Taiping Princess's second husband was Wu Youji 武攸暨 (d. 712), a grandson of Wu Zhao's uncle Wu Shileng 武士讓 (dates unknown). Wu Sansi was rumored to be sexually involved with Empress Wei and Shangguan Wan'er, who, by the return to Tang rule in 705, was one of the most powerful figures at court, responsible for drafting court edicts and organizing courtly cultural activities.

As alluded to by Yang Weizhen, the powerful faction of Wu Sansi, Empress Wei, and the Anle Princess sought to have Anle named heiress apparent to replace the actual heir apparent, her half-brother Li Chongjun 李重俊 (d. 707), Zhongzong's son by a consort other than Empress Wei. In 707 Wu Sansi and Wu Chongxun were murdered by Li Chongjun in the course of the heir apparent's unsuccessful coup, which was prompted by his fear that he would be replaced by his half-sister and which also resulted in Li Chongjun's own death. During this period, an intense rivalry developed between the Wei faction and a faction headed by the Taiping Princess, who was allied with her brother Ruizong. The Wei faction initially managed to pacify their prime political rivals with huge estates and revenues. In 710, the last year of the Jinglong 景龍 reign period (707–10), however, the Anle Princess unwisely attempted to move against the Taiping Princess and Ruizong, leading Taiping to garner strength to retaliate and seek power for herself. Temporarily allying with her nephew Li Longji, Taiping engineered another coup in which the Wei leaders, including Empress Wei, the Anle Princess, and Shangguan Wan'er, were killed. But in the wake of their victory, aunt and nephew grew suspicious of each other, and their mutual mistrust culminated in Xuanzong's execution of the Taiping Princess and her faction in 713.

Inscribing the Women Leaders of the Late Seventh and Early Eighth Centuries

In the collective historical imagination, this tumultuous period is inextricably linked with stories about powerful women leaders, who are some of the most vibrant yet elusive characters to populate the landscape of Chinese history. My choice of the word "characters" is not inadvertent; the compelling nature of these women is closely related to the way in which they have been constructed and reconstructed as characters in historical, quasi-historical, and fictional narratives. Wu Zhao ruled competently, first jointly with Gaozong and then on her own, for about fifty years, quelling internal and foreign rebellion and generally fostering stability. Yet in most later sources, her rule is remembered primarily in terms of excess, cruelty, and dalliance with much younger male consorts.

The decade or so during which politics was dominated by the next generation(s) of powerful women is also retrospectively constructed in terms of female-led aberrance. Although the particulars can and do shift over time, portrayals of these women form into consistent thematic molds, all of which emphasize transgression of gender roles or taboos: their failure to recognize their appropriate cosmological role and, correspondingly, their denunciation by cosmic missives; their greed and conspicuous consumption, especially in the significant form of the landed estate; and a condemnatory focus on sexuality and a sexual culture that is unique to this period. This holds true both for standard histories and collections of historical anecdote purporting to represent things as they really were, and for works—including unofficial histories and various forms of literature—thought to be less concerned with precise notions of historicity.

The early thirteenth-century historian Lü Xiaqing 呂夏卿 (*jinshi* 進士 1215) directly addresses the issue of legitimacy (or de-legitimacy) and female power when he criticizes the tenth-century standard history *Jiu Tang shu* 舊唐書 (Old Tang History) for granting Wu Zhao and Empress Wei (real and de facto heads of state) a measure of legitimacy by including their acts of state in the annals of rulers (*benji* 本紀), which he believes should be reserved for the actions of the (male) emperor alone.[9]

> The actions of empresses are not recorded in the emperors' annals:
>
> For example, in the fifth year of the Xianqing reign [660], Empress Wu banqueted ranked women among her relatives and neighbors in Bingzhou . . . In the second year of the Jinglong reign [708], Empress Wei proclaimed a state-wide amnesty because a five-colored cloud rose from her skirt . . . Events like this are all detailed in the biographies of Empresses Wu and Wei. When the Old History recorded them in the Annals of Gaozong and Zhongzong, this was losing the correct way of history.
>
> 皇后所行之事, 不書于紀:
>
> 如顯慶五年, 武后宴親族鄰里命婦于并州 . . . 景龍二年, 韋后以裙上有五色雲, 大赦天下 . . . 如此之類, 亦皆具武, 韋, 二后傳. 舊史載之高宗, 中宗紀, 失史法也.[10]

When the *Jiu Tang shu* compilers placed their actions in the "wrong" section, they "[lost] the correct way of history"; their subtle moral assessment failed to adequately support Lü Xiaqing's understanding of the moral-gender hierarchy.

The literary-historical tradition through which these women are delegitimized and essentialized into particular typologies underscores their embodiment of transgression, which is often encoded in gendered forms. This study explores portrayals of the key female figures in the complex, shifting factions of the late seventh and early eighth centuries, with an aim to situate them within their contemporary sociocultural context and to understand their retrospective constructions in terms of conceptualizations of their power as women. Central to these portrayals

9. *Jiu Tang shu* was compiled by a committee of historians sponsored by the Later Jin 後晉 (936–45) regime and headed by Liu Xu 劉昫 (887–947). The completed work was presented to the throne in 945.

10. Lü Xiaqing, *Tang shu zhibi*, 2.32.

are sources produced by the elites closest to the operations of power. The women against whom they reacted made use, through surrogates, of religious phenomena and religious literature, providing another body of source material. The tales of female power as revealed in these religious materials, however, do not necessarily embody the same values as literary sources, which project a coherent if partial view reflecting, in particular, the outlook of the well educated. It is this literary-historical tradition that will be the focus of my book. I seek to approach an understanding, first, of what progressions or variants might exist in literary-historical constructions of these women and, second, of what their portrayals tell us about conceptions of gender and sexuality as a metaphor for and actual indicator of sociopolitical position. I analyze in detail the inter- and intra-source similarities and contradictions, focusing on the literary components and functions of these portrayals and the uses of the early Tang female power-holder as a historical example and/or figure of historical myth.

The process of historical construction was, however, accompanied by another process of historical destruction. Many details concerning the actions of powerful women were eliminated from the record, so that it is now easier to describe the images that were created than to look at the history of which they are, even on their own terms, undoubtedly only a partial reflection. The embellishments, prejudicial accounts, and outright fictions that have accumulated around these women can often tell us more about conceptions of their power than can an attempt to define the objective historical "truth" of their lives. This study thus deconstructs cultural image, as revealed through accounts and interpretations of the early Tang women power-holders.

Cultural image is created within particular frameworks of historical interpretation. In his analyses of the relationship between history and narrative, Hayden White has explored the cultural specificity of these interpretive frameworks. Here I make no attempt to apply White's insights to the larger historiographic environment. This must remain a task for the future, especially in view of the research of scholars such as Andrew Plaks, who suggest that Chinese narrative is characterized by structures quite unlike those typical of Western literature.[11] The literary

11. Plaks, "Chinese Narrative Theory."

articulation of the historical period of female power, however, can and should be studied as a discrete topic, bearing in mind what White has argued about the writing of history. White suggests that although "fully realized 'history,'" or narrativized history, presents itself and is understood as being objective, in fact it is distinguished by "its latent or manifest purpose [as] the desire to moralize the events of which it treats."[12] Every narrative has a point of view or judgment; this is equally true of historical narrative as it is of fictional narrative. Our desire to narrativize history bespeaks not the narrative as the form that most naturally represents our experience of events, but rather our need to conceptualize, or "emplot," events in terms of culturally encoded narrative forms.[13]

Essentially, no work of historical narrative is without authorial viewpoint and thus message; the existence of the "hero" and the "villain" is intrinsic to the narrative form. The shape taken by the historical narrative and the judgments meted out therein are rooted in particular cultural environments, suggesting particular perspectives and values. This is not to negate the value of historical accounts in conveying "information," but it indicates an approach not limited to a conception of historical narrative as data and argues in favor of a critical reading method that pays close attention to repeating narrative formulas, tropes, and character types.

The process through which the Tang women's historical images coalesced began with materials compiled during their lifetimes and shortly after their deaths. The images of important political-cultural figures are always subject to some compilation process, and, of course, the critical reader is wise to be particularly suspicious of retrospective materials about the members of losing factions, whose lives are constructed through an unsympathetic lens. Indeed, scholars have long noted that in traditional Chinese historiography, as in all historiographical systems, certain pronounced biases exist. Denis Twitchett and others have analyzed the processes through which historical records were shaped into the sources we have at our disposal today, emphasizing the way in which the worldview of the historians informed their understanding of the function of history.[14]

12. White, "The Value of Narrativity," 13–14.

13. White, "The Question of Narrative," 43; and "Historicism, History, and the Figurative Imagination," 106–7.

14. See, among others, Twitchett, "Problems of Chinese Biography"; Twitchett, *The*

The official history of a regime was compiled after its demise based upon a progressive series of records revised step by step. After the mid-seventh century, the Tang employed two pairs of court diarists. The precise titles changed over the course of the dynasty, but the diarists were always theoretically understood to divide their functions based upon the ancient interpretation of Diarists of the Left and Right, whereby the Diarists of the Left (the *Chunqiu* 春秋/*Zuozhuan* 左傳 tradition) were responsible for recording the ruler's actions, and the Diarists of the Right (following the *Shujing* 書經 and *Guoyu* 國語) recorded his words.[15] As noted by Twitchett, the "basic outline" of the compilation process is no mystery; the court diaries (*qiju zhu* 起居注) and administrative records (*shizheng ji* 時政記), supposed to have been assembled contemporaneous to the events they recorded, were edited into a daily calendar (*rili* 日曆) for each year, which subsequently made up a veritable record (*shilu* 實錄) for each reign.[16] The veritable record was reworked into a national history (*guoshi* 國史), which, after the fall of the dynasty, was edited by the conquering regime into the standard history (*zhengshi* 正史) of the period.[17] The component parts of the standard history—the annals of rulers, tables (*biao* 表), biographies (*liezhuan* 列傳), and monographs (*zhi* 志)—were compiled using different types of source texts. Whereas the *benji*, considered the most authoritative, were put together by a court-appointed group of officials based on the earlier court documents mentioned above, the biographies, at least in the case of positively evaluated figures, were often taken directly from materials, mainly obituary-style "Accounts of Conduct" (*xingzhuang* 行狀), submitted by relatives or disciples of the deceased.

Writing of Official History; Pulleyblank, "The *Tzyjyh Tongjiann Kaoyih*"; Franke, "Some Remarks"; and Hung, "The T'ang Bureau of Historiography before 708."

15. Twitchett, *The Writing of Official History*, 5–8.

16. Twitchett, *The Writing of Official History*, 33.

17. Twitchett, *The Writing of Official History*, 33. The process of editing was generally the purview of the Historiographical Office (*shi guan* 史館), which underwent multiple incarnations over the course of the first century of the Tang. See Hung, "The T'ang Bureau of Historiography before 708," 93–107. Hung discusses how the reigns of Gaozu 高祖 (Li Yuan 李淵; r. 618–26) and especially Taizong also saw the compilation of the standard histories of the majority of the Northern and Southern regimes (*Nan Bei chao* 南北朝; 420–589); these histories are thus the product of the same compilation process and worldview.

The historians who compiled historical records were, of course, aware of the potential for bias inherent in the writing process. Various measures were undertaken to ensure the relative independence of the historical offices from the central government, and Tang historians were certainly conscious of the subjective nature of the "Accounts of Conduct."[18] On an even deeper level, however, the worldview of the compilers mandated a conception of history fundamentally different from our own. The idea of the moral force of history is central to conceptions of the historian's duty.[19] Historical works were meant to provide moral judgments and exemplars of "praise and blame," to the extent that noted historian Liu Fang's 柳芳 (fl. mid- to late eighth c.) *Tangli* 唐曆 (Record of Tang History) was criticized by contemporaries for improper use of "praise and blame" (not for inaccuracy or bias).[20] Arthur Wright has also discussed the conflict engendered by the didactic conception of history; at the same time that historians were anxious to be "recognized as 'good historians' (*liang-shih*)," meaning unbiased historians, their conviction in the historian's moral duty led them to sanction the practice of "appropriate concealment," or biased editing based on their moral interpretation of the past.[21]

The subjective nature of moral judgment exerted a powerful influence over which subjects were included in or excluded from the historical record, as well as how various subjects were treated. In biographies of important individuals, character typology comes into play; the desire to display an individual as a moral exemplar of a particular "type" (virtuous recluse, upright official, chaste woman, evil woman)

18. For example, Twitchett quotes a memorial submitted by Li Ao 李翱 (772–841) in 819 complaining bitterly of the exaggeratedly positive nature of "Accounts of Conduct." Twitchett, *The Writing of Official History*, 71–74.

19. Twitchett, *The Writing of Official History*, 9–11. See also Wright, *The Sui Dynasty*, 16.

20. Twitchett, *The Writing of Official History*, 60. Twitchett is drawing upon the earlier work of E. G. Pulleyblank; see his "The *Tzyjyh Tongjiann Kaoyih*," 460. They are both quoting Liu Fang's biography in *XTS* 132.4536 (時國史已送官, 不可追刊, 乃推衍義類, 倣編年法, 為唐曆四十篇, 頗有異聞. 然不立褒貶義例, 為諸儒譏訕). Pulleyblank and, to a greater extent and in much more detail, Twitchett both list earlier historical sources, now no longer extant, that went into the compilation of extant histories. See Pulleyblank, "The *Tzyjyh Tongjiann Kaoyih*," 448–62, and Twitchett, *The Writing of Official History*, part 2.

21. Wright, *The Sui Dynasty*, 16–17.

is related to the prevalence of narrative "formulas," formulaic episodes long established in the literary-historical tradition that were seen to encapsulate the behavior typical of certain "types."[22] As Twitchett notes elsewhere, such conventions would have been easily recognizable to educated readers.[23] Yet the presence of such formulaic passages highlights the didactic purpose of the standard historical biographies and also evokes their source material, which was, as noted above, always of a more personal and unreliable nature than the source material for the annals and monographs. This is especially true in the case of negative biographies; as Twitchett has pointed out, because Accounts of Conduct would not have been written for "evil" members of losing factions or enemies to the current ruling house, historians in these instances had to rely on biased or suspect accounts.[24] I would add that historians operating under the moral dictum conceptualization of history were not necessarily "forced" to resort to this type of prejudicial or uncorroborated account. Rather, those same prejudices would probably have informed their worldview as well and thus fit into the moral judgments they chose to promulgate.

These scholarly discussions raise important issues about the nature of history that inform my study of the historical constructions of the late seventh- through early eighth-century female power-holders. The situation of negatively evaluated women, however, presents special challenges beyond those involved in portrayals of "evil" male figures. Their identity as women engenders particular types of condemnation based in conceptualizations of appropriate gender roles. The corpus of relatively recent writing on Wu Zhao includes a book entitled, in Chinese (originally in Japanese), *Empress Wu Zetian—Was She an Enlightened Ruler or a Female Disaster?*[25] Try to imagine the same title for a work about a male ruler –

22. See Twitchett in *The Writing of Official History*, 74–76, and "Chinese Biographical Writing," 95–114. See also Franke's discussion of the posthumous historiographical slander of Emperor Shun or Shundi 順帝 (Toghon Temür; r. 1333–68), the last Yuan emperor, in "Some Remarks," 120–22.

23. Twitchett, "Problems of Chinese Biography," 29.

24. Twitchett, "Problems of Chinese Biography," 33–34.

25. Sawada Mizuho, *Zetian Wu hou—shi yingzhu haishi nühuo?* In fact, the translation of Sawada Mizuho's work into Chinese in 1977 seems to be related to the fall of the Gang of Four, which prompted interest in "evil female rulers." See Tien-wei Wu, *Lin Biao and the Gang of Four*, 136.

any male ruler, most beloved or most reviled—*Sui Yangdi—Was He an Enlightened Ruler or a Male Disaster?*—and the gender bias will become glaringly clear. The non–gender-neutral "female disaster" (*nühuo* 女禍) is a specific term within the Chinese tradition and implies transgression by women. This is a recurring category of historical disaster wherein women in positions of "unnatural" power cause disaster different from the problems created by incompetent male rulers (who would be termed non–gender-specific "disasters").[26]

Terms such as *nühuo* are an especially blatant example of the way in which sexism is written into the very rhetoric conceptualizing history and female historical figures. Scholarly awareness of issues surrounding gender and bias in historical compilation is long-standing, and scholars have touched upon these issues in various contexts.[27] As for Wu Zhao and the Jinglong-era women, several scholars, including Jowen Tung and Keith McMahon, have attempted to place Wu Zhao within prevailing gender discourses of the Tang and later periods.[28] No systematic analysis exists, however, of the way in which the powerful women of the early Tang have been negotiated in the literary-historical tradition.

Scholarship on Wu Zhao and the "second generations" of powerful women politicians has, up until now, been split into two main areas of interest. First, scholars have paid considerable attention to the cult of personality of Wu Zhao. Numerous biographies have been devoted to her, and more specifically oriented revisionist studies have attempted to reconstruct previously obscure or misunderstood aspects of her reign.[29] The years in between Wu Zhao's forced abdication in 705 and

26. For a historical discussion of "female disaster" in the pre-Qin through Han periods, see Liu Yongcong (Clara Ho), *De, cai, se, quan*, chaps. 1–3.

27. For a discussion of these issues in relation to perhaps the most famous Tang femme fatale figure, Honored Consort Yang (Yang Guifei 楊貴妃 or Yang Yuhuan 楊玉環, 719–56), see Fan-pen Chen, "Problems of Chinese Historiography."

28. See Jowen Tung, *Fables for the Patriarchs*, 57–72; and McMahon, *Women Shall Not Rule*, 186–204.

29. General and biographical studies often suffer from an over-reliance on the standard histories and an overriding emphasis on evaluation of her effectiveness as a ruler and/or personal morality. See, for example, Luo Longzhi, *Tangdai de houfei yu waiqi*; Gao Shiyu, *Tangdai funü*, 117–22; Dora Shu-fang Dien, *Empress Wu Zetian*, 27–67; and Clements, *Wu*. Among general biographies in Chinese, Zhao Wenrun and Wang Shuanghuai's critical biography, *Wu Zetian pingzhuan*, is noteworthy for its revisionist approach.

Xuanzong's execution of the Taiping Princess in 713 have attracted a different sort of academic attention. Scholars have been drawn to the literary, in particular poetic, developments taking place at Zhongzong's court, especially in relation to the cultural flourishing of the High Tang (712–56) under Xuanzong. Jia Jinhua and others have focused on the development of regulated verse and the sociocultural role of poetry, which was often composed during courtly outings and functioned as a vehicle for both entertainment and political advancement or demotion.[30] While the context of female rule provides the backdrop for these

In terms of more specifically oriented monographs, Guisso's *Wu Tse-t'ien and the Politics of Legitimation in T'ang China China* examines in detail Wu Zhao's policies in regard to religion, the state examination system, and foreign affairs, attempting to "show more clearly the origins of the Empress Wu's historical reputation" and to "draw a more accurate picture" of her reign. Guisso, *Wu Tse-t'ien and the Politics of Legitimation*, 7. Antonino Forte also works in the area of state ideological apparatus, paying special attention to the Buddhist ideology of Wu's regime so as to address and disprove previous misconceptions. See Forte, *Political Propaganda and Ideology in China* and *Mingtang and Buddhist Utopias*. *Mingtang and Buddhist Utopias* deals with the construction and significance of the Mingtang (Hall of Light). On this topic, see also Rothschild, *Rhetoric, Ritual, and Support Constituencies*, 75, 196–97, 316–23.

30. Jia explores the literary output of the prominent court literati of Wu Zhao's and Zhongzong's reigns and attempts to place the poetry of the period in the overall literary-historical development of poetic genre, form, and style. See Jia Jinhua, "The 'Pearl Scholars,'" "A Study of the *Jinglong wenguan ji*," and *Tangdai jihui zongji*, 43–73.

Scholars writing after Jia have continued her focus on the Jinglong court literary culture and *yingzhi shi* 應制詩 (poetry written to imperial command during group courtly outings). Tao Min has further analyzed the background of the *Jinglong wenguan ji* 景龍文館記 (A Record of the Jinglong Literary Institute), in particular, its relationship to the later *Tangshi jishi* 唐詩紀事 (Record of Stories Related to Tang Poems), from which it was reconstructed by Jia. See Tao Min, "*Jinglong wenguan ji* kao." Jie Wu's 2008 dissertation examines group composition during the early Tang, focusing on the literary features of the poetry, as well as the context and social functions of group composition. See Jie Wu, "A Study of Group Compositions." Works on Jinglong-era literary culture tend to reaffirm Jia's conclusions on topics such as the expansion of scope in landscape description in the *yingzhi* poems from Wu Zhao's time on, or the development of regulated verse forms during the period. See Nie Yonghua, *Chu Tang gongting shifeng liubian kaolun*, chaps. 3 and 4; and Sun Qin'an, *Tangshi yu zhengzhi*, chap. 4. See also Ding Yan, "Lüe lun Chu Tang yingzhi shi," 30–33; and Hu Han, "Chu Tang yi gongting nüxing zuojia wei zhongxin zhi youyan shi lüelun," 78–80. Discussion of *yingzhi* poetry also generally involves apologetic attempts to offset the notion that such poems are actually not, in Ding Yan's words, "overall boring, lacking flavor, and lacking artistic value" (在總體上單調乏味及缺乏藝術價值). See Ding Yan, "Lüe lun Chu Tang yingzhi shi," 30.

discussions of literary culture, they are not primarily concerned with attitudes toward gender or rule by women per se.

Monographs devoted to portrayals of women in the Chinese tradition have often focused on the later imperial period, but their approaches to gender issues have proved valuable to me in my research. Yenna Wu's monograph on the development of the "virago" theme in Chinese literature offers an insightful discussion of how to approach portrayals of women in relation to traditional notions of gender roles. Because elements of exaggeration, essentialization, and "fictionalization" are integral to narrative constructions of these women, "[w]hat is at stake is not so much what actually happened but how historians envisaged the roles women played."[31] Judith Zeitlin's work on ghosts and gender in the late imperial tradition likewise emphasizes the importance of an approach focused not on the "question of belief or fictionality," but rather on "the issue of representation" and "the complex meanings, both literal *and* figurative, of these representations."[32] Her definition of the feminine specter as "always an image, culturally and historically constructed" also applies to the narrative figure of the condemned, powerful woman leader.[33]

Narrative Typology and (Re)construction

My analysis takes as its jumping-off point the concepts of narrative construction and reconstruction. How did the images of the female leaders from the Wu-Zhou period of Wu Zhao's dominance (mid-seventh c.–705) through the Jinglong era become crystallized in the rhetoric of history, historical romance, and fiction? What assumptions inform the process of negative "canonization"? I approach the late seventh- through eighth-century period of female rule as an era united not only culturally but also in terms of its reconstruction in the retrospective imagination of history. I seek to understand the cultural lenses through which these

31. Yenna Wu, *The Chinese Virago*, 51.
32. Zeitlin, *The Phantom Heroine*, 10.
33. Zeitlin, *The Phantom Heroine*, 10.

women were portrayed in the years, decades, and centuries after their dominance in government, focusing on their narrative construction as gendered typologies: What tropes are identified with them and how are they reworked and developed over time? How was their legitimacy or lack of legitimacy as women rulers interpreted and appropriated by later writers? What do they represent in the moral-cosmic schemas forming various historical and literary narratives? What is the meaning of "female power" in relation to these women?

In approaching the archetypal representations of this group of female power-holders, I have concentrated mainly on Tang through Southern Song 南宋 (1127–1279) sources. As Guisso has noted, by the Song, their classic conception in the literary-historical tradition was basically fixed.[34] The annalistic, descriptive, and biographical materials found in the standard historical works of *Jiu Tang shu*, *Xin Tang shu*, and Sima Guang's 司馬光 (1019–86) *Zizhi tongjian* 資治通鑒 (Comprehensive Mirror of Government)[35] are, of course, critical sources for Tang history, and they have also been very important to my specific research focus, although I have approached them from the perspective of narrative formulations and what they reveal about attitudes towards gender and power. The material selected during the Five Dynasties 五代 (907–960) and Northern Song 北宋 (960–1126) for inclusion in the standard historical descriptions of these powerful Tang women was culled from a wide variety of historical chronicles, anecdote collections, and circulating legends. In exploring these developments, early anecdote compilations (*biji* 筆記) dating to the eighth through early ninth centuries have proved invaluable sources. I have in particular made use of *Chaoye qianzai* 朝野僉載 (Comprehensive Record of Affairs within the Court and Without), compiled by Zhang Zhuo 張鷟 (ca. 660–ca.740)[36]; *Sui Tang jia hua* 隋唐嘉話 (Table Talk

34. Guisso, *Wu Tse-t'ien and the Politics of Legitimation*, 201–2, note 43. As Guisso discusses in this same passage, there are a few notable dissenting evaluations of Wu Zhao from the mid- to later imperial period from such historians and literary men as Hong Mai 洪邁 (1123–1202) and Li Zhi 李贄 (1527–1602).

35. *Zizhi tongjian* is a chronological record of Chinese history from 403 BCE through 959 CE. The narrative of *Zizhi tongjian* is enhanced by Sima Guang's inclusion of extensive text-critical notes, or *kaoyi* 考異, quoting alternative accounts from sources which are often no longer extant. For further information about Sima Guang and *Zizhi tongjian*, see Ji Xiao-bin, *Politics and Conservatism in Northern Song China*; and Wang Debao, *Sima Guang yu "Zizhi tongjian."*

36. Zhang Zhuo, originally from Luze 陸澤 in Shenzhou 深州 (modern-day Hebei),

from the Sui and Tang), compiled by Liu Su 劉餗 (fl. 742–55)[37]; and *Da Tang xinyu* 大唐新語 (New Words from the Great Tang), compiled by Liu Su 劉肅 (fl. 806–20).[38] While these works contain the greatest amount of lore about Wu Zhao, Empress Wei, the Taiping and Anle Princesses, and Shangguan Wan'er, I have also made use of other Tang collections, such as *Fengshi wenjian ji* 封氏聞見記 (Record of What Mr. Feng Heard and Saw), compiled by Feng Yan 封演 (*jinshi* 進士 756), and *Kai Tian chuanxin ji* 開天傳信記 (Record of News Transmitted from the Kaiyuan and Tianbao Eras), compiled by Zheng Qi 鄭綮 (Tang).

The anecdotal collections initially compiled roughly two to four generations after their deaths played a powerful role in crafting the canonical, transgressive image of these women. The content and some surviving information regarding authorial intent suggest an emphasis on politics, the life of the court, and the moral evaluation of key figures.

---

was a well-known writer whose career spanned the reigns of Wu Zhao, Zhongzong, and Ruizong and the first three decades of Xuanzong's rule. *Chaoye qianzai* is a collection of anecdotes that mainly concentrate on the period of Wu Zhao's dominance and the reigns of Zhongzong and Ruizong, but it also contains sketches from earlier and later times. The collection focuses on historical material, but also includes geographical, zoological, and medical information and episodes that have been characterized as "anomaly" in nature. For Zhang Zhuo, see *JTS* 149.4023–24 and *XTS* 161.4979–80. For the composition of *Chaoye qianzai*, see "Dianjiao shuoming" 點校說明, *CYQZ* 3–5; and Zhou Xunchu, *Tangdai biji xiaoshuo xulu*, 7–14.

37. Liu Su was the son of prominent historian Liu Zhiji 劉知幾 (661–721), who is today perhaps most famous for his opposition to Wu Zhao's desire to tamper with historical records for her own gain. Like his father, Liu Su served as a historian, and, in addition to *Sui Tang jiahua*, was the author of several other now-lost works that seem to have been historical in content. For the biographies of Liu Zhiji and Liu Su, see *JTS* 102.3168–74 and *XTS* 132.4519–23. See also "Dianjiao shuoming," *Sui Tang jiahua*, 3–5 and Zhou Xunchu, *Tangdai biji xiaoshuo xulu*, 1–6.

38. Liu Su was active during the Yuanhe 元和 reign period (806–20), during which he served as a regional official in Jiangdu 江都 and/or Xunyang 潯陽. *Da Tang xinyu* follows the structure of Liu Yiqing's 劉義慶 (403–44) famous *Shishuo xinyu* 世說新語 (A New Account of Tales of the World), a collection of anecdotes about prominent personages and events during the Eastern Jin 東晉 (317–420) dynasty. Like *Shishuo xinyu*, *Da Tang xinyu* is divided into moral categories, under which are given anecdotes about individuals whose behavior was deemed to exemplify those categories. Liu Su's work discusses the period from the beginning of the Tang through the Dali 大曆 reign (766–779) and is politically focused and didactic in nature. For further discussion of the textual transmission and ideological orientation of *Da Tang xinyu*, see Zhou Xunchu, *Tangdai biji xiaoshuo xulu*, 27–31. For a discussion of the *shishuo* tradition, see Qian, *Spirit and Self*.

The preface and postscript to *Da Tang xinyu*, for example, explicitly affiliate the work with the historical tradition of character evaluation and assignation of moral significance.[39] In general, the treatments of the early Tang women power-holders found in these collections delegitimize and condemn them through groups of narratives with repeating themes involving cosmic rejection, conspicuous consumption, and other forms of transgression.

In certain respects, the image of these women created therein was cemented and reaffirmed throughout ensuing generations.[40] In other ways, there are significant areas of contrast between earlier and later representations. Narratives are embellished so as to emphasize the female leader's culpability in a given situation, and her female-identified crimes (corruption, sexual misconduct) become rhetorically enhanced. In this vein, I have evaluated some later sources from Ming 明 (1368–1644) and Qing 清 (1644–1911) times, paying careful attention to developments in specific narratives and in the broader narrative of their perceived place and moral role as characters in the literary-historical tradition.

Because my research focuses on cultural values and especially on gendered perceptions as rhetorically embodied, my source texts are by no means confined to "reliable" works, meaning those works generally judged to be historically accurate. If we discount the worth of "unreliable" works because they are deemed factually inaccurate, we miss key evidence suggestive of worldview and cultural definitions of gender roles. My analysis encompasses explicitly fictional primary sources, including poetry, prose fiction, and pornography, and sources not directly related to these women and/or their era, such as later anecdotal collections and *shihua* 詩話 (notes on poetry or discussions of poetry). It is often in these incidental appearances that we can gauge the nature of their retrospective images and designated cultural-historical roles. In examining

39. See "Da Tang xinyu yuan xu" 大唐新語原序 (Original Preface to *Da Tang xinyu*); *Da Tang xinyu*, 1; and "Zong lun" 總論 (Summation), *Da Tang xinyu*, 202–3.

40. As John Wills has noted, some of the most damning anecdotes about Wu Zhao can be traced back to sources compiled very soon after her death. This information is, however, based upon the claims of eleventh-century historians. Wills surmises that this does not prove the veracity of all of these accounts, but indicates that "in her own time people already were ready to believe the worst about a woman who did not know her place." Wills, "Empress Wu," 132.

the negotiation of these women in the Chinese literary-historical tradition, I have, for reasons of length and scope, focused on the primary sources. I do not engage extensively, for instance, with the rich corpus of Japanese sources pertaining to this period, a direction in research that awaits future work.

My analysis centers on progressively exploring and unpacking the construction of these women's moral-cultural roles vis-à-vis conceptions of history and gender. Some of the most often repeated episodes involving, in particular, Wu Zhao are the extreme "evil woman" episodes, such as her possible murders of her infant daughter and various rivals and her dysfunctional relationships with her adult sons. Discussion of these rather repetitive episodes tends to devolve into an attempt to prove or disprove whether Wu was, in fact, guilty of the crimes of which she has been accused. Though well-known, these episodes are neither the most interesting nor, I would argue, the most important in terms of retrospective images of female power in the era as a whole. My work is thus structured thematically, according to the most central aspects of their typology as it coalesced over time.

The first chapter of this book examines the literary constructions of pre-Tang women leaders to assess the ways in which portrayals of the Tang figures draw upon or depart from existing precedents. Good precedents for female rule do exist in the Chinese tradition, and chapter 1 explores celebrated and censured pre-Tang women in order to understand the circumstances under which female rule was sanctioned versus condemned as transgressive. Positive heroines, even when they were in reality quite powerful, are often praised for their "natural" womanly virtues of chastity, modesty, and knowing their ritual place. Building upon earlier studies, my analysis suggests that a major factor in determining posthumous evaluation is whether or not the woman in question attempted to directly take power herself and/or to rule through her family members. Although Empress Wei and Wu Zhao especially attempted to follow some time-honored traditions of the virtuous empress, they are absolutely not remembered in this way by later generations of historians and writers, who place them within the tradition of the destructive female power-holder, a tradition that attaches specific tropes to this "type" of woman.

The second chapter shifts focus to a complementary perspective on the image-making surrounding these women. This chapter approaches an understanding of their self-image through analysis of the writings, including poetry, prose, and other documents, produced at the courts of Wu Zhao, Zhongzong, and Ruizong either by these women, to their command, or to suit their tastes. Analysis of these laudatory works enables a fascinating glimpse into not only the aesthetic tastes of these women, but also the way in which they preferred to see themselves and their power figured rhetorically. In turn, we can trace the transformation, indeed, the inversion, of these same images and tropes in later portrayals.

Each of the ensuing chapters takes as its focus an important, broad thematic aspect of the rhetorical creation of female power in retrospective accounts of the women who dominated politics during the late seventh through early eighth centuries. The third chapter focuses on the richly varying themes surrounding ritual, signs, and meaning. Cosmic messages are ubiquitous throughout the classical Chinese tradition but acquire a special meaning when deployed in the context of this unique era of female rule. Arthur Wright, Howard Wechsler, and Jack Chen have done discerning work on the legitimation campaigns, including various auspicious signs and events, of famous male rulers such as Emperor Wen of the Sui and Taizong of the Tang.[41] Richard Guisso likewise discusses state symbolism in his analysis of the mechanisms of legitimation utilized by Wu Zhao.[42] Building upon these insightful earlier studies, chapter 3 approaches the issue of legitimacy from a different angle: that is, from the narrative destruction of these women's legitimacy in retrospective materials.

The fourth chapter analyzes the narrative use of conspicuous consumption as a de-legitimizing force in portrayals of the female power-holders of this era. Material memory is a crucial component in their narrative constructions; across all genres, writers have overwhelmingly emphasized their lavish residences, resort complexes, clothes, and other luxury possessions. The disproportionate amount of attention paid to conspicuous consumption, found in some of the earliest sources compiled just decades after the Taiping Princess's death, combines nostal-

41. Wright, *The Sui Dynasty*; Wechsler, *Offerings of Jade and Silk*; and Jack Wei Chen, *The Poetics of Sovereignty*.

42. Guisso, *Wu Tse-t'ien and the Politics of Legitimation*, especially the introduction and chap. 4.

gia for a lost historical moment and condemnation of female-led and -enabled greed. Chapter 4 explores how their greed is interpreted in relation to the growing narrative identification between the private holdings of powerful women and various forms of intrigue.

The fifth chapter centers on the idea of inversion in terms of explicit depictions of gender relations and sexuality. Famous later works of fiction, drama, and pornography emphasize the "scandalous" relationships between older female power-holders, in particular Wu Zhao, and younger male concubines. The chapter traces the development and significance of the "male concubine" theme, arguing that these depictions reinforce, in a particularly graphic manner, the coalescing image of the era as defined by the dangerous reversal of appropriate male and female roles. Sexualized gender inversion completes the image of the "insatiable woman" who usurps unsanctioned symbolic, material, and sexual prerogative.

Throughout, I keep returning to the unifying issues of legitimacy and gender. Utilizing anecdotal, historical, and literary sources about the early Tang women power-brokers, the study explores changing attitudes toward gender and power and the establishment of the rhetorical identification between their power as women and their transgression.

ONE

Female Rule and Its Representation

Gender, Paradigm, and Historical Narrative

The historians and anthologists who sought to portray the powerful, charismatic women of the mid- to late seventh and early eighth centuries worked within a tradition rich in literary lore of female power and full of colorful historical female figures. Their understanding, and hence our versions, of Wu Zhao, Empress Wei, the Taiping and Anle Princesses, and Shangguan Wan'er, as well as the men attached to them, is mediated by layered historical precedents and archetypes of the feminine—in particular, archetypes of the female power-holder. The goal of this chapter is to examine both positive and negative constructions of female rule in the Chinese tradition in order to demonstrate how images of the Wu-Zhou and Jinglong women built upon and departed from earlier models.

In approaching materials on the lives of these pre-Tang women leaders, I view historical writings as a negotiation between what actually happened and what can be found in the discursive tradition, though we should bear in mind that what was eventually left out of the discursive tradition was also an outcome of that negotiation. Like any works of history, relevant materials on the lives of these women are not just neutral documents conveying information, but rather are works operating within an ongoing tradition that placed importance on particular goals, particular types of individuals, and the creation of a particular message.[1] At the same time, however, these sources were never conceived by their creators

1. Twitchett, "Chinese Biographical Writing," 108. See the introduction to this book for a more in-depth discussion of Twitchett's works and issues surrounding historical compilation, bias, and formula.

as fictional accounts bearing only an abstract resemblance to the events and figures of history. A somewhat difficult-to-navigate terrain emerges from this delicate balance between typology and history, and the question of whether certain events actually happened is unanswerable. Perhaps it is not even the right question. Just like the biographies Twitchett discusses in which the writer attempts to present the subject as an upright official, a biography of a woman whom the historian deemed to be an example of the negative type is imbued with its own time-honored ways of signaling destructive womanhood, which the historian believed to have characterized her in history.[2]

In evaluating the rhetorical construction of eulogized and censured female power, this chapter aims to understand traditional cultural-narrative constructions of permissible versus transgressive rule by women. Under what circumstances is a woman allowed or even encouraged to take the throne, and how must she behave as a leader in order to earn posthumous praise in the literary-historical record? Conversely, what behaviors mark the woman ruler as offensive and dangerous?

Scholars have touched upon these issues in varying contexts. In a well-known article, Yang Lien-sheng translates and builds upon Zhao Fengjie's earlier work, which proposes three main situations in which rule by empress dowager was considered permissible: when the rightful emperor was very young, very sick, or had died suddenly and left a posthumous edict placing her in charge.[3] Zhao's insight points to the importance of political stability or instability as a framework through which to understand evaluations of gender roles and, in particular, female political participation. Although Zhao and Yang deal mainly with the imperial period, the complex pre-Qin discourses surrounding gender also often hinged on the importance of sociopolitical order versus disorder. A queen who perfects her role of wife, mother, and helpmate to the king plays a vital role in the moral power of the state; however, a consort who fails to heed the dictates of her proper role is identified with destruction.[4]

Some ancient texts describe *yin* 陰, the female/earth force, and *yang*

2. Twitchett, "Chinese Biographical Writing."

3. Yang Lien-sheng, "Female Rulers in Imperial China," 51.

4. See Goldin, "The View of Women in Early Confucianism"; and *The Culture of Sex in Ancient China*, 48–74.

陽, the male/heavenly force, as complementary, so that the wisest individual is one who embodies both.[5] Already in late Warring States 戰國 (475–221 BCE) and Western Han 西漢 (206 BCE–24 CE) times, however, the increasingly gendered understandings of *yin* and *yang*, with their identification of the *yin* force with passivity and the inner realm, provided the justification for limiting the "appropriate" sphere of activity for women, and *yin* tended to be defined as inferior.[6] Various scholars have suggested that the unification of centralized empire under the Qin 秦 (221–206 BCE) produced profound changes in conceptions of gender roles, changes that tended to disadvantage women in theory and practice through the creation of a tradition associating the feminine with political instability and crisis.[7] Although Hans Van Ess and others have rightly cautioned against oversimplification, especially as regards the Qin–Western Han period,[8] over the course of the Han we begin to see the emergence of prescriptive models of feminine behavior that would become increasingly mainstream over time. Particularly as we move into the Eastern Han 東漢 (25–220 CE) dynasty, there is an emphasis on segregation of the sexes, as ritually codified in the "inner rules" (*neize* 內則) of the *Liji* 禮記 (Record of the Rites), and obedience was frequently lauded as the cardinal virtue in women. The notorious "three obediences" (*sancong* 三從) mandated obedience to father, husband, and son.[9]

It is also during the Han period that we see the appearance of written manuals on female behavior. The first surviving Han work on womanly virtues is *Lienü zhuan* 列女傳 (Categorized/Model Biographies of Women), compiled by Liu Xiang 劉向 (77?–6? BCE). Liu Xiang drew upon earlier accounts about women to craft his work, which provides

5. Goldin, "The View of Women in Early Confucianism," 149–52.

6. See Cutter and Crowell, *Empresses and Consorts*, 26–34; and Bao Jialin, "Yinyang xueshuo yu funü diwei." See also Wills, "Empress Wu," 132–33; and Yenna Wu, *The Chinese Virago*, 20–29.

7. See Hinsch, *Women in Early Imperial China*, chaps. 6–7; Liu Yongcong (Clara Ho), *De, cai, se, quan*, chaps. 1–3; Kinney, *Exemplary Women of Early China*, xv–li; and Cutter and Crowell, *Empresses and Consorts*, 9–25. Qian Nanxiu has discussed conceptions of women in the *Shishuo* 世說 ("tales of the world") tradition; see her *Spirit and Self in Medieval China*, 142–48, 283–318 (on later "Women *Shishuo*").

8. Van Ess, "Praise and Slander," 222.

9. These ideas are also outlined in Yenna Wu, *The Chinese Virago*, 20–29.

biographies of women deemed to exemplify particular virtues.[10] The second well-known Han tract devoted to feminine behavior, *Nüjie* 女誡 (Admonitions for Daughters), by the erudite writer and imperial tutor Ban Zhao 班昭 (ca. 49–120 CE), is the first in a long tradition of moral tracts by women for women. Ban Zhao's preface states that she wrote *Nüjie* as a guidebook to marriage for her daughters who were about to be married, but Ban Zhao's advanced age at the time of composition and her own important political and literary activities have inspired a great deal of scholarly speculation as to her actual impetus for writing *Nüjie*.[11] Regardless of its originally intended purpose, the work was later interpreted as systematically outlining the ideal of feminine submission, a theme that is adopted in subsequent tracts on ideal womanly behavior.[12]

Ban Zhao is, in fact, credited with editing a version of *Lienü zhuan*, though only fragments survive.[13] Of these two most famous Han moral tracts for women, it is *Lienü zhuan* that marks the beginning of the historical-biographical moralizing tradition, whereby biographies are used as models for feminine virtues. *Lienü zhuan* played a foundational role in shaping the development of that tradition and, consequently, conceptualizations of appropriate feminine behavior.[14] Indeed, the structure and style of *Lienü zhuan* exerted a strong influence on the "Hou fei lie zhuan" 后妃列傳 (Biographies of Empresses and Consorts) chapters in subsequent dynastic histories. *Lienü zhuan* is a composite text that draws upon and reworks materials from various earlier sources and also includes stories with no existing predecessor texts.[15] Its chapters are structured according to general virtues (with one chapter about evil women at the end) and divided into sections featuring women deemed to have embod-

10. See Kinney, *Exemplary Women of Early China,* for an annotated translation and discussion of *Lienü zhuan*.

11. Chen Yu-shih has suggested that Ban Zhao wrote *Nüjie* in the tradition of Daoist and military strategy texts as a way of suggesting to women, in particular her famous pupil Deng Sui 鄧綏 (Empress Deng; 81–121 CE), how to survive in the dangerous climate of the court. See Chen Yu-shih, "The Historical Template of Pan Chao's 'Nü Chieh.'"

12. Idema and Grant, *The Red Brush*, 17–42.

13. Kinney, *Exemplary Women of Early China*, 33.

14. Kinney, *Exemplary Women of Early China*, xv.

15. For a detailed discussion of the compilation of *Lienü zhuan*, see Hinsch, "The Composition of *Lienü zhuan*."

ied the particular virtue under discussion.[16] Even a cursory examination of the virtues informing the work's organization reveals an emphasis on prescriptive social roles. The virtuous woman is defined by her perfection of the subservient roles of mother and wife, the evil woman by her transgression of these same roles.

Beginning in the first chapter, "Motherly Exemplars," women are praised above all for upholding the traditional roles ascribed to them by the patriarchal system. Mang Mao of Wei's 魏芒卯 second wife ("Wei Mang ci mu" 魏芒慈母, "The Compassionate Mother of Mang of Wei") is an example of perfect motherhood and wifehood because of her extreme devotion to her husband's children by his first wife, in spite of their rejection of her.[17] Even Ding Jiang 定姜, who is credited with a much more active role in the government, never crossed the gender line to seek power for herself.[18] Duke Zhuang of Chu's 楚莊公 (r. 613–591 BCE) Consort Fan 楚莊樊姬 is praised for her double fulfillment of womanly virtues; she gives good advice to her husband at the same time that she reveals her lack of jealousy, a condemned trait in women because it is threatening to the prevailing marriage ideology. Using the comparison of her own selfless procurement of the most beautiful women for her husband's harem, she criticizes a leading Chu minister's self-serving failure to recommend other worthy men as officials.[19]

Beyond the restrictive emphases on chastity and devotion to the role of mother and wife, there is a disturbing, pervasive current of self-destructiveness in these "model women." Some are lauded for extreme and obsessive adherence to *furen zhi yi* 婦人之義 ("what is proper for women") to the point of self-violence. Duke Gong of Song's 宋恭公 (r. 588–576 BCE) wife Consort Bo 宋恭伯姬 chose to burn to death rather than violate the rule that forbade women from leaving the house at night

16. For a discussion of the historical context, compilation, and structure of *Lienü zhuan*, see Kinney, *Exemplary Women of Early China*, xv–li. See also Hinsch, "The Textual History of Liu Xiang's *Lienü zhuan*" and "The Composition of *Lienü zhuan*."

17. See *LNZ* 1.43–45.

18. She remonstrated harshly with Dukes Ding 衛定公 (r. 588–577 BCE) and Xian 衛獻公 (r. 576–559 BCE) of the state of Wei 衛 (ca. 11th c.–209 BCE) and supposedly tried unsuccessfully to set up Duke Ding's virtuous and gifted younger son on the throne instead of Duke Xian. See *LNZ* 1.18–21.

19. *LNZ* 2.59–61. See Kinney, *Exemplary Women of Early China*, 27–28, for another interpretation of this entry.

without the house mother (*bao fu* 保傅).[20] In a sad and troubling inversion of Mengzi's statement that of course a man could touch his sister-in-law to save her from drowning, King Zhao of Chu's 楚昭公 (r. 515–489 BCE) wife Zhenjiang 楚昭貞姜 chose to drown instead of leaving her place without the official tally.[21]

The influence of this model of female virtue can be perceived in the behavior of generations of empresses, who often penned or ordered the compilation of derivative works on "womanly virtue." Wu Zhao is credited with ordering the compilation of multiple such works outlining normative behavior for women, including *Lienü zhuan* 列女傳 (in one hundred chapters), *Xiaonü zhuan* 孝女傳 (Biographies of Filial Women; in twenty chapters), *Lienü zhuan* 列女傳 (in twenty chapters; this seems to have been an extract of the hundred-chapter version), *Gujin neifan* 古今內範 (Ancient and Modern Rules for Women; in one hundred chapters), and *Neifan yaolüe* 內範要略 (Essential Points of Rules for Women; in ten chapters).[22] All of these works have long been lost, so it is impossible to confirm their specific content, but their titles strongly suggest traditional manuals for female behavior. Regardless of whether or not she believed in or adhered to these traditional models, Wu Zhao clearly saw their compilation as part and parcel of self-legitimation in the course of her rise to power.

This raises the issue of the degree to which women of different eras and geographical areas would have internalized the values perpetuated in this type of work.[23] Certainly educated women of all regions and times would have been aware of these "model women," but, especially in the case of the Northern Dynasties, there existed an established tradition of strong families in which women often played a forceful role. This tradi-

20. *LNZ* 4.133–35.

21. *LNZ* 4.151–53.

22. See Twitchett, "*Chen gui* and Other Works," 37–38 and 55–56, for a detailed discussion of catalogue references to and attributions for these works.

23. In this vein, Chen Jo-shui has discussed possible "proto-feminist sentiments" suggested by the actions taken by Wu Zhao and Empress Wei, especially from the legal standpoint of promulgating measures designed to increase the status of women. See Chen Jo-shui, *Tangdai de funü wenhua*, 201–41 and "Empress Wu and Proto-Feminist Sentiments." Both works contain a useful chronological table of these measures; see *Tangdai de funü zhanghua*, 222–23 and "Empress Wu and Proto-Feminist Sentiments," 92–93.

tion may have supplied alternate models for female behavior more immediate, meaningful, and attractive than the prescriptive roles delineated by works such as the *Lienü zhuan*.

Condemnation of powerful women is certainly not universal in the tradition; the historical tradition praises certain women rulers for their possession of qualities such as intelligence, frugality, and humility. Even some of the "evil women rulers" are also at times lauded for particular actions or particular characteristics. Building upon the work of Zhao, Yang, Kinney, and others, I explore the ways in which virtue and vice are narratively conveyed or manipulated through descriptions of the woman in question's relationship to the prevailing power structure. That is, to make a woman "evil," a writer merely needs to stress her disregard for the interests of her husband, family, and/or dynasty.

In examining portrayals of pre-Tang women leaders who wielded considerable power and yet have also been upheld as moral paragons, I mainly focus on Eastern Han Empresses Ma 馬 (Empress Deming 德明皇后; 39–79 CE) and Deng 鄧 (Deng Sui 鄧綏, also known as Empress Hexi 和西皇后; 81–121 CE). I have chosen these women because they ruled for relatively lengthy periods of time during a dynastic era that, like the Tang, was noted for female rule. Their biographical narratives contain great, yet unrealized, potential for narrative embellishment with the rhetoric of the "destructive woman"; thus, as case studies, they provide fascinating vehicles for comparison and analysis of narrative-moral constructions. Although these women held long-term control of the throne, they were careful to retain the pretense of rule by proxy and demonstrate their "virtue" in forms recognizable from earlier paragons: humility, frugality, selflessness.

In contrast to the women rulers praised for their humility, a desire for personal power is a defining characteristic of women judged to have transgressed their appropriate female roles. Turning to women rulers who were crafted, to a greater or lesser extent, into negative historical archetypes, I mainly deal with portrayals of Western Han Empress Lü 呂 (Lü Zhi 呂雉; 241–180 BCE), Western Jin 西晉 (265–316 CE) Empress Jia 賈 (Jia Nanfeng 賈南風; 257–300 CE), and Northern Wei 北魏 (386–534 CE) Empress Dowager Hu 胡太后 (Empress Ling 靈; d. 528). These empresses all controlled the government, either as regent or jointly with an emperor, and all have been condemned by the historical tradition.

Eastern Han Empress Dou 竇 (Empress Zhangde 章德皇后; d. 97 CE), Northern Wei Empress Feng 馮 (Empress Wenming 文明皇后; 442–90 CE), and Sui 隋 (581–618 CE) dynasty Empress Dugu 獨孤 (Dugu Qieluo 獨孤伽羅, also known as Empress Wenxian 文獻皇后; 544–602 CE) represent fascinating "middle cases" in that their portrayals are an ambivalent mixture of positive and negative typologies.

Our main sources for the history of the northern and southern regimes of the third through sixth centuries are the official or standard histories for these dynasties, most of which were compiled at the early Tang court by committees of historians working under the auspices of the historiographical offices of Gaozu and Taizong.[24] In compiling the dynastic histories of these fallen regimes, early Tang historiographical officers edited and reworked surviving records, including veritable records (*shilu* 實錄) and earlier official and private historical compilations. The potential for bias inherent in the conception of history as moral judgment and the compilation of history by historical "winners" is widely recognized. In the case of histories compiled at the Tang court for dynasties that had fallen as many as three centuries earlier, the issue of the reliability of sources is clearly greatly amplified. The frequent regime changes and periods of disorder characterizing the northern and southern dynastic period further compound the issue of source preservation and integrity.

The issue of regionalism must also be taken into consideration. Scholars have suggested that the greater public visibility of northern elite women, as well as northern "traditions" of female rule, may have influenced the rise to power of Wu Zhao during the Tang, which inherited much of its statecraft power and infrastructure from the preceding northern regimes and which, especially during its first century, was basically a northern dynasty.[25] The idea of a northern "inheritance"

24. *Wei shu* 魏書 (History of the Northern Wei) is mainly a pre-Tang work; see Twitchett, *The Writing of Official History*, Part I.

25. Wills, "Empress Wu," 129–30; Ebrey, *Cambridge Illustrated History of China*, 109. For a sixth-century description of the differences in gender norms between North and South, see Yan Zhitui 顏之推 (531–ca. after 590 CE), *Yanshi jiaxun*, 1.24. For English translations, see Teng Ssu-yü, *Family Instructions for the Yen Clan*, 18–19, and Yan Zhitui, *Yanshi jiaxun—Admonitions for the Yan Clan*, 44–45 (section 5.10). Yan Zhitui, a southerner by birth (but the descendant of a northern regional family), spent the greater part of his adult life in the North due to various political instabilities. After the fall of the Liang 梁 dynasty (502–57 CE) to the Chen 陳 (557–89 CE), he was captured by the northern

for Tang female power-holders is a multifaceted and far from clear-cut issue.[26] However, the portrayals of northern empresses and consorts who assumed a controlling role in government are not paralleled, in terms of degree of political control, in narratives about southern imperial women. In discussing these northern women, I will address the imperial and political structures that facilitated their ascension to power, as well as the rhetorical structures that recorded their rise.

Gender-based condemnation is by no means absolute or unmodulated; some passages laud the achievements of Empress Dugu and Empress Feng in various areas of statecraft even as other passages within the same work follow a typical "destructive woman ruler" progression, accusing them of licentiousness, nepotism, and so on. Such variation may be related to the process of historical compilation through repeated editing and collation of various earlier materials, a process that often spanned generations, and to ambivalence on the part of individual historians or groups of compiling editors. In fact, portrayals of female power are formed through the complex intersection of rumor, generic convention, and historical context at the time of compilation. In this chapter I will begin to navigate this matrix, which continues to inform portrayals of the Wu-Zhou and Jinglong female power-holders.

Exemplars of Female Rule

The placement of "Motherly Exemplars" as the first chapter of *Lienü zhuan* indicates the fundamentality of motherhood to traditional conceptualizations of women's sociocultural role; in classic formulations, this role cuts across class differences to unify women by gender. The *Lienü zhuan* stresses the virtue of the self-effacing mother who spares no effort in her desire to educate and advance her sons. In portrayals of empresses

army and stayed in the North, serving a succession of northern regimes. He was thus uniquely familiar with the ways of life of both the northern and southern elite. For a more detailed discussion of Yan Zhitui's life and thought, see Albert E. Dien, "Yen Chih-t'ui (531–91+ CE)," 43–64.

26. See Pearce, "Nurses, Nurslings, and New Shapes of Power," 290.

and consorts, this typology is often combined with that of the virtuous mate who displays no jealousy towards her husband's other women and treats their children as her own. Given the cardinality of motherhood to conceptions of womanhood, it is not surprising that a woman's obedience or disobedience to exemplary archetypes of motherhood defines her virtue or transgression. Investment in the patriarchal model determines formulations of female character and frames exhortations or warnings about behavior. Rewards and punishments based on behavior include those reaped both during and after the woman's lifetime; posthumous condemnation or praise is crucial to establishing her image in the collective historical memory.

It is no accident that instances of prolonged female rule tended to occur during those periods when the stability of the imperial patriarchy was somehow weakened. During the Eastern Han dynasty, the frequency of child emperors translated into extended periods of rule by women from the position of empress dowager. The lives of Empress Ma, Empress Dou, and Empress Deng all date to this period and all intersect, as the three women were in power within decades of each other. Narrative praise of Empresses Ma and Deng hinges on their fulfillment of patriarchal dictates for womanhood.

The powerful Deng Sui, or Empress Deng, was the second empress of Emperor He 和帝 (Liu Zhao 劉肇; r. 88–105 CE), and she commanded the throne as regent to the young Emperor Shang 殤帝 (Liu Long 劉隆, Liu Zhao's son by a concubine; r. 105–6 CE) and Emperor An 安帝 (Liu Hu 劉祜, Liu Zhao's nephew; r. 106–25 CE). Deng Sui was a highly educated, intelligent woman from an illustrious family. She was the best-known pupil of Ban Zhao, and her portrayal in the *Hou Han shu* 後漢書 (History of the Later [Eastern] Han Dynasty) suggests her great power while demarcating her virtue in terms of her relationships with Emperor He's other women and his children.[27]

From her entry into the palace as a teenager, Deng is described as conscientiously embodying the ideal of non-jealousy and hierarchical respect that was supposed to define the harem (but often did not do so in practice). Deng, then a *guiren* 貴人 (honored lady), "was respectful and

27. *Hou Han shu* was compiled during the Liu-Song dynasty 劉宋 (420–79 CE) by a committee headed by Fan Ye 范曄 (398–445 CE).

circumspect, and her movements were measured. She served Empress Yin [Emperor He's empress at the time] earnestly, trembling day and night. In the hierarchy of the harem, she comforted those of the same rank and often purposefully [lit., overcoming her desires or denying herself] lowered herself; she treated even the lowliest servants of the palace ladies with compassion. As a result, the emperor deeply respected and loved her" (恭肅小心, 動有法度. 承事陰后, 夙夜戰兢. 接撫同列, 常克己以下之, 雖宮人隸役, 皆加恩借. 帝深嘉愛焉).[28] The future Empress Deng's biography reads like a handbook for the virtuous woman: she gently yet firmly chided Emperor He when he demonstrated undue partiality towards her and her family; she eschewed ornaments and flashy clothes; she immediately ran to change her clothes if she and Empress Yin happened to be wearing the same color; and so on.[29]

The conspicuous performance of "wifeliness" and non-jealousy is not just a simple manifestation of virtue; it conveys the woman's devotion to the patrilineage and the patriarchal system. According to their biographies, Empress Ma and Empress Deng both place the imperial male line above their individual or familial interests and, as a result, are rewarded by the imperial patriarchy in which they participate. Empress Ma's elevation to the position of empress is portrayed as a direct consequence of her devotion to furthering the male line: "The Empress [Ma, who had not yet been appointed empress] was always worried because the emperor did not have many sons. She was always recommending her [female] attendants [to the emperor], as if she were afraid that there would not be enough time. If anyone from the rear palace were advanced to attend upon the emperor, she [Ma] would always treat her with increased consideration. If anyone were favored repeatedly, she would then treat her with honor and deference" (后常以皇嗣未廣, 每懷憂嘆, 薦達左右, 若恐不及. 後宮有進見者, 每加慰納. 若數所寵引, 輒增隆遇).[30] Immediately after, we are told that Emperor Ming 明帝 (Liu Zhuang 劉莊; r. 58–75 CE), under pressure to name an empress, chose Ma because of the virtue that she displayed. Importantly, he made this choice following his mother's recommendation;

28. *HHS* 10a.419. For another translation of Empress Deng's biography, see Swann, "Biography of the Empress Teng."

29. *HHS* 10a.419–420.

30. *HHS* 10a.409. *Zhe* 輒, which I have translated as "then," can also carry the meanings of "always" or "immediately."

the empress dowager pinpointed Ma's virtue in supporting the patrilineage in which she herself was also invested.[31] The interface between the two women suggests alternative networks of advancement for women in the palace even while these avenues only existed within the confines of a male-dominated system.

Transgressive Women Rulers

Conversely, accounts of the destructive woman emphasize her disregard for the patrilineage and her prioritization of her own individual and familial interests. Although it is probably not something that any aspiring female ruler would have sought to emulate, within the historical tradition the figure of Empress Lü seems in several respects to be the model of the destructive, transgressive woman. Particularly memorable "snapshots" from portrayals of Empress Lü serve as models for the later portrayals of Wu Zhao. Descriptions of Empress Lü in general focus on her unadulterated violence and calculated quest for power. These dangerous behaviors manifest in her interactions with her unfortunate rival Lady Qi 戚姬 (d. 194 BCE) and Lady Qi's son, the Prince of Zhao Ruyi 趙王如意 (Liu Ruyi 劉如意; 208–194 BCE).

The main historical sources for information about Empress Lü are *Shiji* 史記 (Records of the Historian) and *Han shu* 漢書 (History of the Han Dynasty).[32] In the accounts of these two works, we can see different stages in the development of the historical "characters" of Empress Lü

31. *HHS* 10a.409.

32. The annals (*benji*) of the earlier *Shiji*, completed between 109 and 91 BCE by Sima Qian 司馬遷 (ca. 145 or 135–86 BCE), include the "Lü Taihou benji" 呂太后本紀 (Annals of Empress Dowager Lü); see *SJ* 9. This chapter recounts many of the important anecdotes about Empress Lü's personality and rise to power, including her murder of Lady Qi and Ruyi. In the later *Han shu*, completed by Ban Gu 班固 (32–92 CE) and then finalized by his younger sister Ban Zhao by around 111 CE, the annals are extremely laconic; detailed narrative material regarding her person and ascension to the throne is in most cases removed to the "Gaozu Lü Huanghou" 高祖呂皇后 (Gaozu's Empress Lü) section of the chapter "Wai qi zhuan" 外戚傳 (Biographies of Imperial Relatives by Marriage); see *HS* 97a.3937–40.

and Lady Qi.[33] According to both works, after her father married her off as a young woman to the future Han founder, Empress Lü supported her husband in the process of winning the empire, only to be cast aside by him later for the younger Lady Qi. Empress Lü's own "kind and weak" (*renruo* 仁弱) son, the crown prince and future Emperor Hui 惠帝 (Liu Ying 劉盈; r. 195–188 BCE), likewise lost his father's favor to Ruyi, whom Gaozu considered to be "like himself" (*lei wo* 類我).[34]

Lady Qi proved an active rival to Empress Lü, but she was ultimately unable to unseat Empress Lü's son.[35] Immediately following Gaozu's death, the now-empress dowager imprisoned Lady Qi and summoned Ruyi to court with the intention of killing him. Emperor Hui attempted unsuccessfully to save his half-brother. In the later *Han shu* account, the drama is amplified by Ban Gu's "discovery" of a pathetic song attributed to the imprisoned Lady Qi, an elaboration that, as noted by Idema and Grant, exaggerates the "good versus evil" intensity of the rivalry between the two women.[36] After poisoning the rival son, Empress Lü hideously tortured and murdered her former rival. She mutilated Lady Qi into a "human pig" (*ren zhi* 人彘) and made Emperor Hui look at her.[37] The traumatic experience of viewing the limbless, muted, and poisoned woman was more than he could handle and supposedly led to his own personal unraveling:

> Upon realizing that it was Lady Qi, he cried out in distress, became sick, and was unable to get up for over a year. He sent someone to inform the empress dowager, "This is not something which a human being would be capable of doing. I am the empress dowager's son; there is no way I will ever

33. Idema and Grant, *The Red Brush*, 85. Van Ess has noted that Ban Gu reworked the earlier *Shiji* narrative so as to express greater condemnation for Empress Lü; see Van Ess, "Praise and Slander."

34. *SJ* 9.396; *HS* 97a.3937.

35. *SJ* 9.396; *HS* 97a.3937.

36. *HS* 97a.3937; Idema and Grant, *The Red Brush*, 84–85.

37. "The Empress Dowager cut off Lady Qi's hands and feet, gouged out her eyes and burnt off her ears, made her drink a poison which muted her, and threw her into a vat, calling her the 'human pig.' After several months, she ordered Emperor Hui to go see the 'human pig'" (太后遂斷戚夫人手足, 去眼煇耳, 飲瘖藥, 使居鞠域中, 名曰 "人彘." 居數月, 乃召惠帝視 "人彘"); *SJ* 9.397; *HS* 97a.3938. See Idema and Grant, *The Red Brush*, 83–85.

be able to govern the world again!" Because of this, he drank excessively, debauched himself with women and music, neglected his duty to govern, and died after seven years.

帝視而問, 知其戚夫人, 乃大哭, 因病, 歲餘不能起. 使人請太后曰: "此非人所為. 臣為太后子, 終不能復治天下!" 以此日飲為淫樂, 不聽政, 七年而崩.[38]

As argued by Van Ess, the earlier *Shiji* account creates greater sympathy for Empress Lü by emphasizing her desperation to protect herself and her son against unjust demotion from their rightful positions.[39] Yet we must also note that, in the historical narrative progression, Empress Lü's murder of Ruyi and Lady Qi occurs after the rivalry is, for all intents and purposes, over; Gaozu had died, leaving Empress Lü's son established as Emperor Hui and the empress herself installed in the powerful position of empress dowager to a weak ruler. There is no mention of Lady Qi or Ruyi launching a campaign to overthrow the newly enthroned emperor; thus, their murders serve no purpose other than to brutally express Empress Lü's rage and power.

The actions of Empress Lü certainly suggest intense jealousy. However, she is not described as jealous in the sense of being motivated by infatuation for her husband, but rather as single-mindedly driven to gain ultimate power. In discussing the different motivations for jealousy attributed to women, Yenna Wu notes that one type of jealousy could be prompted by a woman's (justified) fear of losing her position and security, gained through her relationship with her husband, as opposed to fear of losing his love as such (because she loved him, etc.).[40] Empress Lü's biography describes her as "hard/tough and resolute" (*wei ren gangyi* 為人剛毅).[41] Having helped Gaozu to bring about order and found the Han dynasty, she emerges as determined and high-powered, by far the more virile figure

38. As further noted by Van Ess, the *Shiji* account merely states that Emperor Hui became sick and does not indirectly attribute his death to seeing the "human pig." Van Ess, "Praise and Slander," 239–40. See also *SJ* 9.397 and *HS* 97a.3938.

39. See Van Ess, "Praise and Slander," 230–39.

40. Yenna Wu, *The Chinese Virago*, 39–50. See chapters 1 and 2 for a detailed discussion of the psychological underpinnings and development of the trope of the jealous woman in early Chinese literature and historical narrative.

41. *HS* 97a.3937; *SJ* 9.396.

when compared with her son, a compassionate but feeble and ineffectual man. At the most basic level, condemnation of Empress Lü is based on her interactions with the men who are close to her. Just as she destroys the rival woman and the rival son, she equally shows no mercy towards her own son.

The power relations between Empress Lü and the man whom she dominated, her son Emperor Hui, resonate in accounts of the balance of power between authoritative empresses of the later pre-Tang regimes and their male family members. Like Empress Lü, Empress Jia of the Western Jin becomes a model of transgressive femininity in the literary-historical tradition. Her *Jin shu* 晉書 (History of the Jin Dynasty) portrayal[42] likewise establishes her identity as a destructive woman by emphasizing her transgression of the cardinal dictates for women within the patriarchal-imperial hierarchy. Narratives on Empress Jia underline the dangerous, complex factionalism (i.e., fragmentation of the patriarchal system) that was key to her rise and rule, as well as her uncontrolled violence, especially against other women, which is blamed for the Jin's loss of the North and the division of the Chinese realm.

Empress Jia was a formidable force behind the success of her intellectually disabled husband, incidentally also known as Emperor Hui 惠帝 (Sima Zhong 司馬衷; r. 290–307 CE).[43] Empress Jia was the daughter of Jia Chong 賈充 (217–82), a powerful court official and key player in the factional politics of the time. In 272, at the age of fourteen or fifteen, Empress Jia was married to the future Emperor Hui, in spite of the objections of his father, Emperor Wu 武帝 (Sima Yan 司馬炎; r. 266–90).[44] After the death of Emperor Wu in 290, Empress Jia's husband

42. As mentioned above, the *Jin shu*, though no doubt based on earlier historical compilations, is an early Tang historical work. The history was commissioned by the Tang court and presented to the throne in 648. It was completed by a group of scholars led by the then–prime minister Fang Xuanling 房玄齡 (579–648), a talented military and civil official who was an associate of Li Shimin, the Tang founder. For Fang Xuanling's official biographies, see *JTS* 66.2459–67 and *XTS* 96.3853–57.

43. When Sima Zhong was crown prince, his father the emperor, suspicious of the crown prince's intelligence, devised a test for him. The future Empress Jia, with the assistance of the minister Zhang Hong 張泓 (dates unknown), made sure that her husband passed by preparing the answers for him. See *JS* 31.963–4.

44. According to the *Zizhi tongjian*, Jia Chong's clique hatched the scheme of marrying his daughter to the crown prince in order to prevent his appointment to a military

ascended the throne, and she was named empress. In the ensuing years, she treacherously out-maneuvered and removed from power the clan of her mother-in-law Empress Yang 楊后 (Yang Yan 楊艷; 238–74), whose father, Yang Jun 楊駿 (d. 291), initially served as Emperor Hui's regent. During the years in which she held an authoritative role in the government as her husband's regent (having executed Yang Jun), preceding her execution by another coup in 300, Empress Jia built up her own loyal political group, which included the official Zhang Hua 張華 (232–300), her cousin Jia Mo 賈模 (d. 299), her nephew Jia Mi 賈謐 (d. 300), her sister Jia Wu 賈午 (260–300), and a consort of Emperor Wu named Zhao Can 趙粲 (d. 300).

According to all sources, Empress Jia's ruthless political acumen was matched (and impeded) only by her jealous violence. Even from the outset of her marriage to the then–twelve- or thirteen-year-old crown prince, the fifteen-year-old future empress inspired fear in her younger husband, so that "few from the ranks of the royal consorts were advanced to be favored [with sexual attention from the crown prince]" (嬪御罕有進幸者); this situation is obviously the opposite of the atmosphere of intra-female recommendation created by Duke Zhuang of Chu's virtuous Consort Fan from *Lienü zhuan* and, later, by the "virtuous" Eastern Han empresses.[45] Empress Jia's violence is likewise directed towards sexual rivals: "The Crown Princess's [Empress Jia, at that time the crown princess] nature was cruel and violent; in the past she had killed several people by hand. Once she threw a lance at a pregnant concubine, causing her to miscarry" (妃性酷虐, 嘗手殺數人. 或以戟擲孕妾, 子隨刃墮地).[46] Upon learning of her violent insubordination, her father-in-law Emperor Wu became enraged and wanted to remove her, but was convinced by his consort Zhao Can and several other allies to retain her. Zhao Can's words of persuasion are interesting and relevant here: "Consort Jia is young, and jealousy is the natural sentiment of women. When she's older, she'll naturally be different. I wish Your Majesty would reconsider this matter" (賈妃年少, 妒是婦人之情耳, 長自當差. 願陛下察之).[47] Zhao Can,

---

post, and his wife bribed Emperor Wu's Empress Yang 楊后 (Yang Yan 楊艷; 238–74) to win her over to their cause. See *ZZTJ* 79.2518.

45. *JS* 31.963.

46. *JS* 31.964.

47. *JS* 31.964.

another woman of the palace (though a consort of Emperor Wu, not his son Emperor Hui), defended her powerful female ally against charges of repugnant violence directed at a third-party palace woman through recourse to the natural, uncontrollable "sentiment" (*qing* 情) of women. Jealousy, even taken to a vicious extreme, is still more attractive and natural for a woman than would be ambition, anger, or hatred.

This episode can once again be understood in terms of investment in the dynasty. The pregnancy of the concubine represents a rival for status, as the birth of a son automatically raised a harem woman's position and prospects. In brutally preventing the pregnancy, Empress Jia prioritizes her own factional power, as opposed to the stable perpetuation of her husband's line and the dynasty.

Ambiguous Portrayals: The Power and Limits of Typology

Clearly, just as portrayals of Empresses Ma and Deng are wholly positive, the destructive flaws attributed to Empress Jia in these narratives are not mitigated by any redeeming qualities. These relatively unambiguous portrayals establish a clear framework that suggests views of female power in relation to notions of normative womanly roles and dynastic perpetuation. However, it is often in more ambiguous portrayals, that is, portrayals that combine praise and condemnation or that suggest underlying conflict, that we can get a sense of the tensions inherent in the ideological systems informing the narrative's construction. Such tensions drive the rhetorical re-creations of the ways in which Empress Dugu interacts with her husband and her female rivals and are even implicit in descriptions of the conflict between the virtuous Empress Deng and her rival Empress Yin 陰 (d. 102 CE).

In certain respects, the portrayal of Empress Dugu shares the condemnatory language used to censure Empresses Lü and Jia. Zhao Can's persuasion of Emperor Wu, hinging upon the "natural [female] sentiment" of his daughter-in-law, finds an echo in accounts of Emperor Wen's 文帝 (Yang Jian 楊堅; r. 581–604) reaction to his wife Empress

Dugu's murder of a young and beautiful consort whom he had "favored." Like Empress Jia, Empress Dugu was "extremely jealous; no one in the harem dared to approach the emperor" (然性尤妒忌, 後宮莫敢進御).[48] After Emperor Wen found out that Empress Dugu had committed the murder, he galloped twenty miles through rough terrain on a solitary steed. His trusted associate Gao Jiong 高熲 (d. 607) pursued him and, in an effort to pacify the emperor, said: "How can Your Majesty make light of the entire realm for the sake of just one woman!" (陛下豈以一婦人而輕天下!).[49] As in Zhao Can's advice to Emperor Wu, Gao Jiong's comment downplays the brutality of Empress Dugu's crime by relegating it to the inferior realm of women, which is contrasted with the outer, manly realm of politics. Indeed, according to the account, Empress Dugu heard the condescension in his words and came to despise him. As portrayed in the *Sui shu* 隋書 (History of the Sui Dynasty),[50] the power dynamics at play between Emperor Wen and his wife favor Empress Dugu. In Emperor Wen's own words (supposedly): "I am honored as the Son of Heaven, yet I can't do as I please!" (吾貴為天子, 而不得自由).[51]

In spite of the rhetorical and structural similarities between the accounts of Empresses Jia and Dugu, the *Sui shu* account of Empress Dugu's murder of the concubine is noticeably less violent and detailed than the *Jin shu* description of Empress Jia's attack on the pregnant consort.[52] This may well be related to Empress Dugu's demonstration, in other episodes, of appropriate female virtue. The relationship between the empress and her husband, especially during the pre-Sui and early Sui years, is described as one characterized by genuine love and mutual respect. As a young couple, they swore an oath of eternal devotion and

48. *SS* 36.1109.

49. *SS* 36.1109. From the ensuing lines, which explain that Empress Dugu came to hate Gao Jiong because he had called her "just one woman," we understand that the woman Gao Jiong is referring to is Empress Dugu, not the consort whom she murdered.

50. Like the *Jin shu*, the *Sui shu* was put together in the first fifty years of the Tang under a committee of scholars headed in this case by Wei Zheng 魏徵 (580–643), who was, like Fang Xuanling, a favorite of Taizong with northern roots. The history was presented to the throne in 636. For Wei Zheng's official biographies, see *JTS* 71.2545–63 and *XTS* 97.3867–81.

51. *SS* 36.1109.

52. "The empress waited until the emperor was at court and secretly killed her [the consort]" (后伺上聽朝, 陰殺之); *SS* 36.1109.

monogamy, and Empress Dugu (then Lady Dugu) was a great support to the future Emperor Wen in his navigation of the dangerous Northern Zhou 北周 (557–81) court and his bid to establish his own dynasty. The empress was a patroness of Buddhism, a religious preference shared by her husband, and was praised for her intelligence, political acumen, kindness, and modesty. In line with her "virtuous" predecessors, Empress Dugu publicly renounced an official political role, claiming that direct female participation in affairs of state was dangerous to the polity. In actuality she and the emperor constantly decided governmental matters together and were known as the "Two Sages" (*er sheng* 二聖), but the public renunciation is important to the projection of female virtue.[53]

So as to reconcile her virtuous qualities with her apparent murder of the concubine, Empress Dugu becomes a heroine with a fatal flaw, extreme jealousy and obsession with monogamy. It is important to remember that accounts of the inner quarters of the palace are often based on rumor and impossible to verify; we cannot say whether, for example, Empress Dugu really killed the rival consort. Certainly the rhetorical focus on her obsession with monogamy suggests an incongruity with her interpretation of sexual norms as codified in the Tang dynasty. Empress Dugu's insistence upon conjugal faithfulness may reflect northern values stressing the importance of the wife in the elite family.[54] Obviously the value of monogamy did not win out, and in the process of history writing, certain behaviors and values retroactively become "abnormal" and must be reinterpreted and reconciled.

The cultural power of female sexual behavior, according to the interpretations of historians, is seen in the narrative deployment of Empress Dugu's fatal flaw; her "aberrant" sexual preference rhetorically becomes the catalyst for the ruin of the entire Sui state. According to historical accounts, Empress Dugu urged the emperor to banish any official with a pregnant concubine.[55] Within the imperial family, the deteriorating relationship between the empress and the crown prince, Yang Yong 楊勇 (d. 604), is ascribed to his preference for a concubine. Perceiving the possible chance to advance himself, the opportunistic second imperial son, Yang

53. *SS* 36.1108–9.
54. Wright, *The Sui Dynasty*, 74.
55. *SS* 36.1109.

Guang 楊廣 (the future Emperor Yang 煬帝, r. 604–18), easily manipulated his parents by presenting an image of himself as monogamous and virtuous. The *Zizhi tongjian* account of Yang Guang's choreographed reception of his parents at his residence is quite comical: "When the emperor and empress visited his residence, Guang hid all of his beautiful consorts in a separate chamber and only retained the old and ugly ones, dressed in plain silks" (上與后嘗幸其第, 廣悉屏匿美姬於別室, 唯留老醜者, 衣以縵綵).[56] Empress Dugu and Emperor Wen were convinced of their second son's complete accord with his mother's values, and they therefore also believed his slander of his older brother, with the result that Guang replaced Yong as crown prince. Under Yang Guang's rule, the Sui dynasty built by his parents toppled within decades.

The accounts of Yang Guang's successful bid to be made crown prince are meant to emphasize the lethal mistake wrought by Empress Dugu's sexual prerogative. Yet this episode also paradoxically reveals the strong role played by Empress Dugu as one of the "Two Sages" in charge of making key governmental decisions and the confidence placed in her political judgment by the emperor and presumably the court advisors. There is a transparent tension between the historical reality, in which a woman ruler held considerable political clout, her acumen as leader clearly respected, and the negative evaluation that attributes the result of her decisions to the crazy jealousy of an unraveling female.

Empress Dugu's biography represents a fascinating and somewhat manic fusion of narrative markers of womanly virtue and vice. Although the list of virtues is much longer than the list of vices, it is the vices, hinging upon her cardinal relationships with her husband, his other women, and their children, that overshadow her otherwise praiseworthy legacy. In contrast, Deng Sui's biography overall upholds her as a paragon of feminine virtue from a position of power. In the accounts of her rise to power, however, we can intuit narrative elements that might have gone the other way, so to speak, and that contain the rhetorical sprouts out of which the typology of the destructive feminine is often constructed.

According to Empress Deng's biography, her steady rise in Emperor He's estimation brought her into conflict with his first wife, Empress

56. *ZZTJ* 179.5574.

Yin.[57] The competition between Deng and Yin is narratively constructed as a clear-cut conflict between Deng's virtuous humility and Yin's deviousness. As Yin began to lose favor, she and her relatives plotted against Deng, eventually resorting to occult arts (*wugu* 巫蠱).[58] Learning of Empress Yin's hatred for her, a distraught Consort Deng resolved to kill herself but was stopped by fellow palace ladies. Even when Empress Yin's plan against her was uncovered, Deng tried, albeit unsuccessfully, to ask for clemency on Yin's behalf. However, Emperor He had already made up his mind to replace Yin with his new favorite, who happened to be Deng herself. Ever the paragon of humility, Deng pleaded with the emperor and made excuses to try to avoid the honor, but, in the end, she was installed as empress.[59] Emperor He died several years later without having left an adult heir and, in the resultant succession crisis, Empress Deng took full power as regent to one of the deceased emperor's young sons.

The almost extreme emphasis on then-Consort Deng's total blamelessness in the conflict with Empress Yin seems, in a sense, to gloss over a situation that was all too common in the harem: a brutal power struggle for the emperor's affection. In these conflicts, accusations of occult practice were highly common to the point of becoming a narrative cliché.[60]

57. Yin and Deng were actually maternal relatives; Deng's mother was surnamed Yin, and both were descendants of the second empress of the Eastern Han founder Emperor Guangwu 光武帝 (Liu Xiu 劉秀; r. 25–57), the Guanglie Empress 光烈皇后 (Yin Lihua 陰麗華; 5–64 CE). For a discussion of the Eastern Han rulers' choice of empresses from particular clans, see Cutter and Crowell, *Empresses and Consorts*, 21–25.

58. *Wugu* could include the use of curses, effigies, and *gudu* ("*gu* poisoning"). Graphically, *gu* is comprised of the radical for "vessel" placed below the radical for "insect." In pre-Han literature, *gu* is used in several different ways and can indicate disease, evil spirits, a woman tempting a man, a worm-eaten vessel, and a divination symbol. See Feng and Shryock, "The Black Magic in China Known as *ku*," 2. As we move into the Han, *gu* is especially associated with the occult and imperial politics, in particular the imperial harem. As a form of occult practice, *gu* is described as being created when a person with sinister intentions puts insects, snakes, and other reptiles in a jar. The creatures are sealed in there to fight until only one remains; this remaining creature has imbibed the potency of all of its defeated opponents and is used to create the *gu*, which tortures and poisons the human creator's targeted enemy. See Chao Yuanfang 巢元方 (fl. 605–616), *Zhubing yuanhou lun*, 25.135a/b. For discussions of *gu*, see Unschuld, *Medicine in China*, 46–50; Harper, *Early Chinese Medical Literature*, 75–76; and Mollier, *Buddhism and Daoism Face to Face*, 95.

59. *HHS* 10a.420–21.

60. For an analysis of another instance of the role played by occult practice in Han court politics, see Loewe, "The Case of Witchcraft in 91 BC."

Deng Sui, the clear winner in this case, is cast as the virtuous heroine, but Empress Yin's own very terse biography suggests a potential alternative reading of the situation. Yin's biography recounts the *wugu* incident as follows: "*Someone said that* the Empress and Zhu [Deng Zhu, her maternal grandmother] were practicing the occult arts [*jia wugu dao*]" (有言后與朱共挾巫蠱道).[61] That is, the charges were never definitively proven, and their typological nature suggests the influence of gossip or slander between harem rivals. Since Empress Deng is an exemplar of virtue within the literary-historical tradition, the narrative is cast as one of "the jealous rival (Yin) attempts to harm the virtuous favorite (Deng)," not "the power-hungry favorite (Deng) slanders and destroys the hapless rival (Yin)."

Motherhood and the Moral Evaluation of Women Rulers

The sexual politics of the harem, including an empress's desire to control her husband's intercourse with other women, ultimately derives from the idea of the rightful heir and the woman's importance as vessel for that male child. This constantly led to complications involving adoption, manipulation, and murder of children in the precarious environment of the inner quarters. In terms of narrative devices, the ways in which empresses and consorts relate to children are as important as, if not more important than, their interactions with each other in conveying their moral character. Portrayals of "virtuous" empresses and consorts stress their ideal fulfillment of the mother role: they are selfless, compassionate, and utterly disdainful of personal power in serving the patriarchal line. In portrayals of censured powerful women rulers, their abuse of children and stepchildren encapsulates the dangerous ambition inherent in women with too much public power.

In an interaction with his virtuous consort, Empress Ma, Emperor Ming of the Eastern Han himself pinpointed the importance of the

61. *HHS* 10a.417, italics mine.

mother role to securing a woman's prosperity and reputation. When he saw that his favorite consort could not bear children, he gave her the son of her niece, also a palace lady, to raise as her own. His words to her at this point are significant: "A lady need not give birth to her own child, but need only fear that her love and care in raising her charge are insufficient" (人未必當自生子，但患愛養不至耳).[62] The moral is clear; investment in the patriarchal system is of the utmost importance. Uphold the system, and rewards will follow; defy the system, and punishment is never far away. Empress Ma took the lesson to heart and exerted herself to the utmost in raising the future Emperor Zhang 章帝 (Liu Da 劉炟; r. 75–88). She was accordingly rewarded with Emperor Zhang's undying loyalty and a praiseworthy place within the historical memory.

In contrast, Empress Lü's identity as an early historical prototype of the destructive feminine force is demarcated by her role as the anti-mother. Without hesitation, she destroys not only her rivals, but also her own son. By exposing her son Emperor Hui to the horrific sight of the degraded Lady Qi, Empress Lü rendered him so psychologically crippled that he could pose no threat whatsoever to her absolute authority. She is thus blamed for his failure as a ruler; according to these accounts, she turned him into a man who drank, debauched himself, and ignored his responsibilities, instead of the alternative possibility, that is, that she governed on his behalf because he was incompetent. Empress Jia is also known for her un-matronly actions. She was accused of murdering the crown prince, Sima Yu 司馬遹 (278–300), who was not her biological son, when he became a threat to her continued monopolization of power.[63] In addition, she supposedly pretended that she was pregnant and then attempted to pass off as her own the son of her younger sister Jia Wu.[64]

62. *HHS* 10a.409.

63. See *JS* 53.1457–58.

64. See *JS* 31.965–66. The theme of the stolen son is a powerful trope indicating the disorder caused by female power and manipulation. Before Empress Jia, the stolen son scheme was employed by Empress Lü's sonless daughter-in-law Empress Zhang 張 (Zhang Yan 張嫣, also known as Empress Xiaohui 孝惠皇后; d. 163 BCE), the daughter of the Marquis of Xuanping Zhang Ao 宣平侯張敖 (d. 182 BCE). Empress Zhang was actually Empress Lü's granddaughter and Emperor Hui's niece. See *SJ* 49.1969 and 9.402–3.

As in the case of virtuous typologies, what is important is not the biological relationship between mother and child, but rather the mother's obedience to or transgression of the family relationships that were vital to the imperial patriarchy. A woman ruler's defiance of the patriarchal imperial order is matched by the violent reaction of that order against her, once her chaos has been brought under control: by her destruction and posthumous condemnation. The importance of the mother-son bond is seen as so fundamental that devotion to a male charge can mitigate against punishment for other transgressions.

Eastern Han Empress Dou, Emperor Zhang's empress and the adoptive mother of Empress Deng's husband Emperor He, is a case in point. After Zhang's death, she joined with her brother, Dou Xian 竇憲 (d. 92 CE), and other male relatives to build up a powerful faction. When the Dou faction fell from power, she alone was spared execution or posthumous disgrace. In an edict upholding Empress Dou's right to a joint burial with her deceased husband, Emperor He emphasized the mother-son bond: "Although the Dou clan did not obey the law, the empress dowager was always frugal and self-effacing. I have ruled for ten years and deeply respect the fundamental duties and the rites. According to ritual, in the role of minister and son, it has never been considered permissible to be stinting in respecting one's superiors. I cannot bear to be ungrateful for the compassion shown me or remiss in my duty" (竇氏雖不尊法度, 而太后常自減損. 朕奉事十年, 深惟大義, 禮, 臣子無貶尊上之文. 恩不忍離, 義不忍虧).[65] Just as Emperor Ming of the Eastern Han instructed Dou's mother-in-law, Empress Ma, fulfillment of the mother role is key to a woman's negotiation of the imperial patriarchy and demonstration of her virtue.

Narrative depictions of the crucial mother-son relationship suggest broader familial networks, traditional and non-traditional. Empress Ma and Empress Jia are fundamentally opposite narrative types, but, in the accounts of each woman's rise to power, we can intuit the importance of particular familial or alternative familial structures to her success. Empress Ma was named empress due to the support of Emperor Ming's mother; Empress Jia's position was spared through the intervention of Emperor Wu's consort Zhao Can, and her rule was made possible in part by a clique of family members and inner palace supporters.

65. *HHS* 10a.416.

The mother-son or mother-stepson (heir to the throne) relationship, within the rubric of alternative familial structure, likewise plays an important role in accounts of the reigns of powerful Northern Wei rulers Empress Feng and Empress Dowager Hu. Their portrayals in the *Wei shu* 魏書 (History of the Northern Wei Dynasty) reveal the operation of differing cultural and imperial traditions that created alternative avenues of ascension for certain women in the imperial harem to the highest echelons of government. These accounts also represent an attempt to fit these cultural and political norms into the Chinese history format; they are described by historians who either did not understand them or chose to obscure them.

The dates of compilation of the relevant accounts are significant here. The standard histories of both the Northern and Southern Dynasties were, as discussed above, by and large compiled by literati at the seventh-century Tang court. The *Wei shu* is the only pre-Tang history on the Northern Dynasties; it was compiled between 551 and 554 by Wei Shou 魏收 (506–72), a native of Hebei.[66] The original "Biographies of Empresses and Consorts" chapter, however, was lost by the Song dynasty and had to be reconstituted from the later Tang *Bei shi* 北史 (History of the Northern Dynasties)[67] and some other contemporary works that have also subsequently been lost. Thus we can, for all intents and purposes, consider the *Wei shu* chapter on empresses and consorts a later work, probably from the same seventh-century milieu as the *Bei shi*.[68] The uniformity of compilation date might account in part for the vagueness regarding northern customs of succession and imperial marriage practices, which are of critical importance in understanding the women leaders of the period.

Starting in the decades leading up to Empress Feng's appointment as the official empress of Emperor Wencheng 文成帝 (Tuoba Jun 拓拔濬;

66. Wei Shou was a historian, an official, and a literary figure under the Eastern Wei 東魏 (534–50) and Northern Qi 北齊 (550–77).

67. The one-hundred-chapter *Bei shi*, also a standard or state-sanctioned history, is a Tang work and covers the histories of the Northern Wei, Western Wei, Eastern Wei, Northern Zhou, Northern Qi, and Sui dynasties (385–617 CE). The *Bei shi* was completed between 643 and 659 under Li Yanshou 李延壽 (fl. 7th c.).

68. It is, of course, possible that the compilers of the *Bei shi* utilized materials from the *Wei shu* chapter on empresses and consorts, but, given the subsequent loss of the earlier chapter, it is impossible at this remove to determine the relationship between the two chapters. See Holmgren, "Women and Political Power," 35.

r. 452–65), there was a custom of female political operation from the position of the heir apparent's nurse and/or empress dowager among women who were not the biological mother of the ruler. This custom is seen in the cases of Empress Dowager Chang 常太后 (Wencheng's nurse; dates unknown), who was instrumental in appointing Empress Feng, and of Empress Feng herself, and is directly related to the Northern Wei "tradition" of killing the biological mother of the boy appointed heir apparent.[69] As pointed out by various scholars, the first notice of this custom as a Northern Wei "tradition" comes from the purported words of the official Northern Wei founder, Emperor Daowu 道武帝 (Tuoba Gui 拓拔珪; r. 386–409), who claimed that he was executing his unloved consort, a Xiongnu woman née Liu 劉, because he wished to eliminate the influence of the imperial in-laws. Supposedly, Emperor Daowu was following the example of Emperor Wu of the Han 漢武帝 (Liu Che 劉徹; r. 141–87 BCE), who had ordered the mother of the crown prince executed to stop her and/or her family from wresting power from the ruling line.

Although the so-called "tradition" has attracted the attention of many scholars, there is no consensus as to its true provenance and purpose.[70] In regard to the pivotal issue of in-law interference at court, analysis suggests

69. For a detailed discussion of Empress Dowager Chang, see Song Qirui, *Bei Wei nüzhu lun*, chap. 2.

70. Holmgren has argued that Tuoba Gui took the historical example of Emperor Wu seriously and that the violent custom initiated by the first Northern Wei emperor was the result of the growing pains of sinicization. See Holmgren, "Women and Political Power," 58–60. However, it is difficult to believe that a sane ruler would wholeheartedly and immediately adopt such an extreme measure as a tradition intended for himself as well as his descendants after hearing an ancient Chinese story, or that Chinese advisors would suggest this course of action. If we posit that the practice of killing the biological mother of the heir apparent was not a systematic part of Tuoba life before Tuoba Gui's murder of Lady Liu, Song Qirui's argument that Tuoba Gui simply latched on to the ancient historical precedent of Emperor Wu as an excuse to do what he wanted seems plausible here. See Song Qirui, *Bei Wei nüzhu lun*, 101. Based on analysis of prescriptive marriage practices among the Tuoba and other groups, Valentin C. Golovachev believes that the practice did originate among the Tuoba-Xianbei well before the beginning of clear records in the fourth century, during their nomadic pre–Northern Wei period. See Golovachev, "Matricide among the Tuoba-Xianbei." Scott Pearce has refuted Golovachev's argument by drawing attention to the succession crisis that served as background for Tuoba Gui's execution of Lady Liu. See Pearce, "A Response to Valentin Golovachev's 'Matricide during the Northern Wei.'" See also Pearce, "Nurses, Nurslings, and New Shapes of Power."

that in fact, as a tool of eliminating in-law power, the practice was completely ineffective; not only did the violent "custom" do nothing to curb in-law influence, but it actually created avenues to power for alternate "in-law" groups, including a host of powerful women. During the later Northern Wei period (the second half of the fifth century through the fall of the dynasty in 534), execution of the heir apparent's biological mother became a powerful tool that was manipulated by women against women, a potent way to eliminate rivals by invoking the veneer of cultural tradition. The tradition led to the creation of a surrogate or substitute *waiqi* 外戚 (imperial relatives by marriage) group that took the place of the biological mother and her family. The women of these surrogate *waiqi* groups wielded considerable power throughout the later Northern Wei period.[71]

The woman who became Emperor Wencheng's formal empress, Empress Feng, did so precisely because of the operation of this substitute *waiqi* system.[72] She was descended from the royal line of the Northern Yan 北燕 regime (405/407–436), which fell to the Northern Wei in 436. In 456, as a young adolescent, she was made Emperor Wencheng's formal empress. This seemingly was not due to a special love between her and the emperor, but rather to the execution of Wencheng's beloved Consort Li 李, the biological mother of the crown prince, in accordance with the Northern Wei tradition. The decision to kill Consort Li was made by nurse-turned–Empress Dowager Chang, who wielded considerable power in palace affairs.[73] Empress Dowager Chang was a dominant

71. These women included Empress Dowager Chang and Emperor Taiwu's 太武帝 (Tuoba Tao 拓拔燾; r. 423–52) nurse, née Dou 竇, who was appointed first *baotaihou* 保太后 (something like "grand nurse") and then empress dowager. See Song Qirui, *Bei Wei nüzhu lun*, 99–100. For a further discussion of the role played by emperors' wet-nurses in Northern Wei political life, see Li Ping, *Bei Wei Pingcheng shidai*, chap. 3.

72. For a detailed discussion of Empress Feng's life and career, see Song Qirui, *Bei Wei nüzhu lun*, chap. 3; and Li Ping, *Bei Wei Pingcheng shidai*, chap. 4.

73. *WS* 13.331 and *BS* 13.498. Empress Dowager Chang hailed from a higher-class family of Liaoxi 遼西, former Northern Yan territory. She could have entered the Northern Wei harem either as a result of enforced movements of the conquered population or as a servant girl of the youngest daughter of the Northern Yan ruler Feng Hong 馮弘 (Feng Wentong 馮文通; d. 438), grandfather of the future Empress Dowager Feng. Feng Hong's daughter, Empress Feng's aunt, was sent as a last-ditch effort at marriage diplomacy and became Shining Consort Feng 馮昭儀 (dates unknown). After the forced suicide of Crown Prince Tuoba Jun's biological mother, Chang was appointed his nurse

member of a Northern Yan clique in the Northern Wei palace; this clique also included the future Empress Feng's aunt, former Northern Yan princess Shining Consort Feng 馮昭儀 (dates unknown), a consort of Emperor Taiwu, who acted as her niece's surrogate mother and supporter after her entry into the palace.[74]

Virtually institutionalized killing of the crown prince's biological mother might at first seem to contradict a tradition of Northern Wei female power, yet in practice the tradition was just a variation, albeit an unusual one, on run-of-the-mill ruthless harem factional politics. We have here a clear instance of women who held a vested interest in perpetuating the system of killing mothers to potential heirs to the throne. The alternative familial system buttressing the rise to power of women like Empress Dowager Chang and Empress Feng naturally influenced mother-son dynamics within the imperial family, in particular, the heir apparent's relationships with the women who took his mother's place. After the death of Emperor Wencheng, Empress Feng was formally established as regent over the executed Consort Li's son, the twelve-year-old Emperor Xianwen 獻文帝 (Tuoba Hong 拓拔弘; r. 465–71). While acting as Xianwen's legal guardian, she also "personally cared for and brought up" (躬親撫養) his son, the future Emperor Xiaowen 孝文帝 (Tuoba Hong 拓拔宏 or Yuan Hong 元宏, r. 471–99).[75] Like the depiction of Empress Dugu of the Sui, Empress Feng's portrayal is a mixture of positive and negative narrative formulas. The ambiguity that characterizes her portrayal is contingent upon her relationships with Xianwen and Xiaowen, that is, her fulfillment (or lack thereof) of the ideal requirements for the role of mother.

Empress Feng's praiseworthy actions as ruler include the successful pacification of an attempted coup in 465–66, her patronage of Buddhism, and, in the late 470s and early 480s, the institution of various reform

---

and became his surrogate mother. For Empress Dowager Chang's biography, see *WS* 13.327–28 and *BS* 13.495. See also Song Qirui, *Bei Wei nüzhu lun*, 96–99, and Li Ping, *Bei Wei Pingcheng shidai*, 175–93.

74. Shining Consort Feng took the future Empress Feng under her wing after the younger woman entered the palace as a teenager; her aunt gave her an education and, later, supported her bid to become empress. See *WS* 13.328 and *BS* 13.495. For a discussion of Empress Dowager Chang and Shining Consort Feng, see Pearce, "Nurses, Nurslings, and New Shapes of Power," 296–308.

75. *WS* 13.328.

measures that improved the people's quality of life.[76] She was generous to subordinates, laughing instead of punishing a servant who delivered her a bowl of porridge with an insect swimming in it, and she earned a reputation for strict yet fair application of the law.[77] When it comes to narratives of her relationships with her adopted son and grandson, however, she is cast in the role of the destructive woman. Instead of yielding to Xianwen, she is portrayed as assuming full authority as ruler, forcing Xianwen to abdicate to his young son in 471. When she and Xianwen had a falling-out involving Xianwen's murder of her alleged lover, the minister Li Yi 李弈 (d. 470), she did not hesitate to kill the emperor and purge his faction.[78] She and her adopted grandson Emperor Xiaowen lived together at court harmoniously, but the narrative suggests that this was made possible by his willingness to defer to her authority.[79]

In *Wei shu* and *Bei shi*, the conflict between Empress Feng and Xianwen is presented as Xianwen's moral attempt to counteract Empress Feng's immoral behavior. While the *Bei shi* merely states that "the Empress Dowager failed to achieve her intention, so she murdered the emperor" (太后不得意, 遂害帝),[80] the *Wei shu* elaborates in an interesting way: "The empress dowager failed to achieve her intention. [When] Xianzu [Xianwen] died violently, *at the time people said the empress dowager was responsible*" (太后不得意. 顯祖暴崩, 時言太后為之也).[81] This passage admits the possibility that Empress Feng was in fact not responsible for Emperor Xianwen's death, thus acknowledging the power of gossip to damage her reputation by casting her in the archetypal role of the destructive female ruler.[82]

76. Soon after the beginning of Empress Feng's regency, the official Yi Hun 乙渾 (d. 466) carried out his scheme to gain control of the government. However, Empress Feng, with the aid of several other high-ranking court officials, staged a successful counter-coup and defeated his faction. The reform measures that she later instituted were designed to improve the lives of prisoners, lessen the extent of family responsibility for a relative's rebellion, stimulate agriculture, and decrease the taxation burden on the people caused by the rise in serfdom. See *WS* 13.328–29.

77. *WS* 13.329; Song Qirui, *Bei Wei nüzhu lun*, 215–16.

78. *WS* 13.328.

79. *WS* 13.328–9.

80. *BS* 13.495.

81. *WS* 13.328, emphasis mine.

82. The *Wei shu* biography creates the impression that the execution of Li Yi was

As a narrative figure, Empress Feng emerges as an uneasy combination of positive and negative images of the feminine. She ruled competently during a time of stability for the Northern Wei, and this historical background cannot be dismissed as a contributing factor in rhetorical assignations of "virtuous" qualities to her. Several generations later, during the period of Northern Wei decline, Empress Dowager Hu, also known for her exertion of political control, is cast unambiguously as a destructive woman ruler.

Empress Dowager Hu, a consort of Emperor Xuanwu 宣武帝 (Tuoba Ke 拓拔恪, changed to Yuan Ke 元恪; r. 499–515),[83] initially seems to be a potentially positive maternal and patriotic figure. She is described as particularly brave in being willing to give birth to a boy who became crown prince; because of the custom of killing the mother of the crown prince, all of the other imperial consorts prayed to have only princesses or princes with no chance of being named heir.[84] She managed to survive but was separated from her biological son at birth and never allowed to see him. Portrayals of their relationship after he had grown up certainly suggest the alienation caused by this separation, yet narrative accounts of the interactions between Empress Dowager Hu and her son, Emperor Xiaoming 孝明帝 (Yuan Xu 元詡; r. 515–528), do not dwell on such tensions. Rather, they are cast in terms of gendered typologies: Emperor Xiaoming is the moral rightful male ruler who is thwarted by a licentious and power-hungry "unnatural" anti-mother.

Empress Dowager Hu's rule can be divided into two periods. After the death of Emperor Xuanwu, she ruled as regent over Emperor Xiaoming until, in 520, she was deposed for the first time by her brother-in-law

directly followed by the empress's alleged retaliatory assassination of Xianwen. In fact, six years passed between the elimination of Li Yi's faction (with which Empress Feng seems to have been identified) in 470 and the assassination of Xianwen in 476. Eisenberg has argued that the "abdication" of Xianwen in 471 actually occurred at Xianwen's behest and should be understood as an instance of voluntary retired emperorship designed to secure a peaceful succession. According to this reading, Empress Feng did not assume a powerful political role until after Xianwen's death in 476. See Eisenberg, *Kingship in Early Medieval China*, chap. 3.

83. In 496, under Emperor Xiaowen, the imperial surname was changed from Tuoba to Yuan as part of a series of sinicization measures. For a detailed discussion of Hu's life and career, see Song Qirui, *Bei Wei nüzhu lun*, chap. 4.

84. See *WS* 13.337 and *BS* 13.503.

Yuan Cha 元叉 (d. 525), who, acting in concert with the eunuch Liu Teng 劉騰 (d. 523), kept her under house arrest in a separate palace for several years (520–25). According to historical accounts, the notoriously corrupt Yuan Cha and Liu Teng had feared punishment when Empress Dowager Hu and her reputed lover Yuan Yi 元懌 (Prince of Qinghe 清河王; d. 520) launched a campaign to decrease rampant corruption in the administration.[85] Following Liu Teng's death and Yuan Cha's growing inattentiveness as a ruler, Empress Dowager Hu and her faction were finally able to gather enough strength to disarm him and reinstate her.[86]

During the second period of her rule, a power struggle with her son broke out, and, predictably, this is also the point at which her "destructive female nature" comes to the fore. Historical accounts tell us that Empress Dowager Hu again relied heavily upon a lover, Zheng Yan 鄭嚴 (d. 528). This time, we are told, the lover was not virtuous, and Empress Dowager Hu committed the ultimate un-motherly offense of choosing him over her son. Working closely with Zheng Yan and another associate, Xu Ge 徐紇 (dates unknown), she is said to have first killed off all of Emperor Xiaoming's close associates so as to cripple his political power before eliminating the young emperor himself.[87]

According to the more scandalous *Bei shi* account, the three held a banquet at which they poisoned Emperor Xiaoming.[88] When Xiaoming's consort gave birth to a daughter, Empress Dowager Hu falsely proclaimed that the infant was a boy and placed him on the throne. The *Wei shu* biographies of Empress Dowager Hu and Zheng Yan provide alternative but almost verbatim accounts of Emperor Xiaoming's death: "As for Suzong's [Emperor Xiaoming's] death, the affair came out in a hurried and startling manner. *At the time everyone's opinion was that / the whole world said that* Zheng Yan and Xu Ge had done it" (肅宗之崩, 事出倉卒, 時論咸言鄭儼, 徐紇之計; 肅宗崩, 事出倉卒, 天下咸言儼計也).[89] The insinuation of gossip is striking here: "at the time everyone's

85. See *WS* 22.592.

86. *WS* 13.339 and *BS* 13.504–5.

87. *WS* 13.339–40.

88. See *BS* 13.505.

89. *WS* 13.340; *WS* 93.2007 (italics mine). Zheng Yan's biography places the entire blame on Zheng Yan's shoulders ("the whole world said that [Zheng] Yan had done it" 天下咸言儼計也). See also *BS* 35.1315.

opinion was that / the whole world said that" is very different from a simple statement of historical fact. Read with an awareness of gender archetypes, this should at least make us think twice about unquestioning acceptance of the accusations leveled against Empress Dowager Hu as an anti-mother.

The chaos associated with Empress Dowager Hu is ultimately blamed for the fall of the Northern Wei. In a desperate attempt to defeat his mother, Emperor Xiaoming had called upon the Xiongnu general and Bingzhou-based warlord Erzhu Rong 爾朱榮 (493–530) to depose the empress dowager and eliminate her factional allies. Xiaoming's missive to Erzhu Rong precipitated his own death. Erzhu Rong advanced on Luoyang, massacring Empress Dowager Hu and thousands of Northern Wei officials as he took power.[90] In the dramatic narrative of the fall of the Northern Wei, there are various players (Erzhu Rong, Zheng Yan, Emperor Xiaoming) whose responsibility might seem greater than Empress Dowager Hu's. However, her repudiation of the mother role is cast as the dominant factor in setting into motion the disastrous chain of events, and it also becomes the central characteristic in her rhetorical construction as the destructive woman.

Sexually Based Condemnation and Rule by Women

Narratives of powerful female rulers rely on the complex relationship between wives, mothers, and sons within the imperial setting, where every potential regular life tension is exacerbated and new tensions are created due to the stresses surrounding succession and rule. As we have seen, a powerful woman's virtue, or lack thereof, is conveyed through her cardinal relationships within the patriarchal dynastic system. The virtuous woman is defined as one who rules only in the minority or incapacity of the legitimate male authority and one who places the interests of the imperial patriline above her own. Appropriate investment in the system includes fulfillment of the roles of both virtuous mother and dutiful wife.

90. The massacre of Northern Wei officials is known as the Heyin 河陰 Massacre. See Erzhu Rong's biographies in *WS* 74.1643–57 and *BS* 48.1751–76.

Throughout the pre-Tang regimes, women rulers who are condemned by the tradition are accused of sexual misconduct that further encapsulates transgression of the cardinal womanly role.

Sexually based de-legitimation of women rulers differs in several important respects from condemnatory portrayals of male officials or rulers. Although bad male rulers may or may not be accused of sexual misconduct, their sexual crimes are often couched in terms of over-indulgence and are not necessarily seen as the natural expression of character or leadership ability. Even in accounts that criticize these male figures, sexuality remains female-identified and, indeed, a male ruler's sexual depravity is often displaced to or located primarily in his female harem. In the case of condemned women leaders, the typology of sexual misconduct suggests the disorder of the private and public as a defining characteristic of illegitimate female rule. Empress Jia and Empress Dowager Hu are both accused of engaging in multiple sexual affairs with corrupt men.[91] In each case, these relationships rhetorically become major contributing factors in contemporary political disasters. The depictions of the men involved in these relationships are likewise used as foils to reinforce the typology of the powerful women with whom they are associated.

As discussed above, Empress Dowager Hu and Empress Jia are both accused of conspiring with their lovers to assassinate the rightful heir (Empress Dowager Hu's biological son and Empress Jia's stepson, respectively). Empress Jia "became licentious and abandoned" (后遂荒淫放恣) and "caused chaos to manifest inside and out" (亂彰內外) with, among others, imperial physician Cheng Ju 程據 (d. 299), whom she favored and whom she supposedly commanded to concoct poison to assassinate Sima Yu.[92] We should note Cheng Ju's lower status as a medical specialist and his association with devious and improper behavior.[93]

91. Accusations of sexual depravity are not limited to the women under discussion in this chapter. For example, the Liu-Song 劉宋 (420–79 CE) Shanyin Princess 山陰公主 (d. 465) is notorious for demanding a male harem equal to that of her brother, Emperor Qianfei 前廢帝 ("The Former Deposed Emperor," Liu Ziye 劉子業; r. 464–66 CE). See *Song shu* 宋書 (History of the Liu-Song Dynasty), 7.147–48. Unlike the women under discussion in this chapter, all of whom ruled over viable political entities, the Shanyin Princess never seems to have sought political power for herself, and, as his name suggests, Qianfei's reign ended in disaster.

92. *JS* 31.964 and 53.1462.

93. Besides his appearances in the biographies of Empress Jia and Sima Yu, Cheng Ju

Furthermore, *Zizhi tongjian* accuses Empress Jia of extremely bizarre and violent sexual behavior: "She transported young men from the streets into the palace in trunks, but then became afraid that the affair would be discovered, so she often killed them [afterwards]" (又及以簏箱載道上年少入宮, 复恐其漏泄, 往往殺之).[94]

Another account in the *Jin shu* tells a fantastical story of a man's abduction by the empress, which seems to be a specific instance of the behavior described in *Zizhi tongjian*. Once, in Luonan 洛南, a low-level clerk was suddenly found in possession of unusual clothes. Everyone suspected him of thievery, and the matter was investigated. The clerk explained himself by describing a mysterious meeting on the road with an old woman, who told him that a member of her household was ill and that a divination had revealed that they must obtain a young man south of the city to assist in the cure. She promised him great rewards for his assistance. She put him in a large trunk and they traveled for at least ten miles. They passed six or seven doors, after which the trunk was opened and suddenly he saw a gated tower with a fine chamber. He asked what place this was and was informed that he was seeing "heaven" (*tianshang* 天上).[95] Then he was bathed in perfumed water, and fine clothes and delicacies were brought forth. He saw a woman "about thirty-five or thirty-six years old, short with a dark complexion and a mole beside her eyebrows" (年可三十五六, 短形青黑色, 眉後有疵).[96] After he saw this woman, the purpose of his summons became clear to him: "I was detained for several nights, during which we slept together and feasted. When it came time for me to leave, she gave me all the things [which I was accused of having stolen]" (見留數夕, 共寢歡宴, 臨出贈此眾物).[97] When the investigators heard the clerk's description of the woman, they recognized her as Empress Jia and, laughing with embarrassment, discontinued the interrogation and dropped the charges.

is mentioned in the basic annals of Emperor Wu, where he is similarly engaging in the improper behavior of giving the emperor a ritually prohibited coat made of feathers gathered from pheasants' heads. See *JS* 3.69. Emperor Wu prided himself upon the frugality of his government and detested outlandish luxury, so Cheng Ju's gift was especially ill-conceived. See *JS* 45.1272. This example is also referenced in Yang Wanli 楊萬里 (1127–1206), *Chengzhai yi zhuan*, 11.9b.

94. *ZZTJ* 83.2628.

95. *JS* 31.964–65.

96. *JS* 31.965.

97. *JS* 31.965.

The entire story told by the clerk reads like a mock *zhiguai* 志怪 (anomaly account or story of the strange) tale. The hapless and gullible clerk is the "hero" who encounters a divine or spirit female. Here, the magical woman actually turns out to be the unattractive human empress, who has abducted the clerk to satisfy her need for male companionship. Underlying this account is a clear anxiety about what happens when the power relations from the divine woman story type, strongly favoring the woman, are transposed to the reality of a female ruler. Her base impulses are unchecked by any (male) authority and wreak havoc upon the social hierarchy and the sexual integrity of unfortunate men everywhere.

Whereas Cheng Ju and the unnamed clerk are portrayed as, respectively, the henchman and the private servant of Empress Jia, Empress Dowager Hu's coterie of intimate associates gained considerable political clout as a result of their relationships with her. The creation of Empress Dowager Hu's political party is described in terms of sexual liaisons, and her dramatic political life is explained in terms of responses to her colorful sex life. The narrative of the initial coup against her by Yuan Cha is preceded by a revelation of sexual misconduct: "At that time the Empress Dowager was in power, and she forced the Prince of Qinghe, Yi, into a sexual relationship, acting shamelessly debauched and indulging all of her desires. Everyone was repulsed by her behavior" (時太后得志, 逼幸清河王懌, 淫亂肆情, 為天下所惡).[98] In the same paragraph, immediately following her imposition of "forced favor" (*bi xing* 逼幸) on the prince, Empress Dowager Hu is imprisoned by Yuan Cha. Her sexual misconduct is presented as the cause for Yuan Cha's reactive response against her to mete out deserved punishment. This directly contradicts evidence elsewhere in the *Wei shu* and *Bei shi* of Yuan Yi's upright, virtuous character and intention to curb Yuan Cha's corruption.[99] In addition, no evidence is given to substantiate the claim of "forced favor," or even the existence of a sexual relationship between Yuan Yi and the Empress Dowager.[100] The narrative is designed to overwrite any indication of Empress Dowager Hu's political competence with the typology of destructive female power.

98. *WS* 13.339. See also *BS* 13.504.

99. See *WS* 16.404 and 22.591–92 (Yuan Yi's biography); *BS* 16.597 and 19.716–17 (Yuan Yi's biography).

100. Yuan Yi's biographies describe his close alliance with the empress dowager, but do not seem to insinuate a sexual relationship. See *WS* 22.591–92 and *BS* 19.716–17.

After her reinstatement, Empress Dowager Hu reemerged as head of a powerful clique that included two men (Zheng Yan and Li Shengui 李神軌 [d. 528]) rumored to be her sexual partners. At this point, accusations of her bad behavior intensify in historical narratives. The descriptions of Empress Dowager Hu's main partners in crime and sexual favorites during this final period of her rule prefigure in several respects the male sexual favorite type of later historical narrative. This type is generally defined by physicality or sexual attractiveness (as opposed to intellectual substance and talent), advancement through sexual service, and abuse of power.

Prior to his close association with Empress Dowager Hu, Li Shengui held a series of military positions and "very much had the aura of a military leader" (頗有將領之氣).[101] His advancement is shrouded in secrecy and rumor: "During the Xiaochang reign period [525–27], he enjoyed Empress Dowager Ling's [Hu's] favor, and his power towered over court and country. At the time it was said that he was favored in the inner quarters and was a pair with Zheng Yan. Nobody at the time was entirely sure [whether the rumor was true or not]" (孝昌中, 為靈太后寵遇, 勢傾朝野, 時云見幸帷幄, 與鄭儼為雙, 時人莫能明也).[102] The biography of Zheng Yan, the other half of the "pair," follows a similar narrative: "Zheng Yan's style name was Jiran. He was from Xingyang. His appearance was strong and gorgeous. At first he was military aid to the minister of works, Hu Guozhen. Through this, he was favored by Empress Dowager Ling [Hu]. No one at the time knew about it" (鄭儼, 字季然, 滎陽人. 容貌壯麗. 初為司徒胡國珍行參軍, 因緣為靈太后所幸, 時人未之知也).[103] According to his biography, the relationship between Zheng Yan and the Empress Dowager commenced before her house arrest by Yuan Cha. When she regained power in 525, Zheng Yan was granted permission to return to court, after which he, along with Li Shengui, became one of the most powerful officials in the Northern Wei regime.

101. *WS* 66.1475. See the parallel biographical account in *BS* 43.1600.

102. Li Shengui had an upper-class background (his father had been Duke of Chenliu), and after receiving favor, he continued to fill important military posts. He was a leading general in quelling several of the rebellions raging at the time. Upon Erzhu Rong's movement to the Luoyang area, he was again appointed chief commander, but he retreated when he saw that the north was not guarded. He was one of the many Northern Wei officials killed at Erzhu Rong's behest in the Heyin Massacre. See *WS* 66.1475.

103. *WS* 93.2007. See the parallel biographical account in *BS* 35.1315.

Reading between the lines, we can see the operation of rumor in the reconstruction of history: "no one at the time knew about it," but, many years later, the historian somehow came into possession of this privileged information, and it became his duty to share it with readers. The archetype of the "destructive woman in power" again propels the historical account towards the "sexual favorite" narrative, even where no sound evidence for this narrative seems to exist. Acknowledging that the rampant corruption in Empress Dowager Hu's regime was a major contributing factor in Erzhu Rong's invasion and the subsequent fall of the Northern Wei, we must also note that a connection between sexual misconduct and poor leadership skills is implicitly and unfairly assumed. In the accounts of Empress Dowager Hu, licentiousness is synonymous with political corruption and fatal missteps as a ruler, and it is easy to forget that this correlation is not necessary or logical; nor does it necessarily exist in accounts of male rulers.

The portrayals of Zheng Yan and Li Shengui reinforce and reflect the portrayal of Empress Dowager Hu. Likewise, a close analysis of the biography of Empress Feng's important favorite Wang Rui 王叡 (434–81) reveals an intriguing mix of positive and negative formulas that parallel the formulas comprising Empress Feng's own biography. At first glance, the depiction of Wang Rui seems to follow the pattern of the male sexual favorite. He hailed from a family that had a history of official service but that by his time had become impoverished. Wang Rui started out life "carrying on his father's line of work [reading astronomical signs], but he was alluring and strapping. When Gongzong 恭宗 [Tuoba Huang 拓拔晃, Wencheng's father; 428–51 CE] was heir apparent, he saw him and found him remarkable" (叡少傳父業, 而姿貌偉麗. 恭宗之在東宮, 見而奇之).[104] The opening description of Wang Rui's irresistible manly charms is a transparent signal that Wang Rui's future fortunes will be linked to his personal magnetism. Predictably, after receiving appointments through the crown prince's notice, Wang Rui's fortunes increased markedly when Empress Feng gained control of the court as empress dowager. She favored him, and he subsequently received a series of high appointments and drastic increases in rank, which we are made to understand were not just the result of his objective qualifications: "After this

104. *WS* 93.1988. See the parallel biographical account in *BS* 93.3018–20.

[his receiving favor] he participated in internal confidential matters and outside took part in governmental affairs. [The Empress's] love and favor for him grew daily stronger, and the men of the court feared him" (於是內參機密, 外豫政事, 愛寵日隆, 朝士懾憚焉).[105]

The biography thus begins with the classic narrative of the sexual favorite allowed by the besotted ruler to wield a disproportionate amount of power, with disastrous results. Yet, at this point, the entire tenor of the biography changes, and Wang Rui suddenly becomes a hero:

> In the second year of Taihe [478], Gaozu [Xiaowen] and Empress Dowager Wenming [Empress Feng] led all of the officials and foreign emissaries to look at a group of caged tigers. There was an escaped tiger that climbed up the road to the pavilion and almost reached the imperial seat. The attendant courtiers all withdrew in terror, but Rui alone grasped a halberd to fend it off, and the tiger retreated. Thereupon his personal entrustment [from the throne] intensified.
>
> 太和二年, 高祖及文明太后率百僚與諸方客臨虎圈, 有逸虎登門閣道, 幾至御座. 左右侍御皆驚靡, 叡獨執戟禦之, 虎乃退去, 故親任轉重.[106]

Wang Rui soon became one of the most famous men of his time. In the narrative, his fame is matched by his character; two years after he exhibited bravery in defending his empress from the rogue tiger, he revealed his compassion in the aftermath of a failed rebellion plot, preventing over a thousand deaths by pleading for the bloodshed to stop with execution of the ringleaders. Wang Rui's political stance here accords with the policies propounded by Empress Feng during the Taihe era, which were aimed at improving prison conditions and curtailing excessive executions through *menzhu* 門誅, whereby a rebel's entire extended family was put to death for his or her crime.[107] Wang Rui is thus presented as a valuable political ally who participated proactively in the formation of state policy.

Just when we are convinced of Wang Rui's gallantry and strength of character, the biographical narrative twists again. We are told of the explic-

105. *WS* 93.1988.

106. *WS* 93.1988.

107. *WS* 93.1988. These policies are discussed in depth in Song Qirui, *Bei Wei nüzhu lun*, 153–66.

itly sexual nature of Wang Rui's relationship with Empress Feng and of the empress's excessive bestowal of lavish gifts, including luxury items, slaves, and cattle, upon her lover. In order to disguise her special favor for Wang Rui, Empress Feng also supposedly bestowed extravagant gifts on her other great ministers, leading to what must have been a huge collective expense.[108] Echoing the beginning of the biography, the narrative of the sexual favorite's rise to power and subsequent fall due to excessive greed is repeated. The historian has even taken on the tone of secret scandal suggestive of uncorroborated rumor with the comment, "no one was able to find out about it" (人莫能知),[109] which appears especially in the narratives of Empress Dowager Hu's sexual liaisons. However, once again the cautionary tale of the sexual favorite stops as abruptly as it began. Wang Rui became ill and, from his deathbed, sent his benefactress a lengthy and detailed memorial outlining his long-term political advice and vision. This memorial, which is quoted seemingly in full, emerges as a shining, typological example of a document written by a loyal, capable official with the best interests of the state and its people foremost in his mind.[110]

Commensurate with his favor, Wang Rui was given numerous posthumous titles and honors, as well as a lavish burial service. All of the best literary men in the capital composed laments and dirges to honor his passing, and a sacrificial altar, complete with temple and memorial stele, was established for him south of the city. In addition, a pictorial image of Wang Rui fighting the tiger was placed in all of the palaces, with a praise poem commissioned by the throne. Unanimous love of Wang Rui supposedly even led to the creation of a new tune called "Zhongshan Wang yue" 中山王樂 (The Music of the Prince of Zhongshan).[111]

Into the description of the statewide mourning for Wang Rui is inserted a flashback account of his daughters' lavish wedding ceremonies.

108. *WS* 93.1989.

109. *WS* 93.1989.

110. He covers five time-honored fundamentals of benevolent government: exercising restraint in the application of punishments, employing worthy men, being close to the loyal and trustworthy, keeping one's distance from the slanderous and wicked, and banishing and promoting men based on their behavior. He also stresses the importance of adhering to the fine principles laid out in the classics and abolishing heterodox sacrificial practices. See *WS* 93.1989–90.

111. *WS* 93.1990.

This flashback represents another thematic twist, as we turn once again to the language of "[inappropriate] favor." According to this account, Empress Feng personally participated in the marriage preparation and ceremonies. Before the wedding ceremony, the girls went into the palace and were honored with "ritual roughly equal to that [usually accorded to] a princess or the daughter of a prince . . . People of the time said privately that it was the emperor or empress dowager who was marrying off a daughter" (其禮略如公主, 王女之儀 . . . 時人竊謂天子, 太后嫁女).[112] As in the description of the empress's copious bestowal of gifts upon Wang Rui, which "no one was able to find out about," in this passage the narrative of excessive favor is signaled by the intimation of secrecy and misinformation, or rumor, circulating among "people of the time." Yet, at the same time, the fledgling warning narrative never pans out; the excess of the wedding and, later, of the funeral is not connected with any problems. In the generally terse ensuing biographies of Wang Rui's sons, we likewise do not find evidence of bad seed wreaking havoc with the power won for their family by their father's favor.

What are we to make of Wang Rui as male sexual favorite qua brave and compassionate hero?[113] We may be seeing different layers of narrative development preserved in sources no longer available to us, but the tension also stems, on a basic level, from the two conflicting rhetorical identities seemingly combined in the same man. Certainly, available information about Wang Rui's constructive role in Empress Feng's government can partially explain the divergence between his portrayal and those of other reviled male sexual favorites. Part of the confusion also stems from the linguistic ambiguity surrounding literary-historical accounts of sexual favor. In the opening section of his deathbed manifesto, Wang Rui himself seems to spell out the existence of an intimate

112. *WS* 93.1990.

113. The conflicted narrative of Wang Rui's biography is also seen in the biography of Li Chong 李沖 (450–98), another of Empress Feng's close advisors and/or "male favorites." Incidentally, one of Wang Rui's daughters was married into Li Chong's family. His biography claims that Empress Feng showered Li Chong, who was originally from a poor family, with gifts after she began to "favor" him. The tone of rumor and secrecy is likewise used to signal a fledgling "male favorite" narrative: "No outsiders ever found out about it" (外人莫得而知焉); *WS* 53.1180. Yet, like Wang Rui, Li Chong is described as a competent official who never let his private favor negatively affect the way in which he carried out his duties to the state; see Li Chong's biography in *WS* 53.1179–89.

aspect to his "service": "I have served inside the inner quarters, my rank reaching to that of the princes" (內侍幃幄, 爵列諸王).[114] While Wang Rui may well have meant that he had enjoyed the privilege of working closely with the empress in a professional context, phrases such as *neishi* 內侍, "inner service," suggest to the reader accustomed to classical Chinese historical narrative a sexual or illicit type of service. Terms such as *xing* 幸 and *chong* 寵, while often indicating sexual favor, can also indicate the non-sexual favor of a ruler for a subject (based on meritorious or loyal service, aptitude, etc.). Of course, at this remove there is no way to know, for example, whether Empress Feng was indeed intimate with Wang Rui; but we must read these narratives with an awareness of the prejudicial tendency to insinuate a sexual dimension into all close relationships between a female ruler and trusted male associates.

We might also note the relative peace and prosperity of Empress Feng's reign as compared, for example, with those of Empress Jia and Empress Dowager Hu (only a few decades after Empress Feng), both of which were characterized by upheaval and in fact closely preceded the fall of, respectively, the Western Jin and the Northern Wei. Empress Jia and Empress Dowager Hu were two empresses who ruled during chaotic times and did not succeed in stemming the tide of that chaos. Insinuation of sexual impropriety in their relationships with men results from the assumption of a correlation between political failure and sexual deviancy. This is not always the case with unsuccessful male rulers, but it is taken for granted that the misconduct of female rulers must express itself sexually.

It is in the biography of a man like Wang Rui that the tenacious power of this assumption is made glaringly manifest. Empress Feng ruled effectively over a burgeoning polity, and her chosen high ministers, Li Chong and Wang Rui, likewise skillfully accomplished their appointed tasks. Yet, in their biographies, the "sexual favorite" trope repeatedly (though abortively) rears its ugly head, even though it obviously does not fit the narratives at hand. Indeed, the pervasive element of rumor that characterizes insinuations of inappropriate sexual liaisons between empress and minister indicates that we should approach these insinuations with misgiving. Fear of female power, as ruler, over males, as

114. *WS* 93.1989.

ministers, is encapsulated in fear of the free rein of transgressive female sexuality over men and the state.

In this vein, the historiographical grouping of Empress Feng and Empress Dowager Hu is, as discussed by Song Qirui, more a reflection of their being two powerful female rulers of the Northern Wei than of actual similarities in their reigns.[115] In spite of the pronounced differences between them, the preface to the "Biographies of Favorites" (*en xing lie zhuan* 恩倖列傳) chapter in the *Wei shu* lumps them together in parallel prose: "During the [Northern] Wei, Wang Rui was favored at the start of the Taihe reign [477–99], and Zheng Yan was the darling of the Xiaochang period [525–27]. In the first case [the Taihe, or Empress Feng's period of dominance], the [rightful] ruler was young, and in the second [the Xiaochang, or Empress Dowager Hu's period of dominance] the [rightful] monarch was a child. Taking advantage of the opportunity, they [the empresses] spread licentiousness, almost without any fear [of consequences]. They set up factions and obscured the hearing of Heaven [i.e., the rightful ruler]" (魏世，王叡幸太和之初，鄭儼寵孝昌之季，主幼於前，君稚於後，乘間宣淫，殆無忌畏，樹列朋黨，蔽塞天聽).[116] They are grouped together according to chronology, dynasty, and, perhaps most importantly, gender.

An analysis of portrayals of powerful women from the Western Han through Sui eras reveals a set of recurring and archetypal traits of the praised and condemned female leader. Morality or immorality in women rulers is defined by adherence to or rejection of accepted gender behavior in cardinal relationships. The archetype of the overly powerful woman ruler coalesced over time and in response to the intertwining influences of record, rumor, and conceptions of appropriate and inappropriate feminine identity. The portrayals of powerful women raise issues concerning history versus historiography and the movement from event to typology. The narratives create cultural memories, reflect the gender views of writers set in time and place, and reinforce their audiences' attitudes toward the possibility of women in power.

115. Song Qirui, *Bei Wei nüzhu lun*, 213–14.
116. *WS* 93.1987.

As we move into the Tang period, it is important to keep in mind the circumstances under which female rule is considered permissible (when a woman rules as regent for a minor or incapacitated ruler; when she does not seek overt personal or natal familial power) and when it is deemed transgressive (when a woman rules in her own right, suppresses the rightful male heir, and in general rejects the primacy of the imperial patriline). In the late seventh and early eighth centuries, we have a group of women who were collectively and retrospectively deemed to have transgressed all "appropriate" boundaries for women rulers. At the same time, this period can be distinguished from the rules of, for instance, Empress Jia, Empress Dowager Hu, and even Empress Feng because the leadership of Wu Zhao and the women of the next generations ushered in a period of dynastic strength and longevity. Their unprecedented power informs the particular ways in which they are negotiated and refracted through the literary-historical lens.

TWO

(Self)Expression and Gendered Legitimacy

Projection of Identity in Literature of the Late Seventh Century through the Jinglong Era

The retrospective portrayals of pre-Tang female leaders examined in chapter 1 present rhetorical reconstructions of women leaders by historians and compilers. In these recreations, many written several centuries later, the women's actions and voices have often been appropriated so as to accord with the historian-compiler's interpretation of who they were and what they meant. The same holds true of the powerful women of the early Tang. A close examination of the ways in which their images have coalesced into particular censured archetypes enables a far-reaching analysis of attitudes toward their power as women leaders.

Before I move into this analysis in chapters 3 through 5, however, I must note that the overriding theme of transgression that characterizes retrospective portrayals of condemned women leaders was clearly at odds with their desired self-projection. We can gain insight into what themes and images supported their desired self-projections by looking at the prose and poetry that they wrote and that was written in response to their command by courtiers who were both eager to please and well-versed in how to do so. Studying these contemporary writings greatly enriches the analysis of reconstructive portrayals, especially in light of limitations imposed by the loss or destruction of many Zhou through Jinglong materials. Indeed, a full understanding of issues surrounding image, gender, and identity requires knowledge of the rhetorical complexes meant to both praise and defame these women.

Literary Production Under Wu Zhao and Zhongzong

Wu Zhao was an energetic, highly intelligent, and hands-on ruler, and surviving records suggest that she played a direct micromanaging role in the creation of the state propaganda of her rule. Starting from the time when she was Gaozong's shining consort (*zhaoyi* 昭儀), Wu was involved in the compilation of a corpus of works outlining the ideal behavior for people occupying various social positions or roles, including women, officials, and crown princes.[1] She also commissioned multiple histories of her own and Gaozong's reigns.[2] Unfortunately, most of these works, including those that dealt with model female behavior, are long lost.[3] The once-extensive corpus of her personal writings, recorded in Tang and Five Dynasties catalogues as the one-hundred chapter *Chuigong ji* 垂拱集 (Chuigong Collection), is now greatly reduced to a small selection of twenty-eight poems, most of them songs she composed for various state ceremonies, and sixty-five prose pieces.[4]

Of the younger generations of powerful women, Shangguan Wan'er, the literary star of the court scene from the 680s until her death in 710, is the only woman to leave behind a collection of writings, and what remains of it today is also just a small fraction of its original size. Most of her surviving pieces can be dated, based on occasions they reference and often during which they were composed, to the last years of her life, coinciding with the reign of Zhongzong (705–10). Whereas many documents dating from the reign of Wu Zhao were deliberately destroyed after her death, a relatively detailed record survives of courtly occasions, along with corresponding courtly writings, from Zhongzong's rule. This survival is in no small measure pure chance, but it can also be connected, if only as a minor factor, to the importance of literary composition and competition at the courts of Wu Zhao's sons, which ensured that a large corpus of writings was produced.

The literary-cultural undertakings of the time provided aspiring courtiers with a viable avenue of career advancement, leaders with a means

1. See Twitchett, "*Chen gui* and Other Works," 69, 34–43.
2. Twitchett, "*Chen gui* and Other Works," 34–43.
3. Twitchett, "*Chen gui* and Other Works," 37–39.
4. Twitchett, "*Chen gui* and Other Works," 40–43.

of showing their power, and entertainment for all. In 707, Zhongzong, under the direction of Shangguan Wan'er, restructured and broadened a court organization of scholars, called first the Zhaowen guan 昭文館 (Academy for the Illumination of Literature) and then the Xiuwen guan 修文館 (Academy for the Refinement of Literature).[5] On the surface, this group of scholars was a continuation of the national institutes established by Taizu and Gaozong, yet in reality they inherited much from Wu Zhao's Beimen xueshi 北門學士, or North Gate Scholars, in their combination of literary and political roles. The creation of this group grew out of Wu Zhao's need to consolidate her position in relation to opposing groups, including various high-ranking officials and members of the most prestigious clans, whom she had moved against in her quest to secure power. To establish her own base of power independent of these groups, Wu patronized the Buddhist and Daoist clergy and men of letters. In 665, she privately selected and supported a group of scholars who came to be known collectively as the "North Gate Scholars" and who were responsible only to her. The North Gate Scholars assumed duties, such as handling memorials to the throne and making decisions regarding policy, that had traditionally been the duties of the chief ministers.[6] As might be expected of a group assembled under these circumstances, the Beimen xueshi produced various literary works and compilations that supported Wu's political goals, including *Chen gui* and other "normative" works. As part of the empress's inner circle, the Beimen xueshi provided a potent channel through which the Empress could "[circumvent] or [influence] court discussion," and their literary activities were closely linked to her political goals.[7]

5. See Jia Jinhua, "A Study of the *Jinglong wenguan ji*," 227. An organization called the Xiuwen guan was first established by Gaozu in 621. Later that year, the crown prince, the future Taizong (then the Prince of Qin 秦王) founded the Wenxue guan 文學館 (Academy of Literature). In 626, after the crown prince ascended the throne as Emperor Taizong, the Wenxue guan was closed and the name of Xiuwen guan was changed to Hongwen guan 宏文館 (Academy for the Expansion of Literature). Some eighty years later, during the time that Shangguan was involved in the institute's expansion and transformation, its name was first changed to Zhaowen guan, in 705, after which it was returned to its original name, Xiuwen guan, in 706. See *XTS* 47.1209 and *JTS* 43.1848.

6. Twitchett and Wechsler, "Kao-tsung (Reign 649–83) and the Empress Wu," 263.

7. Twitchett and Wechsler, "Kao-tsung (Reign 649–83) and the Empress Wu," 269. For more on *Chen gui*, see Twitchett, "*Chen gui* and Other Works"; and Rothschild, *Rhetoric, Ritual, and Support Constituencies*, chap. 4.

Existing records on the period, including the last years of Wu Zhao's reign and the subsequent reigns of Zhongzong and Ruizong, have emphasized the literary culture of court society, which saw the continuation of the dual political-literary function of high-ranking courtiers. The prominence of the Xiuwen guan scholars in court culture under Zhongzong is described in the biography of courtier Li Shi 李適 (fl. 690–711) in *Xin Tang shu*; when the emperor held banquets and various outings, "only the high ministers and scholars were able to be in attendance" (唯宰相及學士得從).[8] These outings included trips to various scenic locations such as ponds and mountains, visits to stupas and Buddhist temples, and imperial tours of Xinfeng 新豐 District.[9] The courtiers were given various small gifts to mark each occasion.[10] Literary composition, at the behest of the ruler, was a defining part of these outings: "Whenever the emperor was moved by something he would compose a poem, and the scholars would all compose matching poems" (帝有所感即賦詩, 學士皆屬和).[11] More likely, the emperor would have a poem composed for him, probably by imperial ghostwriter Shangguan Wan'er, and as the titles and topics of surviving poems suggest, the literary output was more often centered on the lives of the leading women of the court than on the emotional stirrings of Zhongzong.

Because of the greater availability of data, the literature of the Jinglong era, in particular works reflecting the burgeoning poetic culture, has attracted much more scholarly attention than have works by Wu Zhao and her courtiers. Using extant sources, Jia Jinhua has reconstructed the *Jinglong wenguan ji* 景龍文館記 (A Record of the Jinglong Literary Institute), a work compiled by Wu Pingyi 武平一 (d. ca. 741) not long after the end of the period, which details the activities of the Jinglong court and further indicates the importance of literary composition to

8. *XTS* 202.5748. Li Shi was a prominent scholar and official from the end of Wu Zhao's reign through the reign of Ruizong, when he passed away. Besides being a member of the Xiuwen guan, he participated in the compilation of Wu Zhao's *Sanjiao zhuying* 三教珠英 (Pearls of the Three Teachings) anthology and served in posts such as vice-director in the Ministry of Works 工部侍郎. See also *TSJS* 9.262–64 for a discussion of the Xiuwen guan and a record of literary occasions.

9. *XTS* 202.5748.

10. *XTS* 202.5748.

11. *XTS* 202.5748.

the political and social life of the court.[12] There are multiple records, in historical, anecdotal, and literary sources, describing courtiers composing poems to command in an explicit effort to advance to higher governmental position.[13] The importance of quick and effective poetic composition in the presence of one's peers produced a social climate in which the development of poetic conventions and forms was highly welcome; these developing standards and regulations made the poem into a finely tuned vehicle through which to display cleverness and impress one's audience.[14]

Owing to this environment of literary competition, scholars, led by Jia, have studied the Jinglong literary culture mainly through the lens of the development of regulated verse, which was used widely in its "mature" form beginning with High Tang period. While yielding invaluable results, the formal emphasis of this approach has tended to result in the dismissal of these poems as artistically shallow or limited because they are *yingzhi* poems written to courtly command. However, this value judgment obscures their actual substance and meaning; they are not empty templates of proto-regulated verse, but rather represent the often female leader's preferred self-conception bounced back to her by the most talented and ambitious literary figures of the time. Many of the most important and extravagant sociopolitical court occasions involved in some way the estates and construction projects of the female court leaders, and this is reflected in the topics of the poems and prose pieces composed by courtiers in commemoration of these events. These works celebrate such occasions as group outings to the Anle Princess's mountain villa[15] and the

12. See Jia Jinhua, "A Study of the *Jinglong wenguan ji*." The second chapter of Jia's 2001 volume *Tangdai jihui zongji yu shirenqun yanjiu,* titled "'Jinglong wenguan ji' yu Zhongzong chao wenguan xueshiqun" (43–73), contains much of the same basic information (but written in Chinese).

13. Jia Jinhua, *Tangdai jihui zongji*, 67–70.

14. See Owen, *The Poetry of the Early Tang*, xi–xiv. Chapters 15 and 16 give a detailed account of this climate, as well as the specific nature of the forms themselves.

15. To the titles *Shi yan Anle gongzhu shan zhuang yingzhi* 侍宴安樂公主山莊應制 (In Attendance at a Banquet at the Anle Princess's Mountain Villa: To Imperial Command) and *Feng he xing Anle gongzhu shan zhuang yingzhi* 奉和幸安樂公主山莊應制 (A Respectfully Submitted Companion Piece to His Majesty's Composition, Visiting the Anle Princess's Mountain Villa: To Imperial Command). For a full list of poets with surviving poems that commemorate this occasion, see Jia, "A Study of the *Jinglong wenguan ji*," 219.

Taiping Princess's southern villa;[16] and a banquet at the Anle Princess's new residence.[17] Other poetic series commemorating such holidays as the Double Seventh Day do not mention a princess or empress by name, but their subject matter is clearly well-suited to comparisons between legendary celestial goddesses, such as the Weaving Maid and the moon goddess Chang'e, and leading imperial women. Naturally, the poets constantly exploited these correspondences.

The genre and subject matter of these poems (lavish celebrations held amidst beautiful scenery by stylish court luminaries) has clearly also made them a more popular area of study than, for instance, the archaic-sounding ritual hymns composed by Wu Zhao to honor various court occasions. Yet to approach an understanding of the nature of self-image during this era as a whole (including the important late seventh-century era during which Wu Zhao ruled), it is important to analyze the extant variety of genres and forms, reading them with sensitivity to their original context and purpose. The images evoked by Wu Zhao, Shangguan Wan'er, and courtiers in the genres of ritual writing, poetry, and prose suggest an overarching concern with the projection of harmony and cosmic sanction beyond the expected emphasis in court writings on the harmony of the state. Wu Zhao's ceremonial works stress the unity and interpenetration of *yin-yang*, *qian-kun* 乾坤 (heaven-earth), and other male-female pairings, suggesting her particular identity as a woman ruler and the special challenges this role entailed. Female imagery is deployed

16. *Fenghe chu chun xing Taiping gongzhu nan zhuang yingzhi* 奉和初春幸太平公主南莊應制 (A Respectfully Submitted Companion Piece to His Majesty's Composition, In Early Spring Visiting the Taiping Princess's Southern Villa: To Imperial Command). For a full list of poets who composed poems to commemorate this occasion, see Jia, "A Study of the *Jinglong wenguan ji*," 217–18.

17. Poems under various titles commemorate parties held at Anle's residence. For example, one set of poems commemorates the occasion of Anle's moving into the new residence. See poems to the title *Anle gongzhu yi ru xin zhai shi yan yingzhi* 安樂公主移入新宅侍宴應制 (The Anle Princess Moved into a New Residence: In Attendance at a Banquet to Imperial Command) or the shortened title *Anle gongzhu yi ru xin zhai*. For the poets who composed to this title, see Jia, "A Study of the *Jinglong wenguan ji*," 219–20. Another group of poems was composed on the occasion of a nighttime banquet at the residence. See poems to the title *Ye yan Anle gongzhu xin zhai yingzhi* 夜宴安樂公主新宅應制 (Banqueting at Night at the Anle Princess's New Residence: To Imperial Command), or the shortened title of *Ye yan Anle gongzhu xin zhai*. For the poets who composed to this title, see Jia, "A Study of the *Jinglong wenguan ji*," 219–20.

in late seventh- and early eighth-century works to create the image of a particular brand of far-reaching, generative power possessed and/or desired by the leaders of the time.

Beyond revealing the images and allusions with which the female power-holders wished to hear themselves exalted, as well as the occasions that were deemed worthy of exalting, these works offer a fascinating counterpoint to materials that retroactively defame this image. The rhetorical strategies later used to denigrate these women's power often represent opposite treatments of themes present in the court literature from the Zhou through Jinglong eras. Two important thematic variations exist, surrounding, first, the typical conflation of the imperial, celestial, and natural realms so as to emphasize female divinity, and, secondly, the dominance of imperial power over nature as testimony to royal omnipotence. Royal power is, of course, closely associated with the women who controlled the throne and/or court politics. Whereas the literary materials presented by contemporary courtiers stress the union of the imperial with the divine and nature's yielding response to imperial power, later historical and narrative reconstructions emphasize the unnaturalness of female rule as exemplified by natural and divine rejection and by the female rulers' failure to interpret cosmological signs. Although the early ninth-century anecdote collection *Da Tang xinyu* tells of the minister Wang Qiuli's 王求禮 (d. 706) brave remonstrance against Wu Zhao's celebration of "unnatural" unseasonal snow as "auspicious,"[18] multiple poetic series from the Jinglong period actually celebrate auspicious snowfalls.[19] In retrospective historical and anecdotal sources, female destruc-

18. *DTXY* 9.142. See chapter 3.

19. See, for example, the poetic series *You jin yuan pei xing Wei ting yu xue yingzhi* 遊禁苑陪幸渭亭遇雪應制 (Roaming in the Palace Garden, While in Attendance upon an Imperial Visit to Wei Pavilion We Encountered Snow: To Imperial Command), *Fenghe Ren ri Qinghui ge yan qun chen yu xue yingzhi* 奉和人日清暉閣宴群臣遇雪應制 (A Respectfully Submitted Companion Piece to His Majesty's Composition, On Human Day at Qinghui Terrace All of the Subjects Had a Banquet and Encountered Snow: To Imperial Command), and *Ren ri wan xue yingzhi* 人日玩雪應制 (On Human Day Playing in the Snow: To Imperial Command); for dates, occasions, and poets, see Jia Jinhua, "A Study of the *Jinglong wenguan ji*," 215–16. These poetic series date to wintertime, so they can be seen as conforming to the distinction between "auspicious," i.e., seasonal and in line with proper cosmologically sanctioned rule, and "inauspicious," i.e., unseasonal and symptomatic of cosmological trouble. For a prose piece celebrating snow,

tiveness and greed are rhetorically conveyed through condemnatory accounts of the same estates that Zhou- and Jinglong-era poets sought to immortalize as sites of divinity.

This transposition of perspective on a similar thematic set enables us to think in terms of inversion, a key concept in narrative constructions of these women, and to consider the meaning of gender itself in the decades and centuries in which their images were codified. By "inversion," I am referring to the way in which retrospective portrayals of these women leaders are constructed by depicting in a negative light images or themes found in contemporary praise-filled materials sponsored by them. In negative posthumous portrayals, their power as women itself is defined as the inversion of appropriate and natural gender behavior. This implication likewise belies portrayals of pre-Tang female rulers, but the theme of inversion is particularly striking in materials surrounding the Tang women, and the nature of the existing contemporary and posthumous materials enables comparative thematic analysis of typological constructions.

This chapter approaches these themes through a case study of the *Bao tu* 寶圖 (Precious Diagram) or *Luoshui tu* 洛水圖 (Luo River Diagram), an auspicious divine rock offered to (or, depending upon what we believe, commissioned by) Wu Zhao that functioned as part of the ideological campaign leading up to her establishment of the Zhou. The Luo River Diagram has been the object of both extreme celebration and extreme censure. This chapter deals with contemporary celebrations of the diagram, including Wu Zhao's set of ceremonial songs and prose works by various courtiers. The ensuing chapter provides a complementary examination of works of retrospective condemnation focused on the diagram and similar auspicious stones. An analysis of materials surrounding the Luo River Diagram reveals particular orientations to nature and imperial power, which provide intriguing points of confluence with the surviving works, in particular poetry, produced at the courts of Wu Zhao and her sons. An analysis of representative works written by courtiers to imperial command and of the surviving literary corpus of Shangguan Wan'er, the major literary-cultural "evaluator" of the period, indicates that, as in later

---

see Li Jiao's "Wei Wu Youji he xue biao" 為武攸暨賀雪表 (Celebrating Snow on Behalf of Wu Youji), in *QTW* 243.5b (2455).

historical and anecdotal reconstructions meant to de-legitimate their power as women, the definition of "nature" and "naturalness" is what is most at stake in these power-holders' approved constructions of identity.

The importance of these issues becomes especially clear in the case of ceremonial works, which represent the ruler's attempt to communicate with the broader society and cosmos. As mentioned above, in contrast to Shangguan's more lyrical corpus of poems, Wu Zhao's ceremonial verse has been largely ignored in literary and historical studies. This is primarily due to bias against works deemed to be state-centered and time-specific, that is, works composed at a particular time and for a particular purpose and not necessarily understandable outside of this context. However, the ceremonial works composed by Wu Zhao were instrumental in her campaign to define and project her self-appointed identity as ruler.

The Precious Diagram and the Foundations of Rule

Wu Zhao played an active and creative role in the state ceremonial of the Tang (especially after Gaozong's death in 683) and the Zhou. She deftly crafted the large-scale symbolic and ritual structure of her dynasty, as well as the details of ceremonial song and lyrics. This state structure made brilliant use of the symbolic apparatuses of the Buddhist, Daoist, and Confucian traditions.[20] Wu Zhao's ceremonial songs reference ritual occasions corresponding to unique events in the state ceremonial of her rule. Upon the completion of the Nine Tripods (*jiu ding* 九鼎), created to go in the Tongtian Palace 通天宮, she composed a "Ye ding ge" 曳鼎

20. In spite of generations of scholarly marveling at Wu Zhao's deployment of all three traditions to legitimate her reign, and not to detract from her ingenuity in doing so, the use of iconography from the Confucian, Daoist, and Buddhist traditions is by no means unique to her rule. As discussed by Tiziana Lippiello in her monograph on auspicious signs in the Han through Six Dynasties, invocation of the three traditions was widespread throughout the pre-Tang period, in particular during the northern and southern regimes, as was the appropriation of Daoist and Buddhist imagery for the Confucian legitimization apparatus. See Lippiello, *Auspicious Omens and Miracles,* 197–215, 222–23, and 243–47.

歌 ("Song for Hauling the Tripods").[21] She also wrote groups of songs to celebrate a sacrifice to Heaven ("Tang xiang hao tian yue" 唐享昊天樂 [Music for the Tang Sacrifice to Heaven]; twelve songs), the Mingtang [Hall of Light] ("Tang Mingtang yue zhang" 唐明堂樂章 [Music for the Tang Mingtang]; eleven songs), a Wu family ancestral sacrifice ("Tang Wu shi xiang xian miao yue zhang" 唐武氏享先廟樂章 [Music for the Ancestral Sacrifice to the Wu Clan of the Tang]), and a sacrifice to the Luo River ("Tang da xiang bai Luo yue zhang" 唐大饗拜洛樂章 [Music for the Tang Great Sacrifice to Venerate the Luo River]; fourteen songs).[22] The Luo River celebration directly invokes the issue of cosmic sanction and legitimacy, in keeping with its role in laying the ideological functions for Wu's establishment of the Zhou.

According to various sources, in 688, an otherwise shadowy figure named Tang Tongtai 唐同泰 (dates unknown) and/or Wu Zhao's nephew Wu Chengsi 武承嗣 (d. 698) presented to the throne an auspicious white stone supposedly discovered in the Luo River and carved in red with the inscription: "The Sage Mother looks down upon the water, forever glorifying the imperial seat" (聖母臨水, 永昌帝業).[23] To celebrate the auspicious divine missive, Wu Zhao, among other measures, established a Yongchang 永昌 ("forever glorifying") District,[24] made a suburban sacrifice to Shangdi 上帝 (Lord on High/Supreme Deity), adopted the new title of "Sage Mother Heavenly Emperor" (Shengmu shenhuang 聖母神皇), commissioned "Heavenly Emperor" imperial seals, and renamed the Luo River the Yongchang River.[25] The symbol of the stone, which the empress designated the "Precious Diagram," carries archaic precedents; auspicious river diagrams are associated with the kingships of culture heroes Fu Xi 伏羲 and Yu 禹.[26] The Diagram also

21. Riccardo Fracasso has studied the Nine Tripods and the song; see Fracasso, "The Nine Tripods of Empress Wu"; and Rothschild, *Rhetoric, Ritual, and Support Constituencies*, 309–23.

22. See *QTS* 5.52–57. For more on the Mingtang, see Forte, *Mingtang and Buddhist Utopias*, and Rothschild, *Rhetoric, Ritual, and Support Constituencies*, 75, 196–97, 316–23.

23. *CYQZ* 3.72. As far as I have been able to determine, all references to Tang Tongtai in both anecdotal collections and standard histories revolve around the discovery of auspicious stones; see, for example, *JTS* 6.119, 8.177, and 24.925; and *XTS* 76.3480 and 109.4103.

24. Shortly thereafter, the reign name was also changed from Chuigong to Yongchang.

25. *XTS* 76.3480; *JTS* 24.925.

26. When Fuxi became king, a dragon carried a diagram out of the Yellow River. It

evokes a passage from the *Yijing* 易經 (Classic of Changes) predicting that "when the Yellow River issues forth the Diagram and the Luo River issues forth the Writing, a sage will follow them" (河出圖, 洛出書, 聖人則之).[27] The obvious implication is that Wu Zhao is the awaited sage, and her responding hymns celebrate and stress this identification.

The fourteen "Luo River" hymns employ varying line length. The archaic-flavored four-syllable verse is the most popular and is used for six songs, while the remaining eight are divided between a *Chuci* style using the *xi* 兮 carrier sound (four songs), five-syllable verse (two songs), and six-syllable verse (two songs). Except for the fifth verse, "Bai Luo" 拜洛 (Giving Obeisance to the Luo), the songs all have disyllabic titles ending in *he* 和, "harmony."[28] According to the "Yue zhi" 樂志 (Treatise on Music) in *Jiu Tang shu*, the songs were choreographed to be performed in sequence at various points during the Luo River ceremony.[29] The opening lines of the first hymn, "Zhaohe" 昭和 (Harmony of Illumination), set the tone and suggest the ideological underpinnings

---

was inscribed with writing of the eight trigrams and called the "River Diagram" (*he tu* 河圖). After Yu had succeeded in taming the flood, a spirit turtle brought a deed out of the Luo River. It was made into a map delineating the ancient nine divisions of China and called the "Luo Book" ("Luo shu" 洛書). See Zhao Wenrun and Wang Shuanghuai, *Wu Zetian pingzhuan*, 163–70, for a discussion of Wu's veneration of the Luo River Diagram in the political context of the late 680s. See also Lippiello, *Auspicious Omens and Miracles in Ancient China*, 51–56; Rothschild, *Rhetoric, Ritual, and Support Constituencies*, 189–91, 249–50; and Marlowe, *Empress Wu Zhao*, 35–36. For a discussion of the River Diagram in relation to *chen* prophecy, see Lu Zongli, *The Power of the Words*, 27. Lu has also briefly discussed the River Diagram's role in the legendary history of Chinese writing; see Lu Zongli, *The Power of the Words*, 113.

27. This is noted by Rothschild; see his "An Inquiry into Reign Era Changes under Wu Zhao," 137. See also Lippiello, *Auspicious Omens and Miracles*, 219–20.

28. 昭和, 致和, 咸和, 九和, 顯和, 昭和, 敬和, 齊和, 德和, 禋和, 通和, 歸和, 歸和.

29. The first hymn "Zhaohe" 昭和 was to be sung while the rite was being set up; "Jiuhe" 九和 was meant to accompany Wu's ascent into the carriage and initial progress; "Xianhe" 顯和 was designed to accompany the rite of paying obeisance to the Luo River and accepting the diagram; the second "Zhaohe" was to be used when the Empress (and possibly other participants) ascended the altar to sing; when the *zu* 俎 ceremonial dishes were presented, "Jinghe" 敬和 was to be sung; "Qinhe" 欽和 was to be sung while libations were poured; "Qihe" 齊和 inaugurated the celebratory martial dances, while "Dehe" 德和 saw them off; "Yinhe" 禋和 marked the removal of the *zu* dishes; and the two "Guihe" 歸和 verses both sent off the spirits. *JTS* 30.1113–15.

of the ritual by asserting its cosmic sanction: "Highest Heaven gives a favoring charge, / the Three Sages laid a glorious foundation. // We respectfully follow the directives of old, / we have completed the work on this Bright Terrace [altar]" (九玄眷命, 三聖基隆. 奉承先旨, 明臺畢功).[30]

The hymn represents the Luo River ceremony as the highest exponent of the continuity between the present regime and the mythic, culturally sacrosanct past. The final lines of "Zhaohe" quote the Luo River Diagram inscription: "Forever glorifying the imperial seat, / spreading its pure influence" (永昌帝業, 式播淳風).[31] The "pure influence" of the "imperial seat" is referring to the present imperial seat, that is, Wu Zhao, whose regime was blessed with the Precious Diagram, a manifest sign of cosmic approval. The second hymn, "Zhihe" 致和 (Harmony of [Accompanying?] Presentation), presumably also meant to accompany the opening portion of the ritual,[32] likewise quotes the inscription and stresses cosmic harmonization, effected and demonstrated through the revelation of the Luo River Diagram:

> The divine attainments are unfathomable,
>   circulating *yin* and *yang*,
> encompassing the world, enclosing all directions.
> Heavenly signs have emerged, the imperial seat is glorious;
> we wish to face the brilliant ritual, bringing down
>   auspicious portents.
>
> 神功不測兮運陰陽, 包藏萬宇兮孕八荒.
> 天符既出兮帝業昌, 願臨明祀兮降禎祥.[33]

"The imperial seat is glorious" is, of course, another reference, via the words of the diagram, to the contemporary imperial seat, whose powerful virtue places her in line with the integrated cosmos "circulating *yin* and *yang*."

30. *QTS* 5.55.
31. *QTS* 5.55.
32. No specific directions are given for this song, but it is placed in between the first "Zhaohe" and "Jiuhe."
33. *QTS* 5.55.

The hymns are unified by their emphasis on the ruler's embodiment and synchronization of the complementary forces of the universe. Just as the divine "circulation of *yin* and *yang*" expressed its harmony with contemporary rule by offering up the Luo River Diagram, so, in "Jiuhe" 九和 (Nine Harmonies),[34] "the earth carries the virtue of *kun*, / respectfully following the *qian* spirit" (祇荷坤德, 欽若乾靈).[35] "Dehe" 德和 (Harmony of Virtue) also merges the complementary pairs of auspiciousness, envisioning the emperor (signified by the dragon) and the empress (signified by the phoenix) presiding over a universe interconnected in terms of space, time, and ideology:

At dusk reverentially at one with the dragon accord,
at dawn striving to face the phoenix screen.
Revere the Confucian scholars, practice age-old rules,
laying down arms, follow the directives of old.
Official caps and carriages fly to the ends of the earth,
departing far away, passing over mountains and rivers.
We are fortunate to receive what has been left by the Three Sages,
and joyfully belong to the beginning of a thousand-year reign.

夕惕同龍契, 晨兢當鳳扆.
崇儒習舊規, 偃伯循先旨.
絕壤飛冠蓋, 遐區麗山水.
幸承三聖餘, 忻屬千年始.[36]

The phrase *xianzhi*, "the directives of old," was also used in the first hymn, "Zhaohe," to express continuity with the glorious past. "Dehe" is structured around correspondences (between emperor and empress, past

34. The compound *jiuhe* can refer to autumn or to a type of fragrance. The last line of the hymn references fragrance: "Only desiring to spread forth our reverence, / [would we] dare to make an offering without fragrance?" (惟憑展敬, 敢薦非馨). The *jiu* (nine) here might be shorthand for *jiuxuan* 九玄, "the nine mysteries" or heavens, which appears in the first "Zhaohe." *Jiu* might also be referencing compounds such as *jiutian* 九天 (the highest heavens) and *jiuchong* 九重 (the nine divisions of the celestial realm).

35. *QTS* 5.55–56.

36. *QTS* 5.56.

and present), and the hymn celebrates the way in which these correlative and fundamental opposites are unified. The pairs of emperor-empress and heaven-earth are, like *yin-yang* and *kun-qian*, conceived as gendered. The implication is that Wu Zhao combines in her person the virtues of both halves of each complementary pair; she is both dragon and phoenix. As a female ruler, Wu Zhao felt a special urgency to justify her rule as "natural," cosmically endorsed, and in line with the underpinnings of culture as generally understood among the educated elite of the time; the thematic emphases of the "Luo River" hymns suggest a conception of the ritual songs as playing a role in the legitimization process.

The formal prose pieces offered by prominent courtiers in celebration of the discovery of the Luo River Diagram and/or the resultant ritual employ a similar imagistic and thematic repertoire as does Wu Zhao in her set of hymns. Prominent courtier Cui Rong's 崔融 (653–706) "Jin Luo tu song biao" 進洛圖頌表 (Presenting a Hymn in Praise of the Luo Diagram) emphasizes Wu Zhao's historically unique accomplishment of cosmic harmonization: "Through Your Majesty's sagely force and ample virtue, it [the diagram] has emerged first, responding to the right date, and precious signs are resplendent, as has rarely been heard of through the ages" (伏以陛下聖烈豊懿, 應期首出, 珍符炳鑠, 曠代罕聞).[37] Arguably the most famous pre-Kaiyuan Tang poet Chen Zi'ang 陳子昂 (661–702), known mainly for the gloomy poems he wrote when away from court, was also a major author of pro-Wu propaganda pieces in the late 680s and early 690s.[38] His "Wei Cheng Chubi qing bai Luo biao" 為程處弼慶拜洛表 (Joyously Paying Obeisance to the Luo, Written on Behalf of Cheng Chubi) strikes a similar tone of wonderment and exaltation: "I have seen how Your Majesty's most exalted virtue pairs with Heaven, its transformative force reaching even to the plants and trees. Heaven did not begrudge its treasures; the Luo sent forth the auspicious diagram. The earth did not conceal its riches; the river revealed its mysterious register" (伏見陛下至德配天, 化及草木, 天不愛寶, 洛出瑞圖, 地不藏珍, 河開秘籙).[39] Prominent poet and courtier Li

37. *QTW* 217.6b–7a (2194).

38. Chen Zi'ang's official biographies can be found in *JTS* 190b.5018–25 and *XTS* 107.4067–79. Note the *Xin Tang shu* biography's derisive closing comments about Chen Zi'ang's pro-Zhou writings; *XTS* 107.4079. For more on Chen Zi'ang's role in Wu's regime, see Rothschild, *Rhetoric, Ritual, and Support Constituencies*, 215–23.

39. *QTW* 209.7b (2115). Based on the title and content of the piece, it seems to have

Jiao's 李嶠 (d. 714?) composition "Wei Wei Youxiang he bai Luo biao" 為韋右相賀拜洛表 (Celebrating Obeisance to the Luo, Written on Behalf of Vice-Director of the Department of State Affairs Wei) refers to the archaic origins of the diagram's symbolism and its association with the sage-rulers of the mythic past.[40] Ornate praise of the ruler's virtue is a requirement for court pieces written to celebrate various auspicious occasions or acts by the ruler. However, the topic of the Luo River Diagram is time- and occasion-specific, as is the set of associations, centering on cosmic approval of Wu Zhao's rule, which it embodies.

The Precious Diagram's influence did not stop with its celebration by the court; rather, the diagram as literary device became an allusion of sorts in the court literature of the period, a synecdoche pointing to the auspiciousness and divine sanction of Wu Zhao's rule. Chen Zi'ang's "Wei Chen Yushi shang feng he qiujing guan jing du shi biao" 為陳御史上奉和秋景觀競渡詩表 (Written On Behalf of Censor Chen, A Respectfully Submitted Companion Piece to Her Majesty's Composition, A Poem on Watching the Boat Race in Autumn)[41] is representative of contemporary praise pieces in its invocation of the Luo as a marker of Wu's sagehood and legitimacy:

> Blue clouds emerge from the Luo River, marking the signs of receiving the mandate to rule; a crimson shell illuminates the river, the treasure urging the ruler to take the throne.[42] If not for the utmost divine being of ultimate virtue, who could cause this to happen?

---

had a double purpose; in addition to celebrating the Luo miracle, the work repeatedly praises imperial grace in saving people, including Cheng Chubi, from death, suggesting that Cheng Chubi enlisted Chen Zi'ang's literary talents to express his gratitude to Wu Zhao for sparing him after he committed some offense. Cheng Chubi was the youngest son of civil and military official Cheng Zhijie 程知節 (fl. mid-7th c.). Cheng Chubi's rank reached to General of the Imperial Insignia of the Right (You jinwu da jiangjun 右金吾大將軍), but little further information is available about him. See *JTS* 68.2504.

40. *QTW* 243.16b–17a (2460–61).

41. *QTW* 209.10b–12a (2116–17).

42. The crimson shell is an auspicious sign signaling the king's receiving the heavenly mandate to rule. The origin text is the Han-era *Shangshu zhonghou* 尚書中候 (The Watch Officer's *Shangshu*): "White clouds rise, as swirling winds sway; the dragon horses carry a shell, with crimson writing and green color, emerging from the river. . . . The shell is like the turtle's back, nine feet wide . . . with the measures of the constellations on top, the registers of rulers, recording the calculation of the rise and fall of kings" (白雲起, 回風搖, 龍馬銜甲, 赤文綠色, 自河而出 . . . 甲似龜背, 袤廣九尺 . . . 上有列宿, 斗正之度, 帝王錄, 紀興亡之數); Kong Guanglin, *Shangshu zhonghou Zheng zhu*, 1.3–4.

青雲出洛, 爰開受命之符; 赤甲榮河, 終御興王之寶. 非窮神之至德者, 其孰能與於是哉?).[43]

The piece overall stresses Wu Zhao's unique ability to bring about universal harmony, and the reference to the Luo River is an integral part of this theme.

The Luo River Diagram emerges in these pieces as part of the founding myth of Wu Zhao's Zhou state. The sageliness of the ruler (Wu Zhao) permeates the literary landscape and the cosmic landscapes imagined therein. Chen Zi'ang's "Joyously Paying Obeisance to the Luo, Written on Behalf of Cheng Chubi" describes the "transformative force" of Wu's virtue as "reaching even to the plants and trees." The idea of the ruler's transformative power vis-à-vis nature appears in variations in works not directly connected with formal state ceremony. Indeed, the rhetoric of nature and power, in its various manifestations, played an important role during the period from Wu Zhao's early rise through the reigns of her sons. In the mid-seventh century, talented historian and chancellor Xu Jingzong 許敬宗 (592–672), who played a key role in Wu's rise to power as Gaozong's empress, authored multiple prose pieces celebrating auspicious natural occurrences, such as sightings of "colorful clouds" (*qing yun* 慶雲) and dragons at various locations, as reflections of contemporary rule.[44] These works, submitted to the court with an eye to please the rulers (or perhaps even written at the behest of imperial orders), stress the imperial power of creation. "He Hongzhou qing yun jian biao" 賀洪州慶雲見表 (Celebrating the Manifestation of Colorful Clouds in Hongzhou) depicts the marvelous spiritual force of the ruler permeating the universe, leading to the manifestation of wonders such as the colorful clouds. The power of the ruler surpasses the limits of time and space, taking on the power of creation itself: "If not for skill equal to the transformative force of creation, the Way modeled on Heaven, radiance including all directions, and thoughts extending throughout the world, how could one bring this divine response, this display of spiritual grace?"

43. *QTW* 209.11a (2117).

44. See *QTW* 151.14a–20a (1540–41). Xu Jingzong supported Wu's bid to become empress and made forceful arguments in favor of her vision of the *feng-shan* sacrifices. See his memorial on the rites in *QTW* 151.12a–14a (1539–40).

(自非工倕造化, 道格上蒼, 光含六幽, 思流四海, 安能致茲神感, 式彰靈貺?).[45] The emphasis on the ruler's generative power suggests imperial prerogative over nature and unity with the overarching cosmic design.

Natural Response and Courtly Power

The prose celebration of the colorful clouds is a topic that clearly invites larger-than-life praise of imperial virtue. Yet these same themes manifest themselves in contemporary court literature on landscape. Xu Jingzong's "Yeting shan fu ying zhao" 掖庭山賦應詔 (*Fu* on Yeting Mountain: to Imperial Command) describes the mountain landscape through reference to what Xu sees as the driving creative force, imperial spiritual power.[46] The *fu* 賦 (rhapsody or poetic exposition) closes with an image of harmonious interaction between minister (Xu Jingzong) and ruler, which in turn mirrors the stratified harmony of the landscape:

> [Your Majesty's] virtuous favor enriches the birds and beasts, your brilliant radiance suffuses the plants and trees. The day approaches dusk, and it is getting late. You expand your divine feelings and embody things, recording your flourishing traces with moistened brush. Setting forth your fine words, you pour out the waves of your sea of writing. [Your Majesty] commands your humble servant to compose a matching piece, a *fu* modeled on the "Great Airs" and giving delight.
>
> 德澤加於飛徒, 榮光周於草木. 日云暮, 時稍闌. 暢神襟而體物, 紀盛迹以濡翰. 發詞林之華藻, 瀉筆海之波瀾. 命小臣而並作, 賦 "大雅" 而承歡.[47]

The ensuing closing section of the *fu* continues to describe a harmonious scene presided over by a roaming king (君王兮遊豫) who, passing by in his carriage, witnesses a landscape of flowering forest and singing

45. *QTW* 151.15a (1540).
46. *Yeting* usually refers to the imperial harem.
47. *QTW* 151.8b (1537).

birds and beasts.[48] The particular way in which the animals sing and flowers bloom is worthy of note: "Wild beasts sing, responding to our bells and chimes, / the mountain flowers blossom in the midst of our fine silks" (野獸鳴兮應鍾石，山英開兮間綺羅).[49] Xu Jingzong's *fu* envisions a landscape that responds to courtly mood and unifying presence.

The rhetoric favored by the Jinglong-era poets several decades later represents a variation on the symbolism employed by Wu Zhao and her greatest political supporters to extol her reign and personality cult. The landed estate becomes a microcosmic referent for the exultant courtly rhetoric of generative power and harmonization centered on rulers. It is tempting to see this literary trend as somehow connected to the concomitant splintering of power from a single center (Wu Zhao) to vying factional centers of power during the reign of Zhongzong. While this observation belongs to the realm of conjecture, the transfer of the rhetoric of cosmic power from the imperial cosmos to the estate as micro-cosmos represents an important development in the way in which power came to be conceptualized and extolled.

Courtly dominion over the landscape is nowhere more manifest than in works commemorating visits to luxury properties owned by the women of the court. The very existence and frequency of these poems and prose pieces testify to the material, political, and cultural power of the women. Although the way in which they and their surroundings are depicted rhetorically is not a direct or simple channel into a worldview or a set of cultural attitudes, these materials do provide images of culturally sanctioned conceptions of female power (sanctioned by the most powerful arbiters of culture, the leading women of the court). They enable us to glimpse the ways in which the Taiping and Anle Princesses, Shangguan Wan'er, and other powerful politicians/landowners wanted to hear themselves described: which allusions were chosen as the most flattering and/or apt ways to describe them, what elements of their persons and images were considered most fundamental by the women themselves and their courtiers, and so on.

The prevailing poetic imagery associated with these women's power is elucidated by an examination of a valuable representative poetic

48. *QTW* 151.8b (1537).

49. Here *zhongshi* seems to be referring to the *zhongqing* 鍾磬, a musical stone or chime. *QTW* 151.8b (1537).

series about a court visit to the estate of a powerful woman, in this case, the Taiping Princess. Eight poems survive on the topic of the Taiping Princess's southern villa. The poems are entitled *Fenghe chun chu xing Taiping gongzhu nan zhuang yingzhi* 奉和春初幸太平公主南莊應制 (A Respectfully Presented Companion Piece to His Majesty's Composition, in Early Spring There Was an Imperial Visit to the Taiping Princess's Southern Villa: To Imperial Command); hereafter, *The Taiping Princess's Southern Villa*. The poems commemorate a visit that took place in the second month of 709.[50] The eight poems are attributed to the nine prominent court poets Song Zhiwen 宋之問 (ca. 660–712), Li Jiao, Shao Sheng 邵昇 (fl. 710s?), Shen Quanqi 沈佺期 (ca. 650–729), Wei Sili 韋嗣立 (654–719), Li Yi 李乂 (647–714), Su Ting 蘇頲 (680–737), Zhao Yanzhao 趙彥昭 (fl. ca. 690s–710s), and Li Yong 李邕 (678–747).[51] Though the surviving pieces may well be eight contributions to what was once a larger group of poems, it is nevertheless possible to trace the interplay of images and tropes interweaving through the poems. The reverberation of particular allusions and turns of phrase throughout the series is suggestive of the milieu of group composition and the allusions that would have been expected and pleasing to the objects of praise (the Taiping Princess and imperial family).

Half of the poems begin with explicit descriptions of the princess's residence: "The princess's mountain estate opens abreast of the clouds, / on his spring outing the Son of Heaven arrives, moving the earth" (主家山第接雲開, 天子春遊動地來; Li Jiao);[52] "Early spring returns to the

50. See Jia, "A Study of the *Jinglong wenguan ji*," 217.

51. See, respectively, *QTS* 52.645–46, 61.723, 69.774, 73.804, 91.987, 92.997, 96.1041, 103.1089, and 115.1169. One poem is attributed to both Wei Sili and Zhao Yanzhao, with one minor variation in the first couplet: Zhao's has *jia* 駕 (to drive [a carriage]), while Wei's has *jia* 架 (to suspend). See *QTS* 91.987 and 103.1089. As Jia notes, according to the tenth-century anthology of literature *Wenyuan yinghua* 文苑英華 (Fine Blossoms in the Garden of Literature), the poem should belong to Wei Sili. The poems attributed to Su and Shen are also reversed in *QTS* from the earlier attributions in *Wenyuan yinghua*. Jia believes that the poem attributed to Li Yong might actually have been written by Zhao Yanzhao, since Li Yong was exiled from the court during the Jinglong reign. See Jia, "A Study of the *Jinglong wenguan ji*," 217–18, notes 37–40. See also *WYYH* 176.9b–10b. All of the poems except for the one attributed to both Wei Sili and Zhao Yanzhao have been translated by Stephen Owen; see *The Poetry of the Early Tang*, 225–31. The series is also discussed in Jie Wu, "A Study of Group Compositions," 269–75.

52. *QTS* 61.723.

princess's mountain estate, / the imperial carriage, on a spring outing, encircled by emerald haze" (主家山第早春歸, 御輦春遊繞翠微; Su Ting);[53] "The mountain gate of the princess's estate rises up from the Ba River, / the scenery of the imperial outing enters into the new year" (主第山門起灞川, 宸遊風景入初年; Shen Quanqi);[54] and "From the cliff-side gate of the princess's estate a magpie bridge is suspended, / as from the Gate of Heaven the simurgh horses descend" (主第巖扃架[駕]鵲橋, 天門閶闔降鸞鑣; Wei Sili / Zhao Yanzhao).[55] These openings emphasize the honor of an imperial visit enjoyed by the Princess, whose residence is depicted as a symbiotic part of the natural scenery, "[opening] abreast of the clouds" and "[rising] up from Ba River." As noted by Owen and Wu, the appearance of similar or even identical turns of phrase suggests migration of themes in an atmosphere of group recitation, whereby one poet's composition may have inspired another's.[56] Li Jiao's and Su Ting's poems begin with the same four-character phrase *zhu jia shan di* 主家山第 ("the princess's mountain estate"), while the second lines of the opening couplets all describe the arrival of the emperor, who is on his "spring outing" (*chun you* 春遊; the phrase used in Li Jiao's and Su Ting's poems). Shen Quanqi uses similar phrasing to describe the princess's mountain residence and the imperial visit, including a description of the "imperial outing" (*chen you* 宸遊), which evokes "spring outing" (*chun you*). Song Zhiwen's opening follows the same basic structure: "Green Gate Road connects to Phoenix Terrace, / the imperial outing amidst the white rapids of the Chan River as the dragon cavalry arrives" (青門路接鳳凰臺, 素滻宸遊龍騎來).[57]

This type of opening is quite effective in merging the princess with her landscape. As the poems unfold, they write the princess into the landscape physically and thematically as she is given the identities of immortal women and recluses who are at one with nature. In these poems, the

53. *QTS* 96.1041 under "Shen Quanqi."

54. *QTS* 73.804 under "Su Ting."

55. *QTS* 91.987 and 103.1089. *Luanbiao* 鸞鑣, literally "simurgh bits," refers to the imperial horses. This line is presumably describing the imperial horses' bits, which apparently were shaped like or engraved with images of *luan*, or simurgh, birds.

56. Owen, *The Poetry of the Early Tang*, 225; and Jie Wu, "A Study of Group Compositions," 270.

57. *QTS* 52.645–46.

ancient literary identification between the imperial, the celestial, and the natural is used to convey the way in which the guests and, in particular, the powerful women of the court transcend the everyday human realm both spiritually and materially. Explicit reference to the Taiping Princess and her visitors as immortals is a time-honored means of flattery employed by several poets.[58] But in a significant portion of the poems, the Princess's gendered presence on the landscape is made more explicit through allusions to mythical female figures. Nongyu and the constellation goddess the Weaving Maid are especially popular, and the moon goddess Chang'e also makes repeated appearances.[59] In Shao Sheng's poem, for example, the two royal couples, Zhongzong and Empress Wei and the Taiping Princess and her husband Wu Youji, are each cast as exalted immortal pairs in a mythical paradise: "The beauty of Qin garden outdoes Penglai and Yingzhou, / with emerald walls and scarlet streams encircling the royal capital. // The Two Sages suddenly visit from the simurgh palace, / just as the pair of immortals descends from Phoenix Tower to welcome them" (沁園佳麗奪蓬瀛, 翠壁紅泉繞上京. 二聖忽從鸞殿幸, 雙仙正下鳳樓迎).[60] Zhongzong and Wei are the "Two Sages," while Taiping and Wu Youji are figured as Nongyu and Xiaoshi, the "pair of immortals" on Phoenix Tower.

Allusions to Nongyu and Xiaoshi enable the poets to seamlessly merge the present occasion with the mythical-celestial referents; descriptions of both involve music, phoenix regalia of the royal and immortal kind, and beautiful divine women. We recall that the phoenix is the symbol of the empress, as employed by Wu Zhao in her ritual pieces.

58. See, for example, Li Yi's poem: "Outside of Pingyang Lodge lies the immortal's home, / in the Qin River garden, fine things are lush and flourishing" (平陽館外有仙家, 沁水園中好物華). *QTS* 92.997.

59. Nongyu 弄玉 was the beautiful and gifted daughter of Duke Mu of Qin 秦穆公 (r. 649–621 BCE). Upon Nongyu's marriage to the flute player Xiao shi 蕭史, Duke Mu had a phoenix tower erected for the young couple. Xiaoshi taught Nongyu to imitate the cries of phoenixes when playing the flute, and phoenixes were drawn to their music and gathered around them. One day, they followed the phoenixes and flew away, presumably to become immortals. According to other accounts, Nongyu rode off on a phoenix and Xiaoshi rode off on a dragon. See Liu Xiang, *Liexian zhuan jiao jian*, a.80, 82–83, note 8.

60. Penglai and Yingzhou are the mythical dwelling-places of immortals. *QTS* 69.774. See also the poem attributed to Wei Sili / Zhao Yanzhao in *QTS* 91.987 and 103.1089.

The presence of these particular mythic women in the poems suggests, in addition to female immortality, the princess's possession of special talent and skill (in music and weaving) and perfect love. They also allude to high-mindedness, and an ability to leave the petty concerns of the mortal world behind, in the case of Chang'e possibly for the greater good.[61]

These themes reverberate throughout courtly compositions written to celebrate the women of the court. Lu Cangyong's 盧藏用 (ca. 664–713) "Fenghe xing Anle gongzhu shan zhuang yingzhi" 奉和幸安樂公主山莊應制 (A Respectfully Presented Companion Piece to His Majesty's Composition, Visiting the Anle Princess's Mountain Residence: To Imperial Command) combines the special culturally resonant figures of the Weaving Maid, Chang'e, and the mountain recluse in the personage of the Anle Princess, who is called "the royal daughter": "The royal daughter in the jasper terrace on the shore of the Heavenly River; / beneath the Bridge of Stars and the lunar palace she constructs a residence in the grotto" (皇女瓊臺天漢潯, 星橋月宇構山林).[62] Lu Cangyong hears the immortal sounds of Nongyu and Xiaoshi in the sonic landscape, both man-made and natural, of the Anle Princess's mountain retreat: "The harmonies of the flute tower accord with the chanting of phoenixes" (簫樓韻逐鳳凰吟).[63] In Li Jiao's poem about the Taiping Princess's southern villa, description of the revelry at the courtly outing introduces the presence of mythic lore into the landscape: "Then plucking a zither tune to harmonize with the rocky currents, / we ladle rosy mountain mist into our wine cups. // The simurgh carriage has already left the island of magpies, / but the sound of flute still wafts around Phoenix Terrace" (還將石溜調琴曲, 更取峯霞入酒盃. 鸞輅已辭烏鵲渚, 簫聲猶繞鳳皇臺).[64] "The "island of magpies" and "Phoenix Terrace" evoke the Weaving Maid and Nongyu/Xiaoshi, respectively. Wei Sili / Zhao Yanzhao, Shen

61. According to one version of how Chang'e became the immortal moon goddess, she swallowed the elixir of immortality to prevent her tyrannical husband Houyi from drinking it and forever tyrannizing the world.

62. *QTS* 93.1004. The Weaving Maid and Cowherd constellations are mythologized as star-crossed lovers. Once a year, on the Double Seventh holiday, the Weaving Maid is able to meet her husband, the Cowherd, across a Bridge of Stars made by magpies.

63. "The chanting of phoenixes" refers to compositions by the emperor and empress. *QTS* 93.1004.

64. *QTS* 61.723.

Quanqi, and Su Ting all likewise refer to the Weaving Maid and/or Nongyu.[65]

Both Su Ting and Wei Sili / Zhao Yanzhao follow Li Jiao in highlighting the musical aspect of the allusion and thus the actual atmosphere of the fete. Su Ting describes the divine sounds that naturally enliven the Princess's estate: "It follows that immortals intone phoenix tunes, / together singing and dancing to express gratitude for radiant kindness shown" (自有神仙鳴鳳曲，並將歌舞報恩暉).[66] The "radiant kindness" is that of the imperial couple and the exalted hostess, to whom singing immortals express their gratitude in phoenix songs, evoking the Taiping Princess's mythical referent, Nongyu. Wei Sili / Zhao Yanzhao allude to the artistic talents of Nongyu and another famous royal woman, Wei Zifu 衛子夫 (d. 91 BCE), Emperor Wu of Han's second empress:[67] "The flowers of the forest join in Pingyang's dance, / the oriole in the valley harmonizes with Nongyu's flute" (林間花雜平陽舞，谷裏鶯和弄玉簫).[68]

The mythical women selected by the poets are meant to reflect the Taiping Princess's status as a powerful royal daughter exalted to join the ranks of immortals. Of course, the poets' choices in allusion also indicate the gender of the estate's owner. They imagine a landscape populated with female immortals or, in the case of the Pingyang Princess, a parallel historical personage, a vision both flattering to contemporary female power-holders and indicative of their power.

Indeed, the princess's estate, the poetic and real life playground for "immortals," is a testament to her power to fashion nature to conform to her vision and self-conception. Owing to the vogue for court composition at private landed estates, there was a continued emphasis on the theme of the imperial relationship with nature, transferred to a context of more private ownership that enabled clever rhetorical plays on the concepts of

65. See *QTS* 91.987, 103.1089, 73.804, and 96.1041.

66. *QTS* 96.1041, under "Shen Quanqi."

67. Emperor Wu first fell in love with Wei Zifu, a gifted singer and dancer, at a banquet held by his sister, Princess Pingyang. See *SJ* 49.1978–83. There is also a more recent famous Pingyang Princess, the daughter of Gaozu who aided in the Tang founding with her "Lady's Army" (*Niang zi jun* 娘子軍); see *JTS* 58.2315 and *XTS* 83.3643. Pingyang Lodge (Pingyang guan 平陽館) appears in Li Yi's poem; see *QTS* 92.997.

68. *QTS* 91.987 and 103.1089.

microcosm-macrocosm and imitation-genuine. In the poetic series *The Taiping Princess's Southern Villa*, just as the imperial carriage calls upon the Taiping Princess, spring descends upon her estate. Entrance to the princess's estate is equated with entrance into the early spring season in the poems of Su Ting ("early spring returns to the princess's mountain estate") and Shen Quanqi ("the scenery of the imperial outing enters into the new year"). Song Zhiwen imagines the natural spring scenery of the estate welcoming and hosting the royal guests amidst a scene of cosmic harmony: "Plants in the ravine welcome the fragrant carriage of their own volition, furling together / flowers growing on the cliffs should await the imperial mat to bloom [in honor of the occasion].[69] // Our writings move around the Big Dipper, forming celestial configurations, / wine is held to South Mountain to make a toast for long life" (澗草自迎香輦合, 巖花應待御筵開. 文移北斗成天象, 酒遞南山作壽盃).[70] As in Xu Jingzong's "*Fu* on Yeting Mountain," flowers bloom in response to courtly presence. Song Zhiwen's directive that the flowers "should await the imperial mat to bloom" indicates a world order in which everything conforms to the imperial wish. Processes such as the arrival of spring and the blooming of flowers, which objectively do not follow a human timetable, poetically become the ultimate expressions of imperial centrality and power.

Song Zhiwen's poem goes beyond rhetorical placement of the imperial presence in the heavenly realms to indicate the court's powerful position at the center of the universe. Imperial power is manifested most palpably in poetic rhetoric whereby the imperial prerogative is shown to override nature itself. In implicitly or explicitly placing the imperial court above the celestial and natural spheres, the poems enable the court to appropriate the most awe-inspiring functions of each realm, as well as to play the role of each in relation to the other. Many court occasions of which records survive actually involve acts of imperial "creation" in the form of gifts from the court to the attendant courtiers.[71] A banquet at Daming Palace held on the holiday called Human Day, in 709, was

69. In this line, *shi* 待 can also be understood as "to attend upon," that is, the flowers, like courtiers, attend upon the royal wish.

70. *QTS* 52.645–46.

71. Jia Jinhua discusses these gifts in terms of the female dominance of the court during this time. See Jia, *Tangdai jihui zongji*, 69–70.

accompanied by generous gifts of little silk human cutouts to the courtiers, who responded with celebratory thankful poems.[72] On the occasion of the Cold Food Festival, courtiers were given silk balls and filigree chicks.[73] To celebrate the arrival of spring according to the agricultural calendar, the imperial family gave cut silk flowers to courtiers.[74] In the descriptions of these artificial silk flowers that "bloom" by means of imperial beneficence, royal creation is envisioned as mirroring and supplanting natural processes of creation. The poets envision a world wherein poetic inversion has real-world power; the microcosm of the royal court and the relatively small sampling of artificial flowers, created at the behest of the royal women, take precedence over the macrocosm of the entire natural universe. This particular formulation of power represents the taste and worldview of the female trendsetters of culture and later becomes closely identified, although with a different evaluative emphasis, with the image of female power during this period.

The series of poems composed in February 710 to commemorate the courtly celebration of spring's "arrival" elevates the court to the position of cosmic regulator, able, through its act of artificial creation, to change the course of the natural processes of growth and flourishing. The poems of the series are entitled, with some minor variations, *Fenghe shengzhi li chun ri shiyan nei dian chu jian cai hua yingzhi* 奉和聖制立春日侍宴內殿出剪綵花應制 (A Respectfully Presented Companion Piece to His Majesty's Composition, "On the First Day of Spring, at a Banquet Cut Silk Flowers Were Brought Out from the Inner Palace": To Imperial Command).[75] Most of the participants are familiar from the works

72. Jia, *Tangdai jihui zongji*, 251–53.

73. Jia, *Tangdai jihui zongji*, 70.

74. Jia, *Tangdai jihui zongji*, 209–11, 254.

75. Some poems are preserved under abbreviated titles. See, for example, Li Jiao's poem "Li chun ri shi yan nei dian chu jian cai hua yingzhi" 立春日侍宴內殿出剪綵花應制 (On the First Day of Spring, at a Banquet Cut Silk Flowers Were Brought Out from the Inner Palace: To Imperial Command); Song Zhiwen's poem "Fenghe li chun ri shi yan nei dian chu jian cai hua yingzhi" 奉和立春日侍宴內殿出剪綵花應制 (A Respectfully Presented Companion Piece to His Majesty's Composition, "On the First Day of Spring, at a Banquet Cut Silk Flowers Were Brought Out from the Inner Palace": To Imperial Command); and Shen Quanqi's poem "Li chun ri nei chu cai hua yingzhi" 立春日內出綵花應制 (On the First Day of Spring, Silk Flowers Were Brought Out from the Inner Palace: To Imperial Command). *QTS* 58.691–92, *QTS* 52.631, and *QTS* 96.1029. Jia has

discussed above: Li Jiao, Zhao Yanzhao, Shen Quanqi, Song Zhiwen, Liu Xian 劉憲 (655–711), Shangguan Wan'er, Su Ting, and Wu Pingyi 武平一 (ca. 678–ca. 741). Although the holiday ostensibly marks the first day of the spring season, weather-wise it was still winter; for the court's holiday celebration, flowers were cut out of silk and attached to the bare branches so as to create the illusion of spring. In the poems, the artificial flowers supplant the real flowers, which have not yet blossomed, and, through this act of displacement, alter the speed of nature's development.

Li Jiao's poem is centered on the relationship between the "genuine," *zhen* 真, and the man-made likeness: "Early I heard that the year was about to arrive, / the cut silk [flowers] imitated the fragrant morning. // The strung greens: the remarkable qualities can resemble [the real ones], / the cut reds: their skill closely approximates the genuine" (早聞年欲至, 剪綵學芳辰. 綴綠奇能似, 裁紅巧逼真).[76] The "strung greens" and "cut reds" refer to the silk flowers made by the palace ladies. The artificiality of the silk flowers is clear; they "come out of a box" (*qie li fa* 篋裏發) and are "spring in the hand" (*shou zhong chun* 手中春) and thus represent products owned by the court. Yet, because of the outstanding quality of their imitation, the silk flowers are indistinguishable from "natural" flowers. The closing couplet makes explicit the importance of the silk flowers in demonstrating one's imperial status: "If one does not contest time, / how can one be called a heavenly being?" (不與時光競, 何名天上人).[77] The imperial court derives its high position within the cosmic order from its ability to compete with or even outdo Heaven's act of creation, the onset of spring.

The court's power to arbitrate what counts as genuine emerges as a major unifying theme throughout the *Cut Silk Flowers* series. Shangguan Wan'er's contribution subtly merges artificial and organic acts of creation. The flowers are created in response to the scissors, which bring about their genesis in words that connote actual physical blossoming or birth: *tu* 吐, "spit out," and *shu* 舒, "to unfurl."[78] Other poems in the series

translated Song Zhiwen's contribution and briefly discussed the series. See Jia, "A Study of the *Jinglong wenguan ji*," 234–35.

76. *QTS* 58.692.

77. *QTS* 58.692.

78. *QTS* 5.60. The pairing of *tu* and *shu* is also used in the second regulated verse of the series *You Changning gongzhu liu bei chi: ershiwu shou* 遊長寧公主流杯池二十五首 (Visiting the Changning Princess's Pool for Floating Wine-cups) series; see below.

stress the realness of the cut flowers in terms of their ability to appropriate the function of the "natural" flowers by fooling other creatures of nature with their early "blooming." Zhao Yanzhao describes the way in which the imperial handiwork has mimicked and supplanted the genuine creation of nature: "Cutting silk flowers, she looks up to the early season; / climbing the branches, she indeed traces the genuine" (剪綵仰初候, 攀條故寫真).[79] As proof of the silk flowers' success as artifice, he extols the way in which "their delicate color startles the swallows carrying loam for nesting in their beaks" (嫩色驚銜燕). The cut flowers even succeed in tricking the "lower classes" of humans, the people who pick them: "Their light fragrance fools the pickers" (輕香誤採人).[80] In Song Zhiwen's contribution, the butterflies and bees accept the imperially created flowers as genuine and settle on them.[81]

The power of the courtly flowers goes far beyond a temporary capacity to trick the birds and insects; within the world of the poems, their presence actually succeeds in spurring on the arrival of spring. In Shen Quanqi's poem, the elements of nature, like courtiers who are eager to please, bend to accommodate the imperial will: "Flowers welcome the imperial brush and open, / leaves await the royal banquet to unfurl [or: leaves attend upon the royal banquet and unfurl]" (花迎宸翰發, 葉待御筵披).[82] Zhao Yanzhao's second couplet follows a similar structural and thematic vein: "The flowers are made according to the red of the mind's eye, / the leaves renew to the sentiments of green" (花隨紅意發, 葉就綠情新). Zhao's poem closes by projecting the imperial presence into nature as a sweet-smelling breeze whose touch spurs on the blossoming of spring.[83] Song Zhiwen envisions the cosmic authority of the imperial command as capable of causing spring to begin before its regular or "natural" time: "This year spring has come early; / this must have been because it was urged on by the scissors" (今年春色早, 應為剪刀催).[84]

In Song's poem, the imperial court, allied or conflated with Heaven, possesses prescience and advance experience of seasonal change: "In the

79. *QTS* 103.1087.
80. *QTS* 103.1087.
81. 蝶繞香絲住, 蜂憐艷粉迴. *QTS* 52.631.
82. *QTS* 96.1029.
83. 應為薰風拂, 能令芳樹春. *QTS* 103.1087.
84. *QTS* 52.631.

human realm, they are still unknown, / but in Heaven they suddenly blossom forth before their time" (人間都未識, 天上忽先開).[85] The idea of foresight appears throughout the series as a defining characteristic of imperial supremacy. Liu Xian describes knowledge of the spring season as the court's exclusive provenance.[86] This is directly connected to spring's "earliness," as in Shen's contribution: "Merging around the palace, spring will arrive early, / opening the box, the bright colors are known beforehand" (合殿春應早, 開箱綵預知).[87] Of course, the colors are known beforehand because the palace chose the colors of the silk used to make the flowers; "prediction" is equivalent to power as the artificial flowers supplant organic flowers. In these poems, the identity of the genuine, like that of the controlling force behind nature, is thus displaced; the artificial flowers are, in a sense, more "real" than the organic ones in their imperially vested power to direct the world around them. Shen Quanqi's final couplet suggests the superiority of the "delicate plants" (*qing sheng* 輕生), which, because they have "received the touch of the scissors, will forever accompany the branches of the palace evergreens" (輕生承剪拂, 長伴萬年枝).[88] The normally fragile and short-lived plum and peach blossoms are rendered strong and immortal because they have "received the touch of the scissors" on two levels: they are made out of silk and cannot die, and they have been graced with the imperial touch.

The highest figures of the court emerge as the poetic arbiters of genuineness, an exalted role that has important implications for understanding the conception of power fulfilled rhetorically in these poems and in other contemporary works of court literature. Song Zhiwen's "Taiping gongzhu shan chi fu" 太平公主山池賦 (*Fu* on the Taiping Princess's Mountain Pool) is an even more explicit panegyric on the personal power of the Taiping Princess, power that is again defined through the language of nature and creation: "As for the Princess's birth, / the imperial family was at peace, / soliciting prefectures and kingdoms to select her title, / to correspond to the fine reputation of universal accord;[89] / she embodies the

85. *QTS* 52.631.

86. 上林宮館好, 春光獨早知. *QTS* 71.779.

87. *QTS* 96.1029.

88. *QTS* 96.1029. *Wannianzhi* 萬年枝, literally "ten-thousand-year branches," refers to the trees planted on palace grounds.

89. The phrase *shi yong* 時雍 (universal accord) refers to the "Yao dian" 堯典 (Canon

refined beauty of the immoral maiden / and radiates the pure essence of the Wu Girl constellation . . . she completes construction on the immortal mountain, / equal to the spiritual force of creation" (粵若公主誕生, 皇家太平, 徽郡國以選號, 葉時雍之美名, 孕靈娥之秀彩, 輝婺女之淳精 . . . 構仙山兮既畢, 侔造化之神術).[90] The Taiping Princess not only encompasses the identities of imperial figure and celestial maiden, but also commands the mystical power of nature "equal to the spiritual force of creation."

Song Zhiwen's description of the Taiping Princess, situated within her privately possessed and man-made mountain pool, clearly evokes the rhetoric with which the power of her mother, Wu Zhao, was formulated. In the later *fu* extolling Taiping, however, there is a new emphasis on artifice and microcosmic imitation of nature. In "*Fu* on the Taiping Princess's Mountain Pool," Song Zhiwen describes the princess's pool as embodying the totality of the cosmic marvels that comprise the "spiritual force of creation": "As for its form, it collects weird rocks and towers high; / as for its rarity, it contains pure essence and is cool" (其為狀也, 攢怪石而岑崟, 其為異也, 含清氣而蕭瑟).[91] Song Zhiwen depicts the Taiping Princess's mountain pool as the site of confluence between natural, supernatural, and material wonders, a place where one can "seek magical herbs" (*fang ling yao* 訪靈藥), where "are caged the strange animals of the eight directions / and collected the precious birds of the six meetings" (羅八方之奇獸, 聚六合之珍禽), and where "the divine child," both metaphorical and real, can roam (*dizi you* 帝子遊).[92]

Song Zhiwen's *fu* is designed not merely to praise the Taiping Princess and her mountain pool, but also to express the power manifested therein. Yet the piece does so not by directly describing the money spent or

of Yao) of the *Shang shu* 尚書 (Classic of History): "The black-haired people were transformed to universal accord" (黎民於變時雍). Kong Yingda, *Shang shu zheng yi*, 2.27. See Jie Wu, "A Study of Group Compositions," 260.

90. *QTW* 240.1b (2427). For a translation of the entire *fu*, see Jie Wu, "A Study of Group Compositions," 260–69. See also the discussion of the *fu* on pp. 255–60.

91. *QTW* 240.1b (2427).

92. *QTW* 240.2a–b (2427). "The divine child" appears in the line, "When the mountain pool is complete, the divine child roams" (山池成兮帝子遊); it is referring to both the original opening line about the "Xiang furen" 相夫人 (Lady of the Xiang) in the *Jiu ge* 九歌 (Nine Songs) (帝子降兮北渚) and the Taiping Princess (the emperor's child). See Jiang Shanguo, *Chuci*, 7 (in "Jiu ge" chapter).

human labor amassed, but rather by emphasizing the "naturalness" of the man-made artifice. Artifice at the utmost level overtakes nature by creating microcosmic imitations more perfect and more enjoyable than any naturally occurring river or forest. The contemporary vogue for massive, expensive, and carefully crafted architectural sites, including man-made ponds, landed estates, and other edifices, was, of course, made possible by those who held the highest status and greatest wealth. Yet, in addition to becoming a rhetorical symbol for imperial power, the building of these sites also enabled their creators to effect the temporary literary transcendence of their "everyday" identities – although those identities were far from "everyday" from the perspective of most.

Power and Poetic Persona

In crafting the preferred poetic avatar of the most powerful court women, writers eschewed direct descriptions of wealth in favor of the rhetorical embodiment of the spiritual power of the recluse. Contemporary poems about the residences, banquet halls, and pools of female power-holders combine, without suggestion of contradiction, praise of the possession of both the reclusive impulse and immense material power, suggesting the loftiness of immortals who are able to transcend great wealth. The appeal exerted by the fusion of spiritual and material power is suggested by a quartet of eight-line poems offered by prominent courtier Zheng Yin 鄭愔 (d. 710) to celebrate a banquet held at Shangguan Wan'er's residence.[93] The third poem opens with a direct invocation of Shangguan Wan'er's

93. The series of poems is entitled *Fenghe xing Shangguan Zhaorong yuan xian shi si shou* 奉和幸上官昭容院獻詩四首 (A Respectfully Offered Companion Piece to His Majesty's Composition, "Visiting Shining Consort Shangguan's Hall": Four Poems). See *QTS* 106.1105 and *TSJS* 11.362–63. In *TSJS*, the title is given as *Pei xing Zhaorong yuan xian shi sishou* 陪幸昭容院獻詩四首 (Accompanying Visiting the Shining Consort's Hall: Four Poems). Zheng Yin was a prominent figure during Zhongzong's reign and was associated with other famous partisans of female rulers, including Cui Shi 崔湜 (671–713) and Zong Chuke. However, he was executed for his involvement in the rebellion of Zhongzong's son Li Chongfu 李重福 (680?–710), which occurred just after Ruizong's ascendance to the throne. See *JTS* 86.2835–37; and *XTS* 81.3594.

identity as a woman whose dominion of influence extends from the palace women's quarters to the natural landscape outside: "The worthy talent of the inner quarters is valued, / her lofty high-mindedness and superior attainments lodged in the mountain forest are difficult [to achieve]" (宮掖賢才重, 山林高尚難).[94] Shangguan Wan'er's talent and esteemed place in the life of the court perfectly accord with the natural setting of her estate, and the couplet suggests that she is simultaneously a powerful politician and a "lofty and high-minded" (*gao shang* 高尚) recluse. The final couplet of the first poem reiterates the paradisiacal identity of the home presided over by Shangguan. Zheng Yin exhorts the reader against claims that "we are separated from Qin and Han" (無云秦漢隔) because "we are visiting another instance of flowers of Wuling" (別訪武陵花), both references to Tao Qian's 陶潛 (372?–427) "Tao hua yuan ji" 桃花源記 (Peach Blossom Spring).[95] Without any irony, Zheng Yin locates a paradise defined by ahistoricity and the appeal of an existence uncomplicated by shifting political and societal allegiances at the lavish residence of one of the most powerful political and cultural figures of the day.[96]

The attribution of spiritual power to worldly power considerably increases Shangguan Wan'er's cache. Certainly, the crafted image of one who, though possessed of the greatest political and material force, was nevertheless at heart a "true" recluse most at home in natural surroundings was pleasing to Shangguan's own self-conception and fit perfectly into the vogue for estate building, the products of which represented carefully crafted and extremely expensive man-made "nature." This

94. *QTS* 106.1105.

95. *QTS* 106.1105. According to the famous account, during the Jin dynasty a fisherman from Wuling followed a stream through a grotto opening and discovered an ahistorical village paradise. The residents of the village had fled the disorder at the end of the Qin dynasty and were unaware of historical developments that had occurred in the ensuing centuries. They lived an uncomplicated and satisfied existence and treated the fisherman well. After he left, he could never find his way back to that paradise again. For Tao Qian's account and accompanying poem with annotations and critical discussion, see Yuan Xingpei, *Tao Yuanming ji jianzhu*, 6.479–89. For an English translation of "Peach Blossom Spring," see Hightower, *The Poetry of T'ao Ch'ien*, 254–58. The second poem in Zheng Yin's series also praises the present era as one in which precious peaches, which only bloom once every three millennia, are seen.

96. Shen Quanqi uses the allusion to Peach Blossom Spring in a similar manner in a poem composed at Wei Sili's mountain estate. For a translation and discussion of the poem, see Owen, "The Formation of the Tang Estate Poem," 46–47.

bespeaks a particular relationship involving nature whereby the identities of the court and its leading figures are defined by their power over and chosen place within the natural world.[97] The poetic rhetoric geared towards extolling them expresses and encapsulates this relationship.

Existing works by Shangguan Wan'er herself suggest an idea of power intimately connected with nature and fluidity of identity. Shangguan's best-known surviving work, a series of poems composed during a visit to the Changning Princess's 長寧公主 (680–8th c.) estate entitled *You Changning gongzhu liu bei chi ershiwu shou* 遊長寧公主流杯池二十五首 (Visiting the Changning Princess's Pool for Floating Wine-Cups: Twenty-Five Poems), adopts the voice of a gender-neutral (that is, male) recluse at one with nature.[98] Although this series was written in 710, at the end of the Jinglong era, the poetic identity and values projected by Shangguan Wan'er express a cumulative development in the rhetorical landscape that began in the 670s and 680s. This rhetorical landscape represents a developing perspective on the nature and expression of power, which defines power as the luxury to transcend at will such seemingly fixed aspects of identity as social position and gender.

Shangguan's non-poetic or actual identity is known to us and to all later generations of readers and was surely also very familiar to her contemporaries and co-visitors to the royal estate, who may well have

97. Stephen Owen has perceptively discussed the phenomenon of the early Tang "court recluse," who "retained all the rhetoric of the traditional recluse" without ever actually leaving court society. Owen, "The Formation of the Tang Estate Poem," 44.

98. Owen insightfully argues that one of the most arresting characteristics of Shangguan's "Visiting the Changning Princess" poems is her fluidity in adopting a role (the recluse who espouses the values of simplicity and "naturalness") that, on the surface, is decidedly different from, or even the diametric opposite of, her political and social identity in the real world. Not only does the series contain no "hint that the author is a woman," but, in addition, Shangguan "assumes a private role, ostensibly speaking for herself." Owen thus argues that the series represents a striking departure from the typological banquet poem, characterized by an ornate style and a focus on praise that resulted in less opportunity for individual poetic voice. In this way, the poems in the series can be seen as a declaration of the poet's attainment of the privileged status required to adopt the reclusive poetic persona, in essence announcing her prerogative to determine a shift in poetic fashion and to define and re-define her identity as she sees fit. Owen, "The Formation of the Tang Estate Poem," 52–53. See also Jie Wu, "A Study of Group Compositions," 241 and 244–45. For further translations of eight poems in the series, see Idema and Grant, *The Red Brush*, 69–70.

heard or read the poems soon after their composition. The series is thus an assertion of reclusive identity that also draws together poetic themes found in court poetry written both before and after its composition, and the recluse persona is constructed through reworking tropes already central to elite poetry at the time.

The relationship to nature, and the issue of what constitutes naturalness, is again key in the rhetorical expression of identity. Poems written at banquets to praise the ruler and/or ruling establishment in general often relied upon articulations of imperial power over the generative functions of nature. In Shangguan's series, high status is indicated by one's accord with nature, defined as the capacity for appreciation of nature and attainment of freedom within the "wilds." Shangguan demonstrates her status as a lofty recluse in opposition to the unenlightened state of the "common flock" of people (自不群).[99] Taken as a poetic set written within a particular context of wealth, power, and display, the poems speak for a certain exclusive in-group of which the individual author was an important member. In a form of circular logic, political and material status enables and is proven by the ability to enjoy and profess high spiritual status, or at least to adopt its posture.

In these poems, power is manifested through the subject's privileged and self-conscious freedom from convention (poetic or otherwise) and professed transcendence of material artifice. Shangguan experiments with poetic form in the series, which contains poems with line lengths varying from tetrasyllabic to heptasyllabic, as well as a mixture of quatrains and eight-line poems.[100] This may have been intended as a formal embodiment of the thematic emphasis on "naturalness," meaning spontaneity and unrestraint. We have seen similar experimentation with form in Wu Zhao's Luo River hymns composed in 688; the genre of the works and occasion for which they were composed were certainly different, but this might also suggest general openness to formal experimentation.

Some of the poems recombine the well-known tropes of imperial power over nature and imperial identity with divinity to stress the supe-

99. Fifth pentasyllabic eight-line poem, *QTS* 5.63.

100. It is difficult to discern an original intended sequence to the poems. Although the orderings given in the *Tangshi jishi* and *Quan Tang shi* are different, in both cases the poems are arranged in groups according to form. See *TSJS* 3.62–63 and *QTS* 5.61–63 for the full series.

riority of the courtly world *as the natural world* over mythical celestial paradises. This is made poetically possible as Shangguan Wan'er, a leading court politician, becomes the wise and vocal recluse who eschews worldly values. In one four-syllable quatrain, for instance, the poet instructs the reader to stop speaking of the mythical paradisiacal realms Yuanjiao 圓嶠 and Fanghu 方壺, because "how can they compare to Lu Lodge? / the Immortal Capital is right here" (何如魯館, 即是仙都).[101] There are multiple variations on the poetic evaluation of the poet's present surroundings as superior to any that could be found in various immortal locales, rendering travel to or longing for those locales unnecessary: "What need is there to travel far on the road to the Three Mountains— / I [or: As a human being I] have already reached the home of all immortals" (何須遠訪三山路, 人今已到九仙家);[102] "Send word to the reclusive guest: / don't visit Penglai and Yingzhou anymore" (寄言棲遯客, 勿復訪蓬瀛).[103]

The poet is the vanguard telling all other potential "reclusive guests" where the real site of spiritual fulfillment is. As Jie Wu has noted, this rhetorical posture seems to achieve newfound popularity during this period; Shangguan Wan'er's phrasing and content here are by no means without precedent in the courtly verse of the preceding decade.[104] A poem written by Wu Sansi entitled "Ningbi chi shiyan yingzhi de 'chu shui cha'" 凝碧池侍宴應制得出水槎 (In Attendance at Collected Emerald Pool, to Imperial Command: I Got "Raft Emerging from Water"), combines description of natural beauty with a closing judgment about the nexus of true divinity:

101. *QTS* 5.62. Yuanjiao and Fanghu, also known as Fangzhang 方丈, are three of five legendary immortal mountain-isles connoting reclusion. The other three are Penglai, Yingzhou, and Daiyu 岱輿. Lu Lodge, Luguan 魯館, refers to a dwelling that housed a princess (or other aristocratic woman) after her marriage; given the power of the female imperial family members during this time, it seems to refer to the imperial compound as a whole.

102. Second heptasyllabic quatrain, *QTS* 5.63. The three mountains, Penglai, Fangzhang, and Yingzhou, are the dwelling places of immortals, supposedly located in the Eastern Sea (Donghai 東海). Jiuxian 九仙 refers either to the nine grades of immortals; or to all immortals in general.

103. Sixth pentasyllabic quatrain, *QTS* 5.63.

104. Jie Wu, "A Study of Group Compositions," 187–91, 242–43.

In what era was this wood born,
  and how many years ago was it made into the raft?
If you want to ride the bends of the Silver River [Milky Way],
  first float along the side of the Jade Pool.
The pressing torrents criss-cross the coast,
  in the deep waves the reflections are seen upside down.
Don't trouble yourself to ask the guest of Shu—
  this very place is High Heaven.[105]

彼木生何代, 為槎復幾年.
欲乘銀漢曲, 先泛玉池邊.
擁溜根橫岸, 沈波影倒懸.
無勞問蜀客, 此處即高天.[106]

The extended *Bowu zhi* allusion, of course, fits the poetic subject and would have been a popular choice for anyone drawing the topic "raft" in a group poetic game. The significance of the poem for the present discussion lies in the phrasing and import of the final line, which instructs the reader that there is no need to find out about the heavenly realm from the guest of Shu because the current surroundings (a fete at Collected Emerald Pool) are the true "High Heaven."

The exact dates of Wu Sansi's poem are unclear; since he was killed in 707, he certainly wrote it sometime before Shangguan composed her series in 710. The poetic posture suggested by the closing exhortation of Wu Sansi's poem indicates a self-confident, self-proclaimed superior state of mind. Shangguan's series expands this trope and is full of intimations of self-styled wisdom. A trisyllabic quatrain, for instance, informs the reader: "I follow immortal appreciation, / expanding my sense of

105. Wu Sansi's poem is alluding to a story from Zhang Hua's 張華 (232–300) *Bowu zhi* 博物志 (Record of Broad-reaching Knowledge) about a man who lived on a small island in the ocean. Every year during the eighth month a raft floated by, and one year the man jumped onto it and was carried into the heavens, where he encountered the Oxherd and many weaving maidens. The man on the raft asked what place he had reached and was told by the Oxherd to inquire of Yan Junping, the diviner, when he was in Shu. He followed the instructions and later found out from Yan Junping that he had trespassed into the constellation of the Oxherd. The "guest of Shu" is the skilled diviner Yan Junping. See Zhang Hua, *Bowu zhi*, 10.381.

106. *QTS* 80.866.

separation from the world. // This passes over Mount Kunlun and the Langfeng Peak / and exceeds Penglai" (逐仙賞, 展幽情. 踰崐閬, 邁蓬萊).[107] In a poem written at a princess's southern estate, Wu Zhao's rumored consort Zhang Yizhi 張易之 (d. 705) also "follows appreciation" or "appreciates while following," a phrase that indicates sophisticated contemplation of nature: "Appreciating [the scenery] while following [with the imperial entourage] at Pingyang Estate, / playing the reed whistle east of Shangyuan" (逐賞平陽第, 鳴笳上苑東).[108] The rhetoric of "following immortal appreciation" or "appreciating while following" as part of the recluse's inner contemplation and aloofness from the world is explored most fully in Shangguan's *Visiting the Changning Princess* poems, but it was clearly part of the dominant poetic and cultural discourse in existence prior to the composition of the series (Zhang Yizhi's poem must have been composed sometime prior to his death in 705). This is true whether or not claims of the Zhang brothers' illiteracy are accurate and regardless of who might have actually written poems attributed to them.[109]

In Zhang Yizhi's poem, appreciation is linked with descriptions of landscapes enlivened by famous female figures that are meant to refer back to the princess who owns the estate. "Pingyang Estate" refers to the historical Princess Pingyang, Han Emperor Wu's elder sister. The poem also closes with a description of the courtly musical entertainment as the song of "Qin's flute" (秦簫曲未終), an allusion to Xiao shi and Nongyu, the daughter of Duke Mu of Qin.[110] In Shangguan Wan'er's series, however, there are no female-related allusions, and the emphasis is on an implied contrast between a life of lofty reclusion and a social-courtly life, or materially obsessed existence. The posture adopted by the poet in these lines also paradoxically indicates her elite status; only someone at the very

107. *QTS* 5.62.

108. The poem is entitled "Shi cong guo gongzhu nan zhai shiyan tan de feng zi yingzhi" 侍從過公主南宅侍宴探得風字應制 (In Attendance Passing the Princess's Southern Residence to Attend at a Banquet, I Got the Character "Wind": To Imperial Command). *QTS* 80.867–68.

109. See *QTS* 80.867, which quotes *JTS* 78.2707 claiming that all of the Zhang brothers' poems were actually written by the skilled court poets Song Zhiwen and Yan Zhaoyin. See also chapter 5 for a detailed discussion of these claims of illiteracy.

110. *QTS* 80.868.

top of the sociopolitical hierarchy could afford to rhetorically cast off or place herself outside of that very hierarchy.

Some of Shangguan's *Visiting the Changning Princess* poems disown the material, social, cultural, and even ritual elements of court life. The poet's self-described taste in music and clothes demarcates the line between nature and artifice, genuine and synthetic. The world of sound occupies a significant site of judgment and status-making in Shangguan's series. The "music of song and winds" (*ge chui* 歌吹), that is, the sounds of human artifice embedded within human social interactions, should not be bothered with, as the natural "music" of wind gusting through the pines is "sufficient to delight the emotions" (自足娱情).[111] In keeping with the poetic tradition of "summoning the recluse" (*zhaoyin* 招隱), the music of "civilization" is inherently inferior to the "music of nature," created spontaneously and effortlessly by naturally occurring phenomena.[112] Likewise, in the third pentasyllabic quatrain, the landscape holds the key to uncovering what can be called true music: "If you want to know what truly delights the ear, / just listen to the gurgling of the water" (欲知堪悅耳, 唯聽水泠泠).[113] These lines suggest the poet's unique capacity for discernment; she alone is able to perceive the sounds of true music in the surrounding landscape where others are not, even to the point that she is the instructor in taste and spiritual matters for both the "reclusive guest" ("Send word to the reclusive guest: don't visit Peng and Ying again")[114] and the *Chuci*-esque "prince" ("In the mountains, there is truly much to be enjoyed: / let me go report this to the prince").[115] In an inversion of the famous *Chuci* 楚辭 poem "Zhaohun" 招魂 (Calling Back the Soul), in which a shaman attempts to summon the departed spirit of the prince back from the wilds to the center of civilization, the poetic speaker here urges her prince to leave the constricting inner world of the court, and identifies the natural surroundings as the site of the

111. First quatrasyllabic quatrain; *QTS* 5.62.

112. In particular, Shangguan evokes Zuo Si's 左思 (250–305 CE) poem "Zhao yinshi" 招隱士 (Summoning the Recluse): "There is no need for stringed instruments and pipes; / The mountains and rivers have clear sounds" (非必絲與竹, 山水有清音). Lu Qinli, *Xian Qin Han Wei Jin Nanbei chao shi*, 7.734.

113. *QTS* 5.63.

114. 寄言棲遯客, 勿復訪蓬瀛. *QTS* 5.63.

115. 山中真可玩, 暫請報王孫. Seventh pentasyllabic quatrain; *QTS* 5.63.

most elevated pleasure. As the location of true elite pleasure shifts, the elements of elite culture are relocated or rediscovered in nature: "The wind through the bamboos is like the long flute; / the flowing water serves as the cry of the zither" (風篁類長笛, 流水當鳴琴).[116]

The speaker's self-ascribed perception as to the "genuine" hierarchy of elite values thus translates into the rhetoric of substitution. The speaker conspicuously replaces elements indicative of social interaction and/or the material culture of elite civilization with their "real" forms from the natural realm. As she "wanders around the mountain residence" (遊山第), "lingering and begrudging return" (淹留惜未歸), the speaker turns aspects of the landscape around her into elements of daily life typically considered inherent to traditionally defined civilization: "For books, I draw rattan to make my bookcase; / I take ivy as my clothes. // This is truly a place in which to climb and play; / looking around me, I appreciate its brilliance" (書引藤為架, 人將薜作衣. 此真攀玩所, 臨睨賞光輝).[117] The speaker adopts the privileged position of someone who knows what counts as "truly a place in which to climb and play," someone who is able, where others are not, to define and appreciate what is of value.

Nature also fills the role of companionship: "The mist and clouds inquire after me; / the wind and moon are my understanding friends" (煙霞問訊, 風月相知); "The mountain and forest are my companions; / the pine and cassia are my neighbors" (山林作伴, 松桂為鄰).[118] The natural identity of the recluse actually becomes the most self-conscious indicator of spiritual and physical removal from "the common flock" and their "noisy atmosphere": "Completely unrestrained, I emerge from the mist and clouds, / aloof and untouchable, I am not of the common flock. // Rinsing in the flowing water, I purify the treasury of my thoughts; / leaning on an armrest, I avoid the noisy atmosphere" (放曠出煙雲, 蕭條自不群. 漱流清意府, 隱几避囂氛).[119] As true then as it is now, only the wealthiest and most privileged segment of society can afford to opt out, temporarily and according to whim, of the noisiness of everyday society and regularly lived social roles, not to mention leaving immense tracts of

116. Fourth pentasyllabic quatrain; *QTS* 5.63.
117. Fourth pentasyllabic eight-line poem; *QTS* 5.62.
118. The second couplets of the second and third four-syllable quatrains; *QTS* 5.62.
119. Fifth pentasyllabic eight-line poem; *QTS* 5.63.

land uncultivated for the purpose of periodic roaming and acting out the role of recluse.

Along with self-proclaimed attainment of mental rarity, Shangguan poetically acquires the accoutrements of the "literary recluse" role. The fourth pentasyllabic quatrain, quoted above, refers to her bookcase and robe made of natural products.[120] Other poems further emphasize the recluse role to a stereotypical degree, describing the recluse with his or her most typical prop of the staff, which she or he leans on while roaming and contemplating nature: "Leaning on my staff, I face the peaks with rose-colored clouds; / with careful steps, I descend the frosty footpath" (第杖臨霞岫, 危步下霜蹊).[121] The ninth pentasyllabic quatrain provides the full sense of an elaborate game of dress-up, acquiring and playing with the props of reclusion: "Spreading out leopard-skin mattress crosswise; / wearing deer-womb kerchief at a slant. // May I ask what she is doing— / in the mountains, there is one who is above it all" (橫鋪豹皮褥, 側戴鹿胎巾.借問何為者, 山中有逸人).[122]

"One who is above it all," *yiren* 逸人 or *yike* 逸客, appears elsewhere in the series as a self-referential and self-aggrandizing epithet. The opening of the first pentasyllabic couplet suggests the *yiren*'s unique rapport with nature: "The climbing ivy beckons to the one who is above it all; / the bending cassia accords with my inner emotions" (攀藤招逸客, 偃桂叶幽情).[123] Other poems strongly suggest the self-conscious unrestraint of the recluse role: "My intentions grow calm as I move deeper into the mountains; / my path strays as it follows the bending ravine. // Gradually I sense my mind and spirit soaring free, *beyond it all*; / soon I see the clouds and fog hanging low" (志逐深山靜, 途隨曲澗迷. 漸覺心神逸, 俄看雲霧低).[124] Elsewhere in the series, the posture of reclusive unre-

120. *QTS* 5.62.

121. Sixth pentasyllabic eight-line poem; *QTS* 5.63.

122. *QTS* 5.63. The use of the word *jiewen* 借問 in the third line seems to suggest a third-person perspective, indicating that here Shangguan may be describing an idealized reclusive figure, perhaps as embodied in the estate's owner, the Changning Princess. I would like to thank Professor Hyong Rhew for this suggestion. For an alternate translation, see Jie Wu, "A Study of Group Compositions," 244–45.

123. *QTS* 5.63.

124. Sixth pentasyllabic eight-line poem, second and third couplets; *QTS* 5.63 (emphasis mine). The final line seems to suggest that the speaker is looking down, from an elevated position, upon the clouds and fog.

straint is accompanied by a further fluidity of poetic and gender identity. As noted by Owen, in the third pentasyllabic regulated poem, Shangguan Wan'er envisions herself, a forty-something female politician and court lady, in a pose very uncharacteristic of her typical identity:[125]

> On a fair morning, the air clear and soft,
> I unfasten my robe to appreciate the ivy.
> Tortoise-shell, the congealed colors of spring,
> lapis lazuli ripples atop the waves.
> Standing tiptoe on a stone, I give a long whistle,
> pulling myself along by the pine branches, I burst out in a short song.
> Except for one who is beyond mere things,
> who could cross this path?
> 霽曉氣清和, 披襟賞薜蘿.
> 玳瑁凝春色, 琉璃漾水波.
> 跂石聊長嘯, 攀松乍短歌.
> 除非物外者, 誰就此經過.[126]

Unfastening one's robe, whistling, and spontaneously composing a short song are typical postures of the male recluse as constructed by the literary-cultural tradition.[127] It is tempting to read Shangguan's poetic adoption of the role of the male, or at least non-gender-specific, recluse as an individual woman's rhetorical disavowal or transcendence of the imperatives of gender. Yet, at the same time, Shangguan's poems once again rework tropes permeating the contemporary cultural milieu, tropes that had been integrated into cultural and literary discourse since well before the Jinglong reign period.

In 700, during an outing at Shicong 石淙 on Mount Song in Henan, members of Wu Zhao's poetic entourage drew upon similar phrasing and imagery evoking the recluse in nature when composing works to the imperially set topic of "Fenghe sheng zhi xia ri you Shicong shan" 奉和聖製夏日遊石淙山 (A Respectfully Presented Companion Piece to Her

125. Owen, "The Formation of the Tang Estate Poem," 53–54.
126. *QTS* 5.62.
127. Owen, "The Formation of the Tang Estate Poem," 52–54.

Majesty's Composition, "Roaming on Shicong Mountain on a Summer Day").[128] Li Jiao's contribution to the series precedes Shangguan in proclaiming the beauty of natural versions of pipes and painted screens: "Birds chirp in harmony with the variegated sounds of nature, seeming like tuned pipes, / flowers bloom on thousands of cliffs, resembling painted screens" (鳥和百籟疑調管, 花發千巖似畫屏).[129] Wu Sansi's final couplet likewise connects man-made music, the music of nature, and a particular, valued state of mind: "The bright sun about to set, colliding into the layered cliffs, / the dark clouds on the verge of crossing, being obstructed by the tall peaks. // Facing my wine, playing the zither, I pursue the pleasures of the rustic wilds, / at times hearing clear sounds blowing through the tall pines" (白日將移衝疊巘, 玄雲欲度礙高峰. 對酒鳴琴追野趣, 時聞清吹入長松).[130] Wu Sansi refers to the "pleasures of the rustic wilds" (*ye qu* 野趣) while, in *Visiting the Changning Princess*, Shangguan Wan'er writes of the "pleasures of immortals" (*xian qu* 仙趣),[131] but the thematic milieu and implication of elevated mental state (either *ye* or *yi*) are shared.

Zhang Yizhi's contribution to the Shicong Mountain series likewise paints a secluded landscape in which nature takes the place of man-made luxuries, including silk curtains and music: "A thousand *zhang* of pines and vines intermingle and form a curtain of kingfisher green; / a hillside of mountains and rivers takes the place of the singing zither" (千丈松蘿交翠幕, 一丘山水當鳴琴).[132] Zhang Yizhi's final two couplets link communion with nature, the presence of female divinity (as a figure for Wu Zhao) in the landscape, and the mood or mindset of the "rustic person" (*yeren* 野人): "Blue birds amidst white clouds: the Queen Mother's emissaries; / hanging vines, snapped tendrils: the rustic person's heart. // Dusk in the mountains, amidst the seclusion of the peaks; /

128. Jie Wu has analyzed in detail the compositional context, textual history, and content of the Shicong poems in "A Study of Group Compositions," chap. 4.

129. *QTS* 61.730.

130. *QTS* 80.865. Like Shangguan, Wu Sansi's poem evokes Zuo Si's "Zhao yingshi" 招隱士 (Summoning the Recluse): "There is no need for stringed instruments and pipes; / The mountains and rivers have clear sounds" (非必絲與竹, 山水有清音). See Lu Qinli, *Xian Qin Han Wei Jin Nanbei chao shi*, 7.734.

131. See the third pentasyllabic quatrain, in particular the opening line: "The streams and rocks are full of pleasures of the immortals" 泉石多仙趣; *QTS* 5.63.

132. *QTS* 80.867.

harmoniously the fragrance wafts from the depths of the falling flowers" (青鳥白雲王母使, 垂藤斷葛野人心. 山中日暮幽巖下, 洽然香吹落花深).[133] The "Queen Mother" is the famous and powerful goddess the Queen Mother of the West (Xi wang mu 西王母), meant to refer to Wu Zhao, the "queen mother" of the mortal realm. The "[wafting] fragrance" of the "falling flowers" evokes Pure Land imagery, in which flowers are associated with the Pure Land paradise. The historical context of a female ruler who consciously invoked Buddhist imagery and ideology perhaps makes the reader think, in particular, of the dialogue between the goddess and Shariputra in the *Vimalakirti Sutra* (*Weimojie jing* 維摩詰經). When the goddess sprinkles down flowers, they bounce off of those who are of highest spiritual attainment (bodhisattvas) but remain stuck to those of lower level (including Shariputra, an arhat).[134] The prolonged interaction between the goddess and Shariputra is also famous as an exploration of gender and spiritual attainment. Seeing the goddess's power, Shariputra asks her why she does not "change out of this female body" (汝何以不轉女身), assuming that a female body is undesirable and inferior.[135] Countering that gender is but a "phantom" created by limited and incorrect perspective, she proceeds to temporarily change Shariputra into a woman, whereupon he realizes that, like all illusory worldly phenomena, "the form and shape of my female body does not exist, yet does not not exist" (女身色相, 無在無不在).[136]

The discussion of perspective, gender, and transcendence is apt. Wu Zhao's power is poetically linked to nature and spiritual or otherworldly capacity, which are manifested in the mental state of the "rustic person's heart" (*yeren xin* 野人心). Like Shangguan Wan'er's self-designation of *yiren*, "one who is beyond it all," the *yeren*, "rustic person," denotes a relationship with nature that goes beyond mere communion to express

133. *QTS* 80.867.

134. A bodhisattva, the ideal deity in Mayahana Buddhism, has achieved enlightenment but chooses to remain in the cycle of birth and death (suffering) in order to help others to likewise reach enlightenment. An arhat has realized release from the cycle of suffering individually and is considered by Mahayana believers to be lower than the bodhisattva.

135. *Weimojie suoshuo jing xinzhu*, annotated by Tang Sipeng, 7.180–81; translation is from Watson, *The Vimalakirti Sutra*, 90.

136. *Weimojie suoshuo jing xinzhu*, 7.180–81; Watson, *The Vimalakirti Sutra*, 90–91.

a superior discerning perspective. The court literature of the late seventh and early eighth centuries, as a whole, evinces special fascination with the imperial relationship to nature. Themes involving auspicious signs, cosmic approval of imperial rule, and the court's assumption of the generative powers of the natural realm are all variations on a vision of power whereby the court's supremacy is rhetorically communicated in relation to its power over nature. The rhetorical definition of imperial power as the power to create and refashion at times suggests downplaying of gender distinctions (that is, through the creation or refashioning of identity). Posthumous reconstructions of women leaders' identities as female power-holders ironically indicate the prerogative of later writers to reshape the images of these women in accordance with their own judgments, conceptualizations, and fears.

THREE

Ritual, Signs, and the Interpretation of Female Power

At the end of the Jinglong reign period, an official named Du Pengju 杜鵬舉 died as a result of a mistake in the supernatural bureaucracy. He was taken to the underworld, where he protested and succeeded in having the error rectified. Perhaps as compensation for his suffering, before his return to life he was allowed to look ahead in time, where he saw his unborn sons and, importantly, a vision of the political future. Specifically, he witnessed the ascendance of Ruizong, known to Du Pengju as Prince Xiang 相王. Once back in the human world, he was, some years later, rewarded for his allegiance to Ruizong, and in the "real" imperial court, he recognized the figures from his supernatural experience:

> [In Du Pengju's visit to the underworld] several hundred celestial beings surrounded Prince Xiang. The whole ground was colored clouds and the celestial beings were dressed in immortal clothes, all as if in a painting. In front of Prince Xiang was a woman holding up an incense burner and leading the way. She came close, and he [Du Penju] examined her [and found that] her skirt and belt seemed shredded, [torn in] tiered strips [of cloth]. . . . [After returning to the human realm] . . . [Ruizong] commanded him [Du Pengju] to look at the one holding the incense burner, and when Pengju saw her from far away, she turned out to be the Taiping Princess. He asked her the reason for [the appearance of] her skirt and belt, and she said, "We were just then ironing the imperial dragon robes, when suddenly the fire leapt up, and in the midst of my surprise, I had unknowingly burnt my belt. In the chaos I was not able to change my clothes." The Princess sighed and put forth her praise, saying, "The rise of the sagely Emperor was surely brought about by Heaven."

天人數百, 圍繞相王, 滿地綵雲, 並衣仙服, 皆如畫者. 相王前有女人執香爐引, 行近窺諦, 衣裙帶狀似剪破, 一如雁齒狀. . . .令視執爐者, 鵬舉遙識之, 乃太平公主也. 問裙帶之由, 公主云: "方熨龍袞, 忽為火迸, 驚忙之中, 不覺爇帶. 倉惶不及更服." 公主獻椒陳賀曰: "聖人之興, 固自天也."[1]

This tale is recorded in Zhang Zhuo's *Chaoye qianzai*, an early source for much of our information about court life and culture during the late seventh and early eighth centuries. The tale follows a basic, Buddhist-influenced plotline, popular during the period, of the mistaken journey to the underworld. The opening section of the anecdote informs us that Du Pengju's temporary death was due to an erroneous attribution of bad karma engendered by the killing of a living creature, and his "accuser" is that living creature itself, a horse Du Pengju had slaughtered on the orders of an imperial decree. Because he was acting at the behest of another, the negative karma does not rightly accrue to him, so he does not deserve the punishment of death. Within the worldview assumed by the anecdote, historical developments are predetermined; Du Pengju witnesses the ascendance of Ruizong twice, first in the prerecorded supernatural version and then in the human realm. The Taiping Princess appears here as an ardent and genuine supporter of her brother, and she is also surprisingly down-to-earth as regards her own vanity; she neglects to change her clothes in the urgency of assisting Ruizong.[2]

As will become clear over the course of this chapter, its portrayal of the Taiping Princess is quite startling and anomalous; most retrospective historical and anecdotal sources dealing with her, as well as with the other powerful women who dominated the cultural and political world of the period, emphasize not sisterly loyalty and humility, but greed and lasciviousness. Perhaps from the subject matter (the ascension of Ruizong) and

1. *CYQZ* 6.137–38.

2. In *Taiping guangji*, this passage is also attributed to a work called *Chu shi xiao shi he zuo zhuan* 處士蕭時合作傳. See *Taiping guangji* 300. Our current version of the *Chaoye qianzai* is not the same as the original put together by Zhang Zhuo. The work seems to have been lost after the Song, and a cross-comparison of various bibliographic catalogues and other materials suggests that present versions have been reconstructed from the tenth-century *Taiping guangji* 太平廣記 (Extensive Records from the Era of Great Peace) and other sources. See Zhou Xunchu, *Tangdai biji xiaoshuo xulu*, 7–14.

the sympathetic portrayal of the Taiping Princess we can posit a date close to the time in question, when the Taiping Princess played, together with Ruizong's son Li Longji (the future Xuanzong), a central role in destroying the faction led by her sister-in-law Empress Wei, who was making a bid for power. The contrast between the treatment of the Taiping Princess and that of Empress Wei, who is referred to in this passage by her derogative posthumous epithet "Wei the Commoner" (Wei shuren 韋庶人), is perhaps also suggestive of the mood directly following the violent decimation of the Wei faction, although the historical records are consistently especially hostile to both Empress Wei and her daughter the Anle Princess, who is also known as "The Mutinous Commoner" (Beini shuren 悖逆庶人).

Though couched within a fictional narrative that is of intrinsic interest, this anecdote also touches upon issues surrounding legitimacy, historical memory, and cosmic order. According to the worldview informing the anecdote, the Taiping Princess, as the daughter of two emperors (Gaozong and Wu Zhao) and the sister of two emperors (Zhongzong and Ruizong), is a legitimate member of the ruling line. In contrast, Empress Wei and the Anle Princess are illegitimate usurpers destined for destruction.

The images of these women developed gradually in the decades and centuries after their deaths, drawing from record, rumor, and cultural values (which, of course, are themselves far from static). A small sampling of surviving materials composed very soon after the deaths of the women power-holders, such as Zhang Yue's 張說 (667–730) preface to Shangguan Wan'er's poetry collection, shows that some of these first texts continued the rhetoric of effusive praise used to celebrate them during their lifetimes.[3] In general, however, the process of condemnatory rewriting had already begun in the generation or so after their deaths. This chapter and subsequent chapters dealing with retrospective portrayals trace the development of archetypal image and lore. In some cases, later sources merely quote an earlier anecdote or include a redacted version; in others, however, we can trace stages in a particular story's development, as

3. Zhang Yue's preface has been translated and discussed by several scholars. See Egan, "*Preface to Shangguan Wan'er*," 723–25; and Jie Wu, "A Study of Group Compositions," 214–23.

elements are added and particular points are emphasized. The nature of these developing emphases reveals what came to be seen by historians and compilers as essential to the Zhou through Jinglong women leaders as characters in historical narrative. The selection process of later compilers is also of interest; that is, which anecdotes appealed to later compilers as they gleaned through earlier collections is also expressive of their values and understanding of history.

Narratives of condemnation often represent reverse treatments of the same motifs that underlie praise-filled accounts dating to the late seventh and early eighth centuries. This phenomenon is strikingly evident in narratives concerned with cosmic order, which make up a discourse of richly varying themes surrounding ritual, signs, and meaning in accounts of the powerful women of the period. Writing around the turn of the eighth century, early Tang women and their courtiers used the various genres of court literature as a vehicle to proclaim the natural and heaven-ordained status of their power. In the decades and centuries after their deaths, later writers manipulated the discourse of auspiciousness to express the opposite interpretation of their power, that is, to condemn it as an unnatural violation of the cosmic order.

The prominent role played by the rhetoric of auspiciousness and signs in Chinese historical discourse is well known. Various scholars have discussed the importance of cosmic signs as a means of meting out and influencing historical judgments.[4] Well before we reach the reign of Wu Zhao, auspicious signs were an important component in the legitimation campaign of a ruler, especially a founding ruler. Arthur Wright describes Sui founder Yang Jian's performance of the time-honored steps of thinly veiled usurpation as "[playing] out the scenario of virtuous succession," which included requisite invocation of symbolism and auspicious markers.[5] Wechsler and Lippiello have likewise discussed what Wechsler terms the "management and manipulation of portents" within the context of the ruler's campaign to legitimate his or her assumption of power, a practice that is well attested at least as far back as the Western Han.[6] In any

4. See, for example, Franke, "Some Remarks," 119–20; Wechsler, *Offerings of Jade and Silk*, 56; and Jack Wei Chen, *The Poetics of Sovereignty*, chaps. 1 and 2.

5. Wright, *The Sui Dynasty*, 61–62.

6. Wechsler, *Offerings of Jade and Silk*, 56. See also Lippiello, *Auspicious Omens and Miracles*, chap. 1, 197–215 and 217–23.

regime, a game of auspiciousness, in which contestants for power strove to gain control of the domain of auspicious signs, was at play. These signs included various portents (special stones and gems, remarkable animals, lights, and dreams, among others), astrological phenomena, and unusual weather events, and they were ideally meant, from the perspective of the ruler or potential conqueror, to "predict" and legitimate an impending glorious destiny. Depending upon the historical evaluation of the ruler's legitimacy, those auspicious signs were later judged as authentic expressions of cosmic approval or as inauthentic and harmful forgeries.

It is a platitude of traditional and modern scholarship that celebratory notices of auspicious events are especially prominent in accounts of the reigns of Wu Zhao and Zhongzong. In fact, celebrations of auspicious occurrences are common in the surviving court records, memorials, and literature of most rulers, including the immediate predecessors and successor to the era of female leadership in the seventh through eighth centuries: Gaozu, Taizong, and Xuanzong. In these records, we see celebrations of the same types of miraculous events and signs recorded in reference to the Tang women, such as "auspicious stones" (*ruishi* 瑞石) and "spirit turtles" (*linggui* 靈龜), often miraculously over-written with characters about the ruler and his greatness.[7] Taizong's impressive and lasting success in manipulating his own historical image can be seen in the widespread view of Taizong's government as one focused on the

7. See a record of auspicious events occurring in the first years of Xuanzong's reign in Cen Jian'gong, *Jiu Tang shu yiwen*, 3.1a. The tenth-century anecdote collection *Kaiyuan Tianbao yishi* 開元天寶遺事 (Past Affairs of the Kaiyuan and Tianbao Reign Periods) records an episode in which a jade with the seal-script characters *tianxia taiping* 天下太平 ("the world is at peace") was unearthed in 714; see Wang Renyu, *Kaiyuan Tianbao yishi*, a.1. See Zhou Xunchu, *Tangdai biji xiaoshuo xulu*, 161–63, for detailed information about *Kaiyuan Tianbao yishi*'s transmission history and structure. The famous reign name Tianbao 天寶 (Heavenly Treasure) also supposedly derived from the discovery of a "precious tally" (*bao fu* 寶符). See *KTCXJ*, 5–6. According to *Zizhi tongjian*, Tian Tongxiu 田同秀, an adjutant in the bureau of the Prince of Chen, reported to the throne that Laozi (hailed by the Tang as the ancestor of the imperial Li clan) had come to him and told him that a numinous tally (*lingfu* 靈符) could be found under the former residence of Yin Xi 尹喜, a famous figure in the Daoist tradition who supposedly encouraged Laozi to leave behind the *Daode jing* 道德經. When a tally was indeed unearthed at the indicated location, the reign name was changed to honor the "heavenly treasure." Skeptics also supposedly raised doubts as to the veracity of Tian Tongxiu's claims; see *ZZTJ* 215.6852–53.

fundamentals of statecraft and dismissive of superstitious signs and the discourse of auspiciousness. In fact, Taizong was just as involved in the manipulation of portents and his historical image as was Wu Zhao.[8] The existence of similar works celebrating auspicious events at the courts of rulers posthumously constructed as opposite types indicates that the line between auspiciousness and inauspiciousness, between cosmic sign and forgery, is determined by retrospective evaluations of the moral quality of the figures involved. Retrospective accounts of otherworldly signs and events at the courts dominated by the Tang women rulers are distinguished by their fascination with interpretation, in particular, de-legitimation through interpretation.

Much insightful work has already been devoted to the reconstruction of Wu Zhao's ideological and practical state apparatus.[9] It is not my goal to reexamine the areas already amply explored by these scholars. I am not interested in the precise nature of Wu Zhao's symbolic program, or the symbolic programs of other female leaders, per se; rather, I seek to understand the ways in which their ritual actions were reconstructed in later sources and what these reconstructions tell us about narrative perspective, conceptualizations of gender and power, and the force of rhetoric. Although religious literature was important to the symbolic program, I confine my analysis to reconstructions in secular sources, for the reasons given above. Through an examination of these sources, this chapter deconstructs the condemnatory discourse of signs surrounding the early Tang women. I begin with an examination of general cosmological indictments of female rulers by "upright" officials before turning to specific case studies, including the performance and interpretation of public ceremonies, "auspicious" stones (such as the Precious Diagram or Luo River Diagram) offered to the throne, and dream narratives. My

8. See Jack Wei Chen, *The Poetics of Sovereignty*, chaps. 1, 2, and 7, for detailed discussions of Taizong's ritual-rhetorical performance of good government.

9. For state symbolism in Wu Zhao's reign, see Bokenkamp, "A Medieval Feminist Critique"; Chen Jo-shui, "Empress Wu and Proto-Feminist Sentiments"; Forte, *Political Propaganda and Ideology in China*; Guisso, *Wu Tse-t'ien and the Politics of Legitimation*, chaps. 4–9; Wechsler, *Offerings of Jade and Silk*, 170–94; and Rothschild, *Rhetoric, Ritual, and Support Constituencies*, chaps. 3, 4, and 6. For specific case studies, see Forte, "The Maitreyist Huayi (d. 695) and Taoism"; and Fracasso, "The Nine Tripods of Empress Wu."

analysis focuses on the manipulation and interpretation of signs as a narrative device and meta-narrative goal.

General Cosmological Indictments

Interpretation is of paramount importance in the retrospective condemnation of signs associated with the early Tang female power-holders. A common and seemingly axiomatic source of condemnation is the woman ruler's failure to understand "real" signs or her confusion of "real" and "false" signs. The condemnatory narratives are premised upon particular conceptions of cosmic, gendered order and disorder; the discourse of *yin-yang* and natural resonance is used to construct this period of female rule as one of transgression and misinterpretation. In literature on the period, there are various direct cosmological indictments against female rule along the lines of *yin-yang*, which draw upon much earlier traditions of gender theory. *Chaoye qianzai*, for example, contains notices of the bizarre phenomenon of sex-changing fowl: "After Wenming [684, when Gaozong died and Wu Zhao assumed full control of the throne], throughout the various prefectures of the nation there were presented many cases in which a female fowl transformed into a male. Some of them were changed halfway and halfway not quite transformed. This was a sign of Zetian's direct assumption of the throne" (文明以後, 天下諸州進雌雞, 變爲雄者多. 或半已化, 半未化. 乃則天正位之兆).[10]

The male-identified position of the throne has been illegitimately appropriated by a woman, leading to a severe imbalance at the apex of the human realm. Nature responds to this imbalance with one of its own, the strange and unnatural sexual transformation of female fowl to male. These notices of sex-changing fowl were incorporated during the Northern Song into the *Xin Tang shu*,[11] yet their presence in the eighth-century *Chaoye qianzai* points to an earlier genesis of these rumors in association with Wu Zhao.

An anecdote found in *Taiping guangji* approaches the narrative device

10. *CYQZ* 4.99.

11. *XTS* 34.880. See also Rothschild, "Wu Zhao's Remarkable Aviary," 82.

of bird signs from a different perspective, emphasizing the patent falseness of signs accepted by the female power-holder. The anecdote describes how someone offered a three-legged crow to the throne as an auspicious marvel of nature. A courtier pointed out that one of the legs was fake (*wei* 偽). Wu Zhao responded that it did not matter and instructed them to have the historians record it as an auspicious sign anyway. However, the historian who wrote it down had the last word: "The *Tang History* says, 'In the first year of Tianshou [690], someone presented a three-legged crow to the throne. The Heavenly Empress [Wu Zhao] thought it was an auspicious sign for the Zhou. Ruizong said, "The crow's front leg is fake." The Heavenly Empress was displeased. In a little while, one leg fell off'" (唐書云, 天授元年, 有獻三足烏. 天后以爲周室嘉瑞. 睿宗云, 烏前足僞. 天后不悅. 須臾, 一足墮地).[12] According to the anecdote, somehow, in between the genesis of this episode and its incorporation into the *Tang History*, the anonymous courtier who pointed out the fake leg has turned into Ruizong. This anecdote is fascinating in that it reveals the potential for embellishment in historical narrative, as well as the potential for the ruler's best-laid plans for preservation of her memory to go awry, as the responsibility for recording her legacy is placed in someone else's hands.

Another popular form of indictment, the speech of the "upright official," often touches upon interpretation of the fundamental relationships (between human and natural, male/*yang* and female/*yin*) that order the universe. *Da Tang xinyu*, with its focus on the political realm and character evaluation, is the source for many of the episodes, which are later incorporated into other historical and anecdotal texts. In 675, Gaozong, suffering from ocular problems and possible strokes, proposed to cede the throne to his empress, who was already in charge of much of the day-to-day functioning of the government. Director of the Secretariat Hao Chujun 郝處俊 (607–81), among others, strongly remonstrated against such a course of action.[13] This anecdote appears in multiple

12. *TPGJ* 462.3796. This passage is translated in Rothschild, "Wu Zhao's Remarkable Aviary," 78. As noted by Rothschild, the three-legged crow is an ancient solar symbol. See also Tung, *Fables for the Patriarchs*, 69–70. See Rothschild, *Rhetoric, Ritual, and Support Constituencies*, 117–18, for a possible connection between the three-legged crow and the new characters promulgated by Wu.

13. Hao Chujun started off his career as a presented scholar (*jinshi* 進士) from

sources, of which *Da Tang xinyu* seems to be the earliest.[14] Hao Chujun's impassioned plea relies upon the ancient traditional correlation of male with the outer, *yang* force and female with the inner, *yin* force: "The *Lijing* [Classic of Ritual] says: 'The emperor orders the way of *yang* and the empress orders the moral power of *yin*.' The relationship of emperor to empress is like that of the sun to the moon or *yin* to *yang*; each has its own domain of authority and they cannot appropriate each other's proper functions. If they lose their correct order, Heaven will impose sanctions against you above and disaster will result in the human world below" (禮經云: "天子理陽道, 后理陰德." 然則帝之與后, 猶日之與月, 陰之與陽, 各有所主, 不相奪也. 若失其序, 上則謫見于天, 下則禍成于人).[15] The second half of the anecdote "proves" the truth of Hao Chujun's reasoning. Although in 675 Hao succeeded in temporarily blocking her advance, Wu Zhao did eventually achieve her goal. As she gained power, she exhibited behaviors that further violated her "natural" role as a woman. Together with a Daoist named Guo Xingzhen 郭行真, who "had unlimited access to her inner chambers" (*chu ru gongye* 出入宮掖; literally, "went into and out of her inner chambers," an innuendo of improper sexual relationship), she practiced occult arts and, when exposed, successively executed all those who moved against her, except for Gaozong.[16]

Da Tang xinyu contains a structurally and thematically parallel account directed against Empress Wei. Just a little over a month after Zhongzong's succession, when power should have returned to the "rightful" Li patriline, the situation looked suspiciously similar to that which

Benzhou 本州, whereupon he attracted the notice of high-ranking officials. He gave up service to be a farmer-recluse for a period of time but was recalled to occupy important civil and military posts. For his official biographies, see *JTS* 84.2797–801 and *XTS* 115.4215–18.

14. See *JTS* 84.2799–800, *XTS* 115.4217, and *ZZTJ* 202.6375–76.

15. *DTXY* 2.23–24. In the condensed *Zizhi tongjian* account, Hao Chujun also sets out the traditional identification of male with outer concerns and female with inner affairs: "The emperor orders the outer and the empress orders the inner; this is the natural way sanctioned by Heaven" (天子理外, 后理内, 天之道也); see *ZZTJ* 202.6375–76.

16. *DTXY* 2.24. The first half of this anecdote, comprising Hao Chujun's remonstrance and Gaozong's response, is incorporated into Hao Chujun's official biographies. The second half is not, but this may be more a function of genre than a thematically motivated choice. See *JTS* 84.2799–800 and *XTS* 115.4217.

had prevailed during the period of Wu Zhao's dominance: Wu Zhao's nephew Wu Sansi was back in a high governmental position and Empress Wei had replaced Wu Zhao as the *de facto* female power-holder dominating the male figurehead. Huan Yanfan 桓彥範 (653–706), like Hao Chujun before him, was deeply concerned about what this implied in terms of the dynasty's future: "Your humble servant has taken stock of the generations of rulers and carefully investigated the incidents of past dynasties in which emperors allowed their wives to participate in the plans and affairs of government; in not one case did this [wifely interference in government] not lead to destruction of the state and ruin of the family" (愚臣歷選列辟，詳求往代帝王有與婦人謀及政事者，無不破國亡家).[17] The one precedent not mentioned specifically but looming over the entire discussion is the most recent one of Wu Zhao, Zhongzong's mother. Huan Yanfan then launches into the popularist *yin-yang* philosophy employed by Hao Chujun:

> When *yin* intervenes in *yang*, this violates Heaven; when the female surpasses the male, this violates humanity. To violate Heaven is inauspicious; to violate humanity is not righteous. The *Shu* declares: "The dawn crowing of the mother hen signals the demise of the family." The *Yi* says: "Not far, [her role] is in the kitchen." These passages are saying that women should not be allowed to participate in government . . . [Empress Wei should] exclusively spend her time within the palace, cultivating *yin* [female] teachings, and in this way the propriety of earth [*kun*; also associated with the female, as opposed to *yang*/male/Heaven] will be a model and the dynastic mandate will be renewed.
>
> 以陰干陽, 違天也; 以婦凌夫, 違人也, 違天不祥, 違人不義. 書稱: "牝雞之晨, 唯家之索." 易曰: "無攸遂在中饋." 言婦人不得干政也 . . . 專在中宮, 聿修陰教, 則坤儀式敍, 鼎命維新矣.[18]

The denouement is strikingly similar to that of the *Da Tang xinyu* anecdote about Wu Zhao: "The former monk Huifan and the mountain

17. *DTXY* 2.34. Huan Yanfan held important military and civil posts during the reigns of Wu Zhao, Zhongzong, and Ruizong. He participated in the 705 coup against Wu Zhao that placed Zhongzong on the throne. See his official biographies in *JTS* 91.2927–32 and *XTS* 120.4309–13.

18. *DTXY* 2.34.

men Zheng Pusi, Ye Jingneng, et cetera, all grasped heterodox ways and had unlimited access to the inner palace" (故僧惠範, 山人鄭普思, 葉靜能等, 並挾左道, 出入宮禁).[19] In desperation after their remonstrations were ignored, Huan Yanfan and like-minded men staged a failed rebellion, which led to their executions. The phrasing of "had unlimited access to the inner palace" (*chu ru gongjin* 出入宮禁) is almost identical to that used to describe Wu Zhao's intimate associate, the Daoist Guo Xingzhen (*chu ru gongye* 出入宮掖). In Empress Wei's case, the condemnation is even stronger; the account takes pains to emphasize her promiscuity ("et cetera") with various "mountain men" (*shanren* 山人) a term that here indicates a religious or spiritual inclination.[20] After the surface invocation of popular *yin-yang* philosophy, the later analogue of the "upright" man, that is, the historian or compiler, thus resorts to base attacks of promiscuity to get his point across. An even longer and angrier version of Huan Yanfan's memorial is incorporated into his official biographies, demonstrating the appeal of his convictions to historians several centuries later.[21]

These passages suggest the basic assumptions underlying condemnations of female-led government. This type of rhetoric appears often in narratives about the early Tang period, where it functions to link female rule with various societal problems. Yet, in terms of their general import and clichéd sexist argument, they are not case-specific; they can be, and are, applied to every woman in every historical period interpreted as dangerous and exerting too much public influence. Narratives about the early Tang dynasty are distinguished by their persistent, overriding concern with particular forms of interpretation.

Another anecdote from *Da Tang xinyu* is centered on the time-honored theme of nature's meteorological response to imperial behavior, but it is structured in such a way as to stress the importance of "correct" understanding, that is, the perspective of the male official loyal to the

19. *DTXY* 2.34.

20. The term *shanren* refers to individuals who adopt a "semi-religious lifestyle," without particular sectarian affiliation or full rejection of secular life. See Hobson, *Poems of Hanshan*, 123.

21. See *JTS* 91.2929 and *XTS* 120.4311–12. In this version, Huan Yanfan gives more examples of virtuous versus evil female behavior, mainly culled from the famous Shang and Zhou empresses.

patriarchal ideal. The anecdote begins with some brief historical background: "Zhang Jianzhi had banished Zetian to Shangyang Palace [in the Tang restoration coup of 705], but Zhongzong was still governing the country as crown prince [as opposed to taking the throne as emperor] and making prayers to the Wu clan temple" (張柬之既遷則天于上陽宮, 中宗猶以皇太子監國, 告武氏之廟).[22] That is, although the restoration coup had occurred, Zhongzong still had not assumed the position of emperor and continued to pay ritual homage to the ruling power of his mother. In response, "at that time the sun [kenning for the emperor] was continuously blocked by shade" (時累日陰翳).[23] Censor Cui Hun 崔渾 (fl. 705?) submitted a memorial explaining this situation (which should actually be obvious to a reader familiar with the Chinese literary-historical tradition of resonant weather response to a political situation): Zhongzong's continued reverence of the sovereignty of the Wu temple caused pain to the people and the cosmos, leading to the response of shade blocking the sun, or rightful ruler (Zhongzong). Zhongzong followed Cui Hun's advice and "the shade and clouds lifted in all directions and for ten thousand miles all was perfectly clear. Everyone thought all of this was due to response between the realms of heaven and man" (陰雲四除, 萬里澄廓, 咸以爲天人之應).[24]

In some accounts, the premise of the "response between the realms of heaven and man" is approached from a reverse perspective. If the natural world sympathetically responds to imbalance or injustice at the apex of the human realm, then the ruler's failure to understand the meaning of unusual natural occurrences exposes that ruler's illegitimacy and unfitness for the position she occupies.

During Wu Zhao's reign, snow fell in the third month. "Sycophantic" courtiers such as Su Weidao 蘇味道 (648–705) praised the unseasonal weather as an auspicious sign and submitted a memorial asking for a courtly celebration in its honor. Left Reminder Wang Qiuli[25] halted

22. *DTXY* 2.26. See also *XTS* 120.4324.

23. *DTXY* 2.26.

24. *DTXY* 2.26.

25. Wang Qiuli served as censor under Wu Zhao. He is portrayed as a consummate "upright official" type who submitted many memorials and made many speeches criticizing the immoral actions of his contemporaries. For his official biographies, see *JTS* 101.3154–55 and *XTS* 112.4172–73. The snow incident is redacted in *JTS* 101.3155 and *XTS* 112.4173.

the proceedings and explained the wrong interpretation of signs that underlay the call for celebration: "You, Prime Minister [Su Weidao], are unable to adjust the forces of *yin* and *yang*. When it snows in the third month, this is a disaster, yet you falsely proclaim its auspiciousness! If snow in the third month is auspicious snow, then should thunder during the twelfth month be considered auspicious thunder?" (宰相不能燮理陰陽，令三月降雪，此災也，乃誣為瑞. 若三月雪是瑞雪，臘月雷當是瑞雷耶?).[26] This is a rhetorical question; out-of-season weather, especially thunder, is never auspicious because, according to the theory of cosmic resonance, it always indicates imbalance and abnormality. Consequently, the unseasonal snow is a warning about impropriety or mistakes by the ruler. Wang Qiuli's invocation of *yin* and *yang* forces suggests the nature of this impropriety, that is, the imbalance of female power.

In *Jiu Tang shu*, Wang Qiuli is honored with two biographies, the shorter of which is accorded a placement in the chapter on "Loyal and Righteous Men" (*zhong yi* 忠義). The biographies contain basically analogous versions of the (in)auspicious snow incident, which is situated in the second year of the Jiushi 久視 reign period [701] and used to illustrate his fearless uprightness as a remonstrator.[27] His *Xin Tang shu* biography, however, continues beyond the point where the other accounts cease. Here, Su Weidao does not listen to Wang Qiuli and goes ahead with plans for a celebration of the snowfall. When the celebrants arrive, Wang Qiuli ruins the party with an "acerbic" (*li* 厲) speech: "Now is the season when the *yang* aura should be ascendant, yet *yin* ice is invading through; this is a Heaven-sent disaster. The ruler is uncontrolled and the ministers are wicked and corrupt, the seasons are out of order, the Rong and Di people are throwing the Chinese

26. *DTXY* 9.142. The same basic anecdote is found in Kong Pingzhong's 孔平仲 (1044–1111) *Xu shishuo* 續世說 (Continuation of *Tales of the World*), where the emphasis is mainly on how embarrassed Su Weidao was by this incident. See *XSS* 8.299. *Xu Shishuo*, a collection of anecdotes mainly describing the Sui through Five Dynasties periods, was meant as a continuation of Liu Yiqing's *Shishuo xinyu* (A New Account of Tales of the World), a collection of anecdotes about the Eastern Jin dynasty. For Kong Pingzhong's biography and the compilation of *Xu shishuo*, see "Qianyan," *XSS* 1–2. For a discussion of the *shishuo* tradition, see Qian, *Spirit and Self.*

27. *JTS* 101.3154–55 and 187.4884.

into chaos, bandits are strong, upright officials are few, false officials are many, and the only way to gain entry to officialdom is through bribery. How could a situation like this cause Heaven to send down auspicious signs?" (今陽氣僨升，而陰冰激射，此天災也．主荒臣佞，寒暑失序，戎狄亂華，盜賊繁興，正官少，偽官多，百司非賄不入，使天有瑞，何感而來哉?).[28] Everyone is duly spooked, and Wu Zhao dismisses court.

The correspondences and contrasts established in Wang Qiuli's diatribe are instructive. On the one side, we have *yin*/female, coldness, non-Chinese "barbarian" groups, chaos, lawless banditry, false officials, and bribery; set in distinction to these totally negative forces are things that are *yang*/male, warm, Chinese, orderly, upright, and incorruptible. This conceptual framework also informs, to a greater or lesser extent, the other cases of remonstrance discussed above. In each case, the transgression of female rule is pointed out and condemned by a male official, whose uprightness is defined by his understanding of signs. His ability to interpret cosmological messages is a moral ability, presented as part of his opposition to the female power-holder, whose impropriety is manifest through her failure to perceive the meaning of the sign.

Auspicious weather events, such as auspicious snowfall, were part and parcel of the discourse of naturalness invoked to praise these women during their lifetimes. Later narratives appropriate the rhetoric of naturalness, placing it within a rubric of gender-based (*yin-yang*) criticism designed to denounce the transgression of their rule. This complex of themes informs the narrative alienation of the female ruler from the domain of auspiciousness, as publicly and privately constituted.

28. *XTS* 112.4173. At this time, the Tang was experiencing problems with Qapaghan Qaghan (Ashina Mochuo 阿史那 默啜; d. 716) of Tujue (Eastern Turkic Khaghanate); hence the reference to "the Rong and Di people throwing the Chinese into chaos." For a discussion of this issue, see Skaff, *Sui-Tang China and Its Turko-Mongol Neighbors*, 43–45.

Case Studies in Auspiciousness and Legitimacy

Ritual, Interpretation, and Response

The projection of auspiciousness is closely related to the establishment of legitimacy. In the arena of public declaration of dynastic legitimacy, perhaps no single imperial act was more historically and symbolically resonant, within the Confucian imperial tradition, than the *feng* 封 and *shan* 禪 sacrifices to Heaven and Earth. Wechsler has noted historical changes in the conception of the ritual between the Qin-Han and Tang periods so as to emphasize their public understanding as rites performed for the benefit of both the people and the ruler.[29] The rites' visibility and commanding aura of antiquity made them a powerful tool for imperial display and legitimation, the ruler's public demonstration of his or her cosmic sanction. By the year 666, when Gaozong and Wu Zhao performed the ritual, the *feng* and *shan* had not been performed since the Han. During the joint reign of Wu Zhao and Gaozong, the imperial couple, supposedly at the empress's urging, planned (though ultimately abortively) the sacrifices four times more, in 670, 676, 679, and 683.[30] Wu Zhao finally performed the sacrifice again in 696 when she ruled in her own right as emperor. The frequency of planned *feng* and *shan* sacrifices, especially compared with the previous millennium, reveals the importance of the rituals to Wu Zhao and her investment in their successful completion.

Various scholars have discussed in detail the means by which Wu Zhao earned for herself, and other women of the court, a prominent position as *yaxian* 亞獻, or secondary ceremonial participant, in the 666 *shan* rites carried out on Mount Tai 泰山.[31] Her argument revolved

29. Wechsler, *Offerings of Jade and Silk*, 193.

30. In the first three cases, the ceremonies were cancelled because of problems on the borders with Tibet and Korea; see *ZZTJ* 202.6379 and 202.6391–93. In 683, the ceremonies were cancelled because of Gaozong's ill health. He died before the rescheduled event could take place; see *ZZTJ* 203.6410–11 and 203.6415. See Rothschild, *Rhetoric, Ritual, and Support Constituencies*, 292–309, and Marlowe, *Empress Wu Zhao*, 18–37 and 69–74, for a discussion of the various attempted rites and the 696 ceremony.

31. See Bokenkamp, "A Medieval Feminist Critique," 384–86, Chen Jo-shui, *Tangdai de funü wenhua*, 208–13, Chen Jo-shui, "Empress Wu and Proto-Feminist Sentiments," and Guisso, *Wu Tse-t'ien and the Politics of Legitimation*, 20–21.

around the traditional correlation of the female with the earth, or inner, force, as opposed to the male, heavenly, outer force. She argued for her suitability for the position, as the highest exponent of the human female or inner, central force.[32] As Chen Jo-shui notes, this argument hinged upon a conventional, though probably expedient, view of the role of women.[33] Her argument was accepted, and the *yaxian* of the *shan* ceremony was an exclusively female affair.[34] Even though eunuchs held up curtains to preserve the modesty of the palace women from the collective gaze of the entire male official body, the structure of the ceremony, performed in accordance with Wu Zhao's wishes, indicated the visibility of women, with the empress first and foremost, in the symbolic and ritual foundation of the dynasty.

Historical accounts belittle Wu Zhao's participation in the ceremony by describing how male officials smirked at the spectacle of the female-led ritual.[35] Yet, however discounted the women may have been by later accounts, within this period the ritual and symbolic precedents for legitimate female rule were successfully established by Wu Zhao, with the aid of her trusted allies. These precedents were widely, though not universally, accepted in the years between official return to Tang rule in 705 and Xuanzong's execution of the Taiping Princess and her faction in 713 (that is, the reigns of Zhongzong and Ruizong and the very beginning of Xuanzong's rule).[36]

The success of Wu Zhao's legitimation campaign is perhaps most strongly suggested by the career of her daughter-in-law, Empress Wei. During the reign of Zhongzong, Empress Wei likewise sought to express

32. Bokenkamp, "A Medieval Feminist Critique," 385. See also Chen Jo-shui, *Tangdai de funü wenhua*, 208–11, and "Empress Wu and Proto-Feminist Sentiments," 84–85; and *JTS* 23.886–7.

33. Chen Jo-shui, *Tangdai de funü wenhua*, 210, and "Empress Wu and Proto-Feminist Sentiments," 85.

34. *ZZTJ* 201.6346.

35. See *JTS* 23.888 and *XTS* 14.351. See also Chen Jo-shui, "Empress Wu and Proto-Feminist Sentiments," 85.

36. In 707, Wu family temples, first established in 684 at the suggestion of Wu Zhao's nephew Wu Chengsi, were restored by Zhongzong. His decision to restore the temples was attributed to the successful prayers for rain offered by the empress's son-in-law and nephew Wu Youji and Wu Sansi, but in reality it reflected the continuing power of the Wu family in court politics. See *ZZTJ* 208.6609–10.

her political power symbolically and ritually. In 709, when Zhongzong was preparing for the Southern Suburb sacrifice (*nanjiao* 南郊), another heated debate erupted at court regarding female participation in a historically male-dominated ritual. An analysis of materials surrounding the debate points to the way in which ritual or symbolic measures undertaken by Empress Wei were, later, turned against her to form powerful narratives of condemnation. Chen Jo-shui has noted the striking parallels between this debate and those of the mid-seventh century in terms of the issues at stake and the way in which the debates were later described in historical materials.[37] The debate began when Zhu Qinming 祝欽明 (dates unknown) and Guo Shanyun 郭山惲 (dates unknown), both classical scholars and partisans of Empress Wei, submitted memorials arguing that she should be *yaxian* in the Southern Suburb sacrifice.[38] This would place her in the same prominent ceremonial position in the Southern Suburb sacrifice that Wu Zhao had occupied in the *feng* and *shan* sacrifices of 666. The emperor ultimately followed the arguments of Empress Wei's partisans, although dissenting voices succeeded in blocking the Anle Princess from taking on the role of *zhongxian*.[39]

This episode attests to the continuing culture of female political influence, but the descriptions of the debate in later sources emphasize intrigue and deception. Not surprisingly, Zhu Qinming is portrayed as an unprincipled sycophant, shamelessly "cater[ing] to the Commoner's [Empress Wei's] wishes" (希庶人旨).[40] As described in Zhu Qinming's standard biographies, "In the third year of the Jinglong reign period [709], the emperor was preparing to perform the suburban sacrifice. Qinming and Director of Studies in the Directorate of Education Guo Shanyun secretly did Empress Wei's bidding and stated a phony argument" (景龍三年, 天子將郊, 欽明與國子司業郭山惲陰迎韋后意, 謬立議).[41]

37. Chen Jo-shui, "Empress Wu and Proto-Feminist Sentiments," 94–99.

38. Documents relating to the entire conflict and arguments of each faction are collected together in Wang Pu's tenth-century work *Tang hui yao*, 9a.151–61.

39. *JTS* 51.2173. The *bian* and *dou* ceremonial vessels were held by an aristocratic woman, the daughter of a prime minister.

40. *JTS* 88.2878.

41. *JTS* 109.4104; *XTS* 109.4104. A mid-eighteenth-century comprehensive work on ritual, *Wu li tong kao* 五禮通考 by Qin Huitian 秦蕙田 (1702–64), quotes this passage from the earlier histories. Qin's own opinion is clear; he stresses the abnormality of empress participation in the Southern Suburb rite and reiterates the assessment that

The unquestioned assumption is that Zhu was led by opportunism and not by his understanding of ritual precedent or support of Empress Wei's right as *de facto* co-ruler to participate in the visible and important ritual life of the court.[42]

Unlike the *feng* and *shan*, the Southern Suburb sacrifice had no traditional or previously established correlation with Earth to make it arguably "suitable" for the joint sacrifice by emperor and empress.[43] Zhongzong and Empress Wei were thus following the ritual precedent set by his mother; during his reign the Southern Suburb rite continued to be a sacrifice to both Heaven and Earth, making the same female-earth argument applicable. In arguing for the empress's right to participate in the sacrifice as the *yaxian*, Zhu Qinming refers to passages from the ritual classics that describe the emperor and empress performing ritual sacrifices together.[44] Although, as Chen Jo-shui notes, neither Zhu Qinming nor Guo Shanyun mention the recent and seemingly more relevant precedent of Wu Zhao's innovative alteration of the rite to conform to her identity as a female emperor, this does not necessarily invalidate their interpretation of the rite and the empress's appropriate role therein as purely sycophantic opportunism.[45] Perhaps the recent proximity of the Zhou performance of the Southern Suburb rite made direct mention of it unnecessary, or perhaps Empress Wei's obvious political clout was deemed adequate to substantiate her right to participate in the sacrifice.

The Southern Suburb debate, though particularly controversial, represented merely one instance of Empress Wei's visible and frequent participation in court ceremony. The previous year, in 708, two of her

---

Empress Wei's supporters were "corrupt Confucians" (*fu Ru* 腐儒). See Qin Huitian, *Wu li tong kao*, 9.19–29.

42. As Chen Jo-shui points out, the extent to which Empress Wei was actually pulling the strings behind the requests of supporters such as Zhu Qinming and Guo Shanyun is unclear. Chen Jo-shui, *Tangdai de funü wenhua*, 229, and "Empress Wu and Proto-Feminist Sentiments," 96–97.

43. Because of the difference between the two rites, Chen negatively contrasts Empress Wei's public attempt at symbolic ascendancy with that of Wu Zhao almost half a century earlier. Chen Jo-shui, *Tangdai de funü wenhua*, 230, and "Empress Wu and Proto-Feminist Sentiments," 97.

44. See *JTS* 189b.4965–67; *XTS* 109.4104–5; and Wang Pu, *Tang hui yao* 9a.153–55. See also *QTW* 237.15a–16b (2398–99).

45. Chen Jo-shui, *Tangdai de funü wenhua*, 230.

supporters, Jiaye Zhizhong 迦葉志忠 (fl. 705–10?) and Zhao Yanxi 趙延禧 (fl. 705–10?), submitted memorials requesting that she perform the Original Silkworm (*xiancan* 先蠶) ritual, traditionally performed by empresses.[46] The memorials submitted by Empress Wei's supporters provide a valuable window into prevailing symbolic complexes, both eighth-century and later. The memorials clarify the self-conscious continuity between the rule of Wu Zhao and the restoration government of Zhongzong, but their interest goes far beyond this: the images and themes used in praise by Jiaye Zhizhong and Zhao Yanxi are source texts for specific and widespread narrative forms of retrospective condemnation, in which the "cosmic signs" celebrated by Empress Wei's courtiers become "shameless forgeries."

Jiaye Zhizhong urged Empress Wei to perform the sacrifice to accord with the people's wishes. He placed her in a line of illustrious rulers, beginning with the mythic Yao and then skipping forward to Taizong, Gaozong, Wu Zhao, and the current imperial couple:

> In the past when the Divine Emperor Yao had not yet received the mandate [and become emperor], the world sang "Peaches and Plums"; when the Civil and Martial Emperor [Taizong] had not yet received the mandate, the world sang "The King of Qin Destroys the Ranks"; when the Great Heavenly Emperor [Gaozong] had not yet received the mandate, the world sang "Tang Tang"; when Empress Zetian [Wu Zhao] had not yet received the mandate, the world sang "Wumei niang [Beautiful Charmer]"; when Responding to Heaven Emperor [Zhongzong] had not yet received the mandate, the world sang "Prince Ying at Shizhou"; when Following Heaven Empress [Empress Wei] had not yet received the mandate, the world sang "Mulberry Branches Wei."
>
> 昔神堯皇帝未受命, 天下歌桃李子, 文武皇帝未受命, 天下歌秦王破陣樂, 天皇大帝未受命, 天下歌堂堂, 則天皇后未受命, 天下歌娬媚娘, 應天皇帝未受命, 天下歌英王石州, 順天皇后未受命, 天下歌桑條韋.[47]

46. Wu Zhao first performed the Original Silkworm sacrifice in 656, soon after her installment as Gaozong's empress. She performed the rite three more times during her tenure as empress, in 669, 674, and 675. See Chen Jo-shui, "Empress Wu and Proto-Feminist Sentiments," 79–80, 93; and *Tangdai de funü wenhua*, 222–23.

47. *ZZTJ* 209.6619–20. See *JTS* 51.2173, *XTS* 76.3486, and *QTW* 276.9b–10a (2805–6) for alternate versions of the memorial.

According to classical formulations of kingship, the musical response of the people is a spontaneous identifier of the moral quality of rule. Wu Zhao's rule elicited a song playing upon her surname (武/娬) and her gender ("Beautiful Charmer").[48] Empress Wei's song likewise references her surname and femininity. Mulberry picking and silkworm cultivation were female work, though not work in which Empress Wei, an upper-class woman, would have engaged; Jiaye Zhizhong's memorial urges her, as "mother of the nation" (*guomu* 國母), to fulfill the role of spiritual overseer of mulberry and silkworm cultivation by performing a sacrifice to the "original silkworm."[49]

The theme of the mysterious predictive song or poem, which appears in Jiaye Zhizhong's memorial as a joyful harbinger of sagely rule, is ubiquitous in the classical tradition, starting with the ancient *Shijing* 詩經 (Classic of Poetry).[50] The expressive utterances of "the people," as a mouthpiece for the historian, hold the power to sanction or condemn. The first chapter of *Chaoye qianzai* contains a series of anecdotes about predictive songs that approach these women from a decidedly different interpretive slant than did Jiaye Zhizhong. Far from anticipating positive change, the songs in these anecdotes all predict negative developments.[51] Empress Wei's "Mulberry Branches Song" appears in this context as a harbinger of her destructive presence: "After the Yonghui reign period [650–55], people sang the 'Mulberry Branches Song,' which went: 'Mulberry branch sprouts, the music of Miss Wei.' When it got to the Shenlong years [705–7], the Rebellious Wei responded to this" (永徽年以後, 人唱 '桑條歌'云: "桑條 [艹吊], 女韋也樂." 至神龍年中, 逆韋應之).[52] Half a century after the people were mysteriously moved

48. Sawada Mizuho suggests that *mei* 媚 carries the negative connotation of "beguile" as in "lead astray" (*furen mei dao* 婦人媚道), where *mei* is linked phonetically and in terms of import to *mei* 魅, "demon." However, given the context of this memorial, this seems unlikely. See Sawada, *Zetian Wu hou*, 48–49.

49. *ZZTJ* 209.6620.

50. For a discussion of the predictive song or rhyme in the Jin through Sui periods, see Lu Zongli, *The Power of the Words*, chaps. 4 and 5.

51. Many of the anecdotes describing prophetic songs or rhymes involve verses that foreshadow external attack or internal rebellion; see *CYQZ* 1.8–1.11.

52. *CYQZ* 1.8. Zhao Shouyan, the editor of the Zhonghua shuju 1979 edition of *Chaoye qianzai*, notes that *Jiu Tang shu* has the exact same passage with "Wei" 韋 in place of the unusual character "sprouts" [艹吊]. *Jiu Tang shu* also inserts a *ye* 也 (particle)

to sing this song, it finds its "response" in Empress Wei's rise to power. The correct understanding of how to interpret the response must wait for Empress Wei's failed bid for power and subsequent demonization.

According to the rhetorical image-building tradition, the musical outcries of "the people," if correctly interpreted, foretell the entire story of the Zhou through Jinglong women. Just as a seventh-century popular song foretold her rise, a rhyme popular during the Jinglong reign period supposedly predicted Empress Wei's death at the hands of the coalition led by the Taiping Princess and the future Xuanzong. The Jinglong rhyme is: "The yellow cypress calf pulls its tether till it snaps; its two hooves stamp the ground until its horseshoes snap" (黃栢犢子挽紖斷, 兩腳踏地鞋 [麻需] 斷). The interpretation is as follows: "In the sixth month, the Prince of Ping [Li Longji] executed the Rebellious Wei, who had been plotting insurrection. 'Hooves snap' is referring to the affair [the rebellion] not reaching fruition. Wei was the descendant of the 'yellow calf'" (六月, 平王誅逆韋, 欲作亂. 鞋 [麻需] 斷 者, 事不成. 阿韋是 "黃犢" 之後也).[53] The "yellow calf" refers to another legend, also recorded in *Chaoye qianzai*, defaming Empress Wei's ancestry.[54] Another popular rhyme is said to have presaged the ignominious end of the next generation in the Wei line, the Anle Princess: "It's a pity about Anle Temple, hanging from a stump" (可憐安樂寺, 了了樹頭懸).[55] Soon after, when the princess

after the first "Wei" and a *shi* 時 ("time") before the "Wei" in the second half of the song (桑條韋也, 女時韋也樂). See *CYQZ* 1.23, note 19, and *JTS* 37.1376. See also *CFYG* 894.26b (10588); and *TSJS* 11.364 (both of which have "Mulberry branches Wei, / Miss Wei" 桑條韋也女韋也). *Taiping guangji* incorporates the *Chaoye qianzai* passage; see *TPGJ* 163.1177.

53. *CYQZ* 1.10. See also *TPGJ* 163.1180.

54. *CYQZ* 3.59. According to this anecdote, she was not properly a member of the Wei clan, but rather was the descendant of a slave whose master rewarded him with the family surname of Wei in return for his offering of a yellow calf. The ancestor, originally called Tao Fu 桃符, came to be known as "Yellow Calf Wei" (Huang duzi Wei 黃犢子韋).

55. *CYQZ* 1.10. See also *TPGJ* 163.1179. *Liaoliao* 了了 usually means "bright" or "distinct," but I suspect that in this case it is a substitution for *liaotiao* or *letiao* 了佻, "appearance of hanging." Based on a version of the early dialect dictionary *Fangyan* 方言 (Regional Speech), Xuanying 玄應 (901–75), in his *Yiqie jing yin yi* 一切經音義, elucidates a compound in which an upside-down *liao* is seen in place of the *tiao* found in the compound as preserved in our present version of *Fangyan*. See Xuanying, *Yiqie jing yin yi*, 13.413. The potential for miscopying is clear here, and the meaning of *letiao* makes more sense in the context of the rhyme.

and her mother were executed, their heads were chopped off and hung from bamboo poles. *Shutou* 樹頭, meaning "stump" as a compound, can be divided into *shu*, "tree," and *tou*, "head," to make the prediction; what is "hanging" in the rhyme was actually not the temple, but its unfortunate benefactress's head.

The Precious Diagram and Other Auspicious Stones

Jiaye Zhizhong's memorial thus references sign types that became important in retrospective defamatory constructions of female leaders.[56] Zhao Yanxi's contemporary memorial in support of Empress Wei also raises the issue of sign interpretation in such a way as to evoke fundamental tropes in retrospective condemnations of the Tang female leaders. Zhao Yanxi explicitly conflates the Tang, Wu Zhao's reign (Zhou), and the ancient historical ideal of the Zhou dynasty through allusion to the Precious Diagram (or Luo River Diagram). A condensed version of the memorial is provided in *Zizhi tongjian*:

> Zhou and Tang are a single system, tallying mandates returning together [to the same principle/source]. Therefore, Gaozong enfeoffed Your Majesty [Zhongzong] as Prince of Zhou. During Zetian's time, Tang Tongtai presented to the throne the Luo River Diagram. Confucius said: "That which carries on and inherits the Zhou, even after one hundred generations can still be known." Your Majesty carries on and inherits as Zetian's descendant and for one hundred generations will rule the world.
>
> 周唐一統, 符命同歸, 故高宗封陛下為周王. 則天時唐同泰奏獻洛水圖, 孔子曰, "其或繼周者, 雖百代可知也." 陛下繼則天子孫, 當百代王天下.[57]

As discussed in the previous chapter, the Luo River Diagram was one of the most prominent auspicious signs leading up to Wu Zhao's estab-

56. For another interesting example of this type of narrative, see the tale of He Yuanyou 和元祐, whose vulgar verse is credited with somehow predicting Empress Wei's rebellion and demise. It can be found in sources including *TPYL* 248.9a–b, *CFYG* 549.12b (6594), *TYL* 5.131, and *Jiu Tang shu yiwen* 2.12b–13a.

57. *ZZTJ* 209.6620. A longer version in *Xin Tang shu* lists eight signs of the continuity between Zhou and Tang. See *XTS* 109.4103.

lishment of the Zhou. Auspicious mystical river diagrams are culturally resonant, recognized as powerful signs indicating the cosmic sanction of sagely rule. Like the seventh-century materials discussed in chapter 2, Zhao Yanxi's memorial places the diagram in line with auspiciousness and celebration; the Luo River Diagram is mentioned in connection with Zhongzong's princely enfeoffment and Confucius' praise of the ancient Zhou dynasty.

In retrospective accounts, however, the Luo River Diagram is decidedly inauspicious and, in fact, is an emblematic marker of illegitimacy; it is one of several rocks-as-fabricated signs of auspiciousness that are referenced in many sources dealing with the period.[58] Beginning in the early to mid-eighth century, two main condemnatory traditions surrounding the diagram emerge, one involving its discovery and presentation to the throne and another dealing with its denunciation by a righteous official (defined as righteous because he opposed the diagram and thus Wu Zhao's power). Both narrative threads associate the diagram with gendered manifestations of moral disorder.

According to the early *Chaoye qianzai* account, Tang Tongtai presented to the throne several auspicious prophetic rocks. First he obtained from the Luo River and presented to the throne a white stone with purple writing proclaiming, "The Sage Mother looks down upon the water, forever glorifying the imperial seat" (聖母臨水, 永昌帝業).[59] Wu Zhao, whom we know from another *Chaoye qianzai* anecdote was "fond of auspicious signs" (*hao zhen xiang* 好禎祥)[60] and was especially receptive of those that supported her rule, rewarded Tang Tongtai with a promotion in rank and established a Yongchang 永昌 (Forever Glorifying) District.[61] *Chaoye qianzai* soon relieves us of any doubts as to the genuineness of the Luo River rock: according to the text, the stone submitted by Tang Tongtai was actually just a regular white stone carved with characters that were colored with a purple stone powder mixture. Remarkably, the same trick worked again; we are told of the later "discovery," in a valley in Wen

58. See, for example, *CYQZ* 3.72; *FSWJJ* 4.26; *DTXY* 2.30; *JTS* 6.119, 24.925; *XTS* 76.3480; *ZZTJ* 204.6449; and *TYL* 3.68.

59. *CYQZ* 3.72. Other sources have *ren* 人, "people," instead of *shui* 水, "water"; see below.

60. *CYQZ* 3.72.

61. Shortly thereafter, the reign name was also changed from Chuigong to Yongchang.

River (Wenshui 文水) District, of a stone bearing the words "Rise of Wu" (*Wu xing* 武興).[62] The name of the district was changed to "Rise of Wu," and after these successes, he "often created them [the fake rocks]. Later it became known that they were forgeries and they were no longer accepted, so he stopped" (自是往往作之. 後知其偽, 不復採用, 乃止).[63]

Another early source compiled several decades after *Chaoye qianzai*, titled *Fengshi wenjian ji* (Record of What Mr. Feng Heard and Saw) by Feng Yan, explicitly connects Wu Zhao's response to the Luo River Diagram, or Precious Diagram, with her identity as a female ruler. After the discovery of the Precious Diagram, "all of the officials proposed a reverential title, asking to call [the empress] 'Sage Mother Divine Monarch'" (群臣上尊號, 請稱 "聖母神皇").[64] Afterwards, she added further, even more elaborate, titles such as "Compassionate One [Maitreya], the Peerless, Heaven Appointed Golden Wheel-Turning Sage and Holy Emperor" (Cishi yuegu tiance jinlun shengshen 慈氏越古天冊金輪聖神).[65] By way of explanation of Wu's penchant for titular display, Feng Yan points to her gender: "Zetian ruled court as a female monarch and carelessly acceded to the requests of her underlings at the time, accepting titles of respect and reverence. Thereafter the precedent was set" (則天以女主臨朝, 苟順臣子一時之請, 受尊崇之號, 自後因爲故事).[66] On the one hand, this explanation can be interpreted as recognizing the difficulties that Wu Zhao faced as a woman ruler. On the other hand, Feng Yan's account stains the female-controlled court with an aura of lawlessness. The narrative suggests that desperation led Wu Zhao to "carelessly accede" (*gou shun* 苟順) to the presumably outlandish and

62. Wenshui was also the place of Wu Zhao's family origins.

63. *CYQZ* 3.72. See also *TPGJ* 238.1831.

64. *FSWJJ* 4.26.

65. According to *Jiu Tang shu* and *Xin Tang shu*, Wu Zhao first adopted the title Cishi yuegu jinlun shengshen in spring, during the first month in 695, then simplified it to Cishi yuegu the next month. In the ninth month, she adopted the title Tiance jinlun shengshen huangdi (Heaven Appointed Golden Wheel-Turning Sage and Holy Emperor). See *JTS* 6.124 and *XTS* 4.95. Various scholars have discussed the significance of this title in terms of Maitreyist ideology. See, for instance, Forte, *Political Propaganda and Ideology*, chap. 3; Guisso, *Wu Tse-t'ien and the Politics of Legitimation*, chap. 4; and Marlowe, *Empress Wu Zhao*, 55–56. The translation of the title is adopted, with slight modification, from Guisso, *Wu Tse-t'ien and the Politics of Legitimation*, 45.

66. *FSWJJ* 4.26.

unprecedented requests of her courtiers, thereby establishing a pattern of excess that was never successfully rooted out in later ages. Whereas Wu Zhao intended the titles to proclaim her legitimacy as ruler, Feng Yan's explanation undercuts any sense of imperial legitimacy by interpreting them as the expedient measures of a female-led court, in which patently false signs elicit an exaggerated celebratory response.

In the standard historical sources, material is added to flesh out this anecdote about the Precious Diagram. *Jiu Tang shu* identifies Wu Zhao's nephew Wu Chengsi, later one of the era's most disparaged figures, as the true source behind the forged auspicious rock. The *Jiu Tang shu* basic annals of Wu Zhao's reign inform us that in the fourth month of summer, in the fourth year of the Chuigong 垂拱 reign period (688), "the Prince of Wei Wu Chengsi falsely created an auspicious rock, with an inscription that read, 'The Sage Mother presides over the people, forever glorifying the imperial seat.' He commanded Tang Tongtai of Yongzhou to submit a memorial claiming that he had gotten it from the Luo River. The Empress Dowager was thrilled and named the stone the 'Precious Diagram'" (魏王武承嗣偽造瑞石, 文云: "聖母臨人, 永昌帝業." 令雍州人唐同泰表稱獲之洛水. 皇太后大悅, 號其石為 "寶圖").[67]

Jiu Tang shu's "Liyi zhi" 禮儀志 (Treatise on Ritual) seems to follow the *Chaoye qianzai* account in placing sole blame for the forgery of the "Precious Diagram" on Tang Tongtai.[68] It is unclear when Wu Chengsi became associated with the episode, but internal contradictions in *Jiu Tang shu* point to the circulation of multiple accounts during the period of this history's compilation, or to the Wu Chengsi account as a later insertion.[69] At some point, someone seems to have decided that the devious river diagram scheme was the kind of thing a dishonest type like Wu Chengsi would do and inserted him accordingly into this narrative. *Xin Tang shu* and *Zizhi tongjian* incorporate the inflammatory version involving Wu Chengsi as the mastermind of the Precious Diagram.

67. *JTS* 6.119.

68. *JTS* 24.925.

69. Although *Fengshi wenjian ji* was compiled about two centuries before *Jiu Tang shu*, *Jiu Tang shu* used some sources that were earlier than Feng Yan's time. Therefore, it is difficult to determine when Wu Chengsi became associated with the forgery of the Precious Diagram. See Twitchett, *The Writing of Official History*, part 3, for the compilation of *Jiu Tang shu*.

Jiu Tang shu and *Xin Tang shu* each record a detailed laundry list of the public acts undertaken by Wu Zhao as a result of the discoveries of the Precious Diagram and another counterfeit stone presented by someone from the Si 汜 River vicinity: she made a suburban sacrifice to Shangdi 上帝 (Lord on High/Supreme Deity) to express thanks and praise; held a great gathering of regional military commanders and governors at the capital to give obeisance to the Luo; proclaimed a general amnesty; gave herself the new title of Shengmu huanghou 聖母神皇 (Sage Mother Heavenly Emperor) and had made "Heavenly Emperor" imperial seals; renamed the Luo River the Yongchang 永昌 (Forever Glorifying) River and the Si River the Guangwu 廣武 (Spreading Wu) River; changed the name of the "Precious Diagram" to Tianshou sheng tu 天授聖圖 (the Sage Diagram Conferred by Heaven); and engraved stone for an altar by the Si River that read "Memorial of the Sage Diagram Conferred by Heaven."[70] In *Xin Tang shu*, the description of Wu Zhao's response to the "Precious Diagram" and the Si River stone is placed in her biography and is flanked by descriptions of actions that have been strongly condemned by the historical tradition as landmark examples of her illegitimacy, her cruelty, and her identity as a usurper. Directly before describing Wu Chengsi's creation of the "Precious Diagram," the account relates the establishment of a Chongxian Temple 崇先廟 in Chang'an "to offer sacrifice to the Wu clan" (亨武氏), a clear marker of the impending transfer from Tang to Zhou. Directly after and mixed in with descriptions of the empress's various lavish and visible ceremonial celebrations of the auspicious rocks are accounts of the abortive rebellion against her by Tang princes and its brutal denouement. The unsuccessful rebellion aimed to restore power to Zhongzong and the Li-Tang house, and Wu's swift and ruthless response decimated or exiled large branches

70. *JTS* 24.925 and *XTS* 76.3480. *Jiu Tang shu* further elaborates Wu's response to the "Precious Diagram," describing enfeoffment of the spirit of the Luo River as "Marquis Manifest Divinity" (Xianshen hou 顯神侯), prohibitions on fishing in the river from which the diagram was "conferred by Heaven," the renaming of Song Mountain, in the vicinity of the Luo River, "Divine Peak" (Shen yue 神嶽), and elaborate celebratory ceremonies held by the court. See Rothschild, *Rhetoric, Ritual, and Support Constituencies*, 183–91 and 139–40, for respective discussions of the title "Sage mother" (Shengmu) and of the name Guangwu in the context of Wu's symbolic investment and propagation of her surname.

of the Li imperial family.[71] The narrative placement of the "Precious Diagram" account thus accentuates its patent falseness as manufactured auspiciousness, as well as Wu's cruelty in blithely celebrating the symbol while indiscriminately butchering the Li house.

In addition to variations on this narrative about the diagram's discovery and celebration, multiple sources, starting with *Chaoye qianzai* and *Da Tang xinyu*, record interrelated traditions about the official Li Zhaode's 李昭德 (d. 697) condemnation of several auspicious missives. Li Zhaode held a series of high-ranking posts in the central government under Wu Zhao. He has been uniformly praised for his successful opposition of Wu Chengsi and Wu Sansi's bid to supplant Li Xian as Crown Prince. Li Zhaode was later executed by the empress, who believed "slanderous" memorials accusing him of monopolizing power and plotting rebellion.[72] In the artificially delineated historiographical divide between upright officials who attempted to check the female power-holder's lawlessness and the sycophantic, immoral lackeys who encouraged it, Li Zhaode is placed on the morally correct side.

The *Da Tang xinyu* anecdote describes how Li Zhaode publicly mocked a stone that sounds very similar to the Luo River "Precious Diagram": the stone was discovered in the Luo River and was white with red writing, and the person who discovered it wished to present it to the throne because it had a "red heart" (*chixin* 赤心), a sign of its loyalty.[73] Upon witnessing these proceedings, Li Zhaode retorted, "[Then] are [all the other] stones in the Luo River rebelling?" (洛水中石豈盡反耶?).[74] In *Chaoye qianzai*, Li Zhaode once again debunks a suspicious auspicious sign. A certain Hu Yanqing 胡延慶 from Xiangzhou 襄州[75] discovered

71. The rebellion suffered from disorganization and a total lack of response among the populace and thus was quickly put down. *XTS* 76.3480.

72. See Li Zhaode's biographies in *JTS* 87.2853–57 and *XTS* 117.4255–57.

73. *DTXY* 2.30. *Tang yu lin* incorporates the same passage; see *TYL* 3.68. *Xu Shishuo* provides an analogous passage containing only the story of Li Zhaode's mockery of the red-hearted white stone; *XSS* 8.300.

74. *DTXY* 2.30. *Jiu Tang shu* elaborates and clarifies Li Zhaode's retort: "If 'this stone has a red heart,' how could all the other stones in the Luo River be rebelling?" (此石赤心, 洛水中餘石豈能盡反耶?). *JTS* 87.2855. Basically the same account can be found in *XTS* 117.4256. See Rothschild, *Rhetoric, Ritual, and Support Constituencies*, 341–42, for a brief discussion of this anecdote in the context of Wu's symbolic state-building measures.

75. Hu Yanqing does not seem to appear in either of the Tang histories.

and presented to the throne a tortoise upon whose belly appeared, in red lacquer, the message, "Ten thousand upon ten thousand years for the Son of Heaven" (天子萬萬年). In this anecdote, Li Zhaode does not stop at verbally abusing the auspicious gift, but rather slices it to pieces with a knife and asks to punish Hu Yanqing. Wu Zhao, however, refuses, saying, "It was not done with a malicious heart; just release him and don't inquire further" (此非惡心也, 捨而勿問).[76]

The accounts surrounding the Luo River Diagram and other auspicious stones presented to and, for the most part, accepted by Wu Zhao directly echo an episode recorded in Wen Daya's 溫大雅 (ca. 572–629) *Da Tang chuangye qi ju zhu* 大唐創業起居注 (Court Diaries of the Foundation of the Great Tang), a work compiled prior to 627 that records the various auspicious portents leading up to Gaozu's founding of the dynasty.[77] According to *Da Tang chuangye qi ju zhu*, in the eighth month of 617 an azure stone shaped like a tortoise was found in Taiyuan, the site where Gaozu had been deputed by the Sui to quell unrest. Wen Daya, a propagandist for the Li-Tang cause, records the event in an accepting manner very different from the dismissive and reproving tone with which the auspicious stones of Wu Zhao have been described: "In Taiyuan [they/someone] obtained an azure stone in the form of a tortoise. It had scarlet writing of four characters, saying 'Li will rule for ten thousand generations'" (太原獲青石龜形, 文有丹書四字, 曰: 李治萬世).[78] According to Wen Daya, the skeptical Gaozu initially did not believe in the tortoise's authenticity and ordered his subordinates to scrub off the red inscription. However, even an entire night of scrubbing the tortoise had no effect, and Gaozu was forced to take on the role of the "reluctant ruler" and accept the Mandate of Heaven.[79] Supposedly, Gaozu prevented his ministers from promulgating reports of the auspicious stone, but, as Wechsler notes, the widespread dissemination of the discovery was surely in accord with Gaozu's plan.[80]

76. *CYQZ* 3.72. See also *TPGJ* 238.1831.

77. See Wechsler, *Offerings of Jade and Silk*, 60–62, 283. For more on Wen Daya, see Woodbridge, "Wen Ta-Ya."

78. Wen Daya, *Da Tang chuangye qi ju zhu*, 2.22.

79. Wen Daya, *Da Tang chuangye qi ju zhu*, 2.22. See also Wechsler, *Offerings of Jade and Silk*, 65.

80. Wechsler, *Offerings of Jade and Silk*, 65.

The similarities between the auspicious stones offered to Wu Zhao and the tortoise found in Taiyuan during the months leading up to Gaozu's overthrow of the Sui are clear: in both cases, we have auspicious stones or gems inscribed with red writing predicting the greatness of the founding ruler in question. Clearly, Gaozu and his followers manipulated the domain of auspiciousness just as much as did Wu Zhao in their respective campaigns for legitimacy in the founding of their regimes. The difference lies in later interpretations of these signs, which are completely dependent upon the identity of the ruler manipulating them. In the discourse surrounding the signs, Gaozu's austere skepticism and reluctance to assume high position contrasts sharply with Wu Zhao's shameless acceptance of even the most doubtful auspicious markers. There is perhaps a gendered or sexual undertone here contrasting Gaozu's chasteness and fastidiousness about signs with Wu Zhao's promiscuity and acceptance of any questionable sign that comes her way. The ideology of signs follows a circular logic in which the identity of the interpreter determines the validity of the interpretation and the validity of the sign.

A clear differentiation is thereby made between the "false," self-serving signs accepted by the female ruler and the "genuine" signs revealing her illegitimacy and predicting her downfall. Indeed, in retrospective condemnations, predictions that foretell the fall of female rule are treated reverently as divine missive. In sharp contrast to the unanimous condemnation of "false" signs such as the Precious Diagram is the reception given to a story about another prediction made, according to *Chaoye qianzai*, by the Northern Wei Heavenly Master (Tianshi 天師) Kou Qianzhi 寇謙之 (365–448). In the mid-670s, the local people of Luozhou discovered his carved-stone writings while gathering medicinal herbs on a mountain. Eventually the writings moved up the bureaucratic chain to Gaozong, who deposited them in an inner storehouse. Kou Qianzhi's stone writings were copious and, at the time, indecipherable. In the course of time, however, they were found to have predicted the tumultuous events of the ensuing years, including Wu Zhao's rise to power and Zhongzong's restoration. As an example of the way in which these predictions are interpreted, the cryptic inscription *zhi ge long* 止戈龍 (literally, "stop-spear-dragon") is said to refer to Wu Zhao's rise to the throne because the characters *zhi* 止 and *ge* 戈 combine together graphically to form the character Wu 武.[81] Because other inscriptions were thought to predict the rise of Zhongzong,[82] Kou Qianzhi's stone record was re-presented to the throne upon his ascendance by the son of the district official, Fan Wen 樊文 (fl. 670s?), who had originally presented it to Gaozong. Zhongzong commanded that it be included in the National History records.[83]

Importantly, Fan Wen appears in *Jiu Tang shu* and *Xin Tang shu* in connection with another "auspicious rock" (*rui shi* 瑞石), which is described in the biography of Feng Yuanchang 馮元常 (fl. 670s–before 691), a Li Zhaode "type" official praised for remonstrance against false signs approved by Wu Zhao. Fan Wen presented the auspicious rock to Wu Zhao after she had taken power, in 684, during a time when "many auspicious signs were presented" (多獻符瑞).[84] She wanted to display it to all of her officials, but the occasion was ruined by Feng Yuanchang's protest that the stone was a forgery. The angry empress demoted Feng Yuanchang. Fan Wen is clearly associated with auspicious signs surrounding the imperial house, regardless of whose rule they are said to be supporting. In the case of the auspicious stone, the biographies come out in support of Feng Yuanchang's dismissal of their worth, whereas the stone records of Kou Qianzhi are approached with acceptance and awe ("aren't [these predictions] truthful?" 得不信乎?).[85]

As elucidated by Antonino Forte, the narrative of Kou Qianzhi's predictions is closely associated with another infamous instance of forged prophecy, the new commentary to the *Dayun jing* 大雲經 (Great Cloud Sutra) commissioned by Wu Zhao in the process of legitimizing her rule.[86] Forte dates the original discovery of Kou Qianzhi's writings to 674, as part of the propaganda surrounding the adoption by Gaozong and Wu Zhao of the matching titles of Heavenly Emperor and Heavenly

81. *CYQZ* 5.118.

82. "Li for generation after generation, not moving the ruling house" (李代代, 不移宗者); *CYQZ* 5.118.

83. *CYQZ* 5.118.

84. *JTS* 185a.4800. See also *XTS* 112.4178 and *ZZTJ* 203.6421.

85. *CYQZ* 5.118.

86. Forte, *Political Propaganda and Ideology in China*, 329–32. The prophecy regarding Wu's surname (*zhi* 止 and *ge* 戈 combining to form Wu 武) is directly referenced in the commentary. Forte also discusses variant appearances of the passage in *Taiping guangji*. See also Guisso, *Wu Tse-t'ien and the Politics of Legitimation*, 42.

Empress (Tianhuang 天皇 and Tianhou 天后).[87] Forte suggests that Kou's writings were utilized multiple times as a legitimizing or delegitimizing device: first by Gaozong and Wu Zhao in 674; then by Wu Zhao as she prepared the groundwork for her solo rule; and, finally, retrospectively as a prediction of the Tang restoration (under Zhongzong and then Ruizong) and Xuanzong's reign.[88]

The predictions of Kou Qianzhi are "corroborated" because they are interpreted so as to correspond to events that were planned or that actually occurred; they could just as easily have been censured by an opposing faction as forgeries. An entry in *Chaoye qianzai* brings together these motifs surrounding prediction and the manipulation of fate and/or history. According to this passage, when Taizong was on the throne, a secret or mysterious record predicted that three generations after his reign, a female surnamed Wu would rule. Taizong consulted with an expert official, who determined that the woman in question had already been born and, within thirty years, would almost eradicate the Tang royal house. However, she would ultimately not succeed in destroying the Tang and, if executed now, would only be reborn and follow the same destructive course as a younger, more virile and dangerous woman; it would be best not to disobey the will of Heaven and to let events run their course.[89] The source of this anecdote, and others discussed above, is unclear, leading one to wonder whether, in cases like these, the "earlier predictions" are actually contemporary propaganda. Indeed, a *Kai Tian chuanxin ji* anecdote even gives credence to Wu Zhao's own power of prediction when she foretells the greatness of her grandson Li Longji, who at the time must have been a child or teenager, based upon his brave anti-Wu tirade in court.[90] His tirade was specifically directed against the Taiping Princess's second husband, Wu Youji.[91] In this passage, Wu herself is made into the mouthpiece for the correspondence between a

87. Forte, *Political Propaganda and Ideology in China*, 331.

88. Forte, *Political Propaganda and Ideology in China*, 331–32. See also Marlowe, *Empress Wu Zhao*, 50–51.

89. *CYQZ buyi*.179; see *TPGJ* 163.1180–81 and *XSS* 12.423–24 for analogous accounts. See *CYQZ buyi*.179 for overlap with Hu Qu's 胡璩 (fl. 9th c.) *Tan bin lu* 談賓錄 (Record of Chats with a Guest).

90. *KTCXJ* 3.

91. *KTCXJ* 3.

prediction's condemnation of a female-led faction and its association with perception and greatness.

Dreams, Prediction, and Interpretation

"Correct" interpretation rests on the subject's attunement with the course of history. As an indicator of wisdom and historical attunement, perhaps no narrative conceit is as resonant as the dream interpretation. The narrative device of the dream suggests both the subject's inner psychological state (his or her "true" character) and his or her degree of self-awareness (leading to a "true" or "false" interpretation). In some cases the dream narrative follows a typical trajectory of predictions of glory at birth or impending demise.[92] The emphasis on (mis)interpretation in connection with well-known members of the female-led political factions, however, reflects a general and, in the decades following their deaths, increasing fascination with cosmology and interpretation as a means to accomplish their de-legitimation. Again, many of the earliest accounts of dream narratives come from *Chaoye qianzai* and other eighth- and early ninth-century anecdote collections; by comparing different versions, we can therefore attempt to trace the development of narratives and the values expressed therein.

92. For instance, the future greatness of the talented poet and politician Shangguan Wan'er is foretold in a dream her mother had when pregnant with her. She dreamed that someone gave her a balance and predicted that her baby would wield power over the world. The dream's prediction was later confirmed by Shangguan Wan'er's thirty-odd years of steadily increasing influence at court. This anecdote comes from Zhang Yue's preface to Shangguan Wan'er's literary collection and was incorporated into various later works, including *Taiping guangji* and her historical biographies. See *WYYH* 700.4b–6a; Egan, "*Preface to Shangguan Wan'er,*" 723–25; and Jie Wu, "A Study of Group Compositions," 214–23. In one of the *Taiping guangji* entries on Shangguan, her mother assumes, based on the prediction, that her baby will be a boy and is surprised when she gives birth to a daughter. *TPGJ* 137.986–87. See also *TPGJ* 271.2132–33. In the *Jiu Tang shu* account, people of the time mock the mother when she gives birth to a girl (whom they assume could not possibly be a political power-broker), but they are, of course, later proven wrong; see *JTS* 51.2175–76. *Xin Tang shu* (76.3488–89) adheres more closely to the preface version, as does *TSJS* 3.64.

The prominent courtier Cui Shi 崔湜 (671–713), a confidant of Shangguan Wan'er, Empress Wei, and other women leaders, unwittingly foretold his own ignominious end in a dream. Cui Shi has been depicted as a duplicitous figure. During the height of the power struggle between the Wei and Wu-Li factions, he was somewhat of an unofficial double agent for both groups. In the aftermath of Zhongzong's sudden death and the Taiping/Xuanzong coup against the Weis, Cui Shi had been exiled, along with his associate Lu Cangyong, to the far south. According to the *Chaoye qianzai* account, while stopping along the road in Jingzhou 荊州, Cui Shi dreamt that he was sitting down hearing a sutra lecture and was reflected in a mirror. When he woke up, he asked the skilled diviner Zhang You 張猷 about it. Probably because the meaning of the dream was so unfortunate, Zhang You is depicted as revealing it to Lu Cangyong, not Cui Shi. Sitting down to hear the sutra lecture meant that the law (*fa* 法) was descending upon Cui Shi; the character *jing* 鏡, "mirror," divides into the left and right graphic components of *jin* 金 and *jing* 竟 ("to end"), which Zhang You reads as "about to die" because the homophone of *jin* 金 is *jin* 今, "now/today." Right away a decree arrived ordering Cui Shi to commit suicide.[93]

The *Jiu Tang shu* version of this story embellishes it in such a way as to stress Cui Shi's lack of interpretive ability.[94] According to Cui Shi's *Jiu Tang shu* biography, when he first woke up from his dream, he offered his own totally erroneous interpretation: "The mirror is an image of brightness and illumination; I will be recognized and made resplendent by the ruler" (鏡者明象, 吾當為人主所明也).[95] When he describes his dream to the real diviner Zhang You, he discovers what it really spelled out for his future.[96]

93. *CYQZ* 3.61–62.

94. Again, the compilers of *Jiu Tang shu* made use of early sources, which in some cases predate the anecdote collections. Therefore, it is difficult to date the different versions of the anecdote; we can only compare narrative complexity and embellishment across the various accounts.

95. *JTS* 74.2623–24.

96. Zhang You (written You 由 in *JTS*) offers an abbreviated and slightly altered interpretation of Cui Shi's dream in the historical biography. The part about the lecture hall indicating the arrival of legal punishment is basically the same, but when it comes to the mirror, he merely states that "*jing* (mirror) is written with the components '*li jian jin* 立見金' [immediately see metal]. This is not an auspicious sign" (鏡者於文為 "立

Misinterpretation of dreams and manipulation of dream interpretation are variations upon the themes discussed above in connection with signs and auspiciousness. Female rule and supporters of female rulers are associated with misinterpretation and manipulation of signs and symbols, and this type of delusion is a strong symptom of their being out of sync with the correct cosmic order. Along these lines, the most resonant tale of dream interpretation is actually a complex of dream narratives surrounding a dream or dreams had by Wu Zhao herself. Episodes involving Wu's dreams, which appear in *Chaoye qianzai* and are later incorporated into several other works, touch upon key issues of court symbolism, legitimacy, and gender.

Wu Zhao's dream is inextricable from the political climate of the Zhou court. During the mid- to late 690s, a debate raged over the issue of succession to the throne. As Wu grew older, her nephews Wu Sansi and Wu Chengsi made an aggressive bid to have one of them named crown prince over their cousins, Li Xian (Zhongzong) and Li Dan (Ruizong). According to historical-anecdotal sources, around this time, Wu Zhao dreamed of a parrot with colossal plumage but two broken wings. She asked all of the prime ministers for their opinions on the meaning of her dream, and everyone was silent except for Di Renjie 狄仁傑 (630–700), a decorated military and civil official.[97] Di Renjie's interpretation of the dream directly addressed the pressing contemporary issue: "Wu 鵡 [the second character in the word 'parrot' *yingwu* 鸚鵡, graphically equivalent to Wu Zhao's surname plus the character for bird, *niao* 鳥] is Your Majesty's surname; the two wings being broken is referring to Your Majesty's two sons, the Princes of Luling [Li Xian] and Xiang [Li Dan]. If Your Majesty raises up her two sons, the two wings will be whole" (鵡者, 陛下姓也; 兩翅折, 陛下二子廬陵, 相王也. 陛下起此二子, 兩翅全也).[98] According to the account, Wu Chengsi and Wu Sansi were deeply embarrassed by Di Renjie's pointed interpretation. Wu Chengsi was subsequently removed from power, and, later, Wu Zhao followed Di

見金," 此非吉徵); see *JTS* 74.2624. That is, he divides the *jing* character differently and does not elaborate as to why its particular components are inauspicious. However, as metal was correlated with autumn, the season of execution and withering, perhaps no explanation was deemed necessary.

97. For Di Renjie's official biographies, see *JTS* 98.2885–95 and *XTS* 115.4207–14.

98. *CYQZ* 3.60. See also *TPGJ* 277.2195–96.

Renjie's advice and recalled Zhongzong to the throne, with resoundingly positive and affirming results.[99]

Display is written into this episode. Di Renjie's theatrical interpretation is offered in front of the court and is geared towards his political goal, a return to Tang rule.[100] Yet we are hard-pressed to believe that such crucial matters as the dynastic succession were actually decided based upon an official's spontaneous interpretation of the empress's dream. Actually, by the time this episode is said to have occurred (698), the aging Wu Zhao seems to have become aware of the inevitability of a return to Li rule after her death. As the *Chaoye qianzai* passage indicates, this was partly due to the unrest brought on by foreign conflicts, partly due to the continuing opposition of Tang loyalists, and partly due to symbolic disasters such as the repeated burning of the Mingtang. Indeed, it is unclear whether Wu ever seriously considered her nephews as candidates for the succession.[101] One suspects that if Wu and Di Renjie did actually perform the theatrical demonstration at court, the dream itself was in reality an ingenious "prop" or device invented by Wu.

As elucidated by McMullen, this episode of court theater starring Di Renjie as wise and loyal protector of the Tang also participates in the process through which, after the death of the historical man, the character Di Renjie was gradually transformed into a brave Tang loyalist.[102] In *Zizhi tongjian* he likewise appears in this role; in the depiction of the prolonged court debates surrounding the succession, Di Renjie is very vocal in his

99. According to *Chaoye qianzai*, the newly recalled crown prince was charged to head the Tang army (against the forces of Eastern Tujue leader Ashina Muchuo), and the enemy forces retreated immediately and "scattered of their own accord" (*zei zi tui san* 賊自退散) once they were faced with the virtuous legitimacy of the reinstated crown prince. *CYQZ* 3.60.

100. See McMullen, "The Real Judge Dee," for a discussion of Di Renjie's transformation from historical supporter of Wu Zhao to Tang loyalist to Judge Bao–like figure. McMullen's perceptive discussion of the historical image-making process is also relevant here.

101. See Guisso, *Wu Tse-t'ien and the Politics of Legitimation*, chap. 9, especially 130–32. See also *JTS* 6.126–27, 89.2891, 2895, 183.4729; and *XTS* 4.97, 61.1660, 115.4210, 4212–14, 206.5837–38.

102. McMullen, "The Real Judge Dee," 53, 70–72. In particular, a version of the episode can be traced back to a popular unofficial biography of Di Renjie, *Di Liang gong zhuan* 狄梁公傳 (Biography of Di [Renjie], Duke of Liang), which is first referenced several decades after the An Lushan Rebellion, around the early ninth century.

support of a mother-to-son, as opposed to aunt-to-nephew, succession.[103] Although Sima Guang ultimately rejects this episode,[104] its positioning within the overall narrative is nonetheless instructive. The parrot dream episode becomes the culmination of the hard-fought succession debate, during which Di Renjie has been constantly arguing in favor of the Prince of Luling.[105] When Wu Zhao begins to show signs of responding to his arguments, literally, when "[her] thinking began to become a little more enlightened" (太后意稍寤), she asked Di Renjie about her dream, and he offered his interpretation.[106] Di Renjie's reading of the dream is thus depicted as the finishing touch in his argument, which convinced Wu to reinstate the Prince of Luling as crown prince: "After this, the Empress Dowager did not have the intention to establish [Wu] Chengsi or [Wu] Sansi [as crown prince]" (太后由是無立承嗣, 三思之意).[107]

Other sources, including the early ninth-century *Di Liang gong zhuan* discussed by McMullen, *Xin Tang shu*, and *Tang yu lin*, contain a variant version of this episode, which seems to date back to several sources circulating during the early ninth century in which the basic narrative rubric remains the same but a different dream is substituted:[108] Wu Zhao dreams that she keeps losing at the chess game *shuanglu* 雙陸, and Di Renjie interprets this to mean that "there are no sons [*zi* 子, which can also refer to chess pieces] in the palace" (*gong zhong wu zi* 宮中無子).[109] *Tang yu lin* relates this anecdote in the context of a brief history of chess, whereas *Xin Tang shu* places it in Di Renjie's biography as the starting-off

103. See *ZZTJ* 206.6526.

104. See McMullen, "The Real Judge Dee," 71.

105. *ZZTJ* 206.6526.

106. *ZZTJ* 206.6526.

107. *ZZTJ* 206.6526. In *Zizhi tongjian*, the war proclamation by Ashina Mochuo demanding the return of the rightful heir comes directly after the dream episode. Even though we have already been informed that Wu Zhao no longer entertains any notions about the practicality and/or rightness of installing a Wu nephew as crown prince, as in the *Chaoye qianzai* passage the external threat provides further impetus for the pro-Luling group. After their arguments are presented at court, the matter is finally decided for good, and soon after, the future Zhongzong is called back to the capital. See *ZZTJ* 206.6527–28.

108. The anecdote can also be found in several other sources; see McMullen, "The Real Judge Dee," 70–72, for a detailed discussion. Zhou Xunchu suggests that the anecdote collection *Da Tang shuozuan* 大唐說纂, attributed to Li Zhao 李肇 (fl. 806–20), may be a source text for this anecdote. See Zhou Xunchu, *Tangdai biji xiaoshuo xulu*, 23–24.

109. *XTS* 115.4212.

point for a speech urging the recall of the Crown Prince: "Losing at chess means a lack of pieces/sons [子]. Just look at how Heaven is warning Your Majesty!" (雙陸不勝，無子也．天其意者以儆陛下乎!).[110]

The stories of how Di Renjie saved the Tang state by "correctly" interpreting Wu Zhao's dream suggest the remedial power of interpretation, when that power is placed in the "right" hands. Much of the dynamism and appeal of narratives about sign interpretation in general derive from the power of interpretation to sway and manipulate. Although one might doubt the objective "truth" of particular accounts, on a deeper level the accounts indicate an understanding of interpretation as a powerful force with great destructive or productive potential, depending on the identity of the interpreter.

Coda: Lady Yidu and the Rule of Women

It seems fitting to conclude this chapter with a work that presents an intriguing perspective on the traditional roles of *yin* and *yang* in relation to the possibility of sustained rule by women. "Yidu neiren" 宜都內人 (Lady Yidu) by Li Shangyin 李商隱 (ca. 813–58) is a fascinating, somewhat bittersweet piece of imaginative prose set during the final years of Wu Zhao's reign.[111] The piece, translated in full below, draws upon the stereotypical narrative images associated with female power, but its message represents a twist on the *yin-yang* theory used so pervasively to denigrate women rulers:

> Empress Wu had already usurped the imperial position for a long time, and she frequently indulged her desires, was addicted to inner pursuits, and disrespected the ancestral temple. Rebellions constantly sprang up

110. *TYL* 8.220; *XTS* 115.4212.

111. Chen Jo-shui has referred very briefly to this work in the context of his discussion of measures Wu Zhao implemented that increased the status of women. As Chen notes, Yidu was a county located in modern Hubei; Lady Yidu's title most likely indicates her place of origin. Chen Jo-shui, "Empress Wu and Proto-Feminist Sentiments," 89 and 111n41.

everywhere, and she had to guard against them unceasingly. At that time, Lady Yidu advanced holding the spittoon [at court], [but] her idea was to offer remonstrance. The Empress sat beneath a curtain, leaning against a sandalwood table, and asked her about the affairs of the state. Lady Yidu said, "Does Your Majesty know that in ancient times women were inferior to men?" The Empress said, "I know." The Lady said, "In ancient times there was Nü Wa, who wasn't really a rightful Son of Heaven, but who just helped Fu Xi to order the Nine States. In later generations there were female rulers, some of whom leapt free of their chambers to decide the world's affairs, but none of them achieved legitimacy. Many of them were aiding dim-witted rulers or otherwise were holding onto young sons. Only Your Majesty has revolutionized the imperial surname, cast off your hairpins and bangles, and put on the royal headdress. Auspicious signs come daily, and the great ministers don't dare move against you: you're a true Son of Heaven. But now the ministers with whom you privately dally and your intimates day and night attend you and after a long time you still haven't gotten rid of them. I fear that this is not in accordance with Heaven's will." The Empress said, "Why?" The Lady said, "Female is *yin* and male is *yang*. *Yang* is exalted but *yin* is lowly, so although Your Majesty rules the world with *yin*, you should embody the hard and strong, bright and ardent, to remove all *yang* elements. When *yang* has been removed, *yin* can get what it wants. Now the intimates are coming daily, appropriating Your Majesty's palaces and position; this trend is *yin* seeking *yang*. If *yang* becomes strong then *yin* will correspondingly wane and won't be able to last long. If starting from today Your Majesty is able to get rid of all of your male concubines and stand alone in the world, then the hardness and strength, brightness and ardor of *yang* can be yours. If it can be like this, then after myriad generations, men will be increasingly reduced in power and women will be increasingly powerful. This is my wish." Although the empress was unable to completely make use of [Lady Yidu's policy advice], that very day she did send down a command to execute the builder of the Mingtang.[112]

武后篡既久, 頗放縱, 耽内習, 不敬宗廟, 四方日有叛逆, 防豫不暇. 時宜都内人以唾壺進, 思有以諫者. 后坐帷下, 倚檀几, 與語問四方

112. The "builder of the Mingtang" is Xue Huaiyi 薛懷義 (d. 694), a complex and elusive figure linked sexually to Wu Zhao. His elusiveness is due in large part to a biased and fragmentary historical record. In the late 680s and early 690s, Wu Zhao appointed him architect of the entire Mingtang complex. See chapter 5 for an in-depth discussion. For more on the Mingtang, see Forte, *Mingtang and Buddhist Utopias* and Rothschild, *Rhetoric, Ritual, and Support Constituencies*, 75, 196–97, 316–23.

事. 宜都内人曰: 大家知古女卑于男邪? 后曰: 知. 内人曰: 古有女媧, 亦不正是天子, 佐伏羲理九州耳. 後世娘姥, 有越出房閣斷天下者, 皆不得其正. 多是輔昏主, 不然抱小兒. 獨大家革天姓, 改去釵釧, 襲服冠冕, 符端日至, 大臣不敢動, 真天子也. 然今内之弄臣狎人, 朝夕侍御者, 久未屏去, 妾疑此未當天意. 后曰: 何? 内人曰: 女, 陰也, 男, 陽也. 陽尊而陰卑, 雖大家以陰事主天, 然宜體取剛亢明烈, 以消群陽, 陽消然後陰得志也. 今狎弄日至, 處大家夫宮尊位, 其勢陰求陽也. 陽勝而陰亦微, 不可久也. 大家始今日能屏去男妾, 獨立天下, 則陽之剛亢明烈可有矣. 如是過萬萬世, 男子益削, 女子益專, 妾之願在此. 后雖不能盡用, 然即日下令誅作明堂者.[113]

Multiple levels of contradiction appear in Lady Yidu's advice, which immediately launches into the twin issues of gender and legitimacy. In the tradition of the wise councilor, Lady Yidu begins with a question that she knows will be easy for her ruler to answer: "Does Your Majesty know that in ancient times women were inferior to men?" Lady Yidu begins by reaffirming, as have historians ancient and modern, Wu Zhao's identity as the only woman since the mythic prehistory of Chinese civilization able to rule in her own right as an "official" or "legitimate" (*zheng* 正) monarch, a "true Son of Heaven" (*zhen tian zi* 真天子). The contradiction lies in the fact that the opening has just described Wu Zhao as a long-time usurper (*cuan* 篡), yet, according to Lady Yidu, she is the only legitimate female ruler in history and, in fact, is even more "legitimate" than the mythic culture hero Nü Wa.

Lady Yidu's positive appraisal of Wu as a "true Son of Heaven" is diametrically opposed to the evaluation of her that prevailed in the centuries after the empress's death. Lady Yidu dismisses women who ruled by default as regents to "aid dimwitted rulers" or as empress dowagers "holding onto young sons," the only circumstances under which female rule has traditionally been deemed permissible. Her advice to Wu Zhao entails the construction of an alternative universe, in which *yin* succeeds in subverting *yang* by removing and weakening it. She outlines a program for conquering the danger of "*yin* seeking *yang*," which would sooner or later lead to the former being sabotaged by the latter: Wu Zhao must "embody the hard and strong, bright and ardent, to remove all *yang*

113. Li Shangyin, *Li Shangyin quan ji*, 1058–59.

elements. When *yang* has been removed, *yin* can get what it wants." This process is accomplished by removing intimate male influence, in particular, the empress's male concubines.

Lady Yidu's advice amounts to a long-term vision of female dominance in society. If the female rulers can embody the *yang* usually monopolized by men, the eventual result will be the creation of a social reality in which men are reduced in power and disenfranchised. Of course, as the readers and Li Shangyin know, this result is unlikely if not impossible, and the ending of "Lady Yidu" is reminiscent of historical accounts of wise yet not adopted policy suggestions: "Although the empress was unable to completely make use of [Lady Yidu's policy advice], that very day she did send down a command to execute the builder of the Mingtang."

The entire piece is an inversion of the apprehension regarding undue female influence on the male emperor and the typological scenes of remonstrance it engenders between male minister and ruler. There is a satiric quality to the total reversal of gender roles found in "Lady Yidu." Yet the piece is by no means condemnatory of Wu Zhao and seems almost wistful in suggesting the impossibility of Wu's situation and of the advice laid out by Lady Yidu. According to Lady Yidu, successful and continuous female rule requires generation after generation of empresses to banish all male favorites so as to create a gender-reversed power structure and uproot the "trend of *yin* seeking *yang*." "Lady Yidu" thus perhaps inadvertently suggests the almost insurmountable difficulties faced by the woman ruler in consolidating and maintaining power within the existing system.

Li Shangyin, through Lady Yidu, uses the rubric of *yin* and *yang* to explore the issue of legitimacy, and as in materials discussed above, the piece's primary focus is her unique interpretation of historical circumstances. We have seen that the issue of sign interpretation forms a central concern in narratives dealing with the seventh- through eighth-century period of female political dominance. The omnipresence of accounts stressing false interpretations made or allowed by the female ruler, as well as the fluidity between "sign" and "fraud," "auspicious" and "inauspicious," speaks to a fundamental anxiety regarding signs' potential for manipulation. The misinterpretation and manipulation of signs ("false" signs) are identified with female rule; they rhetorically become manifestations of a space created and controlled by women who overstep their "natural" place.

The interpretation of signs is often closely related to imperial display. That is, court rituals and celebrations of auspiciousness represent public proclamations of legitimacy, and these visible demonstrations are later understood according to different, generally condemnatory interpretive frameworks. The following chapter approaches the interpretive complexes driving retrospective materials about these women from another perspective: analysis of records dealing with their lavish private landed estates, clothing, and other material items. These retrospective accounts, though they purport to provide a window into the material culture, condemn women leaders by interpreting in an opposite, derogatory manner phenomena treated with reverence in seventh- and eighth-century records. Interpretive judgments likewise continue to hinge on the issues of naturalness, gender, and power.

FOUR

Building Power

Symbolic Architecture, Conspicuous Consumption, and Rule by Women

The female power-holders of the late seventh and early eighth centuries are identified with and remembered by the material things they created and possessed. In sources spanning more than a millennium after the Taiping Princess's death, we read about the clothing these women wore, the lavish mansions and landed estates where they feted and plotted, the religious and decorative monuments they commissioned, and the gifts they were given or gave to each other. The poetic topic of the royal estate, the focus of many poems written by courtiers to command during the reigns of Wu Zhao, Zhongzong, and Ruizong, is transformed in the later poet Han Yu's 韓愈 (768–824) quatrain "You Taiping gongzhu shan zhuang" 遊太平公主山莊 (Roaming on the Taiping Princess's Mountain Villa):

Back in those years the Princess
 wanted spring as her own:
on purpose she put terraces and kiosks
 right up to the city's gates.
If you would know how many flowers
 she looked at before her—
all the way to Mount Zhongnan
 belonged to no one else.

公主當年欲占春,
故將臺榭押城闉.

欲知前面花多少,
直到南山不屬人.[1]

The title of Han Yu's poem evokes the titles of many poems written to royal command (*yingzhi* 應制) during the height of the princess's power by the most prominent literary figures of the court. Already by Han Yu's time, around a century after the Taiping Princess's death, the literary-historical image-making process, through which she and contemporary female power-holders became associated with specific types of materiality and conspicuous consumption, was well underway. The poem's theme is possession and the limits of power, as suggested by the princess's doomed attempt to take spring "as her own." As Stephen Owen notes, the compound *zhanchun* 占春, "to take personal possession of spring," is related to a set of variations on commonplace phrases in mid-Tang poetry in which present ownership is used to evoke the absence of previous owners.[2] The Taiping Princess's absence is, in Han Yu's poem, evoked by the description of the extent to which she attempted to cement and take advantage of her "possession."[3] Her tenure of possession and power was, of course, limited, and Han Yu's depiction of her attempt to take private possession of the inherently public sphere of the natural world touches upon key themes involving rule by women and the natural domain.

As we have explored in earlier chapters, the relationship of the early Tang women leaders to nature and "naturalness" is a complex and omnipresent theme. This chapter examines another rhetorical form through which female power during this period is encapsulated and denounced as unnatural: records of conspicuous consumption by Wu Zhao and especially the next generations of Empress Wei, the Taiping and Anle Princesses, and Shangguan Wan'er. The types of information that have had the most lasting attraction in official histories, anecdote collections,

1. *QTS* 344.3853–3854. Translation by Stephen Owen, in Owen, *The End of the Chinese "Middle Ages,"* 25.

2. Owen, *The End of the Chinese "Middle Ages,"* 25.

3. As elucidated by Owen, the Princess wanted "not pure possession but the contemplation of the magnitude of her possessions . . . not merely ownership but a display of ownership for her enjoyment," as she commissioned the construction of terraces and kiosks from which to look at everything that belonged to her. Owen, *The End of the Chinese "Middle Ages,"* 26.

and other literary works are extreme expenditures on luxury sites, luxury items, and imperial occasions. The entrenched legacy of this image of insatiable materiality can still be seen in some recent scholarly works, which tend to repeat historical passages about greedy, arrogant Tang princesses as unquestioned fact.[4] These consumptive behaviors, which are attributed to female leaders and their male associates, are described as destructive to the state, the people, and nature.

There is a close connection between the literary and material cultures of the era.[5] As I have discussed in Chapter 2, the social-literary culture at the turn of the eighth century was characterized by frequent banquets, outings (especially to private estates), and group literary composition. The basic forms taken by these gatherings were by no means invented in the Tang. The courtly entertainments sponsored by Empress Feng and Empress Dowager Hu, for example, bear striking similarities to the activities that were prominent at the courts of Wu Zhao and her sons. Both Feng and Hu were extremely generous patrons of the Buddhist clerical establishment and sponsored the building of numerous lavish temples.[6] In addition, both empresses are described as fond of courtly outings to scenic locations. These outings involved various forms of entertainment, including literary composition and archery.[7] Turning to an even closer precedent, chronologically speaking, group court composition was also a prominent feature of Taizong's court, meant to convey his fairness and largesse as a ruler.[8]

4. See, for example, Gao Shiyu, *Tangdai funü*, 30–38; and Luo Longzhi, *Tangdai de houfei yu waiqi*, 105–6.

5. See the discussion in Jia Jinhua, "A Study of the *Jinglong wenguan ji*" and *Tangdai jihui zongji yu shirenqun yanjiu*, 43–73.

6. A large portion of Yang Xuanzhi's 楊衒之 (d. 555?) *Luoyang qielan ji* 洛陽伽藍記 (Record of Temples in Luoyang) is taken up with describing the gorgeous temples sponsored by Empress Dowager Hu, as well as the turbulent political events occurring around the temple sites. See Yang Xuanzhi, *Luoyang qielan ji jiao zhu*. See *WS* 13.328–29 for a discussion of Empress Feng's acts of Buddhist patronage.

7. For example, Empress Feng led an outing to Spirit Springs Pool 靈泉池 (Lingquan chi) that involved the composition of matching songs by courtiers and visiting dignitaries. See *WS* 13.329. Several passages in Empress Dowager Hu's official biography describe her talent as an archer. See *WS* 13.338–39. Her biography also records one line each from the poems written by her and Emperor Ming on the occasion of an outing to Flowering Grove Garden 華林園 (Hualin yuan). See *WS* 13.338.

8. For an in-depth analysis of Taizong's poetry, see Jack Wei Chen, *The Poetics of Sovereignty*, especially chaps. 4–6.

Yet, though there is clearly a similarity in outward form between the courtly pursuits of previous eras and those of the Wu-Zhou through pre-Kaiyuan period, in the later period courtly entertainment underwent important developments in terms of activity and emphasis. Jia and others have noted that the uniformly mixed-gender courtly outings during this period become more frequent, more elaborate, and more closely tied to factional politics.[9] At the same time, more so than was the case in previous periods, portrayals of court culture played an integral function in the condemnatory rhetorical reconstruction of the era and its leading ladies. Records on the period emphasize in particular the association between these women and specific narrative manifestations of conspicuous consumption.

The vogue for estate-building was not only closely related to faction-building and the creation of loci of power; these sites are portrayed in narrative accounts as embodiments of female excess and greed. Obviously the rich and powerful had always enjoyed grand residences and luxury living, but in accounts of this period the estates of powerful women and their male allies are portrayed as symbolic expressions of female or female-enabled greed, injustice, and intrigue. In these accounts, conspicuous consumption, more broadly defined, is a prominent by-product of the excessive power possessed by women, and the major outflows of their consumption are representative of their transgression of the "natural" hierarchy. Transgression of sumptuary laws is particularly important in this regard. The imperial wedding seems to have been a specifically female-identified manifestation of conspicuous consumption, and as in accounts of ritual, estate-building, and courtly outings, the condemnation is rooted in the power and gender of the bride. As in accounts of the woman ruler's acceptance of many signs, portrayals of the female-led avarice driving the vogue for large-scale, visible conspicuous consumption identify material insatiability with sexual rapaciousness.

Likewise, as in the accounts analyzed in previous chapters, we can see in these materials evidence of the development over time of particular narratives, whereby a narrative core is amplified so as to accord with the objective(s) of individual authors and the accepted evaluation of the "true nature" of the historical actors involved. Analysis of these developments

9. Jia Jinhua, "A Study of the *Jinglong wenguan ji*," 213–28 and 231–36.

enables us to explore how these historical figures are essentialized and what this reveals about evolving conceptions of female power in relation to the Wu-Zhou-Jinglong era.

Luxury Mansions

An often-repeated narrative about Zong Chuke 宗楚客 (d. 710), a high official and a second cousin of Wu Zhao (his mother was Wu's cousin), provides a rich starting point for our analysis. Zong Chuke is always cast in the role of historical villain because of his allegiance first to Wu Zhao and then to Zhongzong's reviled Empress Wei. During the height of his power, at the turn of the eighth century, Zong Chuke constructed a lavish new mansion:

> Zong Chuke completed construction on a new mansion. The beams were made solely of veined cypress wood, and the walls were plastered with aloes wood and red powder, so that whenever the doors were opened the fragrance suffused the air. He had veined stones polished into layered stairs reaching to the ground, so that those wearing *jimo* leather boots tripped and fell.[10] Chuke was implicated by the Prince of Jianchang for accepting

10. *Jimo* 吉莫 is thought to be a Xianbei word. Its earlier appearance is in the "Biography of Xue Rongzong" ("Xue Rongzong lie zhuan" 薛榮宗列傳) in the "Biography of Favorites" (*en xing lie zhuan* 恩倖列傳) section of the *Bei Qi shu* 北齊書 (History of the Northern Qi Dynasty): "Rongzong stepped forward and memorialized, saying: 'In the past I saw Guo Linzong emerging from a tomb, wearing a large hat and *jimo* leather boots and cracking a horse whip. He asked me, "Am I or am I not Azhen [Guo Yuanzhen's father] arriving?"' 榮宗前奏曰:"臣向見郭林宗從冢出, 著大帽, 吉莫靴, 插馬鞭, 問臣, '我阿貞來不?'"; *Bei Qi shu* 50.694. According to the narrative, Xue Rongzong falsely claimed to be able to commune with ghosts. When passing an ancient tomb, the official Yuan Xinggong 元行恭 (dates unknown) jokingly told him it was the tomb of Guo Linzong 郭林宗, the father of Guo Yuanzhen 郭元貞 (dates unknown), a Northern Qi official who had served as Governor of Yangzhou 揚州刺史. Xue Rongzong actually believed this and memorialized about how he had "seen" the ghost. *Jimo* boots have been associated with martial activities, including horseback riding and scaling walls. *Jimo* leather boots are listed in several accounts of tribute items in *Xin Tang shu*; see *XTS* 37.965, 972. *Pu* 仆 means to "trip and fall," but can also be synonymous with *pu* 僕, "servant," so the phrase *yang pu* 仰仆 could conceivably be translated

bribes in excess of ten thousand strings of cash, and he and his brothers were exiled. The Taiping Princess went to look at his mansion and sighed, saying, "When I look at the places where he walked and sat, [I am aware that] we have lived and died in vain." In a year he was recalled to service at court and made an attendant in the secretariat. During the Jinglong reign, he was director of the Secretariat. Upon the defeat of the Wei clan, he was executed.

宗楚客造一新宅成, 皆是文柏為梁, 沉香和紅粉以泥壁, 開門則香氣蓬勃. 磨文石為階砌及地, 着吉莫鞾者, 行則仰仆. 楚客被建昌王推得贓萬余貫, 兄弟配流. 太平公主就其宅看, 嘆曰: "看他行坐處, 我等虛生浪死." 一年追入, 為鳳閣侍郎. 景龍中, 為中書令, 韋氏之敗, 斬之.[11]

As recounted in this anecdote, the incredible concentration of material and human resources required to create the estate soon proved pointless; immediately after the description of the luxurious mansion comes notice of Zong Chuke's embroilment in a corruption scandal for accepting bribes, which had probably paid for the new construction. He was forced to abandon the beautiful new residence for a life in exile, and just a few years later, he was executed.

The entrance of the Taiping Princess into this anecdote signals her prominent association with opulent estate building. Her sigh is one of covetousness; she and other elite court figures (*wodeng* 我等) have been living in vain because their mansions cannot rival Zong Chuke's. Her appearance may also be meant to evoke Zong Chuke's identification with female-led political factions (although after Wu Zhao's deposal he was a follower of the Taiping Princess's enemy Empress Wei). Her assessment of Zong Chuke's mansion makes clear her failure to understand the greater moral suggested by the anecdote, that is, the inevitable ephemerality of ill-begotten wealth and retribution for greed that harms the state and the people.

Chaoye qianzai's lovely opening description of the mansion's arresting beauty contrasts sharply with the fate of its first owner; overall, the passage conveys a conflicted combination of wonder and disapproval.

as "relied on their servants" (that is, because the polished stairs are slippery, those wearing the *jimo* boots had to lean on their servants when ascending or descending).

11. *CYQZ* 3.70. See also *TPGJ* 236.1816.

Chaoye qianzai seems to be the earliest source for this anecdote, as with many episodes involving conspicuous consumption during this period. Condensed versions of the story, recorded in *Zizhi tongjian* and *Xu shishuo*, omit the entire opening section, instead recounting only the bribery scandal and the Taiping Princess's reaction to the mansion.[12] By removing the description of the mansion, these sources also effectively remove the element of aesthetic admiration or nostalgia that is present in the earlier account. Writing three centuries after the compilation of *Chaoye qianzai*, writers such as Sima Guang and Kong Pingzhong saw the description of the mansion as less essential than the narrative of condemnation.

The *Chaoye qianzai* anecdote about Zong Chuke's mansion is not alone in its combination of fascination and antipathy for the profligate and exotic behaviors of female power-holders and members of their factions. By the time the standard histories were compiled, descriptions of the Jinglong women's weakness for extravagantly outfitted, massive landed estates were almost a generic requirement for their biographies. The Anle Princess's *Xin Tang shu* biography describes her estate as follows: "The princess constructed an estate and the Anle Buddhist Monastery. They both followed the model of the imperial compound, but in fineness of skill in construction surpassed it [the imperial compound]" (主營第及安樂佛廬, 皆憲寫宮省, 而工緻過之).[13] *Jiu Tang shu* states with censure that she "constructed an estate on a grand scale; it was excessively extravagant. The Changning Princess and other princesses copied her one after another, and everyone sighed in resentment about it" (廣營第宅, 侈靡過甚. 長寧及諸公主迭相倣效, 天下咸嗟怨之).[14] The narrative establishes a dichotomy of female excess in opposition to good government that puts "the people" first. The dangerous fashion for lavish estate-building is a female craze identified with the princesses, not the

12. *ZZTJ* 206.6538–39; *XSS* 12.434. The very brief *Xu shishuo* entry (just two sentences) seems to have been taken from *Zizhi tongjian*; although providing far fewer details about the scandal, the narrative progression is the same, and *Xu shishuo* uses exactly the same wording as does *Zhizhi tongjian* to describe the princess's sighing statement. However, as Kong Pingzhong's dates are unclear but approximated to the eleventh century, the reverse could be true, or they could both be using an alternative earlier source.

13. *XTS* 83.3654.

14. *JTS* 51.2172.

princes, and the world sends out a collective lament of grief in response to the women's bad behavior.

The Taiping Princess is generally praised for circumspection and perspicacity surpassing her niece, but she too lavished indulgence upon her landed estate:

> The Princess was tall and plump. She had a high forehead, a broad chin, and many schemes and plots. Zetian considered her to be like herself, and she often participated in scheming and planning. The palace compound was strictly secured, and affairs were never allowed to be leaked out. The Princess was also vigilant and self-disciplined; she only aggrandized and adorned her landed estate.
>
> 公主豐碩, 方額廣頤, 多權略, 則天以為類己, 每預謀議, 宮禁嚴峻, 事不令洩. 公主亦畏懼自檢, 但崇飾邸第.[15]

Taiping's *Xin Tang shu* biography goes into greater detail regarding her uncanny ability to anticipate the thoughts and wishes of others, enabling her to remain on her powerful mother's good side where her brothers had failed.[16] Both biographies detail her immense landholdings and the precise nature in which she "aggrandized and adorned" her estate: her fields were all close to the imperial domain and the richest and most fertile soil; the markets of Wu, Shu, and Lingqiao made vessels for her use, and these were transported for her by the states and districts, making for so many convoys that "each could see another [convoy] ahead all along the route" (道相望也); "the rarest delicacies and most beguiling marvels in all the world filled her household, and the procession of musicians and entertainers accompanying her equaled the Emperor's" (天下珍滋譎怪充於家, 供帳聲伎與天子等); and her estate was maintained by tens of thousands of attendants and slaves.[17]

15. *JTS* 183.4738. *Xin Tang shu* likewise notes, often using identical catch words, the Taiping Princess's impressive capacity for inner and outer regulation: "[She] internally plotted with [Wu Zhao] and externally was restrained and fearful. Throughout the empress's reign, she was faultless" (主內與謀, 外檢畏, 終后世無它訾); *XTS* 83.3650.

16. "The princess served Wu Zhao for a long time. She was good at detecting the ruler's [Wu Zhao's] subtlest wishes and according with them; she never missed the mark" (主侍武后久, 善策人主微指, 先事逢合, 無不中); *XTS* 83.3651.

17. *XTS* 83.3651; see parallel (though not verbatim) account in *JTS* 183.4739.

The suffering inflicted upon the people involved in maintaining and transporting goods to the princess's massive estate is once again clearly implied.

Biographical accounts of the most powerful princesses of the era are likewise concerned with the unprecedentedly high enfeoffment stipends granted to these women. *Jiu Tang shu*, *Xin Tang shu*, and *Zizhi tongjian* all record the way in which Taiping's number of allotted households gradually grew, by the turn of the century, to about ten times the amount allowed to princesses according to pre-Yongchun (682–83) regulations.[18] Following her orchestration of the coup that enthroned Ruizong, her wealth continued to increase.[19] The biographies and *Zizhi tongjian* all record with hyperbolic shock the massive accumulation of wealth discovered immediately following her death in 713. According to the *Jiu Tang shu*, "[the victors] assessed her household [and found] wealth and goods piled like mountains, with rare treasures and precious things equal to the imperial treasury. For several years, the revenue from the horse and sheep pastures, fields, and pawnshops could not be located and returned to imperial jurisdiction" (籍其家，財貨山積，珍奇寶物，侔於御府，馬牧羊牧田園質庫，數年徵斂不盡).[20] By all accounts, the revenue formerly hoarded by the Taiping Princess amounted to a substantial detraction from the returns that should have gone towards gainful state purposes.

Although the Taiping Princess's nieces did not quite achieve her level of wealth (mainly because she earned her highest stipend through her pivotal role in orchestrating the coup that dethroned their faction and killed Anle and Empress Wei), the Changning and Anle Princesses nevertheless also greatly exceeded the pre-Yongchun norm of three hundred households per princess. The favored youngest daughter Anle had a fief of three thousand households, while Changning received two

18. See *JTS* 83.4738; *XTS* 183.3650; and *ZZTJ* 204.6466. According to pre-Yongchun imperial regulations, a princess was supposed to be granted three hundred households upon her marriage; by the beginning of Wu Zhao's Shengli 聖歷 reign period (697–700), the Taiping Princess supposedly held approximately three thousand.

19. After playing a leading role in the coup that destroyed the Weis and enthroned her brother as Emperor Ruizong, she gained an additional five thousand households, bringing her total to about ten thousand. See *JTS* 183.4739.

20. *JTS* 183.4740; see also *XTS* 83.3652 and *ZZTJ* 210.6685.

thousand five hundred. The sense of special and inappropriate favor shown to the two daughters of Empress Wei is reinforced by the caustic remark in *Xin Tang shu* that "the Yicheng and Ding'an Princesses were not born to Empress Wei, so their number of households was only two thousand" (宜城, 定安非韋后所生, 戶止二千).[21] Changning and Anle were each given armed guards and large estates after the manner of the imperial precincts. *Xin Tang shu* notes that "no overseer was appointed" (府不置長史) to the two princesses' treasuries, insinuating that the holdings of the favored princesses were not subject to the usual channels of supervision, enabling further corruption and improper accumulation of wealth.[22]

The wealth accumulated by these women is consistently upheld as excessive and harmful to the state. Yet, following the change of government in 705, Ruizong, then Prince Xiang 相王, is recorded as having been awarded the same amount of wealth as was Taiping on that occasion.[23] This passage indicates that her accumulation of wealth was not necessarily in opposition to normative practices of rewarding high-ranking political allies after their participation in a successful maneuver. Her wealth is singled out and condemned because it ties in with negative posthumous reconstructions of her identity and place within history. This negative portrayal is conditioned by particular assumptions regarding gender and power.

Over time, these assumptions seem to almost generate narratives surrounding figures that initially are unpopular in lore on the period. The Changning Princess and her husband Yang Shenjiao 楊慎交 (675–724) were a less politically active couple and, consequently, are less prominent in historical and anecdotal accounts.[24] *Xin Tang shu* includes a biography

21. *XTS* 83.3650.

22. *XTS* 83.3650.

23. See *JTS* 183.4738; *XTS* 83.3650; and *ZZTJ* 214.6596.

24. There is some confusion about Yang Shenjiao's name. In his *Jiu Tang shu* biography, his name is given as Ruijiao 睿交, whereas in his *Xin Tang shu* biography, it is recorded as Shenjiao 昚交; see *JTS* 62.2382 and *XTS* 100.3927. In the princess's *Xin Tang shu* biography, however, his name is given as Shenjiao; see *XTS* 83.3653.

Yang Shenjiao is given only extremely terse biographical entries in *Jiu Tang shu* and *Xin Tang shu*, and in *Jiu Tang shu*, Changning is not given her own biography at all. For Yang Shenjiao's official biographies, see *JTS* 62.2382 and *XTS* 100.3927. Yang Shenjiao appears in a brief entry in the mid-eighth-century *Sui Tang jia hua*, which describes devoted to Changning, notable in that it is taken up almost entirely with descriptions of her and Yang Shenjiao's shared zeal for over-the-top building projects and real estate acquisition. According to the biography, upon their marriage, the couple exhausted the state coffers to build a new residence and, in addition, seized a prodigious amount of real estate belonging to other people.[25] The immense sizes of their palatial compounds in Luoyang and Chang'an are almost difficult to conceptualize. Their Chang'an estate occupied the space in between the city wall and the great thoroughfare, and they had a three-tiered tower built there so that they would be able to survey what they possessed.[26]

This image recalls Han Yu's poem imagining the hubristic Taiping Princess climbing on high to survey her power of possession, and, indeed, the biography impresses first and foremost the power of the favor enjoyed by the princess. She was able to appropriate massive amounts of buildings and land that rightfully belonged to high ministers and the public by sheer force of her mother's penchant for spoiling her: "[The Changning Princess] relied on her mother's love, and her favor was the envy of the whole court" (內倚母愛，寵傾一朝).[27] The biography's brevity and lack of details unrelated to the residences and other pleasure sites constructed by the princess and her husband create the impression of a brief anecdote with a narrow thematic or topical focus and moral message. The fact that *Jiu Tang shu* does not accord a biography to the Changning Princess perhaps suggests that the *Xin Tang shu* compilers pieced together the biography to create a negative moral exemplar. The ending chosen by the historian for the biography evokes the anecdote about Zong Chuke's mansion: "The Luoyang mansion was completed, but before they had even gotten to live in it, the Wei faction lost. Shenjiao was demoted to assistant governor of

---

how the extravagance of the "imperial consorts and princesses' households" (妃主家競為奢侈) enables the wasteful behavior of imperial sons-in-law Yang Shenjiao and Wu Chongxun, Anle's husband. Yang Shenjiao and Wu Chongxun spread oil on a polo field, presumably to create a smoother surface for play. This behavior seems to be an example of wasteful consumption because the oil could have been put to more practical uses, such as cooking. *STJH* c.42. See also *TPGJ* 236.1818.

25. *XTS* 83.3653. Their acquisitions included the former residence of Gao Shilian 高士廉 (575–647), the central yamen of the disbanded Yongchang District in Luoyang, and the former residence of the Prince of Wei, Tai 魏王泰 (Li Tai 李泰; 620–652).

26. *XTS* 83.3653.

27. *XTS* 83.3653.

Jiangzhou, and the princess followed him there" (東都第成, 不及居, 韋氏敗, 斥慎交絳州別駕, 主偕往).[28] After their dismissal to Jiangzhou, the couple sold their Chang'an residence and requested to have their Luoyang residence converted into a shrine. The biography also references the excessive cost of the residences, which was discovered when they were assessed. As in the case of Zong Chuke's mansion, the lavish residence constructed by the Changning Princess and Yang Shenjiao as an edifice of power serves only to illustrate the inherent transience of wealth, power, and ownership.

The denouement to the biography of the Changning Princess describes a fate not nearly as violent as those suffered by her sister, mother, or other powerful court women.[29] The language and motifs of the biography clearly evoke other narratives discussed thus far. Indeed, the biography is significant in that reads like a patchwork of tropes surrounding women leaders and materiality, without the description of personal qualities and actions that provides some sense of individuation in the biographies of women rulers like Empress Wei and the Taiping and Anle Princesses. The biography of the Changning Princess serves primarily to reinforce the association between the imperial women of the era and dangerous forms of conspicuous consumption.

The estate as site of improper conspicuous consumption is further transformed in several stories involving the residences built with the money "earned" by Wu Zhao's favorites, the brothers Zhang Yizhi 張易之 (d. 705) and Zhang Changzong 張昌宗 (d. 705). The brothers are two of the most infamous men in Chinese history, and in accounts of the period, they are certainly the men most remembered in terms of materiality. Yizhi and Changzong were the only Zhang brothers sexually linked to Wu Zhao, but the entire Zhang family benefitted greatly from their favor. *Sui Tang jia hua* and *Chaoye qianzai* contain two similar stories involving warnings received at their mansions by Zhang Yizhi and another brother, Zhang Changyi 張昌儀 (d. 705). As in the above anecdotes, the landed estate serves as the embodiment of corruption,

28. *XTS* 83.3653.

29. The princess and Yang Shenjiao survived well into Xuanzong's reign. Yang died in 724, after which his wife remarried a man named Su Yanbo 蘇彥伯. Yang Wulian 楊務廉 (dates unknown), who oversaw the constructions of their residences as well as the Anle Princess's, was indicted for accepting bribes and disgraced. *XTS* 83.3653.

underscoring its symbolic association with inappropriate annexation of wealth and power.

According to *Sui Tang jia hua*, Zhang Changyi and another brother, "relying on Yizhi and Changzong's favor, lived in a residence that was excessively extravagant, even surpassing that of a prince or princess" (恃易之, 昌宗之寵, 所居奢溢, 逾於王主).[30] During the final year of his life, leading up to the annihilation of the Zhangs in the Li-Tang restoration of 705, Zhang Changyi received an ominous warning: "In his final year, someone wrote on his gate: 'A bunch of silk-strands—for how many days can it be sorted?' As soon as Changyi saw it, he commanded someone to write underneath it: 'A single day is enough.' In a short while, the disaster [of 705] reached him" (末年有人題其門曰: "一絇絲, 能得幾日絡?" 昌儀見之, 遽命筆書其下曰: "一日即足." 無何而禍及).[31] The "bunch of silk strands," of course, stands for Changyi's power, which, as a by-product of his brothers' corruption and sexual service, is doomed; he can only twine it for so long until his fate catches up to him. From the anecdote, it is unclear whether Changyi is aware of this and is content to enjoy wealth and power for a short time, even if it means eventual downfall, or whether he is simply obliviously answering the question at face value. The metaphor of silk cleverly evokes the luxury enjoyed by Zhang Changyi and might be meant to suggest women's work.

The parallel *Chaoye qianzai* anecdote about Zhang Yizhi combines tropes seen in the *Sui Tang jia hua* entry about Changyi and in the *Chaoye qianzai* entry on Zong Chuke's beautiful mansion. Zhang Yizhi constructed a great hall that was "extremely grand and imposing and cost several million. *Red powder plastered the walls*, the columns were made of *veined cypress wood*, and glazed tiles and *aloes wood* served as decoration" (張易之初造一大堂甚壯麗, 計用數百萬. 紅粉泥壁, 文柏帖柱, 琉璃沉香為飾).[32] The overlap between the two passages and the chronological nearness of the sources may indicate a fashion for certain luxury items, a typological rhetorical means of conceptualizing luxury, and/or cross-circulation of lore about the period. The main action portion of

30. *STJH* c.39. See also *TPGJ* 188.1406.

31. *STJH* c.39.

32. *CYQZ* 6.146. I have italicized the phrases that are identical with those used in the description of Zong Chuke's mansion. See also *TPGJ* 143.1025.

the anecdote closely follows the warning-response model of the Zhang Changyi anecdote, but with a supernatural twist. Here instead of an anonymous writer who is nevertheless identified as a person (有人題其門), a ghost writes on Zhang Yizhi's wall at night. The ghost's ominous prediction is a more direct synopsis of the import behind the silk riddle: "How long can it [you/your mansion/your life of luxury] last?" (能得幾時?).[33] Zhang Yizhi ordered the writing removed, but the next day it reappeared. This happened six or seven times, at which point he finally wrote on the wall in reply to the ghostly missive, using phrasing identical, except for the time unit, to that attributed in *Sui Tang jia hua* to his brother: "One month is enough" (一月即足).[34] Apparently this satisfied the ghost; the writing stopped, but less than six months later Zhang Yizhi fell from power.[35]

In each case, the mysterious writing on the gate or wall of his estate elicits or demands an answer from one of the Zhang brothers, and in each case that very answer predicts or even seals his fate. These anecdotes approach the idea of cosmic retribution; the universe condemns the improper wealth amassed by Wu Zhao's minions and, through an unknown eerie agent, prophesies their downfall. In these cases, as in others involving lavish constructions of the era, the mansion represents the builder's nature: excessive, avaricious, and "private," in the most negative sense. The landed estate is simultaneously the site where and medium through which female power-holders and their male supporters are exposed, condemned, and sentenced.

The mansion as a symbol of its owner's transgression easily becomes the mansion as facilitator of that transgression. In the cases of both the Taiping and Anle Princesses, leaders of the two opposing political cliques of the Jinglong period, the private estate is linked with factionalism and

33. *CYQZ* 6.146.

34. *CYQZ* 6.146. Zhang Yizhi's unsuccessful attempt to rub off the supernatural message evokes Gaozu's skeptical attempt to have the auspicious crimson writing on the turtle rubbed out; the interpretation is obviously opposite, but the expression of inevitability is parallel. See Wen Daya, *Da Tang chuangye qi ju zhu* 2.22.

35. In *Zizhi tongjian*, the stories of the two Zhang brothers and their mansions are somewhat conflated; Zhang Changyi tries to remove the anonymous threatening rhyme six or seven times, but it only disappears for good when he responds that a day is enough. The later conflation of the two anecdotes further indicates that they are essentially variants of the same story. *ZZTJ* 207.6581.

clandestine service or favor. In these accounts, the architecture commissioned by the Tang women leaders provides the backdrop for the deployment of their power, as well as becoming a compelling narrative tool through which they are condemned.

Landed Estates and Intrigue

After the ascendancy of Ruizong, the Taiping Princess became a critical decision-maker in state affairs and appropriated the imperial prerogative. *Jiu Tang shu* states that when she chose not to attend court, the prime ministers went to her estate to deliberate whether or not a particular measure was feasible.[36] The impropriety of a private residence supplanting the imperial court as the seat of government is apparent and represents, in the narrative, the disorder of the private and public spheres associated with female rule. In the same vein, Taiping's complex, prolonged bid to unseat Li Longji as Crown Prince and gain control of the public political sphere is described as a clandestine and personal one, carried on slyly outside of the public sphere of the court. We read that "at the time, out of the seven prime ministers, five were the princess's clients. Additionally, General of the Left Palace Guard Chang Yuankai and Palace Guard General Li Ci both privately visited the princess" (時宰相七人, 五出主門下. 又左羽林大將軍常元楷, 知羽林軍李慈皆私謁主).[37] The word *si* 私 implies privacy and secrecy; clientage based upon personal relationship is defined against the public government stage. The negative connotations of the phrase *siye* 私謁 ("to privately visit," or "clientage") are longstanding. "The Biography of Shentu Jia" ("Shentu Jia lie zhuan" 申屠嘉列傳) in *Shiji* clearly establishes the public-private distinction in relation to *siye* and the moral judgment that entails: "[Shentu] Jia was an incorrupt and upright person and did not receive the private visits of clients [*siye*]" (嘉為人廉直, 門不受私謁).[38] If the "incorrupt and upright person" is defined as one who does not receive the private visits

36. *JTS* 183.4739.
37. *XTS* 83.3651; see also *JTS* 183.4739.
38. *SJ* 96.2683.

of clients, then the person who does privately receive clients, in this case, the Taiping Princess, is automatically deemed corrupt and immoral.

In contrast to the public-minded Shentu Jia, the Taiping Princess supposedly rode to the imperial compound and attempted to personally persuade the prime ministers of her cause as they left court.[39] But it is to her estate that historians and compilers accord the most prominent role in the creation of her factional power. After she and, among others, Dou Huaizhen 竇懷貞 (d. 713) formed a close factional alliance aimed at eliminating Li Longji, they tried to entice high official Wei Anshi 韋安石 (651–714) to join them by inviting him to the princess's estate.[40] Whenever Dou Huaizhen left court, he went immediately to Taiping's residence, presumably to report on the latest developments and plan their next move.[41]

Other passages impute a sexual dimension to the private visits of male officials to the estates of female heads of factions. *Zizhi tongjian* describes the popularity of estate building among high-ranking women in the first decade of the eighth century as follows: "Consort Shangguan [Wan'er] and the palace women established many outside residences, from which they came and went unrestrainedly. The men of the court often followed them to pleasure sites to seek advancement. The Anle Princess was the most arrogant and abandoned; from the prime ministers on down, many went out of her gate [as private clients]" (上官婕妤及後宮多立外第, 出入無節, 朝士往往從之遊處, 以求進達. 安樂公主尤驕橫, 宰相以下多出其門).[42] Of course, clientage can and did

39. *ZZTJ* 210.6662.

40. *JTS* 92.2957; *XTS* 122.4350; *ZZTJ* 210.6662. Wei Anshi was a decorated official who served in a variety of posts from the late seventh century until his death. In *Zizhi tongjian* the princess's unsuccessful attempt to court him to her side is dated to 711, the second year of Ruizong's Jingyun 景雲 reign (710–11), during which he served successively as director of the Chancellery, director of the Secretariat 中書令, and vice-director of the Department of State Affairs, concurrently holding third rank in the Secretariat-Chancellery 尚書左僕射, 同中書門下三品. Wei Anshi ultimately sided with the crown prince. For Wei Anshi's official biographies, see *JTS* 92.2955–58 and *XTS* 122.4349–51.

41. *XTS* 109.4100; *ZZTJ* 210.6667.

42. *ZZTJ* 209.6623. Many years later, this passage was incorporated by Hu Wokun 胡我琨 (fl. 17th c.) into his work about money, *Qian tong* 錢通 (A Comprehensive Study of Money), illustrating the lasting power, in the collective historical memory, of the image of the Jinglong women as negative paragons of fiscal irresponsibility; see Hu Wokun, *Qian tong*, 21.18a–b.

exist between male patrons and clients and without any sexual relationship. Yet the sexual innuendo conveyed by the phrase "coming and going unrestrainedly" (*chu ru wujie* 出入無節), literally, "exiting and entering without modesty/restraint," is transparent, especially when coupled with the description of private visits by male courtiers hoping to gain higher positions through pleasing the proprietress.

Source materials reveal that these tropes became attached to the Wu-Zhou through Jinglong women leaders early on; an anecdote from the early to mid-eighth century *Chaoye qianzai* brings together the fundamental themes of greed, private favor, and sexual impropriety as enabled by and embodied in the estate. The anecdote again concerns the Zhang family. Zhang Yizhi had a lavish "Seven Treasure Tent" (Qibao zhang 七寶帳) constructed for his mother, Azang 阿臧. After opening with an inventory of the material luxury of Azang's tent,[43] the passage focuses on the bad behavior of its owner:

> Azang had an adulterous affair with vice-director of the Secretariat Li Jiongxiu. She forced him into it. They would drink together from paired cups, meaning "always follow each other." Jiongxiu feared her power and was repulsed by her decrepitude, so he totally let himself go to drinking unrestrainedly and was always dead drunk, to the point that he could be called repeatedly and wouldn't wake up.
>
> 阿臧與鳳閣侍郎李迥秀通, 逼之也. 同飲以盌盞一雙, 取其常相逐. 迥秀畏其盛, 嫌其老, 乃荒飲無度, 昏醉是常, 頻喚不覺.[44]

By the time this episode was chosen for inclusion in *Jiu Tang shu*, it had amplified to become an even scarier (for men) example of the horrible consequences of female rule. In *Jiu Tang shu*, Wu Zhao actually

43. *CYQZ* 3.69. As in other descriptions of luxury real estate, the anecdote opens with an appraisal of the rare treasures lavished by Yizhi upon his mother: the Seven Treasure Tent overflowed with precious metals and jewels such as "had never before been seen or heard of from far-off antiquity" (曠古以來, 未曾聞見), and only the finest and most unusual furs and whiskers were selected to make up the tent itself.

44. *CYQZ* 3.69. See also *TPGJ* 236.1816. The term "forced" (*bi* 逼) also appeared in chapter 1; Empress Dowager Hu supposedly forced the virtuous and talented prince Yuan Yi into a sexual relationship with her. As in Empress Dowager Hu's case, no evidence is provided to substantiate the claim of sexual coercion.

ordered (*ling* 令) Li Jiongxiu to marry Azang.[45] Repulsed by her decrepitude, he did not treat her well, so "Azang was angry and had Jiongxiu sent away and demoted to governor of Dingzhou" (阿臧怒，出迥秀為定州刺史).[46] According to this embellished narrative, the two older women conspired to sexually exploit younger men. Read from a certain perspective, this episode might strike some readers as humorous. If we probe the reason behind the humor, we find that it might lie in assumptions (both ours and the compilers') regarding "normal" expected gender behavior. If the gender roles were reversed (if an older male power-holder forced a younger female favorite into a relationship), the anecdote would definitely not be at all amusing.

Rule by Women and the Destruction of Nature

In retrospective discourses on the women leaders of this period, the landed estate is perhaps the most prominent and frequently discussed symbol of female excess. Their wealthy male contemporaries also, of course, built landed estates, but it is the estates and pleasure sites commissioned by powerful women that are consistently held up as the epitome of perilous self-indulgence. Destruction of nature is implied in accounts of estate building, which required massive adaptation of the natural environment to suit the proprietress's landscaping tastes. In accounts of the other luxury pleasure sites and items created by the leading women of the Jinglong period, more explicit rhetorical weight is placed on destruction of nature. In these accounts, we further see a negative transformation of the same themes that reverberate throughout the seventh- and eighth-century materials. The theme of the microcosm, in particular, is recast so as to stress the destructive conspicuous consumption in which these women engaged. As in earlier praiseful accounts, the retrospective narratives frequently involve the female power-holder's creation of a

45. *JTS* 37.1377.

46. *JTS* 37.1377. The Zhang brothers' *Xin Tang shu* biography also states that Wu Zhao "decreed that Secretariat Director Li Jiongxiu privately serve [A]Zang" (詔尚書李迥秀私侍臧); *XTS* 104.4014.

smaller-scale, artificial construction, which encompasses and "bests" its natural counterpart—though, in these later accounts, the creation and creator are denounced as transgressive and dangerous.[47]

The Anle Princess is most often and most virulently despised for her rapaciousness, and if we are to take the various accounts as literal fact, she "completely exhausted" the imperial treasury at least five times. The well-known story behind Anle's construction of a scenic pond provides the archetypal expression of her destructive greed:

> Kunming Pool was dug by Emperor Wu of the Han. It was abundant in rushes and fish, and the capital region relied on it. During the reign of Zhongzong, the Anle Princess asked for it. The Emperor said, "Ever since previous dynasties, [the pool] has never been given to anyone. It's not possible." The Princess was displeased, so she assembled a massive amount of conscription workers and dug another pond, which she named "Beats-Kun Pool."
>
> 昆明池者,漢孝武所穿,有蒲魚利,京師賴之. 中宗朝,安樂公主請焉,帝曰:"前代已來,不以與人. 不可." 主不悅,因大役人徒,別掘一池,號曰:"定昆池."[48]

The appeal of the story of Anle and Beats-Kun Pool is evinced by its inclusion in a large number of histories, anecdote collections, and other works from Tang to later imperial times.[49] At least part of the anecdote's attractiveness must lie in the way in which it captures succinctly and perfectly the Anle Princess's arrogance and disobedience as both a daughter and a political figure. Her request for Kunming Pool, a time-honored and well-known public resource, in and of itself reveals total disregard for the welfare of the populace. Making matters worse, she responds to

47. As noted by Owen, passages about microcosmic creations can be seen as part of the set period rhetoric in which a miniature imitation bests the real thing. See Owen, *The End of the Chinese "Middle Ages,"* 94–99, for a discussion of the fascination with miniatures in eighth- and ninth-century literature. For a discussion of the broader background of gardening, see Stein, *The World in Miniature*, 1–112.

48. *STJH* c.42.

49. See, for example, *CYQZ* 3.70–71 and 5.124; *DTXY* 3.45; *TPGJ* 236.1817 and 240.1852; *JTS* 183.4734; *XTS* 83.3654; *ZZTJ* 209.6623–24; Zeng Zao, *Lei shuo*, 54.6b; *TYL* 1.9; Wu Zeng, *Nenggai zhai man lu*, 6.136; *XSS* 10.341–42; Wang Yinglin, *Yuhai*, 171.39b–40a; and Chen Yaowen, *Tianzhong ji*, 10.48a (323) and 28.21b (896).

disappointment by amassing a large conscription labor force to build her own, even better, pond.

There are two main variations on this narrative, both of which can be traced back to early sources, *Sui Tang jiahua*, *Chaoye qianzai*, and *Da Tang xinyu*. Two of them, *Sui Tang jiahua* and *Da Tang xinyu*, both end by describing the aftermath of the pond's completion, when Zhongzong leads courtiers to visit Beats-Kun Pool and compose poems in its honor. One literary courtier, Li Rizhi 李日知 (d. 715), is praised for criticizing the proceedings through his poem.[50] His righteous defiance later earned him the praise of Ruizong after the restoration of "order," that is, the return of male power when the Wei faction was defeated in 710.[51] This is a scene of upright but suppressed men banding together and commiserating over their temporary, inappropriate subjugation by transgressive women. These accounts also criticize Zhongzong's emasculation, as he publically celebrates, with or without comprehension of the broader implications, his daughter's derision of his authority.

The two *Chaoye qianzai* passages on Beats-Kun Pool represent another early narrative tradition, which emphasizes the unlawful seizure of land. One passage about the Anle Princess's "sycophantic" (*chan* 諂) associate Zhao Lüwen 趙履溫 (d. 710) describes Zhao's involvement in the construction of the pleasure site as follows: "[He] seized the people's fields and gardens for the princess to construct Beats-Kun Pool, the name of which signified that it was outclassing the emperor's Kunming Pool. It used up one hundred trillion in cash from the treasury" (為公主奪百姓田園，造定昆池，言定天子昆明池也，用庫錢百萬億).[52] The other passage is set up as an explanation of how the Anle Princess earned the demeaning title of "The Mutinous Commoner" (Beini shuren 悖逆庶人).[53] The emphasis is again on improper appropriation of land and forms of imitation that are

50. Li Rizhi's poem shows his concern for the suffering inflicted upon the conscripted workers who made the pond and its attendant lodge, and ironically criticizes the other members of the celebratory party for their disregard of this issue in the midst of their enjoyment: "I only wish you would consider for now the guests' ease, / be sure not to make known the hardship inflicted upon the builders" (但願暫思居者逸，無使時傳作者勞). *STJH* c.42; *DTXY* 3.45.

51. *STJH* c.42; *DTXY* 3.45.

52. *CYQZ* 5.124.

53. *CYQZ* 3.70.

costly in both material and moral terms.[54] Anle not only designed Beats-Kun Pool to "imitate Kunming Pool" (擬昆明池), but also displayed a penchant for the imitation of various natural and historical wonders: "She had rocks piled into a mountain to mirror Mount Hua and drew water into a torrent to mirror the Heavenly Ford" (累石為山, 以象華岳, 引水為澗, 以象天津).[55] As in the *Chaoye qianzai* version of the Zong Chuke anecdote, part of the passage's appeal lies in the dazzling descriptions of the princess's creations, which were ornamented with precious jewels, silks, and paintings.[56] The seductive language of materiality coexists uneasily with the message of condemnation that seeks to criticize Anle's futile attempt to "possess" scenic sites by using her power and wealth to create her own versions.

Later accounts, including both official Tang histories, often mix together these two narrative strands.[57] In most cases, the main narrative elements that are deemed indispensable are the princess's request for the pond, Zhongzong's denial, and her response by creating her own better pond; few later sources follow *Chaoye qianzai* in excluding the interaction between daughter and father.[58] The point is that, in the words of the *Xin Tang shu*, she "asked to make Kunming Pool [her] private pond" (請昆明池為私沼), and, when denied, went on to make her own replica of a national treasure with no concept of the division between public and private domains.[59]

Records about other pleasure constructions commissioned by the powerful Tang women likewise establish microcosmic imitation as a defining characteristic of their conspicuous consumption. Anle's Nine Bends Pool for Floating Wine-Cups (Jiu qu liu bei chi 九曲流盃池)

54. "She seized the people's residences and gardens" (奪百姓莊園); *CYQZ* 3.70.

55. *CYQZ* 3.70–71.

56. The descriptive passages are later incorporated into multiple works; see *XTS* 83.3654; *ZZTJ* 209.6623–24; and *XSS* 10.341–42. *JTS* 183.4734 includes a very brief mention of the Anle Princess's building of Beats-Kun Pool, but it does not flesh out any details or provide a full anecdotal version.

57. See *JTS* 188.4927; *XTS* 116.4242 (although the poem is not quoted in this account); *TYL* 1.9; and *TSJS* 8.245 for a condensed version.

58. A few do follow *Chaoye qianzai*; see *TPGJ* 236.1817 and Zhang Ying 張英 (1637–1708), *Yuding Yuanjian leihan* 御定淵鑑類函, 313.13. *Taiping guangji* also incorporates the *Chaoye qianzai* anecdote about Zhao Lüwen; see *TPGJ* 240.1852.

59. *XTS* 83.3654.

and its attached Stone Lotus Flower Terrace (Shi lian hua tai 石蓮花臺), for instance, "outdid all that was beautiful in the world" (窮天下之壯麗).[60] The Taiping Princess also had built a lavish pool that is explicitly described as an attempt to artificially create a comprehensive, superior microcosm of nature. After dredging the pool to the west of the capital, she "ransomed" or "redeemed" (*shu* 贖) all types of marine life, released them into the pool, and called it Pool of Liberating Life (Fangsheng chi 放生池).[61] "Liberating life," or *fangsheng* 放生, has the Buddhist connotation of liberating captured living creatures intended for slaughter to accumulate merit. This is very much in keeping with the Buddhist piety of the court under Wu Zhao; for the Taiping Princess it was of course also a family tradition. It is unclear how or from where she redeemed the marine creatures, but the entire project appears to have been religiously geared towards large-scale accumulation of merit and grand display of piety.[62] One might also note that the *Sui Tang jiahua* passage describing the people's "reliance" on Kunming Pool suggests fishing; especially given the particular cultural and familial context, the Anle Princess may have wanted the pond for the similar reason of "liberating" marine life.[63]

According to this passage, the Taiping Princess "liberated" the marine species to the delimited space of her artificially constructed pond. In contrast with the species' original ocean or fresh water environment, her pond is a microcosmic universe that she creates and controls. The theme of the microcosm also appears in records about non-architectural forms of materiality. A *Chaoye qianzai* passage describes the Hundred Treasure Incense Brazier (Baibao xianglu 百寶香爐) commissioned by the Anle Princess for the Luminous Perfected Buddhist Temple (Zhaocheng fo si 昭成佛寺). The Princess again depleted the treasury to make the three-foot brazier, which had four doors, deep red bridges, and balustrades.

60. *CYQZ* 3.71.

61. *STJH* c.46.

62. The cryptic ending of the very brief *Sui Tang jiahua* entry on the Pool of Liberating Life might hint at a certain irony in the implied cost of the Taiping Princess's visible act of piety: "The epitaph says: 'Turtles to the water, milfoils in the market'" (墓銘曰: 龜言水, 蓍言市); *STJH* c.46. Li Gang's 李綱 (1083–1140) *Liangxi ji* 梁谿集 connects the phrase with *fengshui* 風水 and divination practices used to determine an auspicious site at which to build one's home; see Li Gang, *Liangxi ji*, 132.16a–b. However, the meaning of this ending quote from an unspecified epitaph remains unclear.

63. Stephen Owen, private communication.

Utilizing the finest and most intricate workmanship, the brazier was decorated comprehensively with images of every type of plant, bird, and animal life, as well as with heavenly musicians, mythical creatures, and flying immortals. The comprehensiveness of the brazier's decoration extends to the laundry list of precious jewels taken from the treasury to adorn it.[64]

Fashion and Adornment as Conspicuous Consumption

The themes surrounding conspicuous consumption in this period are equally striking in accounts dealing with fashion and personal adornment. Archaeological evidence from tombs has provided a window into the fashions current with the imperial women at the turn of the eighth century. The stone sarcophagus of Zhongzong's daughter, the Yongtai Princess 永泰公主 (d. 701), shows women dressed in lively fashions with low-cut necklines and cleavage.[65] Of course, in material terms, there is much that has not survived of the beautiful robes and skirts described in these sources. However, accounts about imperial women's fashion choices help us to imagine the magnificence of their wardrobes at the same time that they link the women's acts of fashion-related conspicuous consumption with destruction and social disintegration. Chapter 2 discussed the way in which, in Shangguan Wan'er's poetic series, donning the clothes of the recluse indicates embodiment of the positive inner traits associated with reclusion. In retrospective accounts, sumptuary behavior continues to embody moral qualities. The clothes worn by these women are reworked into a condemnatory narrative motif indicating their transgression, in particular, their gendered transgression.

The variety, frequency, and detail of accounts about the excessive personal adornment of women leaders of the late seventh and early eighth centuries indeed suggests the fascination that they generated among both writers and readers. The expensive microcosm theme, whereby the woman wears/embodies the natural world, reverberates in accounts of

64. *CYQZ* 3.70. See also *TPGJ* 236.1817.
65. Wu Hung, *The Double Screen*, 98.

personal adornment. The Anle Princess is again depicted as the worst offender. She had constructed a "hundred-plume skirt" (*bainiao mao qun* 百鳥毛裙) made of the plumage of various species of birds. Her behavior set off a disastrous chain of imitation: "Afterwards all of the officials and common people copied her. They scoured the mountains and disturbed the valleys to find exotic birds and unusual animals of mountain and forest. They swept the ground until nothing was left, to the point that their nets and traps had captured and killed a countless number" (以後百官, 百姓家效之, 山林奇禽異獸, 搜山盪谷, 掃地無遺, 至於網羅殺獲無數).[66] According to traditional conceptions of kingship, a good leader uses his or her powerful moral influence to positively transform his or her subjects. The Anle Princess is portrayed as the opposite of this ideal; she sets a bad example and transforms her subjects in a negative way, leading to immense and pointless destruction.

Over time, the story of the Anle Princess's skirt, which is elsewhere called the skirt "worth a hundred million" (直錢一億), accumulates further lore meant to illustrate her general profligacy.[67] *Zizhi tongjian* describes how, in the making of the skirt, flowers, plants, plumage, and animal furs were woven together as tightly as fine millet grains, creating a captivating optical illusion: "Depending upon whether it was looked at straight-on or from the side, in the sun or in the shade, each time a different color was seen" (正視旁視, 日中影中, 各為一色).[68]

One suspects that this account exaggerates the extent of species extinction brought about by the Anle Princess's hundred-plume skirt, but the analogy of female power's destruction of the natural order with the literal destruction of natural species is a powerfully resonant one. The narrative emphases driving this analogy further represent the pointed inversion or negative transformation of seventh- and eighth-century works extolling the natural cosmic unity of contemporary rule.

A dangerous quest for novelty underlies many of the behaviors of the period that are condemned in later literature. The "Five Phases" (*wuxing* 五行) chapters of the dynastic histories provide a useful and fascinating framework for understanding the moral-material conceptualization of

66. *CYQZ* 3.71. See also *TPGJ* 236.1817.
67. *ZZTJ* 209.6624; *XSS* 10.341.
68. *ZZTJ* 209.6624. See also *JTS* 37.1377.

the early Tang female leaders as it crystallized in the ensuing centuries. The "Five Phases" chapters of *Jiu Tang shu* and *Xin Tang shu* each contain a sub-section entitled "Ornamentation Anomaly" (*fuyao* 服妖). In these chapters, *fuyao* is one of many disaster categories including earthquakes (*dizhen* 地震), mountains crumbling (*shanbeng* 山崩), bizarre animals (*shouyi* 獸異), and poetry anomalies (*shiyao* 詩妖), and explicitly gender-related classical cosmological problems such as "the fowl disaster" (*jihuo* 雞禍, when fowl spontaneously change their sex from male to female because women have too much power).[69] The "ornamentation anomaly" refers specifically to the uncontrollable impulse to ornament with an intense frenzy for the most novel fashions. In accordance with the importance of sumptuary laws in conceptions of social order and decline, the "ornamentation anomaly" is associated with the destabilization of the social hierarchy. Like the advent of natural disasters, the appearance of the ornamentation anomaly is seen as a sign of decline; in discussing examples of the ornamentation anomaly, historians impute a moral message to fashion trends, and the early Tang women are fitted into the moral rubric they construct.[70]

The ornamentation anomaly is defined by excessive and improper focus on superfluous appearances to the detriment of the fundamentals. The passages chosen as examples of *fuyao* indicate the connection between this phenomenon and rule by women, as well as provide further evidence of the way in which these narratives accumulate lore over time. The story of the Anle Princess's hundred-plume skirt is a classic example of *fuyao* and appears in both histories. By the time the episode was included in these later standard historical accounts, the number of hundred-plume garments had multiplied. According to *Jiu Tang shu*, in addition to the skirt, the Anle Princess had two belts made and gave one as a gift to Empress Wei.[71] The *Xin Tang shu fuyao* section states that Anle commissioned two hundred-plume skirts, one for herself and one for her mother.[72] As in other sources, we are told that each of these

69. See *JTS* 37; *XTS* 34, 35.

70. For a discussion of *fuyao* from earliest times through the Yuan, see Ma Duanlin 馬端臨 (1245–1322), *Wenxian tongkao* 文獻通考 (A Comprehensive Examination of Literary Documents), 310.2432–36.

71. *JTS* 37.1377.

72. *XTS* 34.878.

precious articles of clothing wasted hundreds of thousands in cash. Afterwards, mother and daughter commissioned the creation of, respectively, a hundred-fur (*baishou mao* 百獸毛) saddle blanket (made of the furs of and in the form of the hundred animals) and a hundred-plume saddle blanket.[73] To demonstrate the way in which this example is a manifestation of the ornamentation anomaly, the histories echo *Chaoye qianzai*'s claim that entire species were nearly extinguished as a result of people's imitation of the Anle Princess.[74]

Other examples of the ornamentation anomaly from the late seventh century through the reign of Ruizong likewise involve material creations by or for powerful women of the time. For instance, the Seven Treasure Tent built by Zhang Yizhi, the "sexually favored minister" (*bi chen* 嬖臣), for his mother is the example provided from Wu Zhao's Zhou dynasty.[75] According to the moral-conceptual rubric of *fuyao*, moral abnormality is manifested materially. Identity is revealed through attraction to materiality, which itself is identified with women deploying their excessive power. The *fuyao* chapter in the later *Xin Tang shu* is especially concerned with this phenomenon. It demarcates a category called "signs of women participating in government" (婦人預事之象), and these signs are entirely material in that they manifest in changing female fashion.[76]

Two of the examples of *fuyao* explicitly hinge on dangerous reversal of the gender hierarchy in a rite of passage that should impress clear delineation of gender roles, the wedding. The wedding ushers in what should, according to traditional gender theory, be a relationship (the marriage) based on permanent and universally accepted separate roles for the sexes, with the male in the superior position and the female occupying a complementary but firmly inferior role. Narratives about royal weddings, in all their materiality, serve as an appealing didactic motif. A comparison between accounts of the early Tang women's weddings and other accounts about wedding scandals, mainly from the latter half of the Tang, allows for an appraisal of subtle continuities and transformations. The analysis aims

73. *JTS* 37.1377; *XTS* 34.878.

74. *JTS* 37.1377; *XTS* 34.878.

75. *XTS* 34.878; *JTS* 37.1377.

76. *XTS* 34.878. The passage decries the inappropriate public visibility of women as seen in the increasingly revealing horseback-riding fashions that became popular over the course of the first century of Tang rule.

to elucidate the way in which female adherence to or violation of sumptuary law is rhetorically deployed as a key marker of gendered morality, which is in turn a benchmark for overall sociocultural morality.

The actual marriage ceremonies of Wu Zhao and Empress Wei are not discussed in detail in early sources. Shangguan Wan'er's appointments to harem positions, first as *jieyu* 婕妤 (fair concubine) and then as *zhaorong* 昭容 (shining consort), are presented more as promotions reflecting her status at court than as reflections of a relationship between her and Zhongzong.[77] The marriages of the Taiping and Anle Princesses, however, are described repeatedly and in detail in various sources and are pivotal to literary-historical reconstructions of their identities. *Jiu Tang shu*, *Xin Tang shu*, *Zizhi tonjian*, *Tangshi jishi*, and other sources often contain analogous accounts of certain episodes, while other episodes are found only in one or two sources, usually the fullest, most engaging, and most judgmental *Xin Tang shu* biographies. The versions contained in the later history may reflect the growth of rumor and lore surrounding the imperial weddings. Indeed, wedding lore does not appear in the eighth-century anecdotal sources, so the original sources for this material are unknown.[78] Yet although the princesses' weddings themselves are not included in the earliest *biji* sources, themes and personality traits suggested by the wedding accounts reverberate with many early anecdotes. The figure of the transgressive bride is a hard-hitting device for condemning female power-holders, as it combines corruption, greed, and sexual innuendo in a figure that is inherently female. The wedding accounts further construct female prerogative as literally and metaphorically unnatural.

Each princess was married multiple times. The Taiping Princess married Xue Shao 薛紹 (663–88) in 681 and Wu Youji 武攸暨 (d. 712), the grandson of her mother's uncle, in 690.[79] The Anle Princess was

77. Indeed, other than the notices of these promotions, there is no evidence that she and Zhongzong were ever a sexual or romantic item.

78. I have not been able to locate a source earlier than *Jiu Tang shu* that contains these wedding-related materials (though *Jiu Tang shu* certainly made use of many earlier sources that are no longer extant).

79. There are additional accounts of unions that never became full-fledged marriages. When Taiping was a young unmarried woman, for instance, Tibet sought marriage with her, a proposal her parents squelched by appointing her Head Abbess of a Daoist Temple;

also married twice, in each case to a second cousin. She married Wu Chongxun 武崇訓 (d. 707), the son of Wu Sansi, sometime after her father's return to the court from his exile in 698.[80] This marriage came to a premature and violent end in 707, when Anle's half-brother, the Crown Prince Li Chongjun, launched a failed coup in which Wu Chongxun was killed. In 708, she was remarried to her deceased husband's cousin (also her second cousin) Wu Yanxiu 武延秀 (d. 710), the son of Wu Chengsi.

The events leading up to and surrounding the wedding ceremonies of the Taiping and Anle Princesses are described as a series of scandals and inappropriate behaviors by the powerful brides. The *Xin Tang shu* biography relates the background story of how Taiping came to marry Xue Shao. In a striking scene, the princess, clad in the purple robes and jade belt of a military official, comes to dance before Gaozong and Wu Zhao. When her parents ask the reason for her actions, she responds without mincing words: "Can you give this [outfit] to the imperial son-in-law [i.e., a husband for me]?" (以賜駙馬可乎?).[81] The emperor is obedient to her wishes: "The emperor understood her meaning and selected Xue Shao to marry her" (帝識其意, 擇薛紹尚之).[82] According to the *Xin Tang shu* narrative, the princess wielded a great deal of power over important decisions affecting her own life, as well as over her father, the

---

see *XTS* 83.3650 and *ZZTJ* 202.6402. In between her first and second marriages, Taiping was briefly married to her cousin Wu Chengsi, but this marriage was quickly annulled because Wu Chengsi was suffering from an undisclosed "minor illness" (*xiao ji* 小疾); see *XTS* 83.3650. These accounts certainly further indicate the favor and power enjoyed by Taiping.

80. Cen Zhongmian points out a *Quan Tang wen* edict attributed to Wu Zhao and entitled "Le'an junzhu chu xiang zhl" 樂安郡主出降制 (The Marriage of the Le'an Princess [daughter of the crown prince]), in which Le'an junzhu is referred to as the eighth daughter of the crown prince (皇太子, who during Wu Zhao's reign would have been Zhongzong, as Ruizong held the title "imperial descendant," or *huang si* 皇嗣). The man she is supposed to be marrying is Yang Shouwen 楊守文 (dates unknown), son of Assistant of Credentials Yang Chenglie from Hongnong 符節朗弘農楊承烈. A variant version of the edict appears in Song Minqiu's 宋敏求 (1019–79) *Tang da zhao ling ji* 唐大詔令集 (Collected Imperial Edicts from the Tang), in which the princess is referred to as Anle junzhu 安樂郡主 (Anle Princess—*junzhu* again indicates the daughter of the crown prince); see Song Minqiu, *Tang da zhao ling ji*, 43.211. However, no further information about the Anle Princess's possible additional marriage is readily available. See Cen Zhongmian, *Tangshi yushen*, 59–60; and *QTW* 95.16a–b (987).

81. *XTS* 83.3650.

82. *XTS* 83.3650.

emperor.[83] This scene was chosen as an example of *fuyao* in the *Xin Tang shu* because it is a striking example of gender reversal and sumptuary transgression; the Taiping Princess, a young woman, wears clothes appropriate for a male military official.[84] The transparent implication is that just as she did not hesitate to wear clothes appropriate for a man, the Taiping Princess "wore the pants" in all areas of her life.

Accounts of the Taiping Princess's wedding to Xue Shao utilize the motif of natural destruction to condemn her as a figure of transgression and disorder. According to *Zizhi tongjian*, "In autumn, in the seventh month, the Princess married Xue Shao. From south of Xing'an Gate reaching to west of Xuanyang Ward, torches were set out in continuous succession, causing many of the *huai* trees planted on both sides of the road to die" (秋, 七月, 公主適薛氏, 自興安門南至宣陽坊西, 燎炬相屬, 夾路槐木多死).[85] The *Xin Tang shu* biography provides an expanded description of the havoc wreaked upon the city by the lavish wedding procession: "[They] took the Wannian District yamen as the wedding lodge. The gate was narrow and could not accommodate the phoenix [wedding] carriage, so an official demolished the wall to allow them to enter. From Xing'an Gate they set up torches in continuous succession, and the trees on the road all became withered and decayed" (假萬年縣為婚館, 門隘不能容翟車, 有司毀垣以入, 自興安門設燎相屬, 道樾為枯).[86] The striking image of the incredibly long lines of torches flanking the road, creating a scene of temporary beauty but bringing long-term destruction, combines aesthetic allure and moral outrage. Moreover, the rhetoric of destruction reconfigures seventh- and eighth-century positive materials (by Wu Zhao, Shangguan Wan'er, and leading court writers, as discussed in chapter 2) that stress communion with nature.

83. After introducing Taiping as Wu Zhao's favorite daughter, the *Tangshi jishi* excerpt from the biography begins with the sentence, "The Emperor chose Xue Shao to marry her" (帝擇薛紹尚之), thus creating the impression that all decisions regarding the marriage rested with Gaozong; see *TSJS* 1.17.

84. See *XTS* 34.878.

85. *ZZTJ* 202.6402. Hu Sanxing's 胡三省 (1230–1302) commentary to *Zizhi tongjian* informs us that the distance between Xing'an Gate and Xuanyang Ward covered three wards. See *ZZTJ* 202.6402.

86. *XTS* 83.3650; see also *TSJS* 1.17.

Rhetorical constructions of the Anle Princess's marriage to Wu Yanxiu are remarkably similar to those of Taiping's marriage, suggesting the archetypal nature of the image. Anle's marriage to Wu Yanxiu was, by all accounts, a dazzling public display equal to her aunt's. In the accounts there is perhaps a stronger emphasis on her subversion of ritual and sumptuary propriety. As was the Taiping Princess's marriage ceremony, it was a state occasion involving the entire court and drawing heavily on the imperial treasury. She borrowed the empress's carriage to convey her from the palace to her residence (假后車輅, 自宮送至第), and high-ranking court officials presided over the affair.

> The expenditure of money and silk was countless. The next day, there was a great meeting of the royal guards at Taiji Palace. The princess came out wearing her kingfisher clothes and bowed twice to the emperor, then faced south to bow to the officials, who all crouched on the ground and kowtowed in response. Wu Youji and the Taiping Princess performed a partner dance to wish the emperor longevity. The royal guards were each given hundreds of thousands of bolts of silk. The emperor visited Chengtian Gate and proclaimed a general amnesty. He feasted the people for three days, all inner and outer officials were granted merit, and the ritual officials were given increases in rank. She [the princess] seized the Grand Princess Linchuan's mansion to serve as her residence. The emperor destroyed people's homes [to facilitate her new home construction], and their resentful cries resonated. When the mansion was completed, the imperial coffers were completely exhausted.
>
> 捐賜金帛不貲. 翌日, 大會衛臣太極殿, 主被翠服出, 嚮天子再拜, 南面拜公卿, 公卿皆伏地稽首. 武攸暨與太平公主偶舞為帝壽. 賜衛臣帛數十萬. 帝御承天門, 大赦, 因賜民酺三日, 內外官賜勳, 緣禮官屬兼階, 爵. 奪臨川長公主宅以為第, 帝徹民廬, 怨聲囂然. 第成, 禁藏空殫.[87]

In spite of his newly insolvent state, the emperor still hosted a huge courtly literary outing to the princess's new home to celebrate.[88] In addition to the lush description of the wedding pageantry, the passage strongly conveys Anle's indifference for the welfare of the people and the state.

87. *XTS* 83.3654–55.
88. *XTS* 83.3655.

In both official Tang histories, Anle's lavish bridal attire is detailed in the *fuyao* chapter: "When the princess was getting married, Yizhou presented her a dress made of the finest silk and emerald gauze. Gold thread was stitched into flowers and birds. They were as fine as hair strands and as big as grain. Their eyes, ears, mouths, and beaks were all complete, and only those with clear eyesight could see them. These are all examples of *fuyao*" (公主初出降, 益州獻單絲碧羅籠裙, 縷金為花鳥, 細如絲髮, 大如黍米, 眼鼻觜甲皆備, 瞭視者方見之. 皆服妖也).[89] The luxury fashion adopted by the bride, including the hundred-plume garments and wedding skirt, inspired imitators, with disastrous results: "Many households of officials copied her. The furs and feathers of the strange and exotic birds and animals of river and mountain were almost plucked to extinction" (百官之家多效之. 江嶺奇禽異獸毛羽, 採之殆盡).[90]

As discussed above, materiality is not just an indicator of greed, but is also wrapped up in laws of sumptuary and ritual correctness, which are in turn intimately identified with conceptualizations of appropriate gender roles. We should not be surprised, then, that descriptions of scandalous misconduct surrounding the princesses' marriages also emerge. These accounts parallel and reinforce the descriptions of their material excess. Different accounts provide layers of lurid additional details regarding the unions, in particular the second marriages, of both princesses. The scandal surrounding Taiping's remarriage to Wu Youji is the most sensational and condemnatory: "Earlier, during the Yonglong reign period [681], she [Taiping] had married the imperial son-in-law Xue Shao. During the Chuigong reign [685–88], Shao was slandered falsely as having plotted rebellion with a group of princes and was executed, [so] Zetian surreptitiously killed Youji's wife in order to marry him to the princess" (初, 永隆年降駙馬薛紹. 紹, 垂拱中被誣告與諸王連謀伏誅, 則天私殺攸暨之妻以配主焉).[91] In the space of only two sentences, the passage manages to put forth a strong statement of Xue Shao's innocence (被

89. *XTS* 34.878; see *JTS* 37.1377 for the parallel account. In *Jiu Tang shu*, Shu 蜀, not Yizhou, gifted the princess with the skirt. In *Jiu Tang shu*, material concerning the Anle Princess's wedding is scattered in multiple chapters. The wedding carriage and procession are described in Zhongzong's "Basic Annals"; see *JTS* 7.146.

90. *JTS* 37.1377; *XTS* 34.878.

91. *JTS* 183.4738; see also *XTS* 83.3650 and *ZZTJ* 204.6466.

誣告與諸王連謀伏誅) while emphasizing the immoral manipulations perpetrated by the women in control, namely, Taiping and especially Wu Zhao. Even though in reality almost two years passed between Xue Shao's execution and Taiping's remarriage,[92] the biography creates the impression that the two events occurred back to back, perhaps suggesting a causal link (that is, Xue Shao was slandered in order was to make way for a newer, preferred husband for the princess). The brevity and incompleteness of these accounts raise more questions than they answer, and the princess's position in this particular intrigue is never clarified. But certainly the violent scandal casts a pall on the descriptions of lavish wedding festivities.

Historical accounts also scandalize the Anle Princess's marriages by implying an attachment to her second husband that predated her first husband's death. Here we can note a progression, as her behavior becomes more unchaste in later sources. Her second husband, Wu Yanxiu, had been held prisoner in Tujue (Eastern Turkic Khaganate) after having been sent there on an unsuccessful diplomatic mission to marry a daughter of the khan. While there, he learned the Tujue languages and dances, which *Jiu Tang shu* claims contributed to the Anle Princess's attraction to him.[93] *Jiu Tang shu* implies, but does not explicitly state, that Anle immediately began a sexual relationship with Yanxiu upon her first husband's death: "When Chongxun died, Yanxiu got [her] favor and soon married the princess" (及崇訓死, 延秀得幸, 遂尚公主).[94] In the *Xin Tang shu* version, we can note a clear change in tone through the added accusation that the princess and Yanxiu had *already* been having an illicit affair before Chongxun's death: "When Chongxun died, the princess had already been having an illicit affair with Yanxiu, so then she married him [when Chongxun died]" (崇訓死, 主素與武延秀亂, 即嫁之).[95] The roughly contemporary *Zizhi tongjian* injects a further aura of scandal into the Anle Princess's marriages by describing her illicit interest in her second husband not just before her first husband's death, but during her betrothal and wedding to her first husband: "Before, when

92. Xue Shao died at the end of the Chuigong reign, in 688, and the Taiping Princess did not marry Wu Youji until 690. See *ZZTJ* 204.6453 and 204.6466.

93. *JTS* 183.4733.

94. *JTS* 183.4733.

95. *XTS* 83.3654.

Wu Chongxun was going to marry the princess, [Wu] Yanxiu was often able to attend upon her at banquets. Yanxiu was good-looking, with a refined bearing, and was good at singing and dancing, so the princess delighted in him. As soon as Chongxun died, she married Yanxiu" (初, 武崇訓之尚公主也, 延秀數得侍宴. 延秀美姿儀, 善歌舞, 公主悅之. 及崇訓死, 遂以延秀尚焉).[96]

Taken together, the accounts surrounding the Taiping and Anle Princesses' various marital choices play a crucial role in the development of their characters in relation to the historical-moral narrative. In Taiping's biographies, for instance, the marriage accounts are placed at the beginning and act as a sort of initial *xing* 興, if it is possible to borrow the poetic term here, an opening image that "stirs" the reader and indicates, often with indirect imagery, the content and message of the ensuing account. The marriage narratives likewise introduce a striking image that stays with the reader throughout the remainder of the narrative and suggests the way in which it will ultimately play out.

Conclusion: Princess Brides and Moral Rule

The marriages of the early Tang brides, characterized by conspicuous consumption, reversal of gender roles, and scandal—a quintessential affront to nature and the social order—are put in bold relief by a contrasting counter-portrayal involving a princess of the late Tang period. The reign of Xuānzong 宣宗 (Li Chen 李忱; r. 846–59) from the end of the Tang dynasty is a popular source of interesting anecdotes in later compilations such as *Tang yu lin* and *Xu shishuo*. Especially compared with the national power of the Tang state during the reigns of Wu Zhao and her sons, the Tang throne was weak and declining during Xuānzong's rule. Yet he is considered a capable Tang ruler (in fact, the last one) for his introduction of reforms, conciliation with Buddhism after the persecution its followers experienced under his predecessor Wuzong 武宗 (Li Chan 李瀍, later changed to Li Yan 李炎; r. 840–46), and centralization

96. *ZZTJ* 202.6628.

efforts. Anecdotes about him reflect this positive assessment and rhetorically construct his manliness as a ruler and father in control. Accounts surrounding the marriage of his eldest daughter, the Wanshou Princess 萬壽公主 (dates unknown), in particular, create fascinating points of comparison with the narrative constructions of the early Tang women and their various marital escapades.

The Wanshou Princess appears in multiple passages that echo motifs from the lives of the powerful women of the turn of the eighth century. Unlike the women who are the main subject of this study, the Wanshou Princess is described as virtuous, obedient, and modest. Whereas Wu Zhao, Empress Wei, the Taiping and Anle Princesses, and Shangguan Wan'er are used as rhetorical illustrations of the disaster created when women have too much power and freedom, the Wanshou Princess is constructed as an example of correct favor, that is, favor based in education and inculcation of right values. Sources inform us that Wanshou was "loved by the emperor" (主, 帝所愛);[97] as a natural consequence of his love, he took measures designed to ensure that she stayed within her proper humble place as a woman. In contrast to the Anle Princess's appropriation of the imperial carriage for her wedding, Wanshou's father made sure that she always used only a copper carriage to complement his reign's emphasis on frugality. Every time he saw her, he took the opportunity to train her through fear and negative example, warning her, in the time leading up to her wedding, not to "disrespect her husband's household or interfere in government affairs" (無鄙夫家, 無忏時事) and not to follow in the footsteps of the Taiping and Anle Princesses.[98] Finally, he issued an edict forbidding remarriage by princesses. As a result of his endeavors, his daughters, including Wanshou, were deferential and competed with each other to behave well.[99]

Whether the stories of the early Tang women specifically guided the writer of the Wanshou Princess's biography or were influenced by a shared typology, the characters of the Wanshou Princess and Xuānzong are clearly constructed as the opposite archetypes from fathers and daughters in the earlier period. Yet the emphases surrounding the royal women are

97. *XTS* 83.3672.

98. *XTS* 83.3672. These passages praising Xuānzong's instructive and strict love for his favorite daughter and its positive results are included in *TYL* 1.5–6.

99. *XTS* 83.3672.

basically the same: greed versus frugality, conveyed materially; disobedience versus obedience; licentiousness versus chastity. Information regarding her marriage further reveals the transformation and continuity of these emphases. In 850, the Wanshou Princess married Zheng Hao 鄭顥 (d. 860), a *jinshi* graduate and promising young minister from a well-regarded official family. The official wedding notice in Xuānzong's *Jiu Tang shu* "Basic Annals" mentions only Zheng Hao's promotions as a result of his increased status as imperial son-in-law.[100] But a possibly later tradition about the Wanshou Princess's marriage, recorded in the *Xin Tang shu* and *Xu shishuo*, evokes the Taiping Princess's scandalous second marriage to Wu Youji.

Like Wu Zhao's favorite daughter, Xuānzong's beloved Wanshou Princess was bride to an unwilling and unavailable groom. When Xuānzong was looking for a worthy mate for his daughter, the minister Bai Minzhong 白敏中 (792–861) recommended the intelligent and talented Zheng Hao. However, Zheng Hao was "obviously [about to] marry a Miss Lu. He had been just about to take her as his wife when his marriage was annulled. He resented it" (顥與盧氏婚，將授室而罷，銜之).[101] Zheng Hao harbored a strong grudge against Bai Minzhong and used his new position of closeness to the emperor to constantly slander Bai to Xuānzong. When the nervous Bai Minzhong stated his case before the emperor, Xuānzong told him that he had long been aware of the truth of the matter and assured Bai Minzhong that he was under his protection.[102] *Xu shishuo* includes a slightly expanded version of this episode, in which Zheng Hao has already been living in Zhengzhou with Lady Lu when Bai Minzhong recommends him as imperial son-in-law. A placard is pasted on his hall demanding his return to the capital to marry the Wanshou Princess.[103] This anecdote is included under the "Wicked and Evil" (*jianxie* 奸邪) section in *Xu shishuo*, and the passage makes it clear that the wicked and evil party is Zheng Hao. Zheng Hao is condemned for his repeated attempts to slander Bai Minzhong, who had only exerted himself to the fullest in the emperor's service.[104]

100. *JTS* 18b.626.
101. *XTS* 119.4306.
102. *XTS* 119.4306.
103. *XSS* 11.400.
104. *XSS* 11.400.

The story of how Zheng Hao came to marry the Wanshou Princess and what happened afterwards transfers the figure of the unwilling royal son-in-law into a context of strict control by a positively evaluated male emperor. Even though she is the royal bride, the Wanshou Princess has no recorded voice in the anecdote. Zheng Hao might appear to be Wu Youji's counterpart, but his standing in the narrative's moral schematic is very different. While Wu Youji is treated with sympathy as a man whose power of choice and manhood were appropriated by a ruthless woman, Zheng Hao is condemned for attempting to subvert the rightful male imperial power and seeking to harm a loyal servant to the throne.

The accounts of Wanshou's wedding are notable for the lack of alluring description that creates a critical moral point in the portrayals of the early Tang women, their weddings, and related material matters. The mention of the modest copper carriage certainly suggests a less lavish ceremony overall. As we have seen in later historians' portrayals of this princess's Tang predecessors, material finery is treated as a sign of corruption and gender role transgression, an indicator of the proper world turned upside-down and plunged into chaos.

Within these narratives, the women's relationship to materiality functions as a powerful communicator of their morality, that is, the way in which their behavior adheres to or departs from the gender-encoded norms believed to order society. The norms are so deeply ingrained as markers of social order or disorder that within narrative accounts of past events, they even trump the well-known historical reality; as a result, the turn of the eighth century, a period of growth and strength for the Tang empire, becomes an era of chaos, and the late ninth century, which marks the decline of the Tang, becomes a period defined by moral rule. We have seen that the destruction produced by the gender anarchy of female rule permeates these accounts and appears as the outer, material manifestation of inner moral-societal chaos. Gender thus plays a pivotal role in the moral evaluations driving these narrative representations of historical actors and events.

FIVE

Gender Anarchy and the Rhetorical Overthrow of Female Rule

The previous chapters have established the importance of sexual insinuation to the rhetorical condemnation of female power-holders in the late seventh and early eighth centuries. Wu Zhao and Empress Wei's associations with religious specialists are often rhetorically cast so as to suggest promiscuity and improper sexual relationships. In a parallel vein, condemnatory narratives about the women's conspicuous consumption, while certainly emphasizing their fiscal irresponsibility and waste, do not limit themselves to the purely monetary realm. The luxury properties of the women leaders and their male factional allies are constructed in the historical memory as edifices of corruption and "private" (that is, sexual and/or seditious) intrigue. The tendency to insinuate a sexual dimension to some of the transgressive behaviors associated with these women indicates the importance of gender as a theoretical construct in these narratives. As women, Wu Zhao, Empress Wei, the Taiping and Anle Princesses, and Shangguan Wan'er were accused of promiscuity and "private favor" where male rulers would not necessarily have been, but the real issue is not so much sex per se, but conceptions of appropriate gender identity and subversion of expectations of their behavior and desires as gendered (that is, female) beings.

In narratives about these early Tang women and their male associates, sexual transgression becomes over time an increasingly indispensable rhetorical element. The growing emphasis on sexual transgression suggests a change in sexual mores that took place between the period being written about and the period of writing. It has become generally accepted that from the seventh to tenth centuries and onward, gender relations and conceptions of appropriate gender roles changed in such a way as to restrict the freedom of women to remarry and participate in public or mixed-gender settings.[1] This is not, however, just a simple case of historical reactions to cultural change. First, the attitudes of individual male writers differ. Second, as the contents of mid-eighth century works such as *Chaoye qianzai* and *Da Tang xinyu* make clear, rumors about the sexual proclivities of Wu Zhao, Empress Wei, and their daughters were already swirling during their lifetimes; rumors of their affairs survive in written records from less than a full generation after their deaths. The ease with which these rumors develop suggests both anxiety regarding the transposition of gender norms and the linguistic ambiguity associated with accounts about sexual favor.

As discussed in chapter 1, in these narratives, it is impossible to distinguish between a male sexual favorite and a male favorite (minister, court figure, etc.) with whom a condemned woman leader interacted closely in a non-sexual context. The style of the accounts is often very terse, and the terms for "favor" in general and for specifically "sexual favor" are interchangeable. *Chong* 寵 ("favor") can and often is interpreted to indicate "sexual favor" or "[took as a] sexual favorite"; *si* 私 encompasses the meanings of "private" and "sexual"; depending upon the context, *luan* 亂 can indicate either rebellion or illicit sexual activity; various words for "secrecy," such as *qie* 竊 and *mi* 密, are also unspecific as regards the nature of the secret.

The obfuscation of the boundary between lover and political ally is also part and parcel of a major thematic goal of the narratives, that is, condemnation of both the woman leader and her close associates. The inner realm of women is associated with rumor, intrigue, and manipulation; the events of the inner quarters have traditionally been shrouded in a layer of mystery greater than those taking place in public court, even when the inner events had great bearing on political developments. Empress Wei's coup in the wake of Zhongzong's death is largely attributed to fallout from sexual scandals.[2] When Zhongzong died by a suspected

1. See, for example, Gao Shiyu, "A Fixed State of Affairs," 270–314; Gao Shiyu, *Tangdai funü*, 138–62; and Tung, *Fables for the Patriarchs*, "Introduction."

2. Wei Yuejiang's 韋月將 (dates unknown) submission of a memorial indicting Empress Wei for her alleged affair with Wu Sansi is portrayed as a catalyst that set in motion Zhongzong's death and Empress Wei's power play; see *JTS* 96.3031. As for Empress

poisoning, "Ma Qinke [one of Empress Wei's reputed lovers] had been attending upon his sickness, so gossip-mongers blamed the crime on Qinke and the Anle Princess. The empress was terrified. She secretly did not declare mourning and summoned her relatives and close allies to the inner quarters to plot a course of action that would keep them safe" (時馬秦客侍疾,議者歸罪於秦客及安樂公主.后懼,秘不發喪,引所親入禁中,謀自安之策).[3] The passage is important because of what it does not claim: while stating that "gossip-mongers" blamed Ma Qinke and the Anle Princess for Zhongzong's death, the account remains silent as to whether or not the gossip-mongers were, in fact, correct.

The histories in which information about the past is encoded are themselves constructed to serve particular interests and express particular perspectives. These factors combined to encourage historians to rely more on rumor in their accounts of the "women's realm" than they would have if they were writing other types of narrative. If we take away the various moral messages that these narratives are used to serve, the men associated with Wu Zhao and other Tang women leaders emerge as a potentially talented group. Xue Huaiyi 薛懷義 (d. 694) was entrusted with important architectural and military ventures;[4] Cui Shi was a talented literary figure; and historical records even concede that Zong Chuke was "by nature intelligent and perceptive" (楚客性明達) and proved himself

Wei's other rumored lovers, according to *Jiu Tang shu*, "At the time, Chancellor of the Directorate of Education Ye Jingneng was good at talismans and incantations, Cavalry Attendant Ma Qinke often decocted medicinal potions, and Imperial Entertainments Director Yang Jun was employed as a cook. They all had unlimited access to the inner chambers. Jun and Qinke were both favored by the empress. It happened that one after another their mothers passed away, and after a week they all resumed their former vocations" (時國子祭酒葉靜能善符禁小術, 散騎常侍馬秦客頗閑醫藥, 光祿少卿楊均以調膳侍奉, 皆出入宮掖. 均與秦客皆得幸於后, 相次丁母憂, 旬日悉起復舊職); *JTS* 51.2174; see also *XTS* 76.3487. Because the mourning period should last for three years, the writer is implying that they were called back to service with improper speed. In fact, Wu Zhao succeeded in 674 in extending the mourning period for mothers to three years, the same length as that for fathers, whether or not the father was still living; see Chen Jo-shui, *Tangdai de funü wenhua*, 212–16. Again, historical sources adopt a particularly negative stance in describing these men; this attitude does not necessarily reflect the view of Ye Jingneng's contemporaries, especially his co-religionists.

3. *JTS* 51.2174; see also *XTS* 76.3487.

4. Antonino Forte has launched an extensive rehabilitation of Xue Huaiyi; see Forte, *Political Propaganda and Ideology in China*, chap. 2, and *Mingtang and Buddhist Utopias*.

adept at giving discerning advice in sticky situations.[5] Yet despite these underlying hints of talent and despite their seeming diversity in terms of origin and vocation, narrative reconstructions of these men suggest blanket sameness characterized by sexual misconduct and the disordering of traditional gender norms.

Particular understandings of gender inform the portrayals of both the women leaders and the men associated with them. In literary-historical accounts, men such as the Zhang brothers, Xue Huaiyi, Huifan 惠範 (dates unclear), Cui Shi, Zong Chuke and his brothers, and high-ranking members of the Wu clan are immortalized as the emasculated lackeys of un-feminine women: male concubines who are fully controlled by their mistresses politically, financially, and sexually. They are the perfect foil for women who appropriate the roles of men. These narratives are driven by the rhetorical use of inverted gender behaviors, whereby the female usurps the "male" position, forcing the male into the inferior "female" position of concubine or dependent. In these accounts, sociopolitical power trumps biological gender; women become "men," and men become "women."

Because gender roles are defined in social context, the analysis in this chapter focuses on gendered character construction within important relationship typologies. The first section explores portrayals involving the interactions between men, in which each man's behavior towards other men evinces his morality and factional alignment. This section focuses on the case study of the court celebration of Zhang Changzong as the reincarnation of a famous immortal, which suggests attitudes to gender and hierarchy. The second section, dealing with the theme of exchange, examines narratives in which the male favorites exchange women under their care. The act of exchange is sexually inverted in narratives in which the male favorites are themselves the object of exchange by female power-holders; the third section explores this construction of the "male concubine" and what it means in terms of the violation of gender norms. The chapter concludes by extending its exploration of gender norms to evaluate the narrative construction of the male concubines in relation to classical definitions of manliness.

5. *XTS* 109.4102. Zong Chuke saved Wu Zhao from becoming embroiled in a nasty border conflict by correctly and swiftly interpreting the meaning of a deceptive missive; see *XTS* 109.4102–3 for details.

Man to Man: Portrayals Involving the Interactions between Men

Narrative condemnation of male figures from the Zhou and Jinglong period stems from their support of the censured female leaders, but their participation in female-led factions and regimes is often conveyed through their roles in man-to-man interactions. Starting from the earliest surviving retrospective records, reactions to Wu Zhao's male favorites, when viewed collectively, provide a dividing point separating upright officials from immoral sycophants. *Chaoye qianzai* contains several disdainful lists of man-to-man toadying: a man named Zhang Ji 張岌 (dates unknown),[6] who followed behind Xue Huaiyi, lifting his yellow canopy and kneeling on the ground to receive Xue's stirrups; Attendant Censor Guo Ba 郭霸 (fl. 690s), who picked up the excrement of Wu Zhao's notorious Head of Punishments Lai Junchen 來俊臣 (651–697);[7] and the famous literary figure Song Zhiwen, who supposedly collected Zhang Yizhi's urine basin.[8] Supporting "immoral" female leadership means endorsing the hierarchy created by "immoral" female leaders. These narratives are driven by the tension between this hierarchy and the "correct" hierarchy envisioned by the historian-compiler and therefore expressed by the narrative heroes he creates. The Zhang brothers are especially popular subjects for this type of anecdote. When the brothers first made their entrance at court, "their official ranks were still low" (官位尚卑), but the empress's obvious favor for them overrode proper hierarchical decorum.[9] Recognizing the ironic disjunction between their official rank and their actual status, "toadying hangers-on called them 'Fifth Young Master' and 'Sixth Young Master,' and after that it became a commonplace" (諂附者乃呼為五郎, 六郎, 自後因以成俗).[10]

6. No official title or place of origin for Zhang Ji is listed in the *Chaoye qianzai* passage (*CYQZ* 5.124). The passage was incorporated into other works; see, for example, *TPGJ* 240.1853; Xu Yingqiu, *Yuzhi tang tanhui*, 8.31a–b; and Chen Yaowen, *Tianzhong ji* 28.34a (912).

7. Guo Ba first received promotion in 690, as a result of his support of Wu Zhao, and subsequently held various Censorate positions. Like Lai Junchen, Guo Ba's official biography is included in the "Cruel Officials" (*kuli* 酷吏) chapter. See *JTS* 186a.4848.

8. *CYQZ* 5.124.

9. *STJH* c.38.

10. *STJH* c.38. See also *TPGJ* 188.1406.

Episodes that define morality in relation to intra-male interactions often hinge upon identifying a sycophantic man who is an ally of Wu Zhao or another female leader, and a manly man who opposes her. In passage after passage, righteousness is equated with a speech or action directed against a male toady and/or sexual favorite; this type of account is especially popular in biographies aiming to demonstrate how their subject(s) embodied the righteous official type. Many of these anecdotes trace their source to the politically oriented *Sui Tang jiahua* and *Da Tang xinyu*, and later they were incorporated into the official histories and anecdote collections such as *Tang yu lin* and *Xu shishuo*. We have already seen examples of this type of account in previous chapters; a few more examples here will deepen our understanding of the tenor of this narrative convention in relation to intra-male interactions.

One instance is provided by accounts of Wei Yuanzhong's 魏元忠 (d. 707) repeated submission of memorials against the Zhang brothers, for which he was maligned by them yet honored by history. Another well-known example is, in turn, found in records describing the young official Zhang Yue's refusal to give false testimony against Wei Yuanzhong on behalf of the Zhang brothers.[11] There are also multiple accounts of Wei Anshi's dramatic stand against Zhang Yizhi at an inner palace banquet. Wei Anshi's defiance of Zhang Yizhi is explicitly hierarchical; he spoke out against Yizhi's command that some merchants play chess before Wu Zhao on the grounds that such a command defied class laws, according to which merchants, as a "lowly lot" (*jian lei* 賤類), were not allowed to approach the imperial banquet.[12] His classist speech earned him the praise of being a "true prime minister" (*zhen zaixiang* 真宰相) from Attendant in the Secretariat Lu Yuanfang 陸元方 (639–701).[13] In a similar vein, Rectifier Fan Xianzhong 范獻忠 (fl. 705–710?) was "considered strong and manly by the court" (朝廷咸壯之) for taking a dramatic stand against the preferential treatment shown to Empress Wei's favorite Zheng Pusi 鄭普思 (dates unknown), a traitorous individual who had been on the verge of escaping punishment for plotting sedition.[14]

11. *DTXY* 2.31; *JTS* 78.2707 and 92.2952–53; *XTS* 104.4015 and 122.4344–45. See also *DTXY* 4.59–60.

12. *JTS* 92.2956; *XTS* 122.4349; *XSS* 3.153–54.

13. *JTS* 92.2956; *XTS* 122.4350.

14. *DTXY* 2.34. Fan Xianzhong was coming to the aid of another "upright" official,

Interpretations of Fan Xianzhong's manliness and righteousness stem from his open rejection of the sociopolitical hierarchy that had exalted a person like Zheng Pusi in the first place.

Episodes structured according to the typology of the righteous official tend to repeat one another to the extent that the specifics fade into the background; they are notable for using a familiar narrative form to assign morality. A *Chaoye qianzai* passage provides an interesting variation on the typical narrative progression. The anecdote begins by introducing Zhao Lüwen, a man who became powerful through his support of the Anle Princess.[15] What is interesting about the anecdote is that after the brief introduction of Zhao Lüwen, it turns into a diatribe against Zhao and his ilk spoken by the compiler Zhang Zhuo, who here refers to himself in the third person by his style name Wencheng 文成. A guest (*ke* 客) asks him what kind of person Zhao was, and he responds negatively and at length: "A violent petty man, with a heart fawning and sycophantic . . . vicious as a ravenous tiger, greedy as a starving wolf" (猖獗小人, 心佞而陷 . . . 猛若飢虎, 貪若餓狼), and so on.[16]

It might seem strange that Zhang Zhuo would feel the need to quote himself in his own work, which would be a perfect vehicle for him to directly express his opinion. Yet through his "speech," he is retroactively placing himself in the role of the brave upright official who opposes toadies serving transgressive women. Indeed, in all of these passages, the righteous official is actually the mouthpiece of the historian, driving home his judgments about politics, gender, and their intersections.

Records on the period thus display a vested interest in constructing and eulogizing particular definitions of masculinity. One of the most fascinating episodes in this regard comes in the form of a series of narratives about how Zhang Changzong came to be praised as the reincarnation of Wangzi Jin 王子晉, the former Zhou crown prince who cultivated the Dao and rode away on a white crane to become an

---

Su Gui 蘇瓌 (639–710), who had been jailed for speaking out against the nefarious activities of Zheng Pusi and Zheng's wife. For more on this episode, see *JTS* 88.2878 and *XTS* 125.4398.

15. *CYQZ* 5.124. Since part of Zhang Zhuo's diatribe is concerned with Zhao Lüwen's involvement in the construction of Beats-Kun Pool, I mention this passage in chapter 4 in the context of the Anle Princess's lavish building activities.

16. *CYQZ* 5.124.

immortal.[17] Materials touching upon this event are diverse in terms of chronology and genre, and the episode is foregrounded by Wu Zhao's veneration of Wangzi Jin and Mount Song (Songshan 嵩山) as part of the founding ideology of the Zhou. Wu Zhao traced her lineage back to the Zhou emperors and thus identified Wangzi Jin as a remote ancestor. In 690, leading up to the establishment of the Zhou, she visited Gou's Mountain (Goushi shan 緱氏山), refurbished the shrine to Wangzi Jin, and composed a commemorative stele, which still survives.[18] In 696, she performed the *feng* and *shan* sacrifices for the second time, and this time the ceremony was performed on Mount Song. A comparison of Zhou-era and later materials indicates that the Zhang Changzong–Wangzi Jin event, originally intended to complement the ideological climate fostered by Wu Zhao, became, after her death, a means of ridiculing Wu Zhao's court. The Zhang Changzong incident of 700 becomes something of an embarrassing narrative appendage to the significance with which Wu herself imbued the cult of Wangzi Jin.

Early to mid-eighth–century anecdote collections provide brief prose accounts of the Zhang Changzong episode that tally in interesting ways with surviving Zhou materials. The terse *Sui Tang jiahua* account states that because of Zhang Changzong's power and wealth, Wu Sansi "said [Changzong] was the reincarnation of [the immortal] Wangzi Jin and composed a poem to give to him" (謂之王子晉後身，為詩以贈之).[19] According to *Chaoye qianzai*, Wu Sansi wrote a record identifying Zhang Yizhi, Changzong's brother, as the reincarnation of Wangzi

17. Wangzi Jin (also known as Wangzi Qiao 王子喬) was the son and designated successor of King Ling of Zhou 周靈王 (d. 545 BCE). Wishing to abandon worldly existence for spiritual pursuits, he gave up his claim to the kingdom. While roaming around the Yi 伊 and Luo 洛 Rivers, he encountered a Daoist master named Fuqiu gong 浮丘公. Wangzi Jin followed Fuqiu gong to Mount Song (Songshan 嵩山) to cultivate his Daoist practice. After over thirty years, he mounted a white crane on Gou's Mountain (Goushi shan 緱氏山) and rode into the heavens, having achieved immortality. See Liu Xiang, *Liexian zhuan jiao jian*, a.65–68. Both Gou's Mountain and Mount Song are in the vicinity of Luoyang, the seat of Wu Zhao's government throughout most of her rule.

18. For a detailed discussion of Wu Zhao's promotion of Wangzi Jin and the stele, see Pei Jianping and Dong Binglei, "Wuzetian yu 'Shengxian taizi.'" For further discussions of the stele's content and significance, see Li Bincheng, "'Shengxian taizi bei bing xu' kaoshi"; and Liang Hengtang and Liang Puhong, "Shuo Zhou Tang biange zai Shengxian taizi bei shang de liuhen."

19. *STJH* c.39.

Jin. Afterwards, a shrine was erected on Gou's Mountain, and all of the "glib flatterers" (*ningzhe* 佞者) at court composed poems to celebrate.[20] Of the poems composed to commemorate the Zhang brothers' "transformation," Cui Rong's (653–706)[21] was judged to be the best and still survives in *Quan Tang shi* under the title "He Liang wang zhong chuan Zhang Guanglu shi Wangzi Jin hou shen" 和梁王衆傳張光祿是王子晉後身 (Matching the Prince of Liang's "Everyone Says Grand Master of Imperial Entertainments Zhang [Changzong] Is the Reincarnation of Wangzi Jin").[22]

Read in conjunction with other early eighth-century poems on cranes, Cui Rong's depiction of Zhang Changzong provides suggestive points of contrast with later narratives about the crane episode. Cui Rong envisions Zhang as Wangzi Jin descended, once again, to join the imperial world after a long absence in the heavens: "There once was a guest who penetrated into the heavens, / pushing back clouds, he descended into the Emperor's domain. // After three years the exalted guest left, / but a thousand years later he has suddenly come back. // In the past he encountered Master Fuqiu, / Now he's the same as [the immortal] Ding Lingwei" (聞有沖天客, 披雲下帝畿. 三年上賓去, 千載忽來歸. 昔偶浮丘伯, 今同丁令威).[23] Wangzi Jin and Ding Lingwei are both

20. *CYQZ* 5.125. See also *TPGJ* 188.1406 and 240.1853–54. In most cases, Zhang Changzong is identified as the reincarnation of Wangzi Jin, not Zhang Yizhi.

21. Cui Rong was one of the most prominent literary figures at the turn of the seventh century. He is famous for composing mourning songs for Wu Zhao (則天皇后挽歌), as well as her "Mourning Stele" (Ai ce 哀冊). A loyal supporter of the late empress, he supposedly died of grief soon after completing the "Mourning Stele"; see *JTS* 94.3000, *XTS* 114.4196, and *TSJS* 8.253–55.

22. *CYQZ* 5.125; *QTS* 68.767. Here it seems that Guanglu 光祿 is short for Yinqing guanglu dafu 銀青光祿大夫, "Grand Master of Imperial Entertainments with Silver Seal and Blue Ribbon," a title that Zhang Changzong was given during the Wansui tongtian 萬歲通天 reign (697), soon after his initial appointment to Wu Zhao's service. The Prince of Liang is Wu Sansi.

23. *QTS* 68.767. According to *Soushen houji* 搜神後記 (Later Record of In Search of the Supernatural), Ding Lingwei returned to his home district as a white crane many years after achieving immortality. However, disappointed with what he encountered, Ding Lingwei sang a song bemoaning the vagaries of time and encouraging others to follow his lead in cultivating immortality, and then he flew away forever. The "thousand years" in Cui Rong's poem refers to Ding Lingwei's song: "There is a bird, there is a bird: Ding Lingwei, / He left home a thousand years ago and just returned today. // The city walls are the same, but the people are not; / why not learn the ways of the immortal, as

immortal crane figures who, after achieving immortality, returned home one last time before leaving the human realm forever.[24] Cui Rong is thus linking Zhang Changzong with legends about immortal cranes and their return, or "reincarnation." As can be expected from the poem's title, Cui Rong explicitly identifies the returning visitor as Wangzi Jin in the form of Zhang Changzong: "The attendant's [Zhang Changzong] talent and appearance are an exact match, / the Pillar Historian, with a different name" (中郎才貌是, 柱史姓名非).[25]

Wu Sansi's own original poem on this topic has not survived, but *Quan Tang shi* does contain a "Xian heng pian" 仙鶴篇 (Piece on Immortal Cranes) attributed to him.[26] Although it definitely does not belong to the same series as Cui Rong's "Matching the Prince of Liang's 'Grand Master of Imperial Entertainments Zhang Is the Reincarnation of Wangzi Jin,'"[27] the poem draws upon time-honored crane lore that seems to have been popular within the Zhou political and cultural climate. The poem opens with an image of the crane's flight: "The white crane flies into the sky; where does it go? / Green fields and purple carriage canopy always leaning against each other" (白鶴乘空何處飛, 青田紫蓋本相依).[28] "Green fields" (*qingtian* 青田) and "purple canopy" (*zigai* 紫蓋) are not just descriptions of beautiful scenery; together, they unite images of immortal cranes with references to the royal court.[29] Wu Sansi's poem

graves pile up?" (有鳥有鳥丁令威, 去家千年今始歸. 城郭如故人民非, 何不學仙冢壘壘). *Soushen houji*, 1.1.

24. Wangzi Jin supposedly flew past his home district and waved before soaring off again into the heavens. See Liu Xiang, *Liexian zhuan jiao jian*, a.65.

25. *QTS* 68.767. The phrasing in the last line might allude to Ding Lingwei's song (城郭如故人民非). *Tangshi jishi* has *cang* 藏, "hidden," instead of *zhu* 柱, "pillar," as the first word of the second half of the couplet; *TSJS* 8.255. The Pillar Historian is Laozi, who supposedly served as a historian beneath a pillar during the ancient Zhou dynasty; see Crown Prince Li Xian's 李賢 (the second son of Gaozong and Wu Zhao; 653–84) commentary to "Zhang Heng liezhuan" 張衡列傳 (Biography of Zhang Heng), in *HHS* 59.1908.

26. *QTS* 80.865–66.

27. Cui Rong's poem is pentasyllabic, while Wu Sansi's is heptasyllabic. Wu Sansi's poem is also much longer.

28. *QTS* 80.865.

29. Green Fields, or Qingtian, is the name of a mountain, which is one of the thirty-six grotto-heavens in Daoism (三十六洞天之一) and is also known as "Green Fields Great Crane Heaven" (Qingtian da he tian 青田大鶴天). The early Tang encyclope-

alludes to the legends of Wangzi Jin and Ding Lingwei, the same immortal cranes linked with Zhang Changzong in Cui Rong's poem: "Although [the crane of] Gou's Mountain [Wangzi Jin], during the seventh month, left for a long time, / [Ding Lingwei of] the Liao River, after a thousand years, may remember to return" (緱山七月雖長去, 遼水千年會憶歸).[30]

Within the context of his theatrical public praise of Zhang Changzong as a crane immortal, Wu Sansi's choice of topic and usage of particular allusions might suggest that this poem was also meant as some sort of panegyric to Zhang. At the very least, the poem seems to participate in Wu Zhao's veneration of Wangzi Jin as part of the founding lore of the Zhou. In depicting Zhang Changzong as the crane immortal, Cui Rong and Wu Sansi drew on commonplace lore associated with cranes.[31] However, their poems are perhaps particularly focused on the idea of the crane's immortality and return, which thematically ties in with the courtly celebration of Zhang Changzong as Wangzi Jin's "reincarnation."

Later descriptions of the "crane incident" elaborate upon earlier materials in such a way as to twist the event into one of the most memorable scenes of decadence associated with Wu Zhao's court. According to *Jiu Tang shu*, *Xin Tang shu*, and *Tangshi jishi*, Wu Zhao, pleased with "a glib flatterer's" (*ningzhe*; Wu Sansi is not mentioned here) praise of

---

dia *Yiwen leiju* 藝文類聚 (Collected Extracts from Literature) quotes Zheng Jizhi's 鄭緝之 (Liu-Song dynasty) *Yongjua jun ji* 永嘉郡記 (Record of Yongjia District), which describes Zhumu Creek (Zhumu xi 洙沐溪), nine miles from Green Fields. According to this record, a pair of white cranes lived in the creek. Every year they had a baby crane, but as soon as it grew up, it left Zhumu Creek, leaving the parents behind. The cranes were "pure white and very cute, and many said that they were raised by divine immortals" (精白可愛, 多云神仙所養). See Ouyang Xun, *Yiwen leiju*, 90.1565. "Purple canopy" (*zigai* 紫蓋) refers to an imperial standard or carriage.

30. *QTS* 80.865.

31. Li Jiao's classic poem "He" 鶴 (Crane) also refers to the legend of Ding Lingwei, specifically, the "thousand years" it took him to return: "Soaring across myriad miles, / to come and go took him several thousand years" (翱翔一萬里, 來去幾千年). It, too, pairs the crane immortal with the royal court: "Having already rested by the side of Qingtian, / he at times roams before the imperial city" (已憩青田側, 時遊丹禁前). *QTS* 60.719. See also annotations by Xu Dingxiang, *Li Jiao shi zhu*, 105, 236. "Crane" is part of a lengthy, loosely organized series of "poems on things" (*yongwu* 咏物), made up of eight-line heptasyllabic poems on natural phenomena, writing implements, fabrics, fruits, plants, animals, and birds.

Zhang Changzong, had her young favorite wear feathered clothes, play the flute, and frolic around for the amusement of the court.[32] Zhang Changzong thus dressed up to play the role of immortal crane, or crane-riding immortal, returned to strut in the imperial world. Although this narrative only survives in later sources, Cui Rong's poem seems to cleverly reference both the crane legend and the contemporaneous court display: "The imperial guard divides the banners, / next to the royal countenance is [the one wearing] feathered clothes" (天仗分旄節, 朝容間羽衣).[33] The "feathered clothes" seem to function as both a reference to the immortal and a description of the actual clothes supposedly worn by Zhang Changzong, who was never far from the "royal countenance."

An underlying goal of Cui Rong's poem was surely to glorify the imperial court's divine power through reference to the re-enactment of the legend. In Wu Sansi's official biographies, however, his interactions with the Zhang brothers are presented as key evidence of his "extremely fawning" (*qing yu* 傾諛) personality.[34] According to *Xin Tang shu*'s more vitriolic account, "at the time Xue [Huaiyi] and the two Zhangs were spreading around their poison, and Sansi worked his hardest to degrade his virtue [in serving them]. He served as Huaiyi's carriage driver and sang the praises of Changzong, saying that the latter was the reincarnation of Wangzi Jin. He led all the ministers in singing licentious songs. They were all blushing shamefacedly, as any normal person would, but [Wu Sansi] wasn't ashamed" (薛二張方烝蠱, 三思痛屈節, 為懷義御馬, 倡言昌宗為王子晉後身, 引公卿歌咏淫汙, 靦然如人而不恥也).[35] In this passage, the rhetoric of condemnation has intensified and become sexualized. The courtiers do not merely compose normal poems matching Wu Sansi's to celebrate the occasion, but rather sing "licentious songs." Moreover, his obsequious behavior is described as "degrading his virtue" (*qu jie* 屈節), a phrase that carries moral and sexual connotations.

The anecdotal lore connecting the Zhang brothers with cranes is related to an institution established by Wu Zhao in 699 called "Guiding

32. *JTS* 78.2706; *XTS* 104.4014; *TSJS* 8.254–55. *Ningzhe* 佞者 is the same term used in *Chaoye qianzai*.

33. *QTS* 68.767.

34. *XTS* 206.5840.

35. *XTS* 206.5840. In depicting the same incident, *Jiu Tang shu* does not mention the "spreading poison" (*zheng gu* 烝蠱) of Wu Zhao's consorts; see *JTS* 183.4735.

the Immortal Cranes Bureau" (Konghe fu 控鶴府). The name of the bureau was soon after changed to "Palace Service Bureau" (Fengchen fu 奉宸府) and put under the direction of the Censorate.[36] Prominent courtiers such as Wei Yuanzhong, Yan Zhaoyin 閻朝隱 (fl. ca. 690s–710s?), Xue Ji 薛稷 (649–713), and Ji Xu 吉頊 (d. 700) held positions in these bureaus, but the histories claim that they were established solely for the purpose of setting up court positions for the Zhangs.[37] The *Jiu Tang shu* and *Xin Tang shu* biographies of the Zhang brothers both describe the Konghe fu / Fengchen fu as a party group, not a governmental bureau: "Whenever there was a banquet, [Wu Zhao] would command [them / her favorites] to make fun of the courtiers and officials as hilarious entertainment. When there was an inner palace banquet, the two Zhangs and all the Wus would be seated in attendance, engaged in gambling and raucous revelry. The gifts bequeathed [to them by Wu Zhao] were countless" (每因宴集, 則令嘲戲公卿以為笑樂. 若內殿曲宴, 則二張、諸武侍坐, 樗蒱笑謔, 賜與無算).[38] Both biographies describe the crane dress-up scene as occurring in the midst of this hedonistic atmosphere.[39] The vagueness with which the functions of the Konghe fu / Fengchen fu are described enables the imputation that it was nothing more than a "party bureau." At the same time, the vagueness should also cause the reader to question this imputation, if only because it accords so well with the crystallizing image of the female-led government of the time as characterized by excess and corruption.

Descriptions of the crane reincarnation and attendant attitudes towards Wu Zhao's sexual favorites suggest particular perspectives on gender and divinity, which also inform other records on the period. A *Chaoye qianzai* anecdote about Zong Chuke's treatment of Xue Huaiyi closely parallels narratives about Wu Sansi, the Zhangs, and divine reincarnation. Because "Abbot Xue" (Xue shi 薛師, i.e., Xue Huaiyi) currently

36. *JTS* 6.128.

37. "Earlier [Wu Zhao] had established the official positions in the 'Guiding the Immortal Cranes Bureau,' soon changed to the 'Palace Service Bureau,' for her favorites Zhang Yizhi and his younger brother Changzong" (初為寵臣張易之及其弟昌宗置控鶴府官員, 尋改為奉宸府); *JTS* 6.128. See also *XTS* 76.3484 and 104.4014; and *JTS* 78.2706.

38. *JTS* 78.2706.

39. See *JTS* 78.2706; *XTS* 104.4014–15.

benefited from sexual favor,[40] the predictably "sycophantic" (*channing* 諂佞) Zong Chuke composed a record in two chapters saying that Abbot Xue was "a sage descended from heaven. No one knew what era he was originally from, but he was Sakyamuni Buddha's second appearance and the reincarnation of Bodhisattva Guanyin" (論薛師之聖從天而降, 不知何代人也. 釋迦重出, 觀音再生).[41] Zong Chuke was supposedly promoted as a result of this composition.[42] This anecdote clearly follows the same narrative progression as do the accounts about Wu Sansi, Zhang Changzong, and Wangzi Jin. More importantly, the theme of reincarnation is meaningful within the cultural milieu and image of the period. Wu Zhao famously claimed, as part of the propaganda campaign leading up to the establishment of the Zhou dynasty, to be the female incarnation of Maitreya Buddha.[43] This was a campaign in which Xue Huaiyi, as abbot of the White Horse Monastery (Baima si 白馬寺), played an important role. Xue was appointed head of the group of monks commissioned to compose a commentary to the Great Cloud Sutra identifying the empress with a female bodhisattva, the queen Jingguang 淨光, who was an incarnation of Maitreya.[44] The anecdotes about Zhang Changzong and Xue

40. Literally, "held [the type of] favor [formerly held by] Lao Ai" (有嫪毐之寵). Lao Ai (d. 238 BCE) was the sexual favorite of the mother of the first emperor of Qin. The probably apocryphal story of Lao Ai is found in the biography of Lü Buwei 呂不韋 (291–235 BCE), who served the Qin. When Lü Buwei was serving the successor of the heir apparent of Qin, the successor desired Lü Buwei's beautiful concubine, who was then in the early stages of pregnancy with Lü Buwei's child. Lü Buwei gave her to him, and she gave birth to Zheng, the future first emperor of the Qin dynasty. According to the story, the concubine was extremely licentious, and in an attempt to curb her illicit pursuits, Lü Buwei found for her a very well-endowed man named Lao Ai, whom they falsely proclaimed was castrated so as to allow him free access to her chambers. She moved into a separate palace in Yong so as to be able to see him more easily and gave him run of the household. When Lao Ai attempted to seize political power, the affair was exposed, and Lü Buwei was executed along with Lao Ai, his entire clan, and his associates. See *SJ* 85.2508–13.

41. *CYQZ* 5.125.

42. *CYQZ* 5.125.

43. See *JTS* 93.2981 for Censor Guo Ba's submission of a memorial proclaiming Wu Zhao to be the reincarnation of Maitreya Buddha.

44. For detailed discussions of these issues, see Forte, *Political Propaganda and Ideology in China*, chap. 3; and Guisso, *Wu Tse-t'ien and the Politics of Legitimation*, chap. 4. Wu Zhao's use of Maitreyan ideology is reflected in her adoption during the Zhou of the lengthy title "Compassionate One [Maitreya] the Peerless, Golden Wheel-Turning

Huaiyi seem to be part of a vogue for claiming to be the reincarnation of immortal figures or Buddhas. Zong Chuke and Wu Sansi praise the empress's sexual favorites as "matching" her because they are also reincarnations of special mythical and/or religious figures.

The full significance of this reincarnation "matching" becomes apparent when it is considered in tandem with what Guisso terms the "state ideology" of the Zhou, the means by which Wu Zhao justified her reign. Because of the "unprecedented nature" of Wu Zhao's dynasty, she needed to legitimate her reign with an ideology different than those used by her predecessors.[45] Although she drew upon elements of all of the Three Teachings, Buddhist doctrine played an especially important role in establishing Wu Zhao's personal legitimacy. According to the doctrine of reincarnation, a being's identity remains constant in spite of gender change. Wu Zhao's selection of Jingguang as her previous incarnation suggests both her perception of the need to address her gender identity and the possible fluidity or equality of the genders, at least in theory, via the doctrine of reincarnation; the Great Cloud Sutra commentary suggests that Wu Zhao is the reincarnation of not only Jingguang, but also Maitreya Buddha. The anecdotes about the previous incarnations of Zhang Changzong and Xue Huaiyi harken back to the Zhou state ideology and the establishment of Wu's reincarnated identity, which may well have created a rippling effect, whereby other prominent personages were likewise "identified" as the reincarnations of lofty figures. In anecdotes describing the "true" divine identities of Wu's infamous favorites, however, claims hinging on reincarnation are presented by later writers with satirical condemnation, part and parcel of the illegitimacy of the state ideology from which they stemmed.

Sage and Holy Emperor" 慈氏越古金輪聖神皇帝. She held this full title briefly in 695 before simplifying it; see Guisso, *Wu Tse-t'ien and the Politics of Legitimation*, 45 and 226, note 157; *FSWJJ* 4.26; *JTS* 6.124; *XTS* 4.95; and *ZZTJ* 205.6492, 6494, 6497. I adopted the translation of the title, with slight modification, from Guisso, *Wu Tse-t'ien and the Politics of Legitimation*, 45.

45. See Guisso, *Wu Tse-t'ien and the Politics of Legitimation*, 26–28, 34–50.

The Exchange of Women and Constructions of Masculinity

The possibility for fluid gender identity is also undercut by the pervasive emphasis in retrospective records on particular definitions of masculinity, which are conveyed by gendered social interactions. Hierarchical relationships between men traditionally are expressed not only through the ways in which men relate directly to each other, but also through interactions that are mediated by women. These interactions often involve the exchange of women by men.[46] Socially sanctioned exchange or seizure of women cements group solidarity and hierarchies among men, not to mention reinforcing the patriarchal gender hierarchy. In accounts involving the male partisans of the seventh- and eighth-century female leaders, the exchange is never appropriate; these scenes consistently underline the male partisan's disregard for accepted class- or virtue-based hierarchy.

Almost all of these men are accused of some form of sexual misconduct relating to the seizure or improper exchange of women. Some passages weave together the "upright official denounces male sycophant" narrative and the convention of sexual misconduct. The monk Huifan, a partisan of the Wei faction and then the Taiping Princess, "abused his power to forcibly abduct a living man's wife" (恃權勢逼奪生人妻; worse than abducting a widow or unmarried woman because she already "belonged" to a living husband).[47] When local authorities were unable to resolve the issue, the woman's husband brought his grievance before Vice Censor-in-Chief Xue Deng 中丞薛登 (647–719) and Vice Director in the Censorate Murong Xun 侍御史慕容珣 (dates unknown). Murong Xun hesitated to take on the case, but Xue Deng bravely spoke out. He was demoted in official position but exalted in public opinion (*shi yi* 時議) among, of course, those fellow "upright men" whose opinions matter.[48]

In other passages, we can detect a fascination with various forms and layers of gendered exchange. A passage describing Cui Shi's quest for

46. For a theoretical Marxist analysis of women as exchanged commodities, see Irigaray, *This Sex Which Is Not One*, in particular, "Women on the Market."

47. *DTXY* 4.61.

48. *DTXY* 4.61.

high position, for instance, condemns Cui for engaging in exchanges that violate accepted gendered and moral hierarchies:

> Cui Shi sycophantically served Zhang Yizhi and Wei the Commoner [Empress Wei]. When Wei was executed, he attached himself to the Taiping Princess and was her sexual favorite.[49] His wife was beautiful, and he gave her and their two daughters to the harem of the crown prince; thereupon he was made vice director in the Secretariat and manager of affairs. Once someone wrote a placard criticizing him, and it said: "He deputed his mediocre talents to the princess's household and sent his alluring wife to the Spring Palace."
>
> 崔湜諂事張易之與韋庶人. 及韋氏誅, 附太平, 有馮子都, 董偃之寵. 妻美, 與二女並進儲闈, 為中書侍郎, 平章事. 或有人牓之曰: 託庸才於主第, 進艷婦於春宮.[50]

The disdain for Cui Shi stems from his flagrant disregard for sexually encoded gender protocol. Cui Shi doubly forfeits his manhood, first by adopting the female-identified, inferior position of sexual servant and second by violating his duty as husband and father. Although gifting one's daughters to an imperial harem would not have been considered dishonorable, giving one's wife to the harem was highly unusual and would have been deemed shameful. The message on the placard is meant to encapsulate the way in which Cui Shi sold both himself and his wife.

An extended and nuanced example of the way in which men's exchange of women is used as a narrative marker of masculinity and morality is provided by an anecdote that describes Wu Chengsi's tragic seizure of Qiao Zhizhi's 喬知之 (d. 697) favorite slave girl. Versions of the episode are included in *Sui Tang jiahua*, *Chaoye qianzai*, and vari-

49. Literally, "enjoyed favor equivalent to that [formerly] enjoyed by Feng Zidu and Dong Yan." Feng Zidu and Dong Yan are both famous historical male sexual favorites from the Han dynasty. Feng Zidu was the famous general Huo Guang's 霍光 (d. 68 BCE) slave and beloved sexual favorite. Feng Zidu gained a great deal of political power as a result of his relationship with the general, but after his death, he became sexually intimate with Huo Guang's widow. See *HS* 68.2950–55. Dong Yan's mother was a pearl seller who often visited the palace during the reign of Emperor Wu of the Han (r. 141–87 BCE). After her husband died, Grand Princess Dou took the handsome young man as her lover. See *HS* 65.2853–57, 97a.3949.

50. *CYQZ* 5.125. "Spring Palace" refers to the residence of the crown prince.

ous other sources.[51] The terse *Sui Tang jiahua* account omits all details regarding the relationship between Wu Chengsi, Qiao Zhizhi, and the slave girl, whose name is not given: "Rectifier of Omissions Qiao Zhizhi had a favored slave girl who was seized by Wu Chengsi" (補闕喬知之有寵婢, 為武承嗣所奪).[52] *Chaoye qianzai*'s fleshed-out narrative fills in the details while emphasizing Wu Chengsi's deviousness: "Zhou Rectifier of Omissions Qiao Zhizhi had a slave girl named Biyu who was beguilingly beautiful, knew how to sing and dance, and had literary talent. Zhizhi favored her and didn't marry because of her. The false Prince of Wei, Wu Chengsi, borrowed her to teach his concubines how to do their makeup and hair, [but then] he took her for himself and wouldn't return her to Zhizhi" (周補闕喬知之有婢碧玉, 姝艷能歌舞, 有文華, 知之時幸, 為之不婚. 偽魏王武承嗣暫借教姬人粧梳, 納之, 更不放還知之).[53] The *Chaoye qianzai* opening is structured around the issue of status. Obviously the unfortunate slave-girl has the lowest status of all and is destined to be passed from owner to owner. But the hierarchical interplay between Wu Chengsi and Qiao Zhizhi is no less clear; Wu Chengsi, armed with "false" high status, abuses his power to take what "belongs" to another man.

As the episode unfolds, the hierarchical relationship between the two men continues to drive the narrative. According to all accounts, Qiao Zhizhi sent a poem of longing to the girl to express his love.[54] The poem is a love-lament written in the voice of Shi Chong's 石崇 (249–300) concubine Green Pearl (Lüzhu 綠珠), who committed suicide when another, more powerful man wanted to take her away from Shi Chong.[55] The poem

51. See, for example, *BSS* 1.7–8 (under the heading "Qing gan" 情感 [Moved by Emotion]); *JTS* 190b.5012; *TPGJ* 274.2158–59; *XTS* 206.5837; *TSJS* 6.172–73; *QTS* 81.875–76; and Tao Zongyi 陶宗儀 (fl. 1360–68), *Shuo fu* 說郛, 38.3 (2553).

52. *STJH* c.39.

53. *CYQZ* 2.31.

54. In *Chaoye qianzai*, the poem is called "Lüzhu yuan" 綠珠怨 (Green Pearl Lament), though most other sources refer to it as "Lüzhu pian" 綠珠篇 (Piece on Green Pearl). In *Taiping guangji* and *Benshi shi* the poem's title is not mentioned. See *STJH* c.39, *BSS* 1.7–8, *JTS* 190b.5012, *TPGJ* 274.2158–59, *XTS* 206.5837, and *QTS* 81.875–76. In *Benshi shi*, *Jiu Tang shu*, *Taiping guangji*, *Xin Tang shu*, and *Quan Tang shi*, the girl's name is given as Yaoniang 窈娘 instead of Biyu.

55. Green Pearl was one of the "Four Beauties of the Jin Dynasty" and was purchased as a concubine by the wealthy official and literary patron Shi Chong. Like Biyu (or

seems to have been designed to provoke Biyu into committing suicide by reminding her of the "romantic" example of Green Pearl: "Parting from you, I will never be able to bear it, / in vain struggling to hide with my sleeve the harm done to my powder [by her tears]. // A lifetime of the resentment of parting spent in a tall tower, / all at once my complexion lost because of you" (辭君去君終不忍, 徒勞掩袂傷鉛粉. 百年離恨在高樓, 一代容顏為君盡).[56] After reading the poem, Biyu was filled with sadness and did in fact commit suicide by throwing herself into the well. Wu Chengsi found the poem and, as recorded in *Chaoye qianzai*, "was enraged, so he goaded slanderous people to indict him [Qiao Zhizhi]. So [they] beheaded Zhizhi in South Market. His household was destroyed and his registration was removed and his property confiscated" (大怒, 乃諷羅織人告之. 遂斬知之於南市, 破家籍沒).[57]

From today's standpoint, Qiao Zhizhi and Wu Chengsi may both be condemned for treating Biyu as property whose death is meaningful only in terms of how it reflects upon their statuses. In the various accounts of this episode, however, the main focus remains firmly on condemnation of Wu Chengsi and, consequently, on the interplay between the two men. Qiao Zhizhi appears only twice in *Jiu Tang shu* and three times in *Xin Tang shu*.[58] His brief *Jiu Tang shu* biography is almost entirely concerned with the Wu Chengsi–slave girl incident.[59] In Wu Chengsi's *Xin Tang*

Yaoniang), she was beautiful and talented in music. Sun Xiu 孫秀 (d. ca. 301), an associate of the Prince of Zhao, Sima Lun 趙王司馬倫 (d. 301), who then held power, heard of Green Pearl's beauty and wanted to take her from Shi Chong. An armed confrontation below Green Pearl's tower ensued. In order to avoid being taken by Sima Lun, Green Pearl committed suicide by jumping from the tower. See *JS* 33.1008.

56. *CYQZ* 2.31. There are several variant versions of the poem, though the general import is the same. See *STJH* c.39, *Benshi shi* 1.1, *TPGJ* 274.2159, *TSJS* 6.172, and *QTS* 81.875–76.

57. *CYQZ* 2.31. According to *Sui Tang jiahua*, Wu Chengsi was "shocked and upset" (*jingyuan* 驚惋) when Biyu died, and "when he saw the poem, he held a great grudge [against Qiao Zhizhi]. In the end, because of this Zhizhi was maligned and perished" (既見詩, 大恨. 知之竟坐此見構陷亡). *STJH* c.39.

58. He is given a brief biography in *Jiu Tang shu*; *JTS* 190b.5012. His other appearances are confined to a notice of his death in *Xin Tang shu*, inclusion of his literary collection in the bibliographic catalogues of both histories, and, in *Xin Tang shu*, an appearance in Wu Chengsi's biography. See, respectively, *XTS* 4.90; *JTS* 30.2075 and *XTS* 60.1600; and *XTS* 206.5837.

59. *JTS* 190b.5012.

shu biography, the story is quoted as an illustration of Wu Chengsi's evil character: "His nature was violent and he thought nothing of perpetrating disaster" (性暴輕忍禍).[60] The important role played by verse in the tale no doubt led to its incorporation into *Benshi shi* and *Tangshi jishi*. *Tangshi jishi* includes several works by Qiao Zhizhi, but the work that is given by far the most attention is "Green Pearl," no doubt because of its interesting back-story. One gets the impression that, were it not for his supposed involvement in this scandal, almost no information about Qiao Zhizhi would have survived. The various versions of this episode are united by their emphasis on Wu Chengsi's subversion of the "correct" hierarchy, and Qiao Zhizhi is constructed as a sympathetic figure because his rights are appropriated by an illegitimate power-holder.

The tragedy of Biyu reflects particular narrative constructions of masculinity, whereby manhood is defined vis-à-vis conduct within social relationships. Conceptions of masculinity are likewise suggested by more ambivalent cases, such as that of the wily Ji Xu, a partisan of Wu Zhao who served in important posts during the Zhou dynasty.[61] Finding himself out of favor because his father had been condemned to execution for accepting bribes, Ji Xu offered his two younger sisters to Wu Chengsi as a bribe.[62] Wu Chengsi accepted, loaded his booty onto a cattle cart, and drove off with them. They did not speak for three days, and Wu Chengsi, finding this strange, questioned them about it. The sisters cleverly responded in a manner calculated to enlist Wu Chengsi's sympathy for themselves and their family: " 'Our father violated the laws of the state, and we are worried that we won't have anything to rely on anymore.' Since Chengsi was enjoying imperial favor, he pardoned their father from execution. Then he advanced Xu to the Directorate of the Dragon Horses and later promoted him to vice censor-in-chief and vice director of the Bureau of Appointments" ("兒父犯國法, 憂之無復聊賴." 承嗣既幸, 免其父極刑, 遂進項籠馬監, 俄遷中丞, 吏部侍郎).[63]

Ji Xu's sisters skillfully manipulated Wu Chengsi; they first whetted his curiosity by not speaking for three days and then, when finally coaxed to speak, played into his ego by calling attention to their utter helplessness

60. *XTS* 206.5837.
61. For his official biographies, see *JTS* 186a.4848–50 and *XTS* 117.4257–59.
62. *CYQZ* 5.124–25. See also *TPGJ* 240.1853.
63. *CYQZ* 5.125.

and reliance on his mercy. The main and final point, however, concerns Ji Xu: "[Ji Xu] didn't advance through talent, but only because his two sisters implored Chengsi" (不以才昇，二妹請求承嗣故也).[64] Even if we posit the sisters' complicity in some sort of family plot, Ji Xu's means of advancement excludes him from the ranks of upright men. Instead of following a manly course, Ji Xu becomes the procurer for his own sisters; he is dependent upon them for advancement even as he trades them.

Xin Tang shu takes this episode as the opening and character-revealing anecdote of Ji Xu's biography, meant to illustrate the historian's overall assessment of his essential nature as *yinke* 陰克, "succeeding through shady, secret means."[65] The assessment of *yinke* is played out in a somewhat ambiguous manner in the *Xin Tang shu* biography; sometimes Ji Xu appears as a positive trickster figure, and sometimes he is denounced for his sneakiness. In one passage he is described as the empress's confidant who used this important role to sway her in the right direction: "Xu was, moreover, resourceful and sharp-witted, so the empress held him close to her heart" (頊又彊敏，故后倚為腹心).[66] His advice was instrumental, for instance, in swaying Wu to finally execute the cruel official Lai Junchen.[67] Ji Xu is also credited with bringing about, again in a tricky manner, the recall of Zhongzong in the final years of the Zhou, which ensured the eventual return to Tang rule.[68] The biography's closing summary verse (*zan* 贊) further emphasizes artful cunning as Ji Xu's defining characteristic: "Xu advanced in an immoral way, something that the Great Man considers shameful. However, following his feelings, he suppressed the Wu and buoyed the Tang. His help was well-intentioned and upright, so his virtue was far-reaching" (頊進不以道，君子恥之．

64. *CYQZ* 5.125.

65. *XTS* 117.4257. In *Jiu Tang shu*, on the other hand, Ji Xu is placed in the "Cruel Officials" (*kuli* 酷吏) section. See *JTS* 186a.4848–50. In *Taiping guangji*, Ji Xu also appears in the "Cruel and Violent" (*kubao* 酷暴) section (in another anecdote), and the episode involving Ji Xu's sisters is placed in the "Sycophantic and Fawning" (*channing* 諂佞) section. See *TPGJ* 268.2101 and 240.1853.

66. *XTS* 117.4258.

67. See *XTS* 117.4257–58.

68. Ji Xu essentially tricked the Zhang brothers into joining the Li-Tang restoration cause. He advised them that the only way to ensure their safety after Wu Zhao's death was to go with the times and urge Wu to recall her sons. See *XTS* 117.4258–59.

雖然，一情區區，抑武興唐，其助有端，則賢炎遠矣).[69] Ji Xu, a clear partisan of Wu Zhao, is at best an astute opportunist, always second best to men who are unswervingly direct, even to the point of appearing suicidal, in their championing of what is "right."

Gender Anarchy and the Exchange of Men by Women

In these passages, although women are the object of exchange, the real interchange occurs between the men, and the trade is in status and rhetorical-moral manhood. As suggested most explicitly in the *Chaoye qianzai* passage about Cui Shi, a man's willingness to trade in his morality (spiritual or mental manhood) is not so far removed from exchange of his physical manhood in sexual service. Indeed, perhaps the most unique materials on gendered exchange during this period involve the explicit exchange of men by women. These materials are driven by a contextual understanding of gender as defined not so much by biology as by sociocultural status. As Tung notes, the object of desire of a powerful ruler, whether male or female, was inherently considered feminized within the tradition.[70] When women usurp the male identity of leader, along with his attendant political and sexual decision-making power, men are forced into the inferior position identified with the female. Like his female counterpart, the male concubine is traded around between people who control him, with his only chance of advancement lying in sexually pleasing the mistress. These accounts thus accomplish the rhetorical transformation of the era into the reign of gender anarchy, in which the sanctioned positions of male and female are plunged into chaos.

Ironically, gender anarchy is conveyed through the increasing narrative emphasis on the sexuality and physicality of the historical players involved; the maleness of the male concubines is rhetorically feminized, at the same time as it becomes an object of desire and exchange. In the centuries that passed between the composition of anecdotal collections such as *Chaoye qianzai* and *Sui Tang jiahua* and the compilation of the

69. *XTS* 117.4259.
70. Tung, *Fables for the Patriarchs*, 66.

official histories, a body of lore developed that stressed the deviant sexual culture of the Zhou through Jinglong periods, deviance embodied in the portrayals of male favorites such as Xue Huaiyi and the Zhang brothers. The horror inspired in generations of historians and writers by the image of an elderly woman exerting her sexual prerogative over young men is still palpable in more recent scholarly works on the subject, which consistently address the issue of the sexual mismatch between Wu and her favorites.[71] The need to explain the older empress's rumored sex life with young men indicates a continued emphasis on her aberrance or difference as a female emperor; this is not an issue that would ever be seen as requiring comment in relation to a male ruler.[72] These discussions also suggest the importance of exploring the definitions of gender that inform portrayals of the male favorites of the period.

Xue Huaiyi is arguably the most colorful and one of the most notorious of the men who "served" female leaders such as Wu Zhao. His portrayal adheres in many respects to the archetype of the male sexual favorite. His humble origins and lack of qualifications for the positions he came to occupy are an integral element of his portrayals; his lower class background is especially emphasized, with his earlier occupations given, in different sources, as a medicine vendor and crazy vagrant.[73] Analysis of the narrative layers through which his legend grew over the centuries reveals the coexistence of progressive sexualization and attendant emasculation.

Eighth-century sources take a negative attitude towards Xue Huaiyi, but their condemnation is mainly focused on his dishonesty, incompetence, and vulgarity. According to *Chaoye qianzai*, when decorating the lavish Mingtang (Hall of Light) complex, he smeared the head of the Great Image with calf's blood and claimed that it was his own,

71. For example, Sawada Mizuho marvels at Wu Zhao's growing interest in sex as an older woman and wonders if this was related to the freer sexual culture of the Tang era. See Sawada, *Zetian Wuhou*, 174. Zhao Wenrun and Wang Shuanghuai also feel the need to address the issue of sexual mismatch between Wu and her favorites; following Chen Yinke, they suggest that Wu Zhao was not necessarily sexually involved with either Xue Huaiyi or the Zhang brothers and merely established their positions as "male concubines" to demonstrate her prerogative as emperor. See Zhao Wenrun and Wang Shuanghuai, *Wu Zetian pingzhuan*, 213–15.

72. Wills, "Empress Wu," 146.

73. See *ZZTJ* 203.6436 and *XTS* 76. 3479–80.

offered forth in his religious fervor.[74] *Sui Tang jiahua* describes an episode involving Xue Huaiyi that recalls the issues of class and manliness discussed earlier in connection with man-to-man interactions. Xue Huaiyi refused to show Chancellor Su Liangsi 蘇良嗣 (606–90) the proper ritual respect at court, upon which the enraged senior official had members of his entourage attack Xue.[75] Xue Huaiyi seems to have complained to Wu Zhao, who explained his proper role to him: "Abbot, you should enter and exit from the North Gate, while the south yamen is where the prime ministers come and go: don't violate this" (阿師當向北門出入, 南衙宰相往來, 勿犯他).[76] Her response delineates Xue Huaiyi's real status as private hanger-on as opposed to a bona fide public servant. A caustic memorial submitted by Wang Qiuli requesting that Wu Zhao have Xue Huaiyi castrated before granting him access to the inner quarters likewise uncomfortably implies the sexual nature of her relationship with him.[77]

These episodes are clearly extremely unflattering to Xue Huaiyi and certainly reference the sexual nature of his promotion, but their emphasis on Xue Huaiyi's vulgarity and lower-class origins does not depart from earlier portrayals of the male sexual favorite. In the official histories, however, we see a body of sensationalist lore centered on the inappropriate exchange of young men by older and more powerful women:

> [Wu Zhao] ordered that the Qianyuan Palace be destroyed and made into the Mingtang [Hall of Light], with the monk Xue Huaiyi acting as overseer. Huaiyi was from Hu, and his original surname was Feng with the given name Xiaobao [Tiny Treasure]. He was endowed with an imposing appearance and lascivious nature, and he feigned madness in the Luoyang marketplace. Qianjin Princess took him as a sexual favorite and recommended him to the empress, saying, "Xiaobao can go in and serve you." The empress then ordered him in to commence a sexual relationship with her, and she was absolutely delighted with him.

74. *CYQZ* 5.115–16.
75. *STJH* c.37.
76. *STJH* c.37.
77. *CYQZ buyi*.172; the memorial was ignored. Wang Qiuli also appeared in chapter 3 as the official who self-righteously ended the court celebration of unseasonal snow by pointing out its inauspiciousness and connecting it with female rule.

> 詔毀乾元殿為明堂, 以浮屠薛懷義為使督作. 懷義, 鄠人, 本馮氏, 名小寶, 偉岸淫毒, 佯狂洛陽市, 千金公主嬖之. 主上言: "小寶可入侍." 后召與私, 悅之.[78]

After enjoying Feng Xiaobao's services and deeming him fit for a more long-term appointment, Wu Zhao considered it necessary to change his name and occupation so as to normalize his presence in the palace and give him the veneer of a more upper-class background: "Zetian wanted to cover his tracks and facilitate his access to her inner chambers, so she ordained him as a monk. Additionally, since Huaiyi was not from an aristocratic lineage, she changed his surname to Xue and ordered him to associate his family with that of the Taiping Princess's husband, Xue Shao. She ordered Xue Shao to serve him as an uncle" (則天欲隱其跡, 便於出入禁中, 乃度為僧. 又以懷義非士族, 乃改姓薛, 令與太平公主堺薛紹合族, 令紹以季父事之).[79] Wu Zhao creates a fake hierarchy to mask her inappropriate sexual relationship with a lower-class man young enough to be her great-grandson. The implication is that Wu, paralleling her own usurpation of an unnatural position, uses that position to willfully subvert the natural order again to facilitate her sordid desires.

The sources of the later accounts, which describe explicit sexual exchange, are unclear; they may represent reworkings of sensationalist lore found in pornography, rumor-based sources, or rumor. The *Jiu Tang shu* and *Zizhi tongjian* accounts of Xue Huaiyi's introduction to his benefactress are basically similar to that found in *Xin Tang shu*. Sima Guang is less explicit in terms of the sexual trade that is going on, stating tersely that Huaiyi "was advanced through the Qianjin Princess and gained the favor of the Empress-Dowager [Wu Zhao]" (因千金公主以進, 得幸於太后).[80] The *Jiu Tang shu* biography of Xue Huaiyi actually gives the Qianjin Princess a little speech praising Huaiyi's sexual prowess: "Xiaobao has extraordinary talent and is worthy of intimate service" (小寶有非常材用, 可以近侍).[81]

78. *XTS* 76.3479–80.

79. *JTS* 183.4741. See also *XTS* 76.3480 and *ZZTJ* 203.6436.

80. *ZZTJ* 203.6436.

81. *JTS* 183.4741. In *Jiu Tang shu,* Xue Huaiyi initially finds favor with one of Qianjin's attendants, as opposed to the princess herself.

It would be a mistake to interpret the Qianjin Princess's gift as evidence of some sort of sisterhood characteristic of an era in which female leadership somehow translated into sexual liberation and transcendence of jealousy among women. Actually, according to the historical accounts, the Qianjin Princess's male offering was a deft strategic calculation. As a member of the Li royal family, Qianjin was a potential target for Wu Zhao's purge of the imperial Li clan during the late 680s leading up to the establishment of the Zhou in 690.[82] However, with clever maneuvers such as presenting to the throne a handsome young man whose "skills" she had personally tested and approved (千金公主嬖之), she escaped the fate suffered by many of her clansmen and -women: "Only the Qianjin Princess, through clever flattery and well-timed gifts to the throne, survived. She presented a memorial asking to recognize Zetian as her mother, and great favor was bestowed upon her therein. Her title and ranking were promoted to Yan'an Grand Princess, the number of households in her fief was substantiated, and she was granted the surname Wu" (唯千金公主以巧媚善進奉獨存, 抗疏請以則天為母, 因得曲加恩寵, 改邑號為延安大長公主, 加實封, 賜姓武氏).[83] Gender roles were thus reversed, as powerful older women treated young men the way in which powerful older men were understood to have the right to treat young women (as sexual objects that could be traded, for a variety of motives, like other luxury items), and the men accept the arrangement.

A famous and probably fictitious later tradition about Xue Huaiyi's downfall represents the final rhetorical destruction of his manliness, as he is placed in the roles of jealous concubine and victim of gender-inverted violence. In 695, the Mingtang (Hall of Light), a key dynastic and religious edifice built by Xue Huaiyi and intended to be the crowning glory of the Zhou, burned down in a huge fire.[84] Early sources, including *Chaoye qianzai*, *Sui Tang jiahua*, and Wu Zhao's edict following the disaster, either offer no explanation as to how the fire started or, in the case of

82. In *Jiu Tang shu*, Qianjin is identified as a daughter of Gaozu. See *JTS* 61.2362.

83. *JTS* 183.4742.

84. The construction, ideological function, and destruction of the Hall of Light, as well as the role of its head architect in the Zhou symbolic edifice, represent a major topic of interest in scholarship on the era. In particular, see Forte, *Political Propaganda and Ideology in China*, 147–169, and *Mingtang and Buddhist Utopias*.

the edict, provide the practical explanation that smoldering materials left by workers at the site caught fire, igniting the blaze.[85] Yet, in Xue Huaiyi's *Jiu Tang shu* biography and later in *Zizhi tongjian*, an alternate, salacious, and unlikely explanation is given: "Later on, Imperial Physician Shen Nanqiu got [Wu Zhao's] favor. Abbot Xue's favor gradually declined, and his resentment and anger correspondingly grew extreme. During the Zhengsheng reign period [January–October 695], he set fire to the Hall of Light and Hall of Heaven, and both burned down to ashes. Zetian was humiliated and covered up the scandal. She also appointed Huaiyi overseer [of constructing the new Mingtang]" (後有御醫沈南璆得幸, 薛師恩漸衰, 恨怒頗甚. 證聖中, 乃焚明堂, 天堂, 並為灰燼, 則天愧而隱之, 又令懷義充使督作).[86] Afterwards, when Xue Huaiyi grew increasingly arrogant, Wu Zhao came to despise him. She "ordered the Taiping Princess to select several dozen strong women to secretly be on guard against him [Xue Huaiyi]. Someone exposed his surreptitious rebellious plot, and the Taiping Princess's wet-nurse Lady Zhang ordered strongmen to tie him up and strangle him. They used a palanquin to transport his corpse to White Horse Temple. The monks and followers who were associated with him were all banished or fled to far-off and horrible places" (令太平公主擇膂力婦人數十, 密防慮之. 人有發其陰謀者, 太平公主乳母張夫人令壯士縛而縊殺之, 以輦車載屍送白馬寺. 其侍者僧徒, 皆流竄遠惡處).[87]

This later account contains glaring factual holes; for example, why would Wu Zhao reappoint Xue Huaiyi as the overseer of rebuilding of the Hall of Light right after he had purposefully burnt it down?[88] The appeal of this account appears to have lain in its adherence to the narrative of gender disorder that increasingly came to characterize interpretations of the era. Xue Huaiyi is cast as the classic scorned "woman," spurned by

85. *CYQZ* 5.116; *STJH* c.37–38; *QTW* 96.2b (989). See also *TPGJ* 288.2294.

86. *JTS* 183.4743.

87. *JTS* 183.4743.

88. Sawada Mizuho notes the logical inconsistency but suggests that Xue Huaiyi was in fact responsible for setting fire to the Hall of Light and that Wu Zhao re-appointed him so as to avoid embarrassment; see Sawada, *Zetian Wu hou*, 160–62. The decision to reject the most logical explanation (sparks left by craftsmen) in favor of the least logical explanation (Xue Huaiyi as jealous arsonist) is incomprehensible unless we consider the lasting influence of the image of Xue Huaiyi and Wu's relationship as crystallized in the official histories.

the master in favor of a new favorite. His brutal murder vividly captures the gender reversal perceived as the core of his biography and the era of female rule in general. In spite of his arrogance and violence, he remains helplessly trapped in the inferior, female-identified position from the time when he is first selected and exchanged by the Qianjin Princess to his death, which, like his life, is controlled by powerful women.

The motif of gender transposition reverberates throughout accounts of the closest male associates of the early Tang women. According to the standard historical accounts, Wu Sansi likewise came to power through intimate recommendation by powerful women. Wu Sansi was first involved with Shangguan Wan'er and then parlayed this relationship into a personal introduction to Empress Wei: "When [Empress Wei] came to power, she took Shining Consort Shangguan's evil advice and summoned Wu Sansi into the inner palace" (及得志, 受上官昭容邪說, 引武三思入宮中).[89] Empress Wei's *Xin Tang shu* biography more fully explains his motives: "At the time, Shining Consort Shangguan was involved in government affairs, and Jing Hui and his allies were planning to exterminate all of the Wus. Wu Sansi was scared, so he asked the Shining Consort to get him in [to see Empress Wei], and he was favored by the empress" (是時, 上官昭容與政事, 方敬暉等將盡誅諸武, 武三思懼, 乃因昭容入請, 得幸於后).[90] The structure of inter-relationships described here follows the progression found in the story of the Qianjin Princess's gift of Xue Huaiyi as a human bargaining chip, wherein one woman makes a recommendation to another, more powerful woman of a man with whom she has been intimate.

The underlying concern with gendered exchange and role reversal is perhaps most fully explored in narratives about the Zhang brothers. Ironically, the brothers' recent and prominent ancestor was the decorated official Zhang Xingcheng 張行成 (587–653), who served under Gaozu, Taizong, and Gaozong and who appears in several sources as a staunch critic of female political power (in particular, female interference in Gaozong's government) as disruption of the *yin-yang* cosmic order.[91] As a young man, Zhang Yizhi entered the official register through family (*yin* 蔭) privilege,

89. *JTS* 51.2172.
90. *XTS* 76.3486.
91. See *DTXY* 1.6, *JTS* 78.2703–5, and *XTS* 104.4012–14.

whereby the eldest scions of households enjoying a certain rank could automatically enter service at a rank several levels lower than that earned by the last generation.[92] In accounts about their rise to power, the brothers' family background quickly becomes lost in the rhetorical tradition of the sexual favorite's biography, complete with descriptions of their physical charms, the lavish rewards they received from Wu Zhao, and their vulgarity and unworthiness for their newfound fortune. According to *Jiu Tang shu*, "as a young man of slightly over twenty, he [Yizhi] had a fair complexion and an attractive, charming way of carrying himself. He was good at music and singing" (年二十餘, 白皙美姿容, 善音律歌詞).[93] Like Xue Huaiyi, the brothers are the object of exchange between powerful women: "When Wu Zhao was in power, the Taiping Princess recommended his [Zhang Yizhi's] younger brother Changzong, who was chosen for service. Changzong reported [to Wu Zhao] that Yizhi's talent surpassed his and that [Yizhi] was good at smelting medicinal stones. The empress summoned him [Yizhi] and was absolutely delighted with him" (武后時, 太平公主薦其弟昌宗, 得侍. 昌宗白進易之材用過臣, 善治鍊藥石. 即召見, 悅之).[94] Thereafter both brothers enjoyed immediate and extreme favor.

Both biographies detail the inflated government appointments, beautiful clothes, residences, silks, slaves, and livestock lavished upon the brothers by Wu Zhao.[95] The material rewards in status are directly connected with the sexual favor they provided: "After this [Wu's being delighted with Yizhi's service], the brothers both served in the inner chambers. They both applied powder and rouge and wore brocade embroidered clothes. They both received sexual favor" (由是兄弟俱侍宮中, 皆傅粉施朱, 衣錦繡服, 俱承辟陽之寵).[96] As in the case of Xue Huaiyi, the narrative focus

92. *JTS* 78.2706; *XTS* 104.4014.

93. *JTS* 78.2706; see also *XTS* 104.4014.

94. *XTS* 104.4014. The *Jiu Tang shu* account is more explicit about the sexual capacity in which the brothers were recruited. According to the *Jiu Tang shu* biography of the brothers, the Taiping Princess recommended Changzong "to serve in the inner quarters" (太平公主薦易之弟昌宗入侍禁中). *JTS* 78.2706.

95. *JTS* 78.2706; *XTS* 104.4014.

96. *JTS* 78.2706; see also *XTS* 104.4014. Literally, they "received the type of favor shown previously to [the Marquis of] Piyang." The Marquis of Piyang, Shen Yiji 審食其, was a rumored sexual favorite of Empress Dowager Lü during the Western Han. The allusion thus refers to a male favorite of a woman ruler. For Shen Yiji, see *SJ* 8.391–92, 56.260–61; and *HS* 1b.77–80, 16.573.

on the brothers' sexual service emphasizes their (male) physicality yet emasculates them by placing them in the feminine-identified position of concubine, for whom outward attractiveness is paramount.

In the process through which Xue Huaiyi becomes cast as an archetypal sexual favorite, explicitly sexual narratives are superimposed upon an earlier body of literature that stressed his lower-class origins and vulgarity. Similar themes emerge in narratives on the Zhang brothers. However, the brothers' obvious aristocratic lineage complicates narrative imputations of their ignorance, so that descriptions of their ignorance are often structured defensively, designed to counter an imagined opponent's evidentiary claims to the contrary. One might think, for instance, that the brothers' aristocratic official background and participation in courtly cultural activities indicate a certain level of education and ability. After all, they received an imperial commission to compile the massive anthology *Sanjiao zhuying* 三教珠英 (Pearls of the Three Teachings), meant to serve as a comprehensive compendium of Buddhist, Daoist, and Confucian knowledge. But as the historian-compiler's rejoinder counters, the editorial appointment was nothing more than a smokescreen and, as such, should actually be understood as further evidence of their ignorance. As recounted in *Chaoye qianzai*,

> Zhang Yizhi and Changzong's eyes had never recognized a character, and their hands did not know how to write. Whenever they needed to present a memorial or were required to compose something to courtly command, their minions did it for them. As for the *Pearls of the Three Teachings* anthology that they presented to the throne, it was in fact the work of Cui Rong and Zhang Yue's cohort, but Yizhi surreptitiously put his own name on the project as the person in charge.
>
> 張易之, 昌宗目不識字, 手不解書, 謝表及和御製皆諂附者為之. 所進三教珠英, 乃崔融, 張說輩之作, 而易之竊名為首.[97]

The official biographies transform the Zhang brothers' participation in the *Pearls of the Three Teachings* project into an imperial conspiracy.

97. *CYQZ buyi*.172–73. According to the notes in *Chaoye qianzai*, this passage was reconstructed from the thirteenth-century work *Houcun shihua* (Houcun's Notes on Poetry), by Liu Kezhuang. See Liu Kezhuang, *Houcun shihua xu ji*, 3.12a.

After the appearance of the empress's new favorites onto the court scene, she knew that "vile gossip about Changzong was circulating everywhere and she wanted to cover its traces with something nice" (以昌宗醜聲聞於外, 欲以美事掩其迹): she appointed Changzong as figurehead editor to give him an officially sanctioned reason for entering the inner imperial precincts, even though, as a supposedly illiterate man, he was obviously unqualified for the appointment.[98]

The survival of courtly poems attributed to the Zhang brothers could also be proposed as evidence against the claim of illiteracy. *Quan Tang shi*, for example, includes poems attributed to both Zhang Changzong and Zhang Yizhi.[99] Biographical material taken directly from their official biographies, however, is inserted at the beginning of each *Quan Tang shi* entry and serves to completely debunk our faith in the authorship of the ensuing poems attributed to the brothers: "Yizhi and Changzong were both only barely literate in courtly composition, so whenever they were called upon to compose in a group to courtly command, Song Zhiwen or Yan Zhaoyin would compose for them" (易之, 昌宗皆粗能屬文, 如應詔和詩, 則宋之問閻朝隱為之代作).[100] The phenomenon of ghostwriting is by no means unique to the Zhang brothers; in addition to drafting edicts, Shangguan Wan'er supposedly wrote the poetic compositions for the entire imperial family. In the case of the Zhang brothers, the reference to ghostwriters is used to drive home the point that they do not really belong in the circle of high-level literary figures normally invited to court outings.[101]

With regard to the vulgarization of the Zhang brothers, a pornographic work of historical fiction provides a fascinating alternative version of events at the Zhou court. This work, *Konghe jian miji* 控鶴監祕記 (Secret Record of the Director of the Guiding the Immortal Cranes Bureau), is attributed to Zhang Ji 張垍 (mid-eighth c.), but is almost

98. *JTS* 78.2706; see also *XTS* 104.4014–15. The phrasing here is almost identical to that used to describe gossip about Empress Wei's relationship with Wu Sansi (醜聲日聞於外).

99. *QTS* 80.867–69.

100. *QTS* 80.867; originally from *JTS* 78.2707.

101. Zhao Wenrun and Wang Shuanghuai point out other passages in *Jiu Tang shu* in which the Zhang brothers take the lead in the cultural activities of the court. For example, they commissioned painters to paint the portraits of leading court figures. See Zhao Wenrun and Wang Shuanghuai, *Wu Zetian pingzhuan*, 327.

certainly a much later work, possibly originating as late as the eighteenth century.[102] Obviously, the work was not meant as a factual account of court affairs. Yet its focus on the sex lives of the leading women of the court paradoxically challenges the prevailing standard versions in such a way as to somewhat rehabilitate the Zhangs. *Konghe jian miji* opens by explaining how Xue Huaiyi's lower-class origins and uncouth behavior are creating difficulties for Wu Zhao at court. She laments about this to the Qianjin Princess, who immediately replies that she has long been thinking along the same lines and already has a new "male consort" (*nan fei* 男妃) in mind. This lucky man is, of course, Zhang Changzong, and the Qianjin Princess introduces him by contrasting him with Xue Huaiyi, a "petty man of the market" (市井小人) who is easily ridiculed by court ministers: "If Your Majesty could get a scion of an aristocratic household, well-versed in literature and the arts, then how would the ministers dare to humiliate him?" (若得公卿子通曉文墨者, 南衙何敢辱之?).[103]

This portrait of the Zhang brothers is the total opposite of their mainstream image as constructed in most anecdotal and historical sources, yet is much more in keeping with their known identity as "scions of an aristocratic household," descendants of the decorated official Zhang Xingcheng. The author was clearly not attempting to write a particularly praiseful account of Wu Zhao's reign or capability as a ruler, and the less typological portrayal of the Zhang brothers may well be the result of the writer's freedom, as the private writer of a pornography, from the constraints attendant upon the composition of official history or historical anecdote.

102. For Zhang Ji's biography, see *JTS* 97.3058–60 and *XTS* 125.4411–12. The source and accuracy of the attribution to Zhang Ji are unclear; it seems unlikely that Zhang Ji, a respected official and literary figure, would write a pornographic work about the current emperor's grandmother, or that the work would not be attested to earlier than the eighteenth century. The work both circulates independently and appears as "Konghe jian mi ji er ze" 控鶴監密記二則 (The Two Cases of the Secret Record of the Director of the Guiding the Immortal Cranes Bureau) in *juan* 24 of some editions of Yuan Mei's 袁枚 (1716–98) work of supernatural tales, *Zi bu yu* 子不語 (What the Master [Confucius] Didn't Speak About). See, for example, Yuan Mei, *Sui yuan quan ji*, vol. 41, 24.5b–7b. At the beginning of this version, Yuan Mei claims that Zhang Ji compiled *Konghe jian miji*, but most modern editions do not accept the attribution to Zhang Ji. It is possible that *Konghe jian miji* originates with *Zi bu yu*, but, at this point, I have not been able to determine its transmission history.

103. *Konghe jian miji* 1a.

In its emphasis on gendered exchange, *Konghe jian miji* also provides interesting points of comparison with anecdotal and historical accounts. When the Qianjin Princess first recommends Zhang Changzong to Wu Zhao, the empress hesitates. The Qianjin Princess immediately diagnoses the cause of her hesitation and whispers her doubts away: "Your Majesty doesn't need to worry; I also know about Changzong's lower body" (陛下毋過慮，兒兼知昌宗下體矣).[104] She goes on to describe a pool party at which she was able to observe Zhang Changzong's naked body and details the attractiveness of his penis. Wu then asks Qianjin if she has "tried him out" (兒試耶?), and the princess replies that, although tempted, she did not sleep with him herself out of deference for Wu Zhao, but rather had her attendant have sex with him: "[I] sent my attendant to force him" (遣侍兒逼焉).[105] On cue, the Qianjin Princess's servant "memorializes" (*zou* 奏) about Zhang Changzong's exceptional sexual skills.[106]

As discussed earlier, the term *bi* 逼, to force or compel, is used elsewhere in connection with a sexual relationship in which the balance of power is weighted in favor of the woman.[107] Indeed, by far the greater portion of the brief *Konghe jian miji* adopts an imagined female perspective to appraise potential male partners. Explicit discussions of the male member play a prominent role in these appraisals. The work contains an extended conversation between Shangguan Wan'er and her lover Cui Shi, in which he asks her what women look for in selecting men and she gives him a graphic and detailed answer.[108] The first section establishes Zhang Changzong as a perfect specimen by embellishing or rewriting famous episodes about him from the historical tradition. For example, according to the standard historical account given in Shangguan Wan'er's biographies, Wu Zhao had Shangguan branded with a facial tattoo for an undisclosed offense.[109] Other sources dating from the Tang and later

104. *Konghe jian miji* 1b.

105. *Konghe jian miji* 1b.

106. *Konghe jian miji* 1b–2a.

107. For example, it is used to describe Empress Dowager Hu's relationship with Yuan Yi and Azang's relationship with Li Jiongxiu; see, respectively, chapter 1 of this book and *WS* 13.339; and chapter 4 of this book and *CYQZ* 3.69.

108. *Konghe jian miji* 3b–4b.

109. "During Zetian's rule, she committed an offense worthy of execution, [but] Zetian felt pity for her talent and didn't kill her, only tattooing her face [as punishment]" (則天時，婉兒忤旨當誅，則天惜其才不殺，但黥其面而已); *JTS* 51.2175. See

imperial period mostly limit themselves to describing the way in which Shangguan ingeniously covered her disfigurement with a stylish ornament.[110] In *Konghe jian miji*, the irresistible sexual attraction of Zhang Changzong is held responsible for Shangguan Wan'er's disfigurement. Wu Zhao constructs a lavish garden for the Zhangs and holds a party there, at which Shangguan Wan'er is in attendance. Zhang Changzong is lying in a drunken sleep, and Wu Zhao fiddles with his "hibiscus-colored" penis (*se ruo furong* 色若芙蓉), leading to a sudden conflict:

> The empress sighed, saying, "He makes my heart melt." Wan'er was turned on; below her skirt she was totally wet, and involuntarily she stretched out her hand towards Changzong. The Empress was really angry. She picked up a metal dagger and thrust it into [Wan'er's] bangs and said, "You dared get close to the forbidden fillet; your crime is worthy of death!" Sixth Young Master [Zhang Changzong] mercifully intervened [on Wan'er's behalf], and she was able to escape [the death penalty]. But her forehead had a scar [from where Wu Zhao had stabbed her]; therefore in the palace she often wore filigreed flowers [to cover it up].
>
> 后嘆曰:使人之意也消.婉兒心動,裙下皆濕,不覺手近昌宗.后大怒,取金刀插其髻曰:汝敢近禁臠,罪當死.六郎為哀求,始免.然額有傷痕,故於宮中常戴花鈿也.[111]

---

also *XTS* 76.3488: "Starting from the Tongtian reign [Wansui tongtian; 696–97], she was in charge of drafting edicts, and they were all smooth and readable. At one point, she had committed an offense worthy of execution. The empress felt pity for her talent and only tattooed her and didn't kill her" (自通天以來, 內掌詔命, 掞麗可觀. 嘗忤旨當誅, 后惜其才, 止黥而不殺也). It is unclear when Shangguan committed the unspecified offense, but it seems to be a different offense from the crime of her grandfather and to have been committed after she had already started to take on an important function in Wu Zhao's government, or at least after she was old enough to be recognized for her talent.

110. See, for example, Duan Chengshi 段成式 (d. 863), *Youyang zazu* 酉陽雜俎 (Miscellaneous Records from Youyang), 8.61–62; Zhu Shengfei, *Ganzhu ji*, 6.22b (872–393); Zeng Zao, *Lei shuo* 13.14a–b; Tao Zongyi, *Shuo fu* 36.4 (2451); Xu Yingqiu, *Yuzhi tang tan hui*, 29.39b; and Shen Zinan, *Yilin huikao*, 4.10b (125). However, Zeng Zao's *Lei shuo* (12th c.) states that during audiences with high-ranking ministers, Wu Zhao used to have Shangguan hide underneath her couch behind the folds of her skirt to record what was said. One day, Shangguan peeked out to look at the prime ministers. Wu saw her, became very angry, and cut her face with a knife. Zeng Zao, *Lei shuo* 13.14a–b.

111. *Konghe jian miji* 3a–b.

The hierarchical relationships between the main actors in *Konghe jian miji* are striking. Zhang Changzong, the "forbidden fillet" (*jinluan* 禁臠), is an object of desire and possession for the powerful empress and Shangguan. In death, he is similarly objectified. A passage that parodies literary descriptions of the bodies of immortals describes how, after he is killed in the 705 coup against Wu Zhao, Shangguan Wan'er plucks his penis from his corpse in an offering to the empress: "Palace lady Wan'er guessed what was on the empress's mind. From amidst the broken bones, she got [a section of] the stalk [of his penis].[112] It was red and moist as when he was alive. With her hands she offered it to the empress, who wept, saying, 'This is Sixth Young Master'" (宮人婉兒揣后意, 於殘骸中, 收得莖頭半段, 紅潤如生. 手持獻后, 后泣曰: 是六郎也).[113]

Although *Konghe jian miji* is by and large devoid of the direct condemnation that often surrounds male concubines, as in other accounts discussed above the intensive focus on the physical manhood of Zhang Changzong and potential male consorts in general accomplishes their emasculation by placing them in the female-identified position of sex object. In this way, *Konghe jian miji* participates in the narrative encapsulation of the period as one defined by abnormal, reversed gender roles, whereby female rule ("manly" women or women acting as men) begets male servitude. According to the brothers' *Jiu Tang shu* biography, during the late Zhou period, when the Zhang brothers were the empress's current male favorites, she "commanded that beautiful young men be selected to serve as her Left and Right Palace Corral Auxiliaries" (令選美少年為左右奉宸供奉).[114] Alarmed, Left Rectifier of Omissions Zhu Jingze 朱敬則 (635–709) remonstrated against this course of action on the grounds that court decorum had already been adversely affected by Wu Zhao's well-known, or at least widely gossiped about, penchant for younger male favorites. He cautioned the empress to control her amorous impulses: "When it comes to penchants and desires, the foolish and wise are the same [in being stirred, but] the worthy are able to regulate their

112. The Beijing chu ban she edition of *Zi bu yu* (in the Zhongguo wenyan xiaoshuo baibu jingdian series) has *ban duan* 半段 ("half divided/section") instead of *ban jia* 半叚 (literally, "half false"), suggesting that Shangguan got a section or half of Zhang Changzong's member. See Yuan Mei, *Zi bu yu*, 11446.

113. *Konghe jian miji* 3a.

114. *JTS* 78.2706.

emotions and not let them reach an excessive degree" (嗜慾之情, 愚智皆同, 賢者能節之不使過度).[115]

Zhu Jingze details the way in which the examples of Xue Huaiyi and the Zhangs have created a harmful precedent in terms of male behavior: "Recently I have heard that Chief Steward of the Accommodations Service Liu Mo said that his son Liangbin was white in complexion and had a nice moustache and eyebrows, and Left Palace Gate Guard Administrator Hou Xiang said that his penis was big and strong and larger than Xue Huaiyi's. His one and only desire was to advance himself to the position of Palace Corral Auxiliary" (近聞尚舍奉御柳模自言子良賓潔白鬚眉, 左監門衛長史侯祥云陽道壯偉, 過於薛懷義, 專欲自進堪奉宸內供奉).[116] These men self-advertise in terms of attributes that are deemed sexually desirable to women. As vocalized by Zhu Jingze, the point is that the political-cultural climate has degenerated to such an extent that men sexually objectify themselves and seek advancement through conforming to standards determined by female choice.

The nascent power of rhetorical gender reversal is evinced in a fascinating passage from *Da Tang xinyu* about the fawning behavior of some unscrupulous officials towards the Zhang brothers. The passage is a montage of snapshots meant to convey the repulsiveness of the Zhangs and the atmosphere that fostered their power.[117] One such snapshot involves Censor Yang Zaisi's 楊再思 (634–709) sly toadying to Wu Zhao's latest favorites:

> Zaisi further saw that Yizhi's younger brother Changzong had been favored because of his beautiful appearance, so he toadied to them and said: "People say that Sixth Young Master is like a lotus flower, but I don't think they're right; it's really that the lotus flower is like Sixth Young Master."
>
> 再思又見易之弟昌宗以貌美被寵, 因諂之曰: 人言六郎似蓮花, 再思以爲不然, 只是蓮花似六郎耳.[118]

115. *JTS* 78.2706.

116. *JTS* 78.2707.

117. The passage begins with a scene in which another Zhang brother, Zhang Tongxiu 張同休 (d. 705), held a banquet at Sili Temple 司禮寺. As a result of his family's recent rise in station, Zhang Tongxiu presided over all of the officials. He asked Censor Yang Zaisi to perform a Koguryo (Gaoli 高麗) dance because he thought that Yang had Gaoli-like facial features, a request the censor shamelessly obliged. *DTXY* 9.143.

118. *DTXY* 9.143.

Yang Zaisi is, of course, saying that Zhang Changzong is more beautiful than the lotus; he is the apex of beauty and the point of comparison for the flower, not the other way around. Aside from the familiar theme of cronyism, this passage is quite telling as regards gender and linguistic formulations of gender identity. The flower is a common kenning or metaphor for beautiful women, but is almost never used for beautiful men. In this anecdote, Zhang Changzong has rhetorically become female.

The Zhang brothers and Xue Huaiyi, men who are associated with purely sexual service, are generally not given even the most artificial voice with which to speak for themselves. Their actions, personalities, and, inevitably, their crimes are described from the perspective of others, including, of course, the historian or writer. In contrast, men such as Wu Sansi, Zong Chuke, and Cui Shi, while notorious as the male sycophants and rumored lovers of women leaders, also held high government positions, and Cui Shi was one of the most famous literary figures of the period. Perhaps reflecting their slightly higher or at least more "literate" status, the official biographies of these men give them each a short speech summing up what can be loosely termed their philosophy on life. Not surprisingly, their philosophies are always immoral or reveal dangerous moral relativism. They also represent the voice of historical judgment superficially masked as first-person revelation.

Wu Sansi's approach to life is encapsulated by a partisan statement of moral relativism: "As Sansi was very jealous of upright men, he once said, 'I don't know what kind of qualities make someone a good person; only those that are good to me, I count as good people'" (三思既猜嫉正士, 嘗言: "不知何等名作好人, 唯有向我好者, 是好人耳").[119] The account goes on to describe his devious factional activities. In Cui Shi's *Jiu Tang shu* biography, the biographical subject is likewise made to sum up his own greatest vices, lust for power and blind pride:

> Whenever they [Cui Shi and his brothers, all of whom were famous literary men] were banqueting privately together, they compared themselves to Wang Dao and Xie An of the Eastern Jin. [Cui Shi] said to others: "The members of our family have never once, since we started on our official careers, not been number one. A man should prioritize, above all else, occu-

119. *JTS* 183.4735.

pying key important positions in order to control others; how could he stand to quietly and meekly relinquish control to others?"

每宴私之際, 自比東晉王導, 謝安之家. 謂人曰: 吾之一門及出身歷官, 未嘗不為第一. 丈夫當先據要路以制人, 豈能默默受制於人也.[120]

The obvious point is Cui Shi's upside-down priorities; controlling others for the sake of personal power alone is the exact opposite of what a man, at least a good man, should do. Similarly, Zong Chuke's *Xin Tang shu* biography ends by revealing his supposedly secret declaration to his faction of his seditious ambitions: "Earlier, I occupied a lowly position, and I intensely envied the prime ministers; when I became a prime minister myself, I began to set my sights even higher for the position of emperor; if I could face south for just one day, it would be enough" (始, 吾在卑位, 尤愛宰相; 及居之, 又思天子, 南面一日足矣).[121]

The likelihood of the historical record accurately preserving Zong Chuke's "secret" traitorous comment, or, for that matter, the perverse life philosophies attributed to Wu Sansi and Cui Shi, is very low. The importance of these accounts lies not in the information they convey, but in the issues they raise: why are the male partisans of these female power-holders treated with such negativity and, at the same time, such undeniable uniformity? The fundamental underlying question is what these particular thematic emphases say about conceptions of masculinity and femininity in relation to female power during this period.

The presence of so many male figures explicitly defined as, or insinuated to have been, sexual partners of Wu Zhao, Empress Wei, the Taiping or Anle Princesses, or Shangguan Wan'er was surely meant to negatively impress future generations with their promiscuity and corruption. Yet beyond gossipy accusations about their sex lives, some passages suggest the climate of social chaos fostered by these women leaders. *Da Tang xinyu*, for instance, characterizes Wu Zhao's rule as one in which "many slaves were involved in relationships with outsiders" (奴婢多通外人), leading to total disorder and violence as many of them falsely accused

120. *JTS* 74.2624. This speech is also found in *TPGJ* 184.1378, 240.1854, and 265.2072.

121. Facing south denotes the position of the emperor towards his subjects. *XTS* 109.4103.

their masters of treasonous conduct.[122] A passage in Empress Wei's *Jiu Tang shu* biography describes a similar scene, in which the imperial couple loses many palace women to outside liaisons during a group outing.[123]

Thus, although the accusation of promiscuity is a ubiquitous, easy, and conventionally gender-specific way of defaming women leaders, such accusations are neither the most vivid nor the most defining element in the rhetorical de-legitimation of the female power-holders of the era. Instead, we have seen that the core underlying issue is gender as it relates to conceptions of social and cosmic order. Their rhetorical de-feminization and the attendant emasculation of their male associates reveal the pull of gender inversion as a narrative construct. These accounts invent and explore a particular gender anarchy characterized by "male" women and "female" men. These figures are narratively deployed to construct an upside-down and dangerous world created by female rule.

The literary-historical enchantment with specific gendered constructs has led to the erasure of much information about these women that is deemed to fall outside of the artificially delimited narrative purviews. Some passages provide fleeting glimpses of a much wider circle of powerful women who survive only as names. Empress Wei's *Jiu Tang shu* biography describes a mixed-gender Jinglong political climate that is much more complex than is generally suggested by the surviving historical record:

> At the time, Shining Consort Shangguan and her mother née Zheng and the Palace Ladies née Chai and Helou planted and deployed close factions. They widely accepted bribes and sent down edicts enfeoffing "slanted" officials. Some rose from the ranks of slaves, butchers, and vendors and gradually came to occupy an exalted class. Furthermore, they summoned the Shamaness Zhao to have unlimited access to the inner palace. She was enfeoffed as Lady Longxi, and her power was equal to Shangguan's.

122. These slaves were supposed to remain within the confines of the palace, and it was improper for them to have dealings with outsiders. *DTXY* 4.57.

123. Empress Wei and Zhongzong went to the market by night to view the brightly lighted lamps. They brought with them several thousand palace women, who apparently made ample use of the opportunity afforded them to get out of the palace precincts: "They roamed by night, dissolutely viewing [the lamps]. As a result they formed secret illicit liaisons with men from outside the palace and absconded without returning" (夜遊縱觀, 因與外人陰通, 逃逸不還); *JTS* 51.2174.

時上官昭容與其母鄭氏及尚宮柴氏, 賀婁樹用親黨, 廣納貨賂, 別降墨敕斜封授官, 或出臧獲屠販, 累居榮秩. 又引女巫趙氏出入禁中, 封為隴西夫人, 勢與上官氏為比.[124]

Passages mentioning Lady Longxi, the palace ladies Chai and Helou, and the women from "several dozens of in-law clans" (姻聯數十族) suggest a wide, now nebulous world of mixed gender participation in court and mixed gender possession of power.[125] Duan Tali 段塔麗 has likewise discussed recently excavated memorial tablets of unnamed palace women describing their support of the Li-Tang cause in contemporary factional struggles.[126] Taken together, these records indicate the suppression of information regarding this wider cultural-political realm at the same time that they suggest the reasons behind the suppression. Historical and anecdotal records have transformed the Zhou and early Tang female power-holders into transgressive typologies that embody unnaturalness, greed, and sexual deviance.

This chapter has demonstrated that the concept of gender inversion is the key to understanding the condemnatory rhetorical construction of female power during the late seventh and early eighth centuries. Sources dealing with this period are distinguished by the way in which they construct relationships between men and women. In some accounts, the trope of sexual exchange is inverted to place the woman leader in the

124. *JTS* 51.2173. See also *XTS* 112.4173. During this time, a major divisive issue at court was the existence of the *xiefeng guan* 斜封官, literally "slantingly enfeoffed officials," meaning officials granted position outside of the regular government channels. *Xiefeng guan* were posts, often on the princesses' staff, that could be purchased for an exorbitant sum. They were written in black ink, as opposed to the official red-inked brush, and were submitted "slantingly" to the side gate of the Secretariat. The term connotes moral depravity similar to that suggested by the phrase *siye* 私謁, or "clientage"; the *xiefeng guan* are closer to cronies than government servants selected for their talent and loyalty to the state. According to various sources, the appointment of *xiefeng guan* was rampant during Zhongzong's reign, was briefly outlawed by Ruizong, was reinstated at the behest of the Taiping Princess, and then finally died out altogether during the reign of Xuanzong. *Xiefeng guan* are discussed in many different sources; see, for example, *CYQZ* 1.7; *DTXY* 2.27; *TPGJ* 186.1389–90; *TYL* 3.67; *JTS* 7.156 and 77.2682; and *XTS* 5.117–18, 45.1176, 83.3654, 112.4173–74, and 118.4279. See also Guisso, "The Reigns of the Empress Wu, Chung-tsung and Jui-tsung (684–712)," 325–32.

125. *XTS* 112.4173.

126. Duan Tali, *Tangdai funü diwei yanjiu*, 77–80.

position of power, the exchanger of men as opposed to the exchanged. Masculinity is constructed as opposition to female power, and men who gain their status through closeness to women leaders are rhetorically feminized. The power of rhetorical de-legitimation reveals intense anxiety regarding female appropriation of male roles, but it also indicates the power of narrative, its rhetorical forms, tropes, and modes of operation, to set and condition expectations for gendered identities and behaviors.

Conclusion

As memorial inscriptions go, Shangguan Wan'er's is rather brief. She, Empress Wei, and the Anle Princess were all executed in 710 as members of the "rebel," or losing, faction. However, the posthumous treatment that she received during the reigns of Ruizong and Xuanzong was considerably better than that accorded the Wei women. The title of shining consort (*zhaorong* 昭容) was restored to her by imperial edict in 711, and this period also saw the imperially sanctioned compilation of her literary collection, with a preface written by eminent literary man Zhang Yue, also the author of her memorial inscription.[1] Zhang Yue's eulogy refers to Shangguan's political roles as leader of the official body, critical decision-maker, and counselor to the throne. In bringing up Hou Yi and the Three Worthies, he alludes obliquely to her violent death,[2] thus skirting the issue of the factional conflicts that led to Shangguan Wan'er's demise and in which Xuanzong was deeply embroiled. Her memorial reads as follows:

Heaven sends down timely rain, the mountains and river send forth clouds. From this was born the numinous beauty, bringing prosperity to our sagely

1. Although traditionally Xuanzong has been credited with ordering the compilation of Shangguan's literary collection, in a recent article Zheng Yaru has argued that Shangguan's positive posthumous treatment, including the compilation of her collection, occurred under Ruizong at the behest of the Taiping Princess. See Zheng Yaru, "Chong tan Shangguan Wan'er." See also the discussion in Rothschild, "'Her Influence Great,'" 135.

2. "It's like those nine suns, which caused Hou Yi to meet with violence; it's like the Three Worthies, that Qin mourned them therein" (如彼九日, 羿焉暴之; 如彼三良, 秦焉悼之); *QTW* 231.6b (2337).

lord. Her way was refined and subtle; brilliantly radiant were her literary gifts. The Three Lights of Sun, Moon, and Stars move forward together;[3] the shining consort governed them. The prime ministers all met together; the shining consort ordered them. Outside, she planned on behalf of the state; inside, she counseled the emperor. Her concern lay in presenting worthies to the throne; her thoughts revolved around seeking many court gentlemen. When the heart is moved by loyalty and filiality, Heaven rewards accordingly; auspiciousness and inauspiciousness each have their allotments, so even Confucius prayed in such cases.[4] It's like those nine suns, which caused Hou Yi to meet with violence;[5] it's like the Three Worthies, that Qin mourned them therein.[6] When the Han palace selected talents, Lady Ban was the most outstanding; that the Chu historian could record the hegemony was due to Beauty Fan's strength. Majestic, the Duke of Qi exalted her brilliant virtue. We sigh about the "red brush":[7] this should serve as mirror and example.

3. The phrase *san guang* 三光, "the Three Lights," originally comes from "Discourse on Swords" ("Shuo jian" 說劍) in the *Zhuangzi* 莊子: "Above, it takes its model from the roundness of Heaven, following along with the three luminous bodies of the sky. Below, it takes its model from the squareness of earth, following along with the four seasons. In the middle realm, it brings harmony to the wills of the people and peace to the four directions" (上法圓天以順三光, 下法方地以順四時, 中和民意以安四鄉); *Zhuangzi ji jie*, 8.272. Translation from Watson, *The Complete Works of Chuang Tzu*, 342–43.

4. This refers to *Analects* 7.35: "The Master was seriously ill. Zilu asked permission to offer a prayer. The Master said, 'Was such a thing ever done?' Zilu said, 'Yes, it was. The prayer offered was as follows: pray thus to the gods above and below.' The Master said, 'In that case, I have long been offering my prayers'" (子疾病, 子路請禱. 子曰: "有諸?" 子路對曰: "有之. 誄曰: '禱爾于上下神祇.'" 子曰: "丘之禱久矣"). Translation by D. C. Lau, in Confucius, *The Analects*, 91.

5. During the time of King Yao 堯 in the legendary past, there were ten suns that scorched all plants and crops, as well as predatory animals and monsters that terrorized the people. The heroic archer Hou Yi 后羿 shot down nine of the suns and killed various monsters and fearsome animals. For Hou Yi, see "Surveying Obscurities" ("Lan ming xun" 覽冥訓) and "The Basic Warp" ("Ben jing xun" 本經訓) in Liu An, *Huainanzi ji shi*, vol. 1, 485–502, especially 500–502, and vol. 2, 574–78. Translation of chapter titles from Liu An, *The Essential* Huainanzi.

6. The "Three Worthies" are the three worthies of Qin 秦: Yanxi 奄息, Zhonghang 中行, and Qianhu 鍼虎. In the *Shijing* 詩經 poem "Yellow Bird" ("Huang niao" 黃鳥) from the "Airs of Qin" ("Qin feng" 秦風), they are human sacrifices for Duke Mu of Qin. See Cheng Junying and Jiang Jianyuan, *Shijing zhu xi*, 350–53.

7. "Red brush," or "red tube," is a reference to another *Shijing* poem, "Quiet Girl" ("Jing nü" 靜女) from the "Airs of Bei" ("Bei feng" 邶風): "The quiet girl is beautiful, she gave me a red brush/tube" (靜女其孌, 貽我彤管). See Cheng Junying and Jiang Jianyuan, *Shijing zhu xi*, 115–17. Tradition has linked the "red brush" with female historians of high antiquity; it is thus an allusion to Shangguan.

天降時雨, 山川出雲. 乃生靈媛, 祚我聖君. 精微其道, 煥炳其文. 三光錯行, 昭容綱紀. 百揆繁會, 昭容條理. 外圖邦政, 内諗天子. 憂在進賢, 思求多士. 忠孝心感, 天焉報之; 吉凶有數, 丘焉禱之. 如彼九日, 羿焉暴之; 如彼三良, 秦焉悼之. 漢宮選才, 班氏其特; 楚史書霸, 樊姝之力. 彧穆齊公, 敘其明德, 嗟爾彤管, 是鑒是則.[8]

Perhaps the most intriguing aspect of the memorial is the historical exemplars to which Zhang Yue compares the Shining Consort. The honorable Lady Ban is a staple complimentary allusion for works about women; Zhang Yue pinpoints Ban's talent, and there is a parallel between two gifted and learned women who played an important role in the government.[9] The allusion to Consort Fan, however, seems misplaced unless we consider Zhang Yue's purpose in so crafting the memorial. Consort Fan was mentioned briefly in chapter 1's discussion of classic models of female behavior as codified in *Lienü zhuan*.[10] The crux of Consort Fan's virtue is located in her championing of the dynastic patriarchy. The main episode of her *Lienü zhuan* entry involves her damaging (and correct) character assessment of her husband's minister Yu Qiuzi 虞丘子 (dates unknown) based on an analogy between herself and Yu Qiuzi; whereas she always procures beauties for the king, Yu Qiuzi is selfish and monopolizes favor for himself and his intimates.[11] The story

8. Zhang Yue, "Zhaorong Shangguan shi bei ming" 昭容上官氏碑銘 (Memorial Tablet for Shining Consort née Shangguan), *QTW* 231.6b (2337).

9. I believe that the allusion is to Ban Zhao and not to Consort Ban, Emperor Cheng's 成帝 (Liu Ao 劉驁; r. 33–7 BCE) consort, who is remembered for her virtue and defense of herself against charges of occult practice brought by the Zhao sisters, the "un-virtuous" new harem favorites who supplanted her. See *HS* 97b.3983–88; and Idema and Grant, *The Red Brush*, 77–82. Although Consort Ban also wrote or is attributed with writing several famous poems, of the two famous Ban women Ban Zhao is probably the more well-known "female literary talent" and the one with the most important governmental role. Thus she would seem to be a more appropriate figure for comparison to Shangguan Wan'er.

10. Consort Fan was the wife of King Zhuang of Chu, and *Lienü zhuan* hails her as an example of a "virtuous and perspicacious" (*xianming* 賢明) woman. King Zhuang was not a particularly gifted or moral ruler, but as a result of Consort Fan's remonstrance he curtailed his overindulgence in hunting and applied himself diligently to affairs of state. See *LNZ* 2.59.

11. King Zhuang was pleased with his consort's words and related them to Yu Qiuzi the next day. Mortified, Yu Qiuzi repented and recommended the talented and worthy

of Consort Fan hinges upon the clichéd analogy between two cardinal hierarchical relationships: husband is to wife as king is to minister. On a deeper level, Consort Fan's virtue lies not just in her role as wise advisor to her husband, but also in her active support of a system that devalues her. She acts against her own individual desires and interests ("how could I not want to monopolize your love and favor?"),[12] and it is this self-effacement that defines her as a "virtuous and perspicacious" woman.

One might argue that in the context of Shangguan Wan'er's memorial inscription, Consort Fan is merely a stock literary allusion about a woman who somehow benefited the government. Yet this misses the import of the allusion; it writes over Shangguan Wan'er as bold political power-holder with the image of a woman who conforms to the model of selfless helpmate. This sort of narrative re-casting is the only way in which Zhang Yue can rescue Shangguan Wan'er from historical judgment; his memorial inscription reveals the power of history and genre to remake the figures and events of the past. The force of ingrained narrative typology indicates that the process of narrative reconstruction can potentially even proceed unconsciously, without particular authorial intent. In Zhang Yue's case, certainly his "Preface to Shining Consort Shangguan's Literary Collection" evinces singular respect for her talent and nostalgia for the era over which she presided.[13] Shangguan's recently unearthed tomb has also yielded the discovery of a new epitaph, which further suggests the respect accorded to Shangguan in the years immediately following her death and challenges the orthodoxy or immutability of her received image as posthumously constructed.[14]

This study of the narrative repertory with which the women leaders of the Zhou through Jinglong era have been cast and re-cast has returned time and again to the issue of narrative typology and formula.

Sunshu Ao 孫叔敖 (ca. 630–593 BCE), who guided the king towards ordering his state and achieving the position of hegemon within three years. See *LNZ* 2.60.

12. 妾豈不欲擅王之愛寵哉?; *LNZ* 2.60.

13. In this work, he praises her as "the most talented of her generation, astute and erudite" (才華絕代, 敏識聰聽). He narrates her amazing rise to power and her skillful execution of a wide range of important government responsibilities from the 680s until her death; see *WYYH* 700.4b–6a. See also chapter 2 for recent scholarly discussions of this work.

14. For a translation and discussion of the epitaph, see Rothschild, "'Her Influence Great.'"

The study's approach is grounded in the theoretical understanding of history as a type of culturally situated narrative that engenders particular types of plot structures and historical characters designed to guide readers towards particular moral messages. Underlying this approach is the belief that when we investigate historical characters constructed from complex intersections of record, cultural value, and rumor, any definitive objective truth about the historical facts and specific details of their personal lives remains highly elusive. A more fruitful and satisfying approach, and, I believe, one that is more wide-ranging in its implications, seeks to understand the nature of these intersections, how cultural biases and archetypes are formed over time, and how thorny and multifaceted cultural sites such as gender, power, and kingship are negotiated, assimilated, and interpreted. Following this approach, my study has placed the images of these Tang women in the historical discourse of female power and moral-cosmic conceptualizations of gender. The sociocultural phenomenon of gender anarchy exists in historical works because it is perceived and defined as such by historians and writers who find attitudes or institutions in the past at odds with their understanding of sociocultural norms. Therefore, the writers describe them as unnatural, and narrative embellishments tend to stress their judgments.

In this vein, my study raises the important issue of how portrayals of these women differ from portrayals of condemned male rulers, whose presence is certainly felt in the tradition. Although male rulers are accused of excess and greed, in the accounts that condemn them we do not see the lingering, detailed descriptions of specific instances of material excess that are ubiquitous in narratives on the early Tang women power-holders. In accounts of the evil male ruler, his material and especially sexual transgression is described in terms of overindulgence in prerogatives, as opposed to indulgence in activities that are fundamentally inappropriate. Furthermore, condemnations of male rulers often displace their transgression to the imperial harem, so that their misdeeds are framed in terms of dissipation in the feminine.

My initial analysis of portrayals of pre-Tang women leaders revealed the development of prototypes of female power. Historical and anecdotal narratives demarcate models of transgression and virtue in women leaders, whereby a woman's moral worth is determined by her level of self-effacing investment in the patriarchal ruling structure. Portrayals of female power-holders categorized as transgressive rely more heavily on rumor and insinuation than do portrayals of other historical narrative types. The power of narrative formulas is evident in critical analysis and cross-examination of these portrayals, which often sound suspiciously repetitive. Even in the case of Empress Feng of the Northern Wei, a capable ruler who presided over a prosperous state, we see the tropes of the destructive woman assert themselves in the form of insinuations of improper sexual behavior. The biographies of the successful high-ranking male ministers of her court often totter uneasily between the "sycophantic sexual favorite" narrative and the "virtuous and loyal official" narrative.

Historical, semi-historical, and fictional narratives hinge upon a negotiation of viewpoints and worldviews, and portrayals of historical figures in particular represent convergences of contemporary and retrospective perspectives, positive and negative propaganda, and rumor. My examination of the shift from contemporary to retrospective accounts of the same personages and events has demonstrated the fluidity of narrative images, the ease with which the same basic image or event can be recast to accord with an opposite interpretation of its meaning. The celebration of cosmic approval, harmony, and imagery of the divine female, found in seventh- and early eighth-century materials, is later reworked into a condemnatory discourse emphasizing their transgression as figures that violate their "natural" roles as women. In seventh- and early eighth-century materials, we read of commoners spontaneously bursting into song to praise the beneficent rule of Wu Zhao and Empress Wei; in *Chaoye qianzai*, the joyful songs have become ominous predictive songs, which obliquely foretell the dreadful rise of female rule. The works of poetry and prose produced at the courts of Wu Zhao and Zhongzong extol the physical and spiritual beauty of the landed estates and their owners, often the leading ladies of the court; later writers identify what they see as the destructive nature of these women with their lavish residences and possessions.

Condemnatory narratives define their rule itself as inversion from the correct norm, as a source of destabilization based upon a reversal of gender roles that are perceived as natural. In these narratives, biology is not as important as socio-cultural position in determining rhetorical gender, and the perceived disordering of socially sanctioned gender roles is associated with cultural decline and chaos. The dangerous materiality of the feminine, in particular, is echoed in various literary-historical discourses and is often important for conveying character evaluation. Within the timeframe of the late seventh and early eighth centuries, two other women, Xuanzong's sisters the Jinxian 金仙 (689–732) and Yuzhen 玉真 (692–762) Princesses, emerge as interesting counterpoints to the women who have been the subject of this study. The sisters were ordained as Daoists and were appointed abbesses of their own temples. Surviving records on the princesses' shared ordination ceremony stress the lavish expense and cast powerful Daoist cleric Shi Chongxuan 史崇玄 (d. 713), who presided over the ceremony, in a manner that evokes Xue Huaiyi and Huifan.[15] The rhetorical and historical baggage of the Taiping Princess looms large in these portrayals; like her nieces, she received a Daoist ordination, and Shi Chongxuan's condemnation is probably in large part due to his association with her.[16] How, then, did the princesses avoid the full exponent of rhetorical blame and emerge as sincere Daoist abbesses? A simple answer might lie in the fact that neither woman seems to have participated in a prolonged manner in political power plays.[17] Yuzhen's self-conscious renunciation of her secular property and titles (in 744, after decades of enjoying them) enabled her to further extricate herself from potential blame.[18]

In a sense, the very fact that the narratives about greed and corruption begin, through abortively, in connection with women who never participated meaningfully in politics actually indicates the trenchant

15. For a translation of cleric Zhang Wanfu's document describing the ordination preparations, see Benn, *The Cavern-Mystery Transmission*, 115–20. Benn also analyzes the document in detail.

For Shi Chongxuan, see *TPGJ* 288.2292; *JTS* 7.141; and *XTS* 59.1520 and 83.3656–57. Supposedly, Shi was "allowed unlimited access to the imperial quarters" (得出入禁中); *XTS* 83.3656. The favor he enjoyed seems to have caused a group of Buddhist monks to become jealous, and, in an ill-conceived scheme, they bribed an insane man to proclaim himself emperor and claim that Shi Chongxuan made him do it; see *XTS* 83.3656–57; and Benn, *The Cavern-Mystery Transmission*, 18–19. Shi Chongxuan was ultimately executed when Taiping fell from power.

16. See Benn, *The Cavern-Mystery Transmission*, 10–11, 16–19.

17. Benn records instances in which Yuzhen came to the defense of maligned ministers and presided over Daoist rituals in her capacity as a high-ranking Daoist cleric, but her level of political engagement never came close to that of Taiping and Anle. See Benn, *The Cavern-Mystery Transmission*, 12–16.

18. *XTS* 83.3657; Benn, *The Cavern-Mystery Transmission*, 15.

nature of the narratives. The appeal of these narratives is borne out in their continuation and transformation in later discourses surrounding the early Tang women leaders.

The Powerful Women of the Early Tang in Later Literature and Other Media

Long after the first accounts were written about them, the powerful women of the early Tang and their male associates continued to capture the imaginations of generations of writers and readers. These later works often share the concern with gender roles and sexuality. In particular, Wu Zhao has been a popular subject with writers throughout the later imperial and modern periods. During the Ming and Qing dynasties, she was the subject of famous novels and works of crime fiction and pornography. The pornographic work *Ruyijun zhuan* 如意君傳 (Biography of Lord Ruyi ["As You Like It"])[19] follows the sexual relationship between Wu Zhao and her fictional favorite, the well-endowed Xue Aocao 薛敖曹, who seems to be based most closely on Xue Huaiyi.[20] Wu Zhao and Xue Huaiyi also star in *Wu Zetian si da qi'an* 武則天四大奇案 (Four Great Cases of Wu Zetian), a crime drama featuring the famous judge Di Renjie.[21] The work closes with Judge Di meting out justice to all offenders, including the empress's lover.

The at-best ambiguous image of early Tang female power and natural response is given a somewhat more positive treatment in Li Ruzhen's 李汝珍 (ca. 1763–ca. 1830) novel *Jinghua yuan* 鏡花緣 (Flowers in the Mirror). The majority of the novel follows protagonist Tang Ao's 唐敖 (Arrogance of Tang) travels to various lands in which social norms are

19. *Ruyi* is a play on words referencing Wu Zhao's Ruyi reign period (692) and the protagonist's sexual service of Wu Zhao ("as you like it"). This is also a Buddhist term meaning "staff" or "wand," referring to the protagonist's penis.

20. Xue Huaiyi is mentioned briefly as a previous lover. See Stone, *The Fountainhead of Chinese Erotica*, 139. Stone's work provides a translation and study of *Ruyijun zhuan*.

21. For a loose English translation, see van Gulik, *Dee goong an*. For discussion of the work, see Idema, "The Mystery of the Halved Judge Dee Novel."

somehow reversed from those of China, but the frame story is set at Wu Zhao's court. Tipsy after drinking with the Taiping Princess and other court ladies, Wu Zhao issues a decree ordering all the flowers to bloom at the same time by the next morning, even though it is not natural for all of them to bloom together. The flower spirits are cowed into following the decree, only to be punished by the gods for blooming out of season. Their punishment is to temporarily live on earth as mortal women. There, the talented flower fairy incarnations successfully take part in the imperial examinations for women held by Wu Zhao. At the end, they join with their husbands and brothers in the coup deposing the empress and restoring power to Zhongzong, the point presumably being that the cosmic disorder of female rule is, like the mortal incarnations of the flower fairies and Tang Ao's habitations of various socially reversed lands, inherently temporary.[22]

In twentieth-century China, May Fourth and Communist thinkers discovered in Wu Zhao a champion of the working class and women's rights. The revival of interest in Wu Zhao and other famous historical women in the twentieth century was especially linked to the Maoist reevaluation of historical figures. This was a process in which Jiang Qing played an important role.[23] Guo Moruo's 郭沫若 (1892–1978) play *Wu Zetian* 武則天, published in 1963, is representative of the tenor of Maoist reevaluation. The work extols her brave opposition to the entrenched aristocrats and the feudal class system. In an unintentionally humorous episode of anachronism, when the teenage Shangguan Wan'er asks Wu Zhao why she had executed her father and grandfather, the empress explains that it was because they represented the aristocratic feudal class that wanted to oppress women and the people in general. Since Wu Zhao was opposed to this negative class allegiance, they rebelled against her and she had to eliminate them.[24] She is also depicted as proud of her lower-class origins and disapproving of Luo Binwang's 684 declaration of war against her on the grounds that he does not attempt to speak on

22. For studies of *Jinghua yuan*, see Epstein, *Competing Discourses*, ch. 6; Roddy, *Literati Identity and its Fictional Representations*, ch. 8; and Brandauer, "Women in the *Ching-hua Yuan*."

23. See MacFarquhar and Schoenhals, *Mao's Last Revolution*, chaps. 1, 2, and 5.

24. Guo Moruo, *Wu Zetian*, 22.

behalf of the people.[25] Ironically, Jiang Qing herself has been cast as the archetypal "destructive female power-holder." Beginning in the 1960s (in Taiwan and Hong Kong) and intensifying after the fall of the Gang of Four, there appeared an entire genre of works dedicated to exposing Jiang Qing's "amorous adventures" and tracing her quest to realize her "dreams of becoming a female emperor" along the lines of Wu Zhao.[26]

The legend of China's only female emperor spread beyond China to be taken up by American, European, and Asian-American writers. Modern novels on Wu Zhao often follow quite closely the standard historical sources. *Lady Wu*, by the famous translator and writer Lin Yutang (1895–1976), is notable for adopting all of the most prejudicial and far-fetched episodes found in *Jiu Tang shu*, *Xin Tang shu*, and/or *Zizhi tongjian* and, in some cases, embellishing these with extra salacious details.[27] For instance, the novel depicts Xue Huaiyi as being inspired to identify Wu with the Buddha Maitreya after seeing her "naked protruding belly" (which later became part of the iconography of Maitreya) during sex.[28] Likewise, Su Tong's 蘇童 (1963–) 1994 novel *Wu Zetian* for the most part follows faithfully the standard historical account.[29] Eleanor Clooney and Daniel Altieri's *Deception: A Novel of Murder and Madness in Ancient China* (1993) takes more liberties with the historical narrative, but fabricated episodes are geared towards portraying her as an evil, insane, and illiterate shrew.[30]

25. Guo Moruo, *Wu Zetian*, 69, 72.

26. See, for example, Zhang Ganping 張贛萍, *The Vile History and Amorous Adventures of Jiang Qing* 江青的醜史與艷聞 (1969); Le Xin 樂欣, *Jiang Qing's "Dreams of Being a Female Emperor"* 江青的"女皇夢" (1986); Wei Shaochang 魏紹昌, *The Unofficial History of Jiang Qing* 江青外史 (1986); and Zhu Zhongli 朱仲麗, *"Dreams of Being a Female Emperor": The Unofficial Biography of Jiang Qing* "女皇夢": 江青外傳 (1988).

27. For example, Lin includes the claim that Xue Huaiyi burned down the Mingtang in a jealous rage. See *JTS* 183.4743.

28. Lin Yutang, *Lady Wu*, 162. The imagery is anachronistic; the iconography of the fat-bellied Maitreya does not predate the tenth-century "Laughing Buddha" Budai. I am indebted to the anonymous reader of this manuscript for this point.

29. Although the novel shifts perspective on several occasions to adopt the standpoints of three of Wu Zhao and Gaozong's sons (Li Hong, Li Xian, and Li Dan), characters and events are portrayed according to the standard historical accounts.

30. See, for example, descriptions of Wu Zhao's disregard for the people in Clooney and Altieri, *Deception*, 88–89, 92–94.

In the twenty-first century, Beijing-born author and French émigré Shan Sa's 山颯 (Yan Ni 閻妮; 1972–) 2003 novel *Impératrice*, translated into English in 2006 by Adriana Hunter and entitled *Empress*, adopts a wholly positive spin on Wu's life and career. The novel is written from Wu Zhao's perspective, beginning when she was in her mother's womb and ending some time after her death. In order to eliminate troublesome elements in traditional sources on Wu, Shan Sa refers, through the empress's voice, to the prejudices against her in standard accounts and also changes those accounts. For example, according to Shan Sa's account, Empress Wang actually might have murdered Wu's infant daughter, and officials opposed to her rule slandered her by suggesting she was the murderer.[31] Wu's brutal murder of her rivals is likewise transformed into the vengeful act of Concubine Xiao against unnamed harem rivals.[32]

In more recent times, a television series, *Da Ming Gong ci* 大明宮詞 (Palace of Desire, or literally "Palace Lyrics of the Great Hall of Light"), proved immensely popular with Chinese audiences. Focusing on the relationship between Wu Zhao and her daughter the Taiping Princess, the series portrayed the powerful princesses of the turn of the eighth century as positive, endearing figures. The Taiping Princess, in particular, is transformed once again; she is neither a spiritually lofty immortal nor a destructive, power-hungry woman, but rather a tragic romantic heroine.[33]

Even a cursory description of these works reveals the same underlying issues that inform my study: we see the way in which these women are fashioned and refashioned as historical characters based upon the cultural lens of the writer-interpreter. The image of the medieval Chinese female power-holder thus continues to be shaped by writers to accord with their own particular cultural perspectives and contemporary concerns. This realization, in turn, has implications for the way we approach history itself, in particular, the relationship between history and collective identity formation. The way in which we define ourselves in the present is premised upon generally accepted interpretations of the past. This is

31. Shan Sa, *Empress*, 119. See also pp. 317–18 for a description of the way in which she was posthumously slandered.

32. Shan Sa, *Empress*, 101–2.

33. An appendix to Jonathan Clements's *Wu: The Chinese Empress Who Schemed, Seduced, and Murdered Her Way to Become a Living God* briefly introduces several other recent novels, movies, and television series; see pp. 188–96.

perhaps especially true in regards to pre-modern elite Chinese society, in which historical precedent plays such an essential and culturally defining role. The increasing denunciation of the early Tang women leaders as we move into the Five Dynasties and Song periods not only indicates the clear gender bias of male historians, but also suggests changing modes of self-definition, which gave these men a new and different stake in image-making surrounding the Tang women. A systematic examination of portrayals of the Tang female leaders in relation to identity formation among the literati is beyond the scope of my study. I hope, however, that this book has opened a dialogue about the interconnectedness between historical image-making, collective (male) identity, and changing conceptions of gender.

Bibliography

Ban Gu 班固. *Han shu* 漢書 (History of the Han Dynasty). Beijing: Zhonghua shuju, 1962..

Bao Jialin 鮑家麟. "Yinyang xueshuo yu funü diwei" 陰陽學説與婦女地位 (*Yinyang* Doctrine and Female Position). In *Zhongguo funü shi lunji xu ji*中國婦女史論集 續集 (Essays on Chinese Women's History), edited by Bao Jialin, vol. 2, 37–54. Taibei: Daoxiang chubanshe, 1988.

Benn, Charles D. *The Cavern-Mystery Transmission: A Taoist Ordination Ritual of A.D. 711*. Honolulu: University of Hawai'i Press, 1991.

Bingham, Woodbridge. "Wen Ta-Ya: The First Recorder of T'ang History." *Journal of the American Oriental Society* 57, no. 4 (Dec. 1937): 368–74.

Bokenkamp, Stephen R. "A Medieval Feminist Critique of the Chinese World Order: The Case of Wu Zhao (r. 690–705)." *Religions* 28 (1998): 383–92.

Brandauer, Frederick. "Women in the *Ching-hua Yuan:* Emancipation toward a Confucian Ideal." *Journal of Asian Studies* 36, no. 1 (1977): 647–60.

Cen Jian'gong 岑建功. *Jiu Tang shu yiwen* 舊唐書逸文 (Lost Passages from *Jiu Tang shu*). Appended to Luo Shilin 羅士 琳, Liu Wenqi 劉文淇, and Cen Jian'gong, *Jiu Tang shu jiaokan ji* 舊唐書校勘記. Dingyuan fangshi 定遠方氏, 1872.

Cen Zhongmian 岑仲勉. *Tangshi yushen* 唐史餘瀋 (Supplement to the Tang Histories). Beijing: Zhonghua shuju, 1960.

Chao Yuanfang 巢元方. *Zhubing yuanhou lun* 諸病源候論 (Comprehensive Discussions of the Causes and Symptoms of All Illnesses). Beijing: Renmin weisheng chubanshe, 1993.

Chen, Fan-pen. "Problems of Chinese Historiography as Seen in the Official Records on Yang Guei-fei." *T'ang Studies* 8–9 (1990–91): 83–96.

Chen, Jack Wei. *The Poetics of Sovereignty: On Emperor Taizong of the Tang Dynasty*. Cambridge, MA: Harvard University Asia Center, 2010.

Chen Jinhua. "Sarira and Scepter: Empress Wu's Political Use of Buddhist Relics." *Journal of the International Association of Buddhist Studies* 25, no. 102 (2002): 33–150.

Chen Jo-shui 陳弱水. "Empress Wu and Proto-Feminist Sentiments in T'ang China." In *Imperial Rulership and Cultural Change in Traditional China*, edited by Frederick P. Brandauer and Chun-chieh Huang, 77–116. Seattle: University of Washington Press, 1994.

———. *Tangdai de funü wenhua yu jiating shenghuo* 唐代的婦女文化與家庭生活 (Tang Women's Culture and Family Life). Taibei: Yunchen wenhua, 2007.

Chen Yaowen 陳耀文. *Tianzhong ji* 天中記 (Record from Tianzhong Mountain). Taibei: Wenyuan shuju, 1964.

Chen Yu-shih. "The Historical Template of Pan Chao's 'Nü Chieh.'" *T'oung Pao* 82.4/5 (1996): 229–57.

Cheng Junying 程俊英 and Jiang Jianyuan 蔣見元, eds. *Shijing zhu xi* 詩經注析 (The Classic of Poetry, with Notes and Analysis). Beijing: Zhonghua shuju, 1991.

Clements, Jonathan. *Wu: The Chinese Empress Who Schemed, Seduced, and Murdered Her Way to Become a Living God*. Phoenix Mill: Sutton Publishing, 2007.

Clooney, Eleanor, and Daniel Altieri. *Deception: A Novel of Murder and Madness in Ancient China*. New York: Avon, 1993.

Confucius. *The Analects*. Translated by D. C. Lau. London: Penguin, 1979.

Cutter, Robert Joe, and William Gordon Crowell. *Empresses and Consorts: Selections from Chen Shou's Records of the Three States with Pei Songzhi's Commentary*. Honolulu: University of Hawai'i Press, 1999.

Dien, Albert E. "Yen Chih-t'ui (531–591+): A Buddho-Confucian." In *Confucian Personalities*, edited by Arthur F. Wright and Denis Twitchett, 43–64. Stanford: Stanford University Press, 1962.

Dien, Dora Shu-fang. *Empress Wu Zetian in Fiction and in History: Female Defiance in Confucian China*. Hauppage, NY: Nova Science Publishers, 2003.

Ding Yan 丁燕. "Lüe lun Chu Tang yingzhi shi" 略論初唐應制詩 (On Early Tang *yingzhi* Poetry). *Shang qiu shifan xueyuan xuebao* 商丘師范學院學報 (Journal of Shangqiu Teachers' College) 23, no. 8 (August 2007): 30–33.

Dong Hao 董浩 et al. *Quan Tang wen* 全唐文 (Complete Prose of the Tang). Beijing: Zhonghua shuju, 1983.

Duan Chengshi 段成式. *Youyang zazu* 酉陽雜俎 (Miscellaneous Records from Youyang). Beijing: Zhonghua shuju, 1985.

Duan Tali 段塔麗. *Tangdai funü diwei yanjiu* 唐代婦女地位研究 (Research on the Status of Tang Women). Beijing: Renmin chubanshe, 2000.

Ebrey, Patricia Buckley. *Cambridge Illustrated History of China*. Cambridge: Cambridge University Press, 1996.

Egan, Ronald. "*Preface to Shangguan Wan'er*, Shangguan Zhaorong wenji." In *Women Writers of Traditional China: An Anthology of Poetry and Criticism*, 723–25. Edited by Kang-i Sun Chang and Haun Saussy. Stanford: Stanford University Press, 1999.

Eisenberg, Andrew. *Kingship in Early Medieval China*. Leiden: Brill, 2008.

Epstein, Maram. *Competing Discourses: Orthodoxy, Authenticity, and Engendered Meanings in Late Imperial Chinese Fiction*. Cambridge, MA: Harvard University Asia Center, 2001.

Fan Ye 范曄 et al. *Hou Han shu* 後漢書 (History of the Later Han Dynasty [Eastern Han Dynasty]). Commentary by Li Xian 李賢. Beijing: Zhonghua shuju, 1965.

Fang Xuanling 房玄齡 et al. *Jin shu* 晉書 (History of the Jin Dynasty). Beijing: Zhonghua shuju, 1974.

Feng, H. Y., and J. K. Shryock. "The Black Magic in China Known as *ku*." *JAOS* 55.1 (1935): 1–30.

Feng Yan 封演. *Fengshi wen jian ji jiaozhu* 封氏聞見記校註 (Record of What Mr. Feng Heard and Saw). Beijing: Zhonghua shuju, 1958.

Forte, Antonino. "The Maitreyist Huayi (d. 695) and Taoism." *Tang yanjiu* 唐研究 (Tang Studies) 4 (1998): 15–29.

———. *Mingtang and Buddhist Utopias in the History of the Astronomical Clock: The Tower, Statue, and Armillary Sphere Constructed by Empress Wu*. Roma: Instituto italiano per il Medio ed Estremo orientale: Ecole française d'Extrême –Orient, 1988.

———. *Political Propaganda and Ideology in China at the End of the Seventh Century: Inquiry into the Nature, Authors and Function of the Dunhuang Document S.6502, Followed by an Annotated Translation*. Kyoto: Scuola Italiana di studi sull'Asia orientale, 2005 [revised from the original 1976 edition].

Fracasso, Riccardo. "The Nine Tripods of Empress Wu." In *T'ang China and Beyond: Studies on East Asia from the Seventh to the Tenth Century*, edited by Antonino Forte. Kyoto: Instituto Italiano di Cultura, Scuola di Studi sull'Asia Orientale, 1988: 85–96.

Franke, Herbert. "Some Remarks on the Interpretation of Chinese Dynastic Histories." *Oriens* 3 (1950): 113–22.

Gao Shiyu 高世瑜. "A Fixed State of Affairs and Mis-positioned Status: Gender Relations During the Sui, Tang, Five Dynasties, and Song Dynasty." In *The Chalice and the Blade in Chinese Culture: Gender Relations and Social Models*, edited by Min Jiayin. Beijing: China Social Sciences Publishing House, 1995: 270–314.

———. *Tangdai funü* 唐代婦女 (Women during the Tang Dynasty). Xi'an: San Qin chubanshe, 1988.

Goldin, Paul Rakita. *The Culture of Sex in Ancient China*. Honolulu: University of Hawai'i Press, 2002.

———. "The View of Women in Early Confucianism." In *The Sage and the Second Sex: Confucianism, Ethics, and Gender*, edited by Chenyang Li, 133–61. Chicago: Open Court, 2000.

Golovachev, Valentin C. "Matricide Among the Tuoba-Xianbei and Its Transformation During the Northern Wei." *Early Medieval China* 8 (2002): 1–42.

De Groot, J. J. M. *The Religious System of China: Its Ancient Forms, Evolution, History and Present Aspect, Manners, Custom and Social Institutions Connected Therewith*. Taipei: Ch'eng Wen Publishing Company, 1976.

Guisso, R. W. L. "The Reigns of the Empress Wu, Chung-tsung and Jui-tsung (684–712)." Chapter Six in *The Cambridge History of China Volume 3*, edited by Denis C. Twitchett, 290–332. Cambridge: Cambridge University Press, 1979.

———. *Wu Tse-t'ien and the Politics of Legitimation in T'ang China*. Bellingham: Western Washington University Press, 1978.

Guo Moruo 郭沫若. *Wu Zetian* 武則天. Beijing: Zhongguo xiju chubanshe, 1963.

Hanyu da cidian 漢語大詞典. Beijing: Shangwu yinshuguan, 2003.

Harper, Donald. *Early Chinese Medical Literature: The Mawangdui Medical Manuscripts*. New York: Kegan Paul International, 1998.

Hightower, James Robert. *The Poetry of T'ao Ch'ien*. Oxford: Clarendon, 1970.

Hinsch, Bret. "The Composition of *Lienü zhuan*: Was Liu Xiang the Author or Editor?" *Asia Major*, 3rd series, 20.1 (2007): 1–23.

———. "The Textual History of Liu Xiang's *Lienü zhuan*." *Monumenta Serica* 52 (2004): 95–112.

———. *Women in Early Imperial China*. Boston: Roman & Littlefield Publishers, 2002.

Hobson, Peter. *Poems of Hanshan*. Walnut Creek, CA: Altamira, 2003.

Holmgren, Jennifer. "Race and Class in Fifth Century China: the Emperor Kao-tsu's Marriage Reform." *Early Medieval China* 2 (1995–96): 86–117.

———. "Women and Political Power in the Traditional T'o-pa Elite: A Preliminary Study of the Biographies of Empresses in the *Wei-Shu*." *Monumenta Serica*, vol. 35 (1981–83): 33–73.

Hu Han 胡菡. "Chu Tang yi gongting nüxing zuojia wei zhongxin zhi youyan shi lüelun." 初唐以宮廷女性作家為中心之游宴詩略論 (On Early Tang Banquet Poems Centered on Court Women Authors). *Chifeng xueyuan xuebao* 赤峰學院學報 (Journal of Chifeng University) 28, no. 5 (2007): 78–80.

Hu Wokun 胡我琨. *Qian tong* 錢通 (A Comprehensive Study of Money). Yingyin Wenyuan ge Siku quanshu. *Shibu* 13, *Zhengshu lei* 3. Taibei: Taiwan shangwu, 1983.

Hung, William. "The T'ang Bureau of Historiography before 708." *Harvard Journal of Asiatic Studies* 23 (1960–61): 93–107.

Idema, Wilt. "The Mystery of the Halved Judge Dee Novel." *Tamkang Review* VII (1977): 155–70.

Idema, Wilt, and Beata Grant. *The Red Brush: Writing Women of Imperial China*. Cambridge, MA: Harvard University Asia Center, 2004.

Irigaray, Luce. *This Sex Which Is Not One*. Translated by Catherine Porter with Carolyn Burke. Ithaca, NY: Cornell University Press, 1985.

Ji Xiao-bin. *Politics and Conservatism in Northern Song China: the Career and Thought of Sima Guang (A.D. 1019–1086)*. Hong Kong: Chinese University Press, 2005.

Ji Yougong 計有功. *Tangshi jishi* 唐詩紀事 (Record of Stories Related to Tang Poems). Beijing: Zhonghua shuju, 2007.

Jia Jinhua 賈晉華. "The 'Pearl Scholars' and the Final Establishment of Regulated Verse." *T'ang Studies* 14 (1996): 1–20.

———. "A Study of the *Jinglong wenguan ji*." *Monumenta Serica*, 47 (1999): 209–36.

———. *Tangdai jihui zongji yu shirenqun yanjiu* 唐代集會總集與詩人群研究 (A Study of Tang Dynasty Group Collections and Poetry Groups). Beijing: Beijing daxue chubanshe, 2001.

Jiang Shan'guo 蔣善國. *Chuci* 楚辭 (Songs of Chu). Taibei: Xin wen feng chubanshe gongsi, 1982.

Kinney, Anne Behnke. *Exemplary Women of Early China: The Lienü zhuan of Liu Xiang*. New York: Columbia University Press, 2014.

Kong Guanglin 孔廣林. *Shangshu zhonghou Zheng zhu* 尚書中候鄭注 (The Watch Officer's *Shangshu*, with Zheng Xuan's Commentary). In *Yi wei tong gua yan (ji qi ta san zhong)* 易緯通卦驗及其他三種 (An Examination of the Hexagrams in the *Book of Changes*, with three other titles). Beijing: Zhonghua shuju, 1991.

Kong Pingzhong 孔平仲. *Xu shishuo* 續世說 (Continuation of *Tales of the World*). Shanghai: Dongfang chuban zhongxin, 1996.

Kong Yingda 孔穎達. *Shang shu zheng yi* 尚書正義 (The Correct Significance of the *Shangshu* [Classic of History]). Beijing: Beijing daxue chubanshe, 1999.

Konghe jian miji 控鶴監祕記 (Secret Record of the Director of the Guiding the Immortal Cranes Bureau). Xie chun yuan, Min guo chu 寫春園, 民國初, between 1912 and 1930.

Le Xin 樂欣. *Jiang Qing de "nühuang meng* 江青的"女皇夢" (Jiang Qing's "Dreams of Being a Female Emperor"). In *Huo zhuo "Si ren bang" nei mu* 活捉"四人幫"內幕 (Capturing the Inside Story of the "Gang of Four"). Suo Guoxin 所國心 and Le Xin. Jiulong: Xin xiu chubanshe, 1986.

Lei Jiaji 雷家驥. *Wu Zetian zhuan* 武則天傳 (Biography of Wu Zetian). Beijing: Renmin chubanshe, 2001.

Li Baiyao 李百藥. *Bei Qi shu* 北齊書 (History of the Northern Qi Dynasty). Beijing: Zhonghua shuju, 1972.

Li Bincheng 李斌城. "'Shengxian taizi bei bing xu' kaoshi" "升仙太子碑並序" 考釋 (A Textual Analysis of the "Stele for the Crown Prince Who Ascended as an Immortal [Wangzi Jin] and Preface"). In Wang Wenchao and Zhao Wenrun, *Wu Zetian yu Songshan*, 29–40.

Li Fang 李昉 et al., comps. *Taiping guangji* 太平廣記 (Extensive Records from the Era of Great Peace). Beijing: Zhonghua shuju, 1961 (2010 reprint).

———. *Taiping yulan* 太平禦覽 (Imperial Readings from the Era of Great Peace). Beijing: Zhonghua shuju, 1960 (1963 reprint).

———. *Wenyuan yinghua* 文苑英華 (Fine Blossoms in the Garden of Literature). Beijing: Zhonghua shuju, 1966.

Li Gang 李綱. *Liangxi ji* 梁谿集 (Liang Brook Collection). Yingyin Wenyuan ge Siku quanshu. *Jibu* 4, *Bieji lei* 3. Taibei: Taiwan shangwu, 1983.

Li Juan 李娟. *Wu Zetian* 武則天. Beijing: Guojia tushuguan chubanshe, 2010.

Li Ping 李凭. *Bei Wei pingcheng shidai* 北魏平城時代 (The Pingcheng Era of the Northern Wei Dynasty). Beijing: Shehui kexue wenxian chubanshe, 2000.

Li Ruzhen 李汝珍. *Jinghua yuan* 鏡花緣 (Flowers in the Mirror). Beijing: Zhongguo wenlian, 1998.

Li Shangyin 李商隱. *Li Shangyin quan ji* 李商隱全集 (The Complete Collection of Li Shangyin). Edited by Feng Hao 馮浩 et al. Zhuhai: Zhuhai chubanshe, 2002.

Li Yanshou 李延壽 et al. *Bei shi* 北史 (History of the Northern Dynasties). Beijing: Zhonghua shuju, 1974.

———. *Nan shi* 南史 (History of the Southern Dynasties). Beijing: Zhonghua shuju, 1975.

Li Yipeng 李宜蓬. "Lun Shangguan Wan'er" 論上官婉兒 (On Shangguan Wan'er). *Suihua xueyuan xuebao* 綏化學院學報 (Journal of Suihua University) 27, no. 5 (Oct. 2007): 61–65.

Liang Hengtang 梁恒唐 and Liang Puhong 梁普紅. "Shuo Zhou Tang biange zai Shengxian taizi bei shang de liuhen" 說周唐變革在升仙太子碑上的留痕 (On the Remaining Traces of the Zhou-Tang Transition, as Seen in the "Stele for the Crown Prince Who Ascended as an Immortal [Wangzi Jin]"). In Wang Wenchao and Zhao Wenrun, *Wu Zetian yu Songshan*, 189–93.

Lin Yutang. *Lady Wu*. New York: G. P. Putnam's Sons, 1965.

Lippiello, Tiziana. *Auspicious Omens and Miracles in Ancient China: Han, Three Kingdoms and Six Dynasties.* Sankt Augustin: Monumenta Serica Institute, 2001.

Liu An 劉安. *Huainanzi ji shi* 淮南子集釋 (Master Huainan, with Collected Interpretations). Edited by He Ning 何寧. Beijing: Zhonghua shuju, 2010.

———. *The Essential* Huainanzi. Edited and translated by John S. Major et al. New York: Columbia University Press, 2012.

Liu Kezhuang 劉克莊. *Houcun shi hua* 後村詩話 (Houcun's Notes on Poetry). Taibei: Guangwen shuju, 1971.

Liu Su 劉餗. *Sui Tang jiahua*隋唐嘉話 (Table Talk from the Sui and Tang). Beijing: Zhonghua shuju, 1979.

Liu Su 劉肅. *Da Tang xinyu* 大唐新語 (New Words from the Great Tang). Beijing: Zhonghua shuju, 1984.

Liu Xiang 劉向. *Lienü zhuan jinzhu jinyi* 列女傳今註今譯 (Biographies of Model Women, with New Notes and Translation). Edited and translated by Zhang Jing 張敬. Taibei: Taiwan shangwu, 1994.

———. *Liexian zhuan jiao jian* 列仙傳校箋 (Model Biographies of Immortals, with Commentary). Notes by Wang Shumin 王叔岷. Beijing: Zhonghua shuju, 2007.

Liu Xu 劉昫 et al. *Jiu Tang shu* 舊唐書 (Old Tang History). Beijing: Zhonghua shuju, 1962.

Liu Yongcong 劉詠聰 (Clara Ho). *De Cai Se Quan: Lun Zhongguo gudai nüxing* 德才色權: 論中國古代女性 (Virtue, Talent, Sex, Power: On Pre-modern Chinese Women). Taibei: Maitian chuban gufen youxian gongsi, 1998.

Loewe, Michael. "The Case of Witchcraft in 91 BC: Its Historical Setting and Effect on Han Dynastic History." *Asia Major* 15 (1970): 159–96.

Lu Qinli 逯欽立. *Xian Qin Han Wei Jin Nanbei chao shi* 先秦漢魏晉南北朝詩 (Poems of the Pre-Qin, Han, Wei, Jin, and Northern and Southern Dynasties). Beijing: Zhonghua shuju, 1993.

Lü Xiaqing 呂夏卿. *Tang shu zhibi* 唐書直筆 (The Upright Brush on the Tang Histories). Congshu jicheng chubian, vol. 378. Beijing: Zhonghua shuju, 1985.

Lu Zongli. *The Power of the Words: Chen Prophecy in Chinese Politics, A.D. 265–619*. Oxford: Peter Lang, 2003.

Luo Longzhi 羅龍治. *Tangdai de houfei yu waiqi* 唐代的后妃與外戚 (Tang Consorts and Imperial Relatives by Marriage). Taibei: Guiguan tushu, 1978.

Ma Duanlin 馬端臨. *Wenxian tongkao* 文獻通考 (A Comprehensive Examination of Literary Documents). Beijing: Zhonghua shuju, 1986 (1991 reprint).

MacFarquhar, Roderick, and Michael Schoenhals. *Mao's Last Revolution*. Cambridge, MA: The Belknap Press of Harvard University Press, 2006.

Marlowe, Britt. *Empress Wu Zhao, Son of Heaven: Uses of Religious Patronage and Propaganda to Secure Support and Quell Dissension during the Tang Dynasty*. M.A. Thesis, University of Colorado, 2008.

McMahon, Keith. *Women Shall Not Rule: Imperial Wives and Concubines in China from Han to Liao*. Lanham: Rowman and Littlefield, 2013.

McMullen, David. "The Real Judge Dee: Ti Jen-chieh and the T'ang Restoration of 705." *Asia Major*, 3rd series, vol. 6, part 1 (1993): 1–41.

Meng Qi 孟棨. *Benshi shi* 本事詩 (Original Stories Relating to Poems). Shanghai: Shanghai guji chubanshe, 1991.

Min Jiayin, ed. *The Chalice and the Blade in Chinese Culture: Gender Relations and Social Models*. Beijing: China Social Sciences Publishing House, 1995.

Mollier, Christine. *Buddhism and Daoism Face to Face: Scripture, Ritual, and Iconographic Exchange in Medieval China*. Honolulu: University of Hawai'i Press, 2008.

Nie Yonghua 聶永華. *Chu Tang gongting shifeng liubian kaolun* 初唐宮廷詩風流變考論 (An Examination of Changes in Early Tang Court Poetry). Beijing: Zhongguo shehui kexue chubanshe, 2002.

O'Hara, Albert Richard, ed. and trans. *The Position of Woman in Early China According to the Lieh nü chuan, "The Biographies of Eminent Chinese Women."* Westport, CN: Hyperion, 1981 [reprint; 1945 original].

Ouyang Xiu 歐陽修. *Xin Tang shu* 新唐書 (New Tang History). Beijing: Zhonghua shuju, 1975.

Ouyang Xun 歐陽詢. *Yiwen leiju* 藝文類聚 (Collected Extracts from Literature). Shanghai: Shanghai guji chubanshe, 2007.

Owen, Stephen. *The End of the Chinese "Middle Ages": Essays in Mid-Tang Literary Culture*. Stanford: Stanford University Press, 1996.

———. "The Formation of the Tang Estate Poem." *Harvard Journal of Asiatic Studies* 55, no. 1 (June 1995): 39–59.

———. *The Poetry of the Early Tang*. Melbourne: Quirin Press, 2012.

Pearce, Scott. "Nurses, Nurslings, and New Shapes of Power in the Mid-Wei Court." *Asia Major*, 3rd series, 22.1 (2009): 287–309.

———. "A Response to Valentin Golovachev's 'Matricide during the Northern Wei.'" *Early Medieval China* 9 (2003): 139–44.

Pei Jianping 裴建平 and Dong Binglei 董炳磊. "Wu Zetian yu 'Shengxian taizi'" 武則天與 "升仙太子" (Wu Zetian and the "Crown Prince Who Became an Immortal" [Wangzi Jin]). In Wang Wenchao and Zhao Wenrun, *Wu Zetian yu Songshan*, 194–98.

Peng Dingxiu 彭定求 et al. *Quan Tang shi* 全唐詩 (Collected Poems of the Tang). Beijing: Zhonghua shuju, 1960.

Plaks, Andrew H. "Chinese Narrative Theory: Towards a Critical Theory of Chinese Narrative." In *Chinese Narrative: Critical and Theoretical Essays*, edited by Andrew H. Plaks, 309–52. Princeton: Princeton University Press, 1977.

Pulleyblank, E. G. "The *Tzyjyh Tongjiann Kaoyih* and the Sources for the History of the Period 730–63." *Bulletin of the School of Oriental and African Studies, University of London*, vol. 13, no. 2 (1950): 448–73.

Qian Nanxiu. *Spirit and Self in Medieval China: The Shih-shuo hsin yü and Its Legacy*. Honolulu: University of Hawai'i Press, 2001.

Qin Huitian 秦蕙田. *Wu li tong kao* 五禮通考 (A Comprehensive Examination of the Five Rites). Yingyin Wenyuan ge Siku quanshu. *Jingbu* 4, *Lilei* 5. Taibei: Taiwan shangwu, 1983.

Roddy, Stephen. *Literati Identity and its Fictional Representations in Late Imperial China*. Stanford: Stanford University Press, 1998.

Rothschild, Norman Harry. "'Her Influence Great, Her Merit Beyond Measure': A Translation and Initial Investigation of the Epitaph of Shangguan Wan'er." *Studies in Chinese Religions*, vol. 1, no. 2 (2015): 131–48.

———. "An Inquiry into Reign Era Changes under Wu Zhao, China's Only Female Emperor." *Early Medieval China* 12 (2006): 123–49.

———. *Rhetoric, Ritual, and Support Constituencies in the Political Authority of Wu Zhao, Woman Emperor of China*. Ph.D. diss., Brown University, 2003.

———. "Wu Zhao's Remarkable Aviary." *Southeast Review of Asia Studies*, vol. 27 (2005): 71–88.

Sawada Mizuho 澤田瑞穗. *Zetian Wu hou—shi yingzhu haishi nühuo?* 則天武后—是英主還是女禍? (Empress Wu Zetian—Was She an Enlightened Ruler or a Female Disaster?). Translated by Li Tiansong 李天送譯. Xi'an: San Qin chubanshe, 1977.

Shan Sa. *Empress*. Translated by Adriana Hunter. New York: Regan Books, 2006.

Shen Yue 沈約. *Song shu* 宋書 (History of the Liu-Song Dynasty). Beijing: Zhonghua shuju, 1974.

Shen Zinan 沈自南. *Yilin huikao* 藝林彙考 (A Collected Examination of Literature and the Arts). Beijing: Zhonghua shuju, 1988.

Sima Guang 司馬光. *Zizhi tongjian* 資治通鑒 (Comprehensive Mirror of Government). Beijing: Zhonghua shuju, 1956.

Sima Qian 司馬遷. *Shiji* 史記 (Records of the Historian). Beijing: Zhonghua shuju, 1964.

Skaff, Jonathan Karam. *Sui-Tang China and its Turko-Mongol Neighbors: Culture, Power, and Connections*. Oxford: Oxford University Press, 2012.

Song Minqiu 宋敏求. *Tang da zhao ling ji* 唐大詔令集 (Collected Imperial Edicts from the Tang). Taibei: Dingwen shuju, 1972.

Song Qirui 宋其蕤. *Bei Wei nü zhu lun* 北魏女主論 (The Female Rulers of the Northern Wei Dynasty). Beijing: Zhongguo shehui kexue chubanshe, 2006.

Stein, Rolf. *The World in Miniature: Container Gardens and Dwellings in Far Eastern Religious Thought*. Stanford: Stanford University Press, 1990.

Stone, Charles R. *The Fountainhead of Chinese Erotica: The Lord of Perfect Satisfaction (Ruyi jun zhuan)*. Honolulu: University of Hawai'i Press, 2003.

Su Tong 蘇童. *Wu Zetian* 武則天. Taibei: Maitian chuban gufen youxian gongsi, 1994.

Sun Qin'an 孫琴安. *Tangshi yu zhengzhi* 唐詩與政治 (Tang Poetry and Politics). Shanghai: Shanghai renmin chubanshe, 2003.

Swann, Nancy Lee. "Biography of the Empress Teng: A Translation from the Annals of the Later Han Dynasty." *Journal of the American Oriental Society* 51, no. 2 (June 1931): 138–59.

Tao Min 陶敏. "*Jinglong wenguan ji* kao" 景龍文館記考 (An Examination of the *Jinglong wenguan ji*). *Wen shi* 文史 48 (1999): 221–36.

Tao Qian 陶潛, attr. *Soushen houji* 搜神後記 (Later Record of In Search of the Supernatural). Beijing: Zhonghua shuju, 1981.

Tao Zongyi 陶宗儀. *Shuo fu* 說郛 (Collected Sayings from the Classics). Taibei: Taiwan shangwu yinshu guan, 1972.

Teng Ssu-yü. *Family Instructions for the Yen Clan*. Leiden: Brill, 1968.

Tian Xiaofei. "From the Eastern Jin through the early Tang (317–649)." In *The Cambridge History of Chinese Literature*, edited by Stephen Owen, 199–285. Cambridge: Cambridge University Press, 2010.

Tung, Jowen. *Fables for the Patriarchs: Gender Politics in Tang Discourse.* Lanham: Rowman and Littlefield, 2000.

Twitchett, Denis. "*Chen gui* and Other Works Attributed to Empress Wu Zetian." *Asia Major* vol. 16, part 1 (2003): 33–109.

———. "Chinese Biographical Writing." In *Historians of China and Japan*, edited by W. G. Beasley and E. G. Pulleybank. London: Oxford University Press, 1961: 95–114.

———. "Problems of Chinese Biography." In *Confucian Personalities*, edited by Arthur F. Wright and Denis Twitchett, 24–39. Stanford: Stanford University Press, 1962.

———. *The Writing of Official History under the T'ang.* Cambridge: Cambridge University Press, 1992.

Twitchett, Denis, and Howard J. Wechsler. "Kao-tsung (Reign 649–83) and the Empress Wu: The Inheritor and the Usurper." Chapter Five in *The Cambridge History of China Volume 3*, edited by Denis C. Twitchett, 242–89. Cambridge: Cambridge University Press, 1978.

Unschuld, Paul. *Medicine in China: A History of Ideas.* Berkeley: Univ. of California Press, 1985.

Van Ess, Hans. "Praise and Slander: The Evocation of Empress Lü in the *Shiji* and *Hanshu*." *Nan Nü* 8.2 (2006): 221–54.

van Gulik, Robert, trans. *Dee goong an: Three Murder Cases Solved by Judge Dee: An Old Chinese Detective Novel.* Tokyo: Toppan Print, 1949.

Vimalakirti Sutra. Translated by Burton Watson. New York: Columbia University Press, 1997.

Wang Dang 王讜. *Tang yu lin* 唐語林 (Tang Forest of Words). Taibei: Taiwan shangwu yinshu guan, 1968.

Wang Debao 王德保. *Sima Guang yu "Zizhi tongjian"* 司馬光與"資治通鑒" (Sima Guang and "*Zizhi tongjian*"). Beijing: Zhongguo shehui kexue chubanshe, 2001.

Wang Hongjun 王洪軍. *Wu Zetian pingzhuan* 武則天評傳 (A Critical Biography of Wu Zetian). Ji'nan shi: Shandong daxue chubanshe, 2010.

Wang Pu 王溥. *Tang hui yao* 唐會要 (Institutional History of the Tang). Beijing: Zhonghua shuju, 1955.

Wang Qinruo 王欽若 et al. *Cefu yuangui* 冊府元龜 (Book Prefecture of the Primordial Tortoise). Taibei: Taiwan Zhonghua shuju, 1967.

Wang Renyu 王仁裕. *Kaiyuan Tianbao yishi* 開元天寶遺事 (Past Affairs of the Kaiyuan and Tianbao Reign Periods). *Minghuang za lu: fu buyi, jiao kan ji (ji qi ta wu zhong)* 明皇雜錄附補遺校勘記及其他五種 (Assorted Records about the Reign of Xuanzong, with appended passages and annotations, and five other titles). Beijing: Zhonghua shuju, 1985.

Wang Shuning 王殊寧. "Tang Jinglong nianjian xiuwen guan xueshi kaolüe" 唐景龍年間修文館學士考略 (An Examination of the Xiu wenguan Scholars During the Jinglong Reign). *Shehui kexue luntan* 社會科學論壇 (Social Sciences Forum), vol. 7 (*xia*) (2006): 153–55.

Wang Wenchao 王文超 and Zhao Wenrun 趙文潤, eds. *Wu Zetian yu Songshan* 武則天與嵩山 (Wu Zetian and Mount Song). Beijing: Zhonghua shuju, 2003.

Wang Xianqian 王先謙 and Liu Wu 劉武. *Zhuangzi ji jie* 莊子集解 (Zhuangzi, with Collected Commentaries). Paired with *Zhuangzi ji jie nei pian bu zheng* 莊子集解內篇補正 (Zhuangzi, with Collected Commentaries and Textual Corrections on the Inner Chapters). Xin bian zhu zi ji cheng. Beijing: Zhonghua shuju, 1987 (2004 reprint).

Wang Xiumei 王秀梅, ed. *Shi jing* 詩經 (Classic of Poetry). Beijing: Zhonghua shuju, 2010.

Wang Yinglin 王應麟. *Yuhai* 玉海 (Jade Ocean). Taibei: Taiwan Huawen shuju, 1967.

Watson, Burton. *The Complete Works of Chuang Tzu*. New York: Columbia University Press, 1968.

Wechsler, Howard J. *Offerings of Jade and Silk: Ritual and Symbol in the Legitimation of the T'ang Dynasty*. New Haven: Yale University Press, 1985.

Wei Mojie suoshuo jing xinzhu 維摩詰所說經新注 (Vimalakirti Sutra, with New Notes). Annotated by Tang Sipeng 唐思鵬. Beijing: Huawen chubanshe, 2006.

Wei Shaochang 魏紹昌. *Jiang Qing waishi* 江青外史 (The Unofficial History of Jiang Qing). Jiulong: Zhongyuan chubanshe, 1986.

Wei Shou 魏收. *Wei Shu* 魏書 (History of the Northern Wei Dynasty). Beijing: Zhonghua shuju, 1974.

Wei Zheng 魏徵 et al. *Sui Shu* 隋書 (History of the Sui Dynasty). Beijing: Zhonghua shuju, 1973.

Wen Daya 溫大雅. *Da Tang chuangye qi ju zhu* 大唐創業起居注 (Court Diaries of the Foundation of the Great Tang). Congshu jicheng chubian, vol. 378. Beijing: Zhonghua shuju, 1985.

White, Hayden. "Historicism, History, and the Figurative Imagination." In *Tropics of Discourse: Essays in Cultural Criticism*, 101–20. Baltimore: The Johns Hopkins University Press, 1978.

———. "The Question of Narrative in Contemporary Historical Theory." In *The Content of the Form: Narrative Discourse and Historical Representation*, 26–57. Baltimore: The Johns Hopkins University Press, 1987.

———. "The Value of Narrativity in the Representation of Reality." In *The Content of the Form: Narrative Discourse and Historical Representation*, 1–25. Baltimore: The Johns Hopkins University Press, 1987.

Wills, John. "Empress Wu." *Mountains of Fame: Portraits in Chinese History*. Princeton: Princeton University Press, 1994: 127–48.

Wright, Arthur F. *The Sui Dynasty: The Unification of China, A.D. 581–617*. New York: Alfred A. Knopf, 1978.

Wright, Arthur F., and Denis Twitchett, eds. *Confucian Personalities*. Stanford: Stanford University Press, 1962.

———. *Perspectives on the T'ang*. New Haven: Yale University Press, 1973.

Wu Hung. *The Double Screen: Medium and Representation in Chinese Painting*. Chicago: University of Chicago Press, 1996.

Wu, Jie. "A Study of Group Compositions in Early Tang China (618–713)." Ph.D. diss., University of Washington, 2008.

Wu, Tien-wei. *Lin Biao and the Gang of Four: Contra-Confucianism in Historical and Intellectual Perspective*. Carbondale: Southern Illinois University Press, 1983.

Wu, Yenna. *The Chinese Virago: A Literary Theme*. Cambridge, MA: Council on East Asian Studies, Harvard University: Harvard University Press, 1995.

Wu Zeng 吳曾. *Nenggai zhai man lu* 能改齋漫錄 (Casual Records from the Nenggai Studio). Beijing: Zhonghua shuju, 1960.

Wu Zhen 吳縝. *Xin Tang shu jiumiu* 新唐書糾謬 (Errors in the New Tang History). Congshu jicheng chubian, vol. 378. Beijing: Zhonghua shuju, 1985.

Xu Dingxiang 徐定祥. *Li Jiao shi zhu; Su Weidao shi zhu* 李嶠詩注; 蘇味道詩注 (Li Jiao's Poetry, with Notes; Su Weidao's Poetry, with Notes). Shanghai: Shanghai guji chubanshe, 1995.

Xu Yingqiu 徐應秋. *Yuzhi tang tan hui* 玉芝堂談薈 (Abundant Talks from Jade Mushroom Hall). Shanghai: Shanghai guji chubanshe, 1993.

Xuanying 玄應. *Yiqie jing yin yi* 一切經音義 (Pronunciation and Meaning in All Sutras). Taibei: Taiwan shangwu yin shu guan, 1981.

Yan Zhitui 顏之推. *Yanshi jiaxun* 顏氏家訓 (Admonitions for the Yan Clan—A Chinese Classic on Household Management). Translated by Zong Fuchang 宗福常. Beijing: Foreign Languages Press, 2004.

———. *Yanshi jiaxun* 顏氏家訓 (Family Instructions for the Yan Clan). Edited by Xia Jiashan 夏家善. Tianjin: Tianjin guji chubanshe, 1995.

Yang Hsüan-chih. *A Record of Buddhist Monasteries in Lo-yang*. Translated by Yi-t'ung Wang. Princeton: Princeton University Press, 1984.

Yang Lien-sheng. "Female Rulers in Imperial China." *Harvard Journal of Asiatic Studies*, vol. 23 (1960–61): 47–61.

Yang Wanli 楊萬里. *Chengzhai Yi zhuan* 誠齋易傳 (Chengzhai's Commentary on the *Yijing* [*Classic of Changes*]). Taibei: Taiwan Zhonghua shuju, 1970.

Yang Weizhen 楊維楨. *Tieyai gu yuefu zhu* 鐵崖古樂府注 (Old-Style *yuefu* of Iron Coast, with Notes). Edited by Lou Buchan 樓卜瀍 (fl. 1774). Shanghai: Zhonghua shuju, ca. 1930–39.

Yang Xuanzhi 陽衒之. *Luoyang qielan ji jiao zhu* 洛陽伽藍記校注 (A Record of Buddhist Monasteries in Luoyang, with Annotations). Taibei: Mingwen shuju, 1980.

Yuan Mei 袁枚. *Sui yuan quan ji* 隨園全集 (Complete Collection of Yuan Mei's [Sui yuan's] Work). Shanghai: Wenming shuju shi yin ben, 1918.

———. *Zi bu yu* 子不語 (What the Master Didn't Speak About). In *Zhongguo wenyan xiaoshuo bai bu jing dian* 中國文言小說百部經典 (Classics of Chinese Classical Fiction), vols. 16–17. Edited by Liu Lihong 劉麗紅. Beijing: Beijing chubanshe, 2000.

Yuan Xingpei 袁行霈. *Tao Yuanming ji jianzhu* 陶淵明集箋注 (The Collected Poems of Tao Yuanming, with Notes). Beijing: Zhonghua shuju, 2003.

Zeitlin, Judith. *The Phantom Heroine: Ghosts and Gender in Seventeenth-Century Chinese Literature*. Honolulu: University of Hawaii Press, 2007.

Zeng Zao 曾慥. *Lei shuo* 類說 (Comprehensive Sayings). Taibei: Yi wen yi shu guan, 1975.

Zhang Ganping 張贛萍. *Jiang Qing de choushi yu yanwen* 江青的醜史與艷聞 (The Vile History and Amorous Adventures of Jiang Qing). Hong Kong: You chou chubanshe, 1969.

Zhang Hua 張華. *Bowu zhi* 博物志 (Record of Broad-reaching Knowledge). In *Zhongguo wenyan xiaoshuo bai bu jing dian* 中國文言小說百部經典 (Classics of Chinese Classical Fiction), Vol. 1. Edited by Liu Lihong 劉麗紅. Beijing: Beijing chubanshe, 2000.

Zhang Ying 張英 et al. *Yuding Yuanjian leihan* 御定淵鑑類函 (Imperial Edition of Deep Mirror of Extracts). Yingyin Wenyuan ge Siku quanshu. *Zibu* 10, *Leishu lei*. Taibei: Taiwan shangwu, 1983.

Zhang Zhuo 張鷟. *Chaoye qianzai* 朝野僉載 (Comprehensive Record of Affairs within the Court and Without). Beijing: Zhonghua shuju, 1979.

Zhao Wenrun 趙文潤 and Wang Shuanghuai 王雙懷. *Wu Zetian pingzhuan* 武則天評傳 (A Critical Biography of Wu Zetian). Xi'an: San Qin chubanshe, 2000.

Zheng Qi 鄭棨. *Kai Tian chuanxin ji* 開天傳信記. (Record of News Transmitted from the Kaiyuan and Tianbao Eras). In *Minghuang za lu: fu buyi, jiao kan ji (ji qi ta wu zhong)* 明皇雜錄附補遺校勘記及其他五種 (Assorted Records about the Reign of Xuanzong, with appended passages and annotations, and five other titles). Beijing: Zhonghua shuju, 1985.

Zheng Yaru 鄭雅如. "Chong tan Shangguan Wan'er de siwang, pingfan, yu dandagi pingjia" 重探上官婉兒的死亡平反與當代評價 (A Reevaluation of Shangguan Wan'er's Death, Rehabilitation, and Contemporary Appraisals). *Zaoqi Zhongguo shi yanjiu* 早期中國史研究 4, no. 1 (2012): 111–45.

Zhou Xunchu 周勛初. *Tangdai biji xiaoshuo xulu* 唐代筆記小說敘錄 (Descriptive Catalogue of Tang Anecdote Collections). Nanjing: Fenghuang chubanshe, 2008.

Zhu Shengfei 朱勝非. *Ganzhu ji* 紺珠記 (Scarlet Pearl Record). Yingyin Wenyuan ge Siku quanshu. *Zibu* 10, *Zajia lei* 5. Taibei: Taiwan shangwu, 1983.

Zhu Zhongli 朱仲麗. *"Nühuang meng": Jiang Qing waizhuan* "女皇夢": 江青外傳 ("Dreams of Being a Female Emperor": The Unofficial Biography of Jiang Qing). Beijing: Dongfang chubanshe, 1988.

Index

HARVARD-YENCHING INSTITUTE MONOGRAPH SERIES

(most recent titles now in print)

37. *The Korean Singer of Tales*, by Marshall R. Pihl
38. *Praying for Power: Buddhism and the Formation of Gentry Society in Late-Ming China*, by Timothy Brook
39. *Word, Image, and Deed in the Life of Su Shi*, by Ronald C. Egan
41. *Studies in the Comic Spirit in Modern Japanese Fiction*, by Joel R. Cohn
42. *Wind Against the Mountain: The Crisis of Politics and Culture in Thirteenth-Century China*, by Richard L. Davis
43. *Powerful Relations: Kinship, Status, and the State in Sung China (960–1279)*, by Beverly Bossler
44. *Limited Views: Essays on Ideas and Letters*, by Qian Zhongshu; selected and translated by Ronald Egan
45. *Sugar and Society in China: Peasants, Technology, and the World Market*, by Sucheta Mazumdar
49. *Precious Volumes: An Introduction to Chinese Sectarian Scriptures from the Sixteenth and Seventeenth Centuries*, by Daniel L. Overmyer
50. *Poetry and Painting in Song China: The Subtle Art of Dissent*, by Alfreda Murck
51. *Evil and/or/as the Good: Omnicentrism, Intersubjectivity, and Value Paradox in Tiantai Buddhist Thought*, by Brook Ziporyn
53. *Articulated Ladies: Gender and the Male Community in Early Chinese Texts*, by Paul Rouzer
55. *Allegories of Desire: Esoteric Literary Commentaries of Medieval Japan*, by Susan Blakeley Klein
56. *Printing for Profit: The Commercial Publishers of Jianyang, Fujian (11th–17th Centuries)*, by Lucille Chia
57. *To Become a God: Cosmology, Sacrifice, and Self-Divinization in Early China*, by Michael J. Puett
58. *Writing and Materiality in China: Essays in Honor of Patrick Hanan*, edited by Judith T. Zeitlin and Lydia H. Liu
59. Rulin waishi *and Cultural Transformation in Late Imperial China*, by Shang Wei
60. *Words Well Put: Visions of Poetic Competence in the Chinese Tradition*, by Graham Sanders
61. *Householders: The Reizei Family in Japanese History*, by Steven D. Carter
62. *The Divine Nature of Power: Chinese Ritual Architecture at the Sacred Site of Jinci*, by Tracy Miller
63. *Beacon Fire and Shooting Star: The Literary Culture of the Liang (502–557)*, by Xiaofei Tian
64. *Lost Soul: "Confucianism" in Contemporary Chinese Academic Discourse*, by John Makeham
65. *The Sage Learning of Liu Zhi: Islamic Thought in Confucian Terms*, by Sachiko Murata, William C. Chittick, and Tu Weiming
66. *Through a Forest of Chancellors: Fugitive Histories in Liu Yuan's* Lingyan ge, *an Illustrated Book from Seventeenth-Century Suzhou*, by Anne Burkus-Chasson
67. *Empire of Texts in Motion: Chinese, Korean, and Taiwanese Transculturations of Japanese Literature*, by Karen Laura Thornber
68. *Empire's Twilight: Northeast Asia Under the Mongols*, by David M. Robinson
69. *Ancestors, Virgins, and Friars: Christianity as a Local Religion in Late Imperial China*, by Eugenio Menegon

70. *Manifest in Words, Written on Paper: Producing and Circulating Poetry in Tang Dynasty China*, by Christopher M. B. Nugent
71. *The Poetics of Sovereignty: On Emperor Taizong of the Tang Dynasty*, by Jack W. Chen
72. *Ancestral Memory in Early China*, by K. E. Brashier
73. *'Dividing the Realm in Order to Govern': The Spatial Organization of the Song State*, by Ruth Mostern
74. *The Dynamics of Masters Literature: Early Chinese Thought from Confucius to Han Feizi*, by Wiebke Denecke
75. *Songs of Contentment and Transgression: Discharged Officials and Literati Communities in Sixteenth-Century North China*, by Tian Yuan Tan
76. *Ten Thousand Scrolls: Reading and Writing in the Poetics of Huang Tingjian and the Late Northern Song*, by Yugen Wang
77. *A Northern Alternative: Xue Xuan (1389-1464) and the Hedong School*, by Khee Heong Koh
78. *Visionary Journeys: Travel Writings from Early Medieval and Nineteenth-Century China*, by Xiaofei Tian
79. *Making Personas: Transnational Film Stardom in Modern Japan*, by Hideaki Fujiki
80. *Strange Eventful Histories: Identity, Performance, and Xu Wei's* Four Cries of a Gibbon, by Shiamin Kwa
81. *Critics and Commentators: The* Book of Poems *as Classic and Literature*, by Bruce Rusk
82. *Home and the World: Editing the Glorious Ming in Woodblock-Printed Books of the Sixteenth and Seventeenth Centuries*, by Yuming He
83. *Courtesans, Concubines, and the Cult of Female Fidelity*, by Beverly Bossler
84. *Chinese History: A New Manual, Third Edition*, by Endymion Wilkinson
85. *A Comprehensive Manchu-English Dictionary*, by Jerry Norman
86. *Drifting among Rivers and Lakes: Southern Song Dynasty Poetry and the Problem of Literary History*, by Michael Fuller
87. *Martial Spectacles of the Ming Court*, by David M. Robinson
88. *Modern Archaics: Continuity and Innovation in the Chinese Lyric Tradition, 1900-1937*, by Shengqing Wu
89. *Cherishing Antiquity: The Cultural Construction of an Ancient Chinese Kingdom*, by Olivia Milburn
90. *The Burden of Female Talent: The Poet Li Qingzhao and Her History in China*, by Ronald Egan
91. *Public Memory in Early China*, by K. E. Brashier
92. *Women and National Trauma in Late Imperial Chinese Literature*, by Wai-yee Li
93. *The Destruction of the Medieval Chinese Aristocracy*, by Nicolas Tackett
94. *Savage Exchange: Han Imperialism, Chinese Literary Style, and the Economic Imagination*, by Tamara T. Chin
95. *Shifting Stories: History, Gossip, and Lore in Narratives from Tang Dynasty China*, by Sarah M. Allen
96. *One Who Knows Me: Friendship and Literary Culture in Mid-Tang China*, by Anna Shields
97. *Materializing Magic Power: Chinese Popular Religion in Villages and Cities*, by Wei-Ping Lin
98. *Traces of Grand Peace: Classics and State Activism in Imperial China*, by Jaeyoon Song
99. *Fiction's Family: Zhan Xi, Zhan Kai, and the Business of Women in Late-Qing China*, by Ellen Widmer
100. *Chinese History: A New Manual, Fourth Edition*, by Endymion Wilkinson
101. *After the Prosperous Age: State and Elites in Early Nineteenth-Century Suzhou*, by Seunghyun Han
102. *Celestial Masters: History and Ritual in Early Daoist Communities*, by Terry F. Kleeman
103. *Transgressive Typologies: Constructions of Gender and Power in Early Tang China*, by Rebecca Doran
104. *Li Mengyang, the North-South Divide, and Literati Learning in Ming China*, by Chang Woei Ong